MW01093800

LITTLE BOOK OF

CHANEL
BY LAGERFELD

Published in 2022 by Welbeck
An imprint of Welbeck Non-Fiction Limited,
part of Welbeck Publishing Group.

Based in London and Sydney
www.welbeckpublishing.com

A CIP catalogue record for this book is available from the British Library.

ISBN 978-1-80279-016-0

Printed in China

10 9 8 7 6 5

FSC
www.fsc.org

MIX
Paper | Supporting
responsible forestry
FSC® C020056

LITTLE BOOK OF

CHANEL
BY LAGERFELD

The story of the iconic fashion designer

EMMA BAXTER-WRIGHT

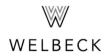

WELBECK

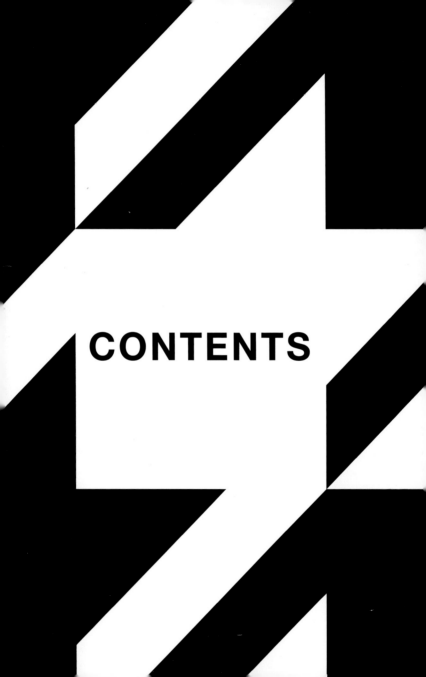

CONTENTS

INTRODUCTION.. 06

EARLY YEARS.. 10

THE CHANEL CHALLENGE............................. 26

EVOLUTION OF THE BRAND 40

A GLOBAL IDENTITY 62

THE CHANEL MUSES 82

THE ART OF THE ATELIER 96

THE ICONIC ADVERTISING CAMPAIGNS ...116

THE GREATEST SHOWS ON EARTH 130

INDEX 156

CREDITS...160

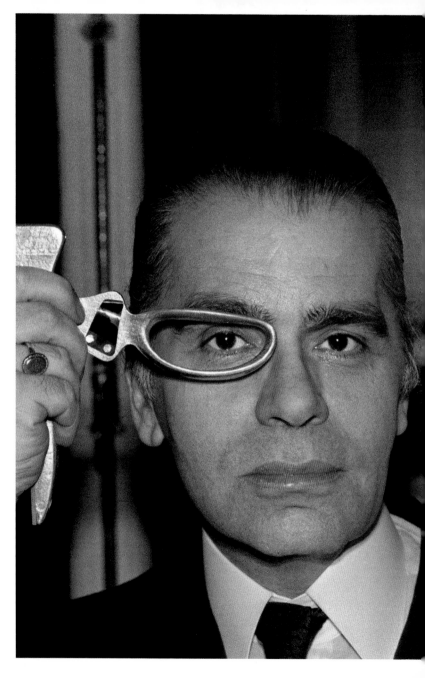

INTRODUCTION

"People like to think fashion is about being the star,
but it isn't."
KARL LAGERFELD

From his early forays at the age of 21 into the world of haute couture, the flamboyant German designer Karl Lagerfeld was prolific in his ambitious output, refusing to be confined to a single genre and subsequently inventing his role as a creative chameleon, who influenced trends in many fields. "I would like to be a one-man multinational fashion phenomenon," he confidently stated to *WWD* in 1984, before establishing himself as the leading authority in a global fashion industry that he dominated for the next 35 years. His dedicated work ethic, aligned with an unfailing ability to tap into the zeitgeist of an era, proved a triumphant formula. The only secret to his outstanding success? Hard work and discipline. "Life and Destiny don't owe us anything, you have to work for it," he told Rodolphe Marconi in 2007, looking back on his career.

Insistent on complete artistic freedom, he created the blueprint for the luxury-sector freelance designer, but his name became synonymous with the House of Chanel, his most successful and lucrative contract, which was scheduled to run until 2045. Early on in his career a fortune teller told Lagerfeld

OPPOSITE Looking serious in the design studio in 1987, without his signature shades.

that his life would really begin when it stopped for others, and so it transpired. The fashion revolution that Gabrielle "Coco" Chanel ignited in 1910 evolved into a multibillion-dollar industry, with universal appeal, under his inspired direction, while simultaneously propelling his personal fame and reputation to that of superstar celebrity. His vision for Chanel when he took over in 1983 was to incorporate the signature details while deconstructing the traditional aesthetic; "Respect never works," he said. By introducing a healthy dose of irreverence, manifested in the form of quilted clogs, sequinned miniskirts and monogrammed bikinis, he quickly turned the house into one of the world's most desirable brands. Then, with the dawn of a new century, he was the first to recognize the seismic shift in fashion's digitally influenced landscape and introduced jaw-dropping theatricality into his experiential catwalk shows, creating cinematic moments for a new online audience.

Renowned for his razor-sharp repartee, and a wicked sense of humour that seemed to increase with age, Lagerfeld offered unflinchingly honest opinions ("Sweatpants are a sign of defeat"). These earned him the nickname Kaiser Karl, in an industry where his influence was so profound, he could adjudicate on matters of good and bad taste with impunity. As self-proclaimed king, he was something of an enigma, rarely seen without his closest companion Choupette, a fluffy Birman cat he adopted in 2011, famous for her own product line and over 200,000 Instagram followers. Lagerfeld revelled in his larger-than-life persona, unwavering in his daily uniform of white shirt, signature shades, pompadoured ponytail and fingerless biker gloves adorned with golf ball-sized Chrome Hearts rings, a carefully conceived caricature that ensured protection from personal scrutiny. Beyond fashion, his inexorable energy was channelled into costumes for the opera, photography, film, designs for hotels, furniture, musical instruments, and beautiful illustrations; he was an exceptionally talented political satirist (he called his drawings "Karliatures") and published regularly in the monthly German magazine *Frankfurter Allgemeine Zeitung*.

Beyond all Lagerfeld's achievements, though, he will be best remembered as the diamond in Chanel's exceptionally sparkling crown – his longstanding modernization of the house through dynamic branding instantly recognizable, and his personal prominence as the most influential designer of the twentieth and twenty-first centuries unsurpassed.

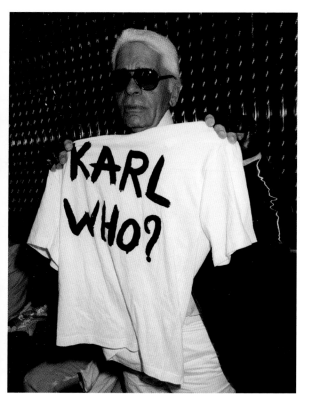

LEFT Recognized as the most famous designer in the world and well known for his wicked sense of humour, Karl Lagerfeld was never afraid to make fun of himself.

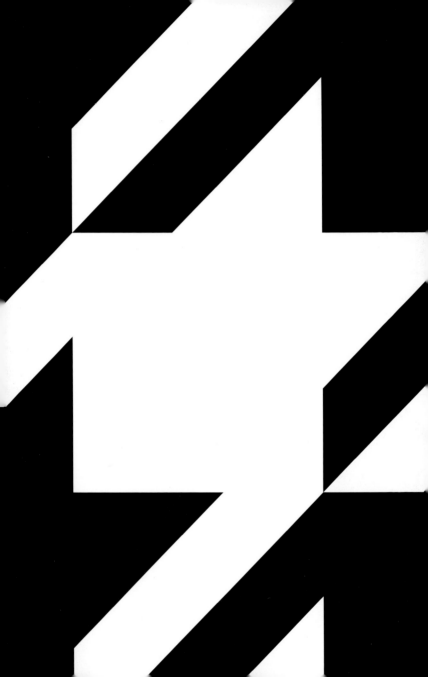

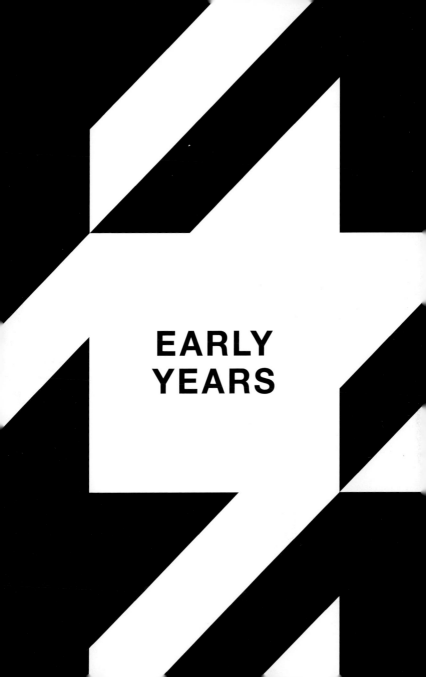

EARLY
YEARS

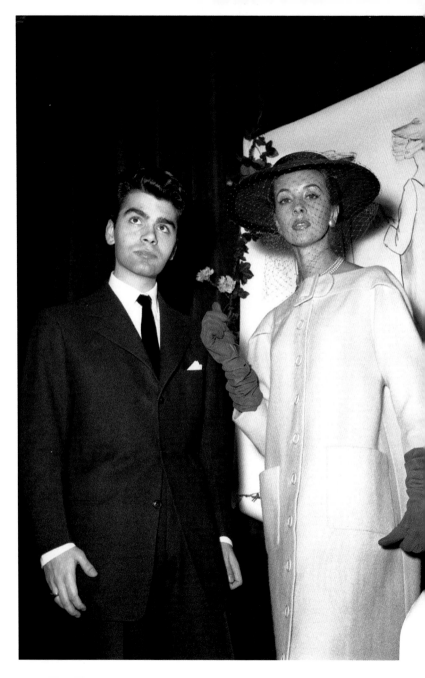

A SINGULAR AMBITION

The thriving, international port of Hamburg, located on the muddy banks of the River Elbe in northern Germany, provided the childhood setting for a young Karl-Otto Lagerfeldt, who was born to elderly parents on 10 September 1933.

His mother often spoke to him of Hamburg as "a gateway to the world", but for a precocious little boy who was convinced from an early age that he would become famous, the port was simply a way out.

Hamburg-born businessman Otto Lagerfeldt was a 49-year-old widower with a young daughter, Thea, when he married an attractive divorcée from Prussia in 1930. Elisabeth Lagerfeldt (née Bahlmann) was 17 years his junior and gave birth the following year to a little girl, Martha Christiane, known as Christel, and two years later their son, Karl-Otto Lagerfeldt, arrived. Initially the family lived in the affluent Baurs Park area of the city, but made a calculated decision to move out before 1939 to a spacious house in the small country town of Bad Bramstedt in Schleswig-Holstein, 40 km (25 miles) northeast

OPPOSITE Pictured alongside his exquisite coat design in 1954, winner of the International Wool Secretariat competition that took place annually in Paris. The prize secured his first professional employment with Pierre Balmain.

of Hamburg. Young Karl was a bright, studious boy, proficient in reading and writing in his native tongue by the age of five, but also able to speak adequately in French and English (a skill he learnt to understand what his parents were saying when they did not want him to hear their conversations). Obsessed with sketching and drawing, he cut a solitary figure at the Jürgen-Fuhlendorf-Schule he attended in Bad Bramstedt, often wearing a formal shirt and tie and by the age of 10 cultivating longer hair; he did not want to look like his fellow classmates, or engage in any of their childish games. Speaking years later to *ID* magazine about his childhood, he reiterated his deliberate preference for isolation: "I hated children. I didn't play with children. I never had toys, I only wanted notepads, pencils and books. I never wanted anything else in life."

Adored and protected by his quick-witted and artistic mother, to whom he was closer than his absent father (who earned his fortune promoting condensed milk for the German branch of the American Milk Products Company and was often away), Karl was taken to his first fashion show in 1950 at the Palais Esplanade in Hamburg. In a post-war atmosphere that was crying out for beauty and escapism, Elisabeth and her 17-year-old son attended a glamorous show presented by the Parisian couturier Christian Dior, who had recently achieved worldwide fame with the elegant lines of his revolutionary New Look collection. The event made a big impression. "I loved it, the mood, what it projected, the idea of a life," he told John Colapinto from the *Observer* in 2007, so much so that the adolescent made the decision to go to Paris and try to make a living out of fashion.

Although he hadn't finished his final high school exams, Karl persuaded his parents to let him leave home and finish his education at the Lycée Montaigne in Paris, where he majored in history and drawing. With Germany's economy in tatters, the

OPPOSITE Fluid lines and an imaginative use of colour exemplified Karl Lagerfeld's work for Chloé, where he built his reputation as a visionary designer throughout the seventies.

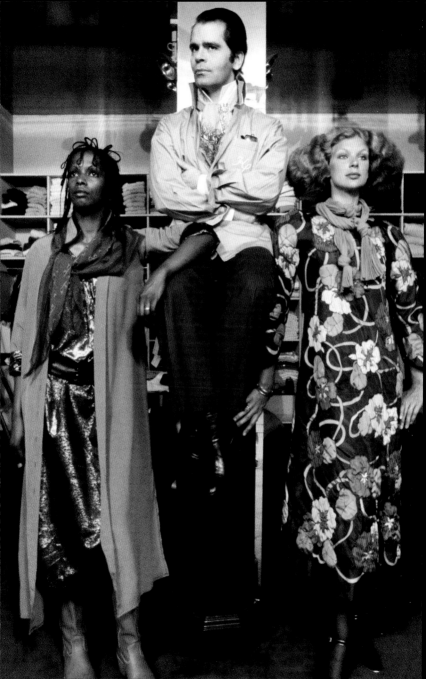

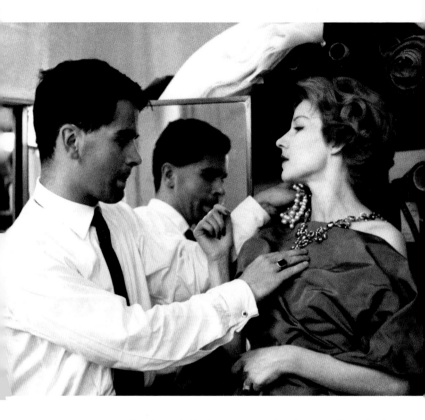

family needed little convincing that their son's future lay beyond the provincial countryside of his homeland. Elisabeth was confident that her gifted boy, who had a strong survival instinct, knew exactly what he wanted to do. Besides, his father also had an office in Paris, so the city didn't seem too far away. In Paris came reinvention: he dropped the "t" from his surname and it was not long before his talent was recognized. The International Wool Secretariat organized a prestigious fashion competition every year, and this time, in 1954, the judging panel included Hubert de Givenchy and Pierre Balmain. Amid fierce contention from 6,000 other aspiring fashion designers, the young German submitted sketches and fabric samples for several designs and was celebrated as a winner in the Coat category for his daring, daffodil-yellow, knee-length wool coat, cut squarely across the collarbone with a large buckle detail. A painfully shy 19-year-old Yves Saint Laurent was also singled out as winner, of the Dress category, for an elegant black evening frock. For a long time the two young men, photographed together as competition winners, and both rising stars in the same profession, were great friends. Pierre Balmain now offered Lagerfeld an assistant position at his successful maison, the first tentative steps in a career in haute couture, which provided an invaluable experience in understanding the mechanisms of the atelier.

"I started at Balmain as a studio artist, you had to sketch the existing dresses for the buyers and the clients. You had to sketch them dress by dress, every embroidery, every button, every flower. Do that for three years and you know how to draw," he told Susannah Frankel in 2015. Promotion to Balmain's assistant came quickly but, after three and a half years, Lagerfeld was ready to move on to Jean Patou. Designing under the name Roland Karl, he was responsible for producing two collections of 65 dresses a year, which he recalls as "not a lot for a young man" in "not the trendiest house in the world".

His experience at Patou taught Lagerfeld about technique, learning from the head premiere who had been running the atelier since 1919 when the house first opened. "French material was the best in the world, names like Rodier and Lesur, I learnt all the techniques of the 1920s. Perhaps I lost my time there in terms of creativity, but certainly not in terms of knowledge, and learning on the job." After five years in the rarefied atmosphere of the couture salon, Lagerfeld was ready to move on, "bored to death" by the slow pace at Patou, but also attuned to the emergence of something more immediate and exciting in the

form of new ready-to-wear collections that provided a total
look. In 1963, Lagerfeld started a freelance career designing for
a number of different clients, providing not just women's clothes
but shoes, bags and accessories for a variety of European labels
such as Max Mara, Ballantyne and Charles Jourdan, as well as
Krizia, which Lagerfeld recalled "in those years with Mariuccia
Mandelli was like the Prada of today." He was the first designer
to operate in this freelance manner and it was a business model
that he adopted very successfully for the next 50 years, juggling
multiple work commitments and never offering his talent as an
exclusive commodity to any one company. As he explained to
Bridget Foley from *WWD*, "I did a lot of freelancing and I loved
it because I hate to be bound to one thing."

In 1963 he took some sketches to Gaby Aghion, a stylish
French-Egyptian living in Paris, who had launched an upmarket
ready-to-wear label called Chloé, which produced two collections
a year designed by a number of different *stylistes* directed by her
overall artistic vision. At first, Lagerfeld contributed just one
or two designs to each collection, but he rapidly established a
brilliant working relationship with Madame Aghion, and as the
other designers slipped away (often to start their own lines), she
entrusted him to take over by naming him Design Director.
Fashion was changing rapidly: the labour-intensive production of
haute couture, which required several fittings to perfect a formal
elegance, now seemed dull and outdated. The modern pieces
Lagerfeld designed for Chloé attracted a different type of customer
who demanded off-the-peg simplicity, providing clothes that
looked clean cut and were easy to wear. Developments in mass
production ensured factories could utilize new technology working
with contemporary fabrics, allowing them to deliver accessible
prices while still maintaining exceptional production values.
Lagerfeld was prolific in his output, instinctively had a commercial
understanding of what would sell, and took inspiration from a

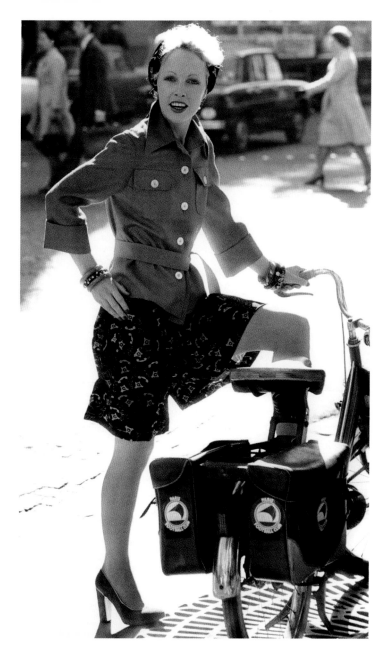

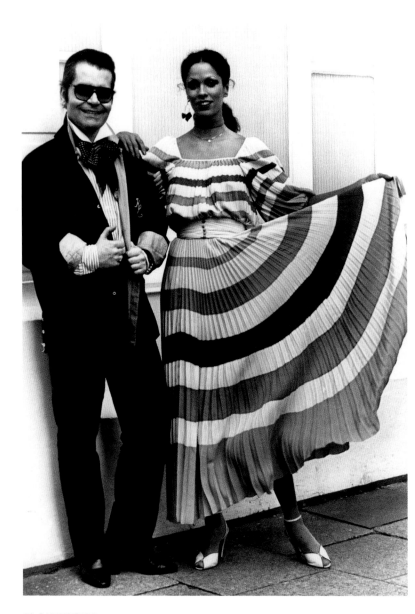

myriad of different sources: art, literature, architecture, even his observations of students on the streets of Paris.

Two years later, in 1965, Lagerfeld began a lifetime collaboration with Fendi, a small family-run business in Rome that had a reputation within Italy as an established luxury label. Working for the five Fendi sisters, whose parents Adele and Edoardo had created the company, Lagerfeld was given a remit to revamp the couture fur collection, breathing new creativity into what had become a predictably uninspired range of classic mink coats worn by wealthy clients who represented a bygone era. Incorporating dyed colours and wildly playful ideas such as plaiting and knitting fur, painting on fur, lining fur with fur and shaving pelts into patterned tufts, Lagerfeld instigated the idea of Fun Fur for Fendi, and also skilfully incorporated the skins into accessories and many ready-to-wear items. The iconic inverted double-F monogram was sketched out by Lagerfeld in a couple of seconds at his first meeting with the sisters; it signalled a radical new direction for the Italian house, and has since become a global signifier for a luxury brand that specializes in leather and fur.

Within the elite Parisian fashion world, Lagerfeld was establishing a reputation as a successful ready-to-wear designer and a flamboyant personality about town. Often surrounded by a coterie of glamorous young people, he presented himself as a confidant Teutonic aristocrat, often in full-length fur, seen at Café de Flore in Boulevard Saint-Germain or Le Sept nightclub located on rue Saint-Anne.

OPPOSITE Tapping into a trend for nostalgia, Chloé became one of the most covetable labels of the 1970s, although Lagerfeld was never named as the designer of the collections.

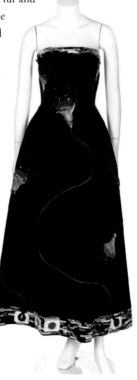

BELOW Strapless grosgrain evening gown with pink and white plastic lightbulbs appliquéd onto the dress and beaded plug sockets embroidered onto the hem for Maison Chloé.

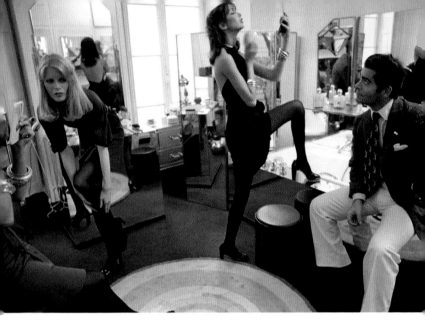

His every move was made to impress, sporting longer hair
(sometimes tied back in a ponytail with a bow), sitting behind
the wheel of a conspicuously flashy Bentley, wearing made-
to-measure suits designed to flatter his muscular frame, and
accessorizing with a silk cravat and ostentatious monocle.
He was starting to develop a visual persona that confidently
projected the swagger of brilliance; passionate about history
(although simultaneously curious about the present), he lived
in a series of impressive apartments furnished with valuable
tapestries and priceless antiques, mostly from his favourite
periods of the eighteenth century. As the sophisticated literary
leader of his band of creatives (Antonio Lopez, Juan Ramos,
Corey Tippin, Pat Cleveland) Lagerfeld was an extraordinarily
generous friend and sponsor, providing lavish gifts and holidays
and always picking up the tab at the end of the evening for his
favoured fashion clique. Like Andy Warhol, Lagerfeld innately

understood the importance of creating an impenetrable image to present to the world. The two men met in Paris in 1972, when Warhol arrived to shoot an underground art film called *L'Amour*, using the designer's Left Bank apartment on the rue de l'Université as a location and casting him as a German aristocrat. On a work trip to Japan, Lagerfeld picked up a bamboo-covered folding fan and subsequently, for over 20 years, amassed an extraordinary collection for which he became known, rarely seen in public without one. Lagerfeld's adoption of a fan as accessory established an immediately identifiable trademark that both consolidated the mystique of the designer and conveniently acted as an aesthetic method of self-protection.

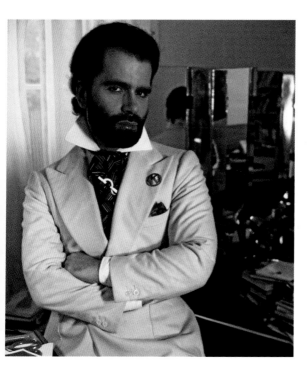

LEFT Sporting shorter hair and a full beard, Karl Lagerfeld was known in Paris as a sartorial dandy –here is early evidence of the high collars and decorative tie pins that would come to identify his style 50 years later.

BELOW Posing
backstage at a show
in Japan in 1977.
It was here that
Lagerfeld first picked
up a bamboo fan,
an accessory that
became synonymous
with the designer for
more than 20 years.

Chloé in particular gained cult status as a chic fashion label in the 1970s (his Art Deco-inspired collection of 1972, presenting bias-cut dresses that mixed exuberant florals with graphic black and white prints, received international acclaim), but Lagerfeld's successful relationships with the multiple companies for which he was designing usually remained discreet. He unashamedly embraced commercialism, happy to create a multitude of different products for numerous brands in Europe, America and Japan; shoes, bags, textiles, leather goods and knitwear were all created using lucrative freelance contracts, without the need to promote his own name. Empire building was never an ambition, although his stature within the fashion industry was clearly on an upwards trajectory. His next appointment, which he accepted under the terms of a "life contract", brought fame, wealth, adulation and unparalleled recognition, as he became the most famous international designer of his era.

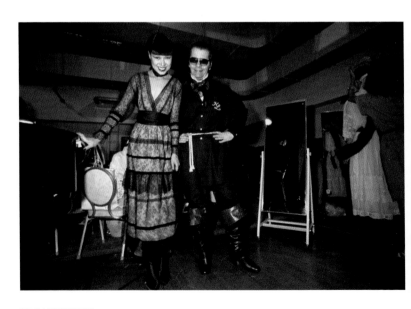

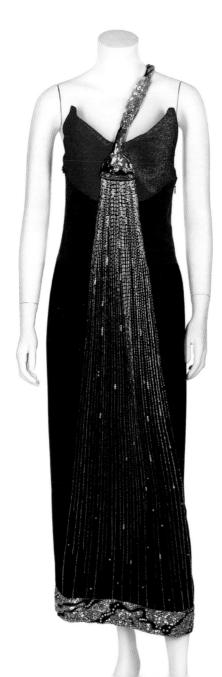

LEFT Visual witticisms are a Lagerfeld trademark, as seen here in his final Chloé collection. The silver shower spray is made from sequins and faceted stones, with bugle beads and rhinestones cascading down the front of the evening gown.

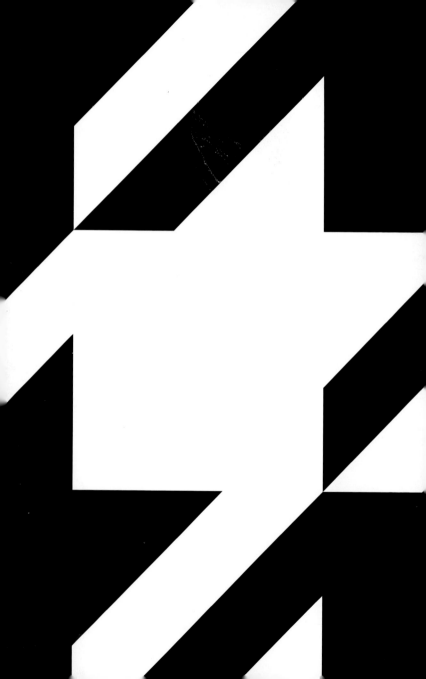

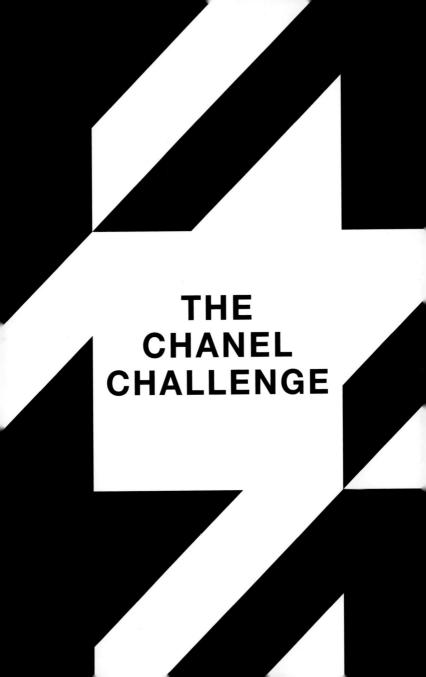

THE
CHANEL
CHALLENGE

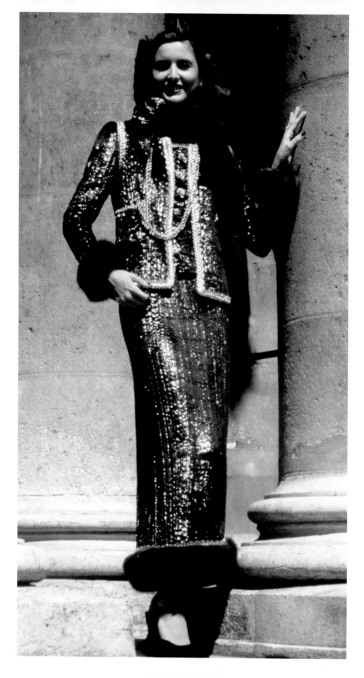

THE REBIRTH OF A COUTURE HOUSE

In 1982, after months of rumours, it was announced that Karl Lagerfeld had been hired by the House of Chanel, with a remit to reignite the fusty haute couture collections and take over the ready-to-wear and accessory ranges.

With the indomitable force of its founder Mademoiselle Gabrielle Chanel long gone, the house had floundered, dependent solely on an ageing clientele who remained loyal to the classic tweed suits first introduced in her 1950s comeback collections. For 11 years the family-run company, owned originally by Pierre Wertheimer, and now by his grandson Alain, had lurched onwards, reliant on steady cosmetics and perfume sales (Chanel N°5 was still a popular fragrance) and various merchandise deals to produce off-the-peg collections, mostly for an American market. Before Lagerfeld arrived at the dormant maison, the two fashion sides of the business had been run as separate entities, with leading designers Monsieur Jean Cazaubon and Madame Yvonne Dudel overseeing declining sales of haute

OPPOSITE High-octane glamour for Chanel, in this full-length, night-blue, cellophane-velvet three-piece evening suit for Autumn/Winter 1983. It features gold embroidery details and lustrous zibeline trims, usually made from soft alpaca or camel hair.

couture and Phillipe Guibourge in charge of a ready-to-wear line that was promoted in boutiques throughout America, Canada and Europe.

Alain Wertheimer was an astute businessman with ambitious plans for the company that had already made his family extraordinarily wealthy. He intended to stop the copious licensing deals and control all future design, manufacturing and distribution by bringing every aspect of the process back in-house, and ultimately to reinstate the exclusivity of the label to its former glory. New York-based Kitty d'Alessio, hired by Wertheimer in 1980 to oversee Chanel operations in America, suggested Lagerfeld: she greatly admired his prolific output of work both in Europe and the United States, and argued that he was uniquely qualified for the job. Despite previous declarations that luxury ready-to-wear, not haute couture, collections were the future of fashion, Lagerfeld accepted the position, against a tsunami of advice from friends and associates who told him to reject the offer. "When I took over everybody told me: 'Don't touch it. It's dead', but this was an interesting challenge, and the owner said to me 'You can do what you want'," Lagerfeld recalled nearly 40 years later, talking to journalist Tyler Brûlé about a decision that at the time sent shockwaves through Paris. How on earth could a German designer, best known as a successful pioneer of popular modern style, ever truly engage with the painstakingly slow process of haute couture and step into the revered shoes of Coco Chanel, widely acknowledged as one of France's greatest couturières?

The appointment of Lagerfeld held additional significance within the competitive one-upmanship of the Parisian fashion industry in the 1980s. While the prospect of reigniting the Chanel label was compelling, it also gave the designer an opportunity to finally elevate his own reputation to that of Yves Saint Laurent. His former friend (and now bitter rival) had built his own

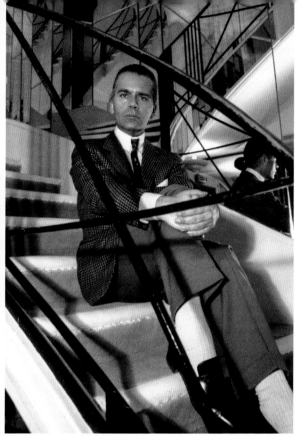

spectacularly successful house allied to Chanel's principles of androgynous style over ostentatious extravagance. In the months prior to her death, Chanel herself had named Yves Saint Laurent as her rightful heir, and now at the age of 49 it was Karl Lagerfeld who was appointed as Artistic Director, in charge of all creative decisions and given a free rein to do what he wanted, with the aim of attracting a new generation of loyal customers.

Lagerfeld set to work in the legendary Chanel headquarters in rue Cambon towards the end of 1982, with the original sign "Mademoiselle – Privé" firmly intact on the studio door. In preparation for his first haute couture collection, a handful of his own associates arrived at rue Cambon to help smooth the transition into a new era. Recruited to help were Hervé Léger and Eva Campocasso, both former assistants; leggy brunette model Mercedes Robirosa, who shook up the staid team at the press office; and Paquito Sala, famous for his exquisite tailoring skills at Pierre Balmain. With absolutely no intention of simply reproducing the predictable vintage Chanel style that had become so associated with the label, Lagerfeld made it clear that the pastel, boxy suits would not be reappearing.

OPPOSITE Having studied the Chanel archives in detail, early collections showed new interpretations of the classic suit, with a longer-length belted jacket and "windmill" slit skirts.

"A very static image has emerged based on Chanel's last years," he explained to Christopher Petkanas from *WWD* before his first collection was revealed. "So I've looked over her whole career and found something much more interesting." To familiarize himself with all the great couturière's work, which had long since been forgotten, Lagerfeld studied the archives, cutting out images of every Chanel item he could find from his personal collection of fashion magazines. He compiled detailed scrapbooks that visually referenced a framework of essential elements and aesthetic codes which signified the whole career of Chanel, and let it be known that he would acknowledge the spirit of the past without being overtly reverential. Firmly focused on establishing a new direction, Lagerfeld spun the connective threads of Chanel's history into something surprisingly modern – inspired, he claimed, by the words of Goethe, the German writer and poet: "To make a better future with a large element of the past."

The first couture collection by Lagerfeld, presented to an invited audience of elite guests who included Bernadette Chirac, Paloma Picasso, Isabelle Adjani and André Leon Talley, took place on Tuesday, 25 January 1983, in the first-floor salon at rue Cambon. Set to a soundtrack of Edith Piaf and Charles Trenet, the show opened with a trio of elegant suits, reimagined in a

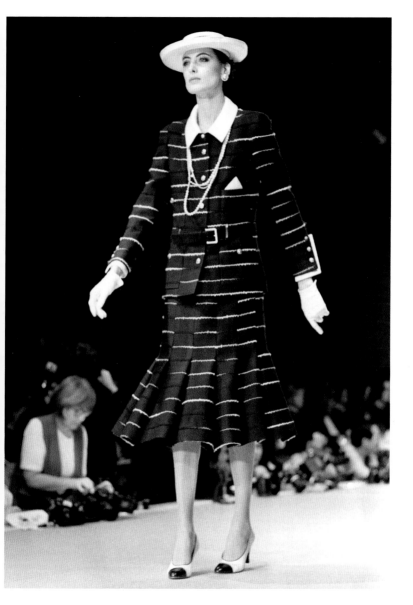

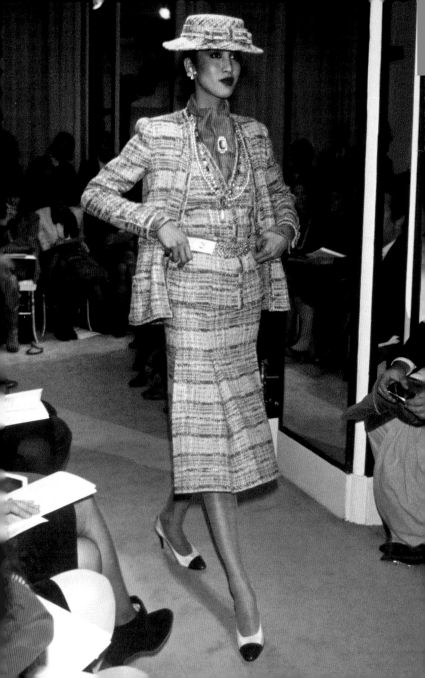

striking palette of red, white and blue, an emphatic reference to the national colours of the French Tricolore. The braid-edged suits, reproportioned with broader shoulders and shorter, double-breasted jackets, were accessorized with an abundance of costume jewellery, multiple chain belts at the waist and shown with longer "windmill" slit skirts and two-tone shoes. Opening the show alongside Inès de la Fressange and Anne Robart was top New York model Diane DeWitt, a well-known face in the United States. Her inclusion in the line-up suggested an acknowledgment by Lagerfeld that it was the American market who were instrumental in backing Chanel's 1954 comeback, and implied that this fresh interpretation of the label would also be a winning choice for the modern American woman.

The show referenced a myriad of ideas taken from Chanel's 60-year career and her personal style. The fluid lines of the 20s and 30s were playfully reimagined in the form of hip-length

BELOW The Autumn/Winter haute couture collection in 1985 featured beautiful evening wear with lavish sequin and embroidery detailing, all executed by hand by Maison Lesage.

OPPOSITE Chanel's original signatures remained intact in a 1983 collection that showed updated tweeds, gilt buttons and jauntily placed boater hats.

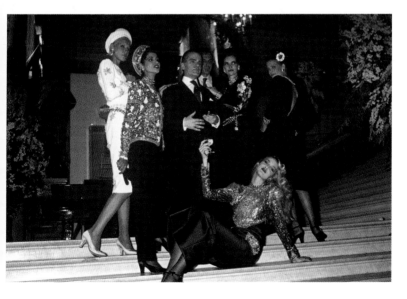

BELOW Early
interpretations of the
classic suit introduced
unfamiliar colourways,
such as this dark
purple tweed suit,
which featured 1980s
statement shoulder
pads to create a
broader silhouette.

silk cardis, striped waistcoats, unstructured skirts and long ropes of pearls. Elegant navy-and-white striped tops and wide-legged, double-fronted sailor pants with conspicuous gold buttons were reminiscent of the chic Deauville days, while an understated pink cotton suit was clearly a reference to the one Jacqueline Kennedy wore in Dallas in 1963.

"We want to modernize the Chanel image," Lagerfeld told *Vogue* magazine. Inès de la Fressange, who became a favourite house model for Lagerfeld at Chanel, spoke to fashion commentator Loïc Prigent about her memories of that first collection, saying, "Karl thought it was important to show that a 25-year-old girl could be dressed in Chanel."

The recognizable house codes were reintroduced: the white camellia pinned to a jacket lapel, simple black boater hats with white ribbon bows and multiple chain belts worn like necklaces were all given a stylish makeover to appeal to a contemporary audience. The reviews, though not ecstatic, were favourable. French socialite Marie-Hélène de Rothschild, a loyal devotee of Chanel, offered this prescient observation: "No one could have done it on the first try. It will come."

OPPOSITE The inaugural collection for Chanel opened with a trio of reimagined suits that echoed the patriotic colours of the French national flag, with head-to-toe outfits in blue, white and red echoing the vertical bands of the Tricolore.

OVERLEAF Throughout his life Karl Lagerfeld owned many homes, some of which he rarely visited. His apartment in Monaco was fitted out entirely by the influential Milanese design group Memphis, with a bed that was designed as a boxing ring.

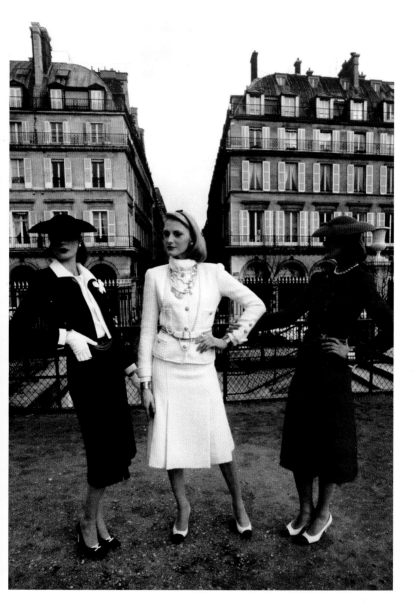

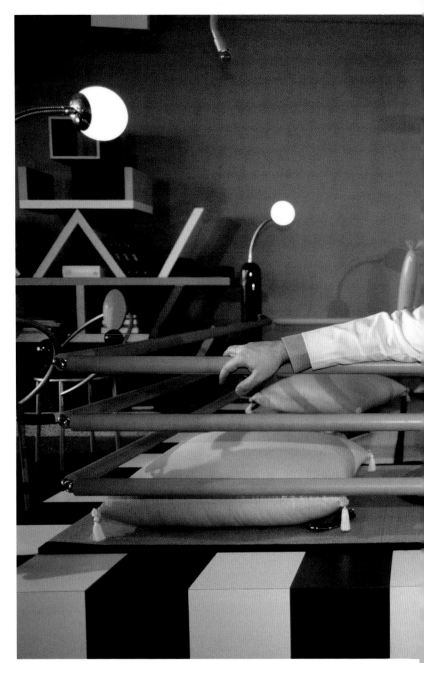

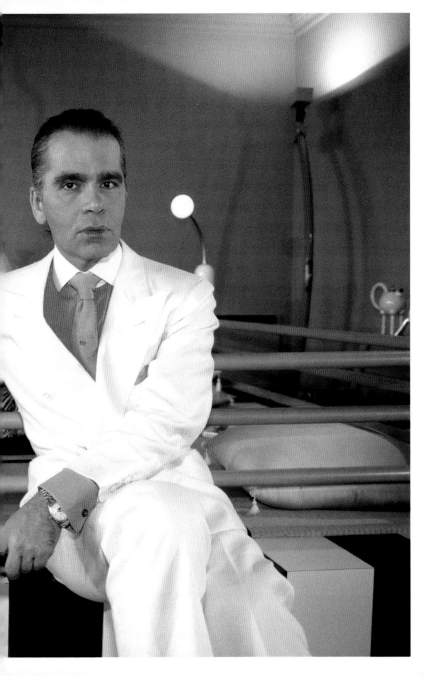

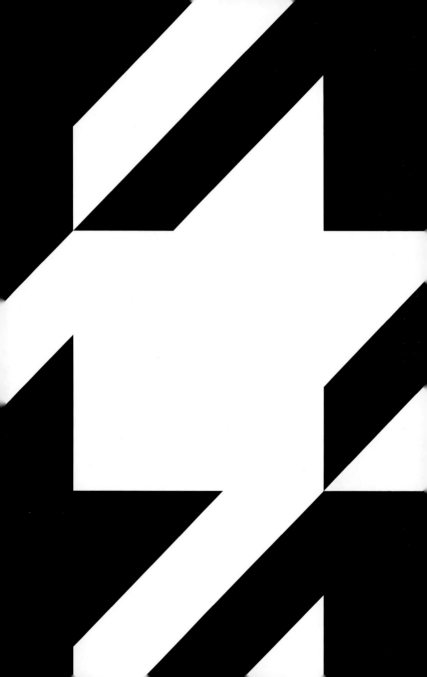

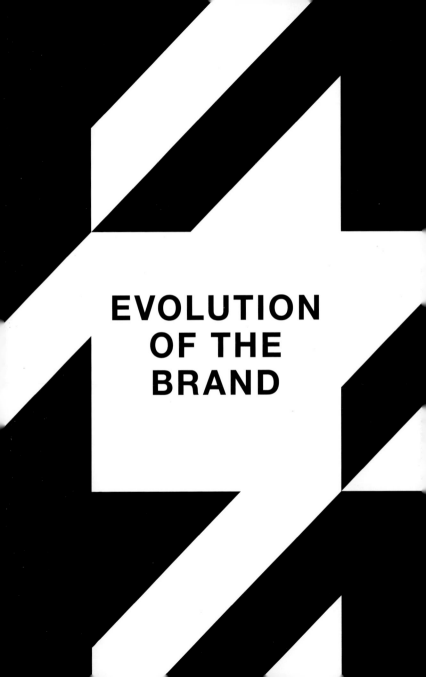

EVOLUTION
OF THE
BRAND

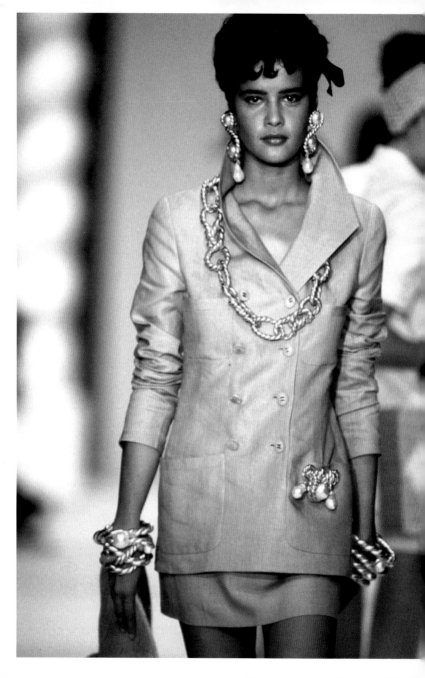

REINVENTION OF THE CLASSICS

> "My job is not to do what she did, but what
> she would have done."
> KARL LAGERFELD

From his acceptance of the job as Creative Director, Lagerfeld quickly shifted the perceived aesthetic of Chanel onto a brand-new path, the basis of which was determined by his encyclopaedic research of the entire back catalogue of her oeuvre. Dutiful reproduction would result in disaster for the company; instead, he instinctively embraced the idea of focusing on details of the famous iconography of her legacy, reworking the significant signature codes of Chanel in a visually creative way that had not been previously attempted. His aim from the beginning was to target his collections to a younger generation of modern consumers, and to appeal to them through a lighter touch, using wit and humour in his designs. His revolutionary intentions to deconstruct the familiar, and by now rather tired, templates of Chanel's heritage and to reinvent them with huge injections of irreverence became strikingly evident very early on.

OPPOSITE Classic suit shapes were reimagined; jackets got longer and skirts shorter, while the styling details of chunky gilt chains and oversized earrings captured the excess of 1980s style.

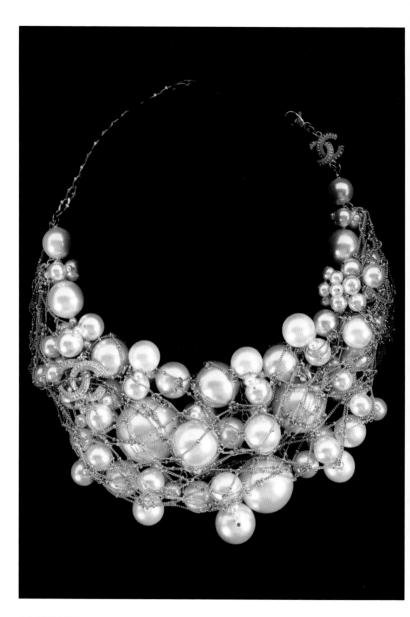

Some critics recoiled at his blatant rebranding of Chanel's understated style, but Lagerfeld himself was unrepentant. "To survive you have to cut the roots to make new roots. Fashion is about today. You can take an idea from the past, but if you do it the way it was, no one wants it," he told journalist John Colapinto. Successfully tapping into the "more is more" zeitgeist of the 1980s, Lagerfeld exaggerated the established tropes of Chanel. Visually he styled his collections with eye-catching gimmicks: super-sized ropes of pearls, clanking layers of gilt chains and massive camellia adornments, all perfectly pitched as high-end status symbols for the yuppie generation obsessed with conspicuous consumption. For his first Spring/Summer Ready-to-Wear collection in 1984, Lagerfeld introduced denim into his collections, using it both for modern day dresses with red contrast top stitching, and elegant suits with an emphasis on bold shoulders and jaunty fedora hats. He had found a way to be respectful to the legacy of Chanel, while simultaneously introducing an identifiable stamp of kitsch, exemplified through dynamic styling and bold accessories. With each subsequent collection that followed, Lagerfeld became more confident in his creativity, playing with fresh new proportions, creating luxury tweeds using metallic threads in vibrant colour combinations, and branding much of his output with the instantly recognizable double-C logo. His strategy to distance himself from the collections of the past was a calculated risk that paid off. "If you look at the 1950s collections, [at] the end of the 1950s there are very few chains, there is no CC, and no camellias, but in the 1980s we had to pull out all the stops because otherwise it would just have been a posh, unassuming tweed suit with a little bow," he told journalists later.

Lagerfeld opened every show with an updated version of a classic Chanel suit, executed with a brilliant Lagerfeld twist, while the striking colour combination of black and white so

OPPOSITE Clusters of faux pearls and glittering double-C insignia designed to evoke a fisherman's catch are caught in a tangled net of fine white gold chains in this surreal choker necklace.

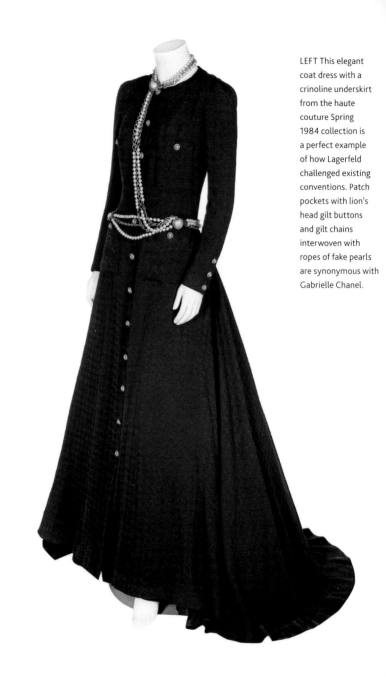

LEFT This elegant coat dress with a crinoline underskirt from the haute couture Spring 1984 collection is a perfect example of how Lagerfeld challenged existing conventions. Patch pockets with lion's head gilt buttons and gilt chains interwoven with ropes of fake pearls are synonymous with Gabrielle Chanel.

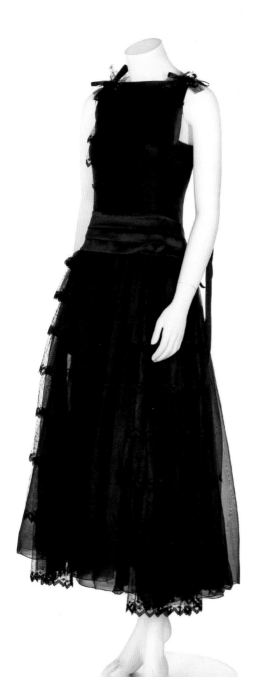

LEFT By mixing modernism in the form of black silk and spandex with a romantic silhouette from the 1920s, Lagerfeld ensures lace, ribbons and flouncy tulle petticoats are given a contemporary twist.

BELOW Chanel runway shows are always visually entertaining. Here, an exact copy of the classic Chanel suit is scaled down to a matching "mini- me" size in 1985.

OPPOSITE Paying homage to the ornate rococo style of French artist Jean-Antoine Watteau, Jerry Hall models an extravagant haute couture gown for the Spring/Summer 1985 collection.

OVERLEAF Lagerfeld presented an updated collection of wide-legged trouser suits in strong vibrant shades, inspired by the fluid pants Chanel first wore in the 1920s.

successfully utilized by Coco remained an integral part of each collection and now became an identifiable signature of the house – but he also thrilled his audiences with so much more. In 1985, the Spring/Summer haute couture show paid homage to the influential French artist Jean-Antoine Watteau (1684–1721) who was known for his theatrical, rococo-style paintings mostly executed in delicate pastels. Lagerfeld indulged his love of romance, dressing Texan model Jerry Hall in an ice-blue, full-length taffeta skirt, with delicate ruffles sweeping around her neck and décolletage, under a short, cinched-in, yellow leather jacket. This fantasy version of femininity, strongly influenced by historical artworks, was not a silhouette normally associated with the brand. He dramatically expanded the previously limited Chanel colour palette, showing coats and jackets in bold clashes of hyacinth blue, emerald green, burnt orange, raspberry pink and mauve in the Autumn/Winter 1998 show, and included city

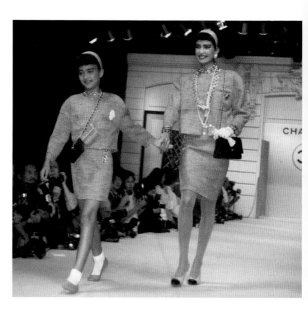

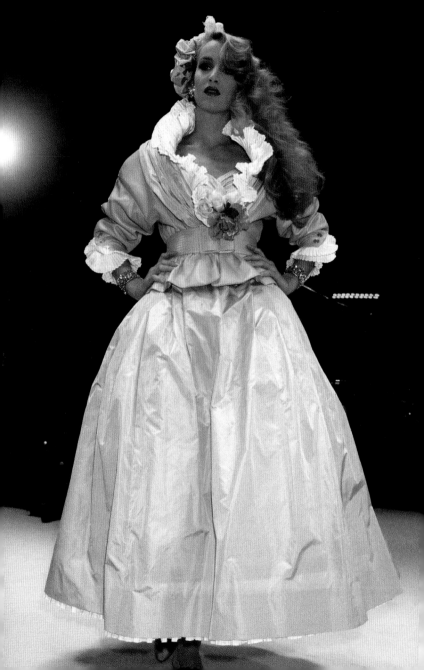

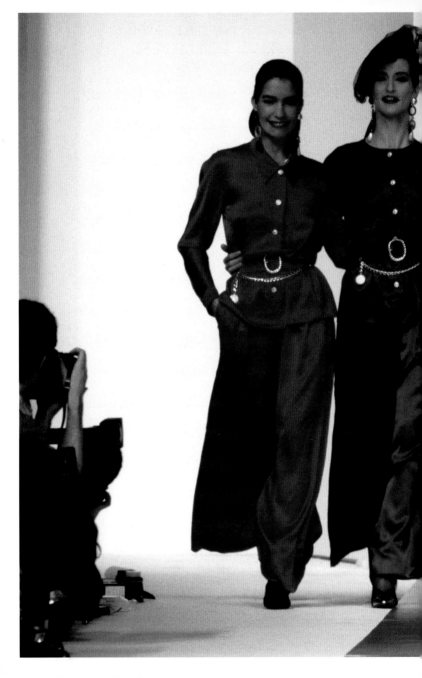

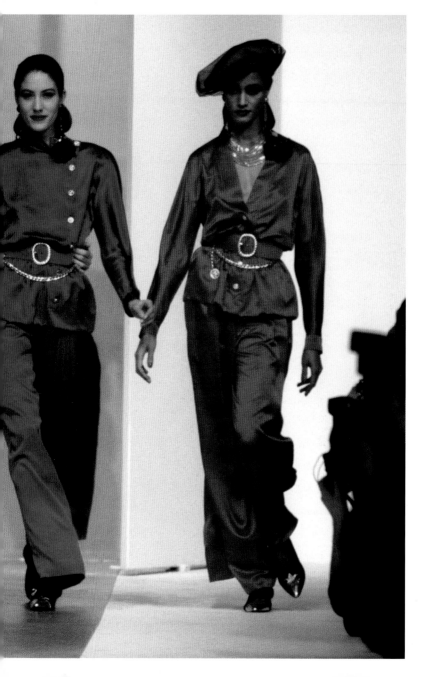

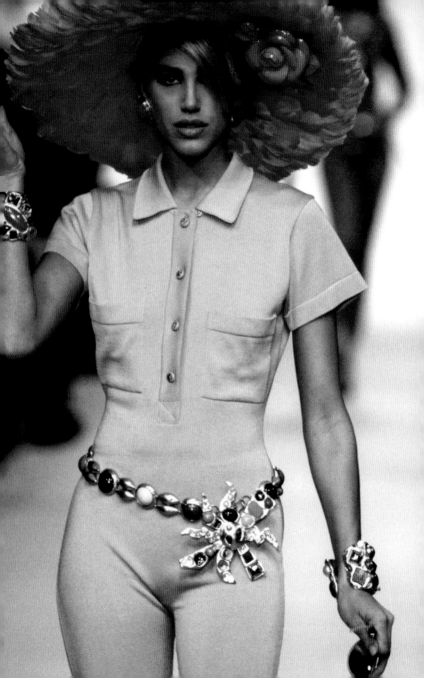

shorts and figure-hugging vest dresses embellished with chunky chain jewellery in skin-tight black leather in 1987.

Overt sex appeal was not an obvious trope of the existing Chanel aesthetic, which usually favoured understated style as opposed to blatant sensationalism. Lagerfeld promised his first collections would be "modern and street-sexy, not Las Vegas sexy", an idea he pursued throughout his tenure at the house, attuned to the fanfare of publicity created by a show that shocked the audience and created great newspaper headlines. Mixing fashion's historical timelines, he showed girls in towering Marie Antoinette beehive wigs in the early 90s, with locs falling

BELOW Yasmeen Ghauri, a favourite Chanel model, shows off the gold lamé lining of her full-length, fitted wool coat, embellished with ornate buttons and elaborate waist detailing and worn over a matching shortie mini skirt, on the catwalk in 1990.

OPPOSITE Swedish model Emma Sjöberg walks the runway in an all-in-one, body-hugging cycling-shorts suit from 1991, part of a colourful spring collection that was dubbed the "city surfer".

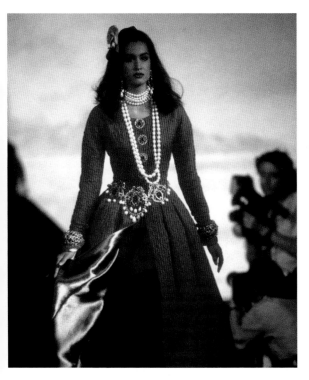

RIGHT The "Paris-Shanghai" collection from 2010 showcased a sleek, fitted evening dress, overlaid with floral prints in floaty silk chiffon, and neat rouleaux button detailing.

OPPOSITE Wearing a veil similar to the one Chanel herself had been photographed in, and smoking her cigarette in the same way, Inès de la Fressange was encouraged to emulate the effortless style of the rebellious Coco on the catwalk.

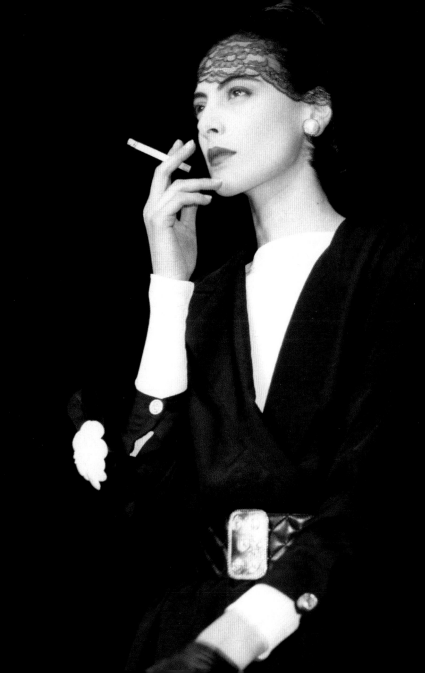

down around their shoulders as they strutted down the catwalk in layers of see-through mesh body suits that they peeled off as they walked. Ingrid Schissy from *Interview* magazine recognized the brilliance of his calculated strategy. "I mean how much more dramatic can you get than a total see-through thing, where the tush is visible!"

During these early years, the aristocratic French model Inès de la Fressange was signed up by Lagerfeld with a contract for Chanel that demanded she worked for the house exclusively. "I only worked for Chanel, and that's what I wanted," she said in 2020. With her dark, messy bob, flashing eyes and toothy grin, Lagerfeld presented Inès as a living embodiment of the spirit of Mademoiselle; she opened every show, was given more outfits to wear than any other girl and was seen alongside the designer as he took to the catwalk to accept the final applause. Lagerfeld introduced a carefree mood to his runway shows for Chanel, de la Fressange walking with a distinct swagger, hands placed casually on her hips, winking at the audience. She wore a veil in a similar style to that of Mademoiselle Chanel, and was asked to study pictures of her smoking, to hold a cigarette in the same way. Thoroughly French and effortlessly chic, de la Fressange was the irrefutable star of the show, but Lagerfeld was determined always to include a diverse range of models from Japan, China, Brazil and America to ensure that the appeal of Chanel should not be limited only to French women. From the late 80s, the best models in the world were walking for the house: women such as Pat Cleveland, Yasmin Le Bon, Jerry Hall and Naomi Campbell were seen having fun on the catwalk. Lagerfeld's momentous challenge to reignite the house he called a "sleeping beauty" was universally hailed by the fashion press as a great success.

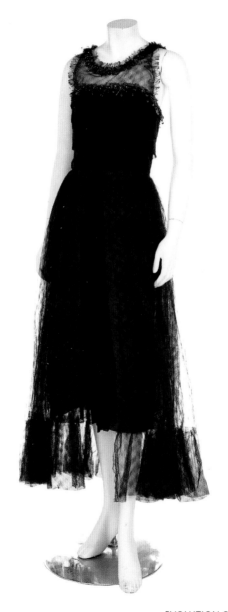

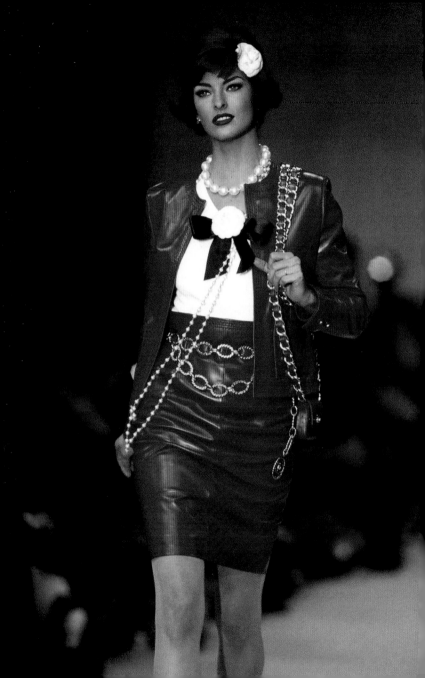

Unlike Chanel herself, who never picked up a pencil and created her innovative pieces by working with toiles and fabric, reshaping the clothes using her famous scissors to cut and manipulate the fabric into submission, Lagerfeld was a prolific and talented draughtsman. Since childhood he had spent hours absorbed with notepads, pencils and books, and now his detailed sketches, which provided fluid representations of complete outfits, with every button, dart and seam accurately placed, were precise enough for the design teams to interpret his visions perfectly and bring them into reality. "I was born with a pencil in my hand and I can't remember ever wanting to do something other than what I do today," he told *Vanity Fair* in 1992. With an extraordinarily disciplined work ethic (throughout his tenure at Chanel he continued to design for Fendi and for his own label KL, as well as accepting one-off commissions for other artistic projects), Lagerfeld followed the same creative routines each day. Working from home every morning on new designs for the upcoming collections, he sketched furiously on a pad of A4 lightweight paper in a quick-fire process that saw many of his inventive ideas relegated to the wastepaper bin. Listening to music and dressed always in a fresh white cotton piqué robe, worn to protect his clothes from the chalky residue of the pastel colours he used, Lagerfeld discovered in later years a preference for the vibrant shades of Shu Uemura eyeshadow to add colour. He explained the methodology of his working process to Bridget Foley from *WWD*: "I'm a sketching artist because I like to sketch. But my fashion sketches are easy to read. When I see old sketches from the 50s there are no details. I give on my sketches every technical detail and it still looks like a trendy illustration. But this is what I like. I spend hours doing it."

BELOW Lagerfeld introduced the idea of sex appeal to the Chanel customer, as in this transparent, gauzy top, embellished with diamond shaped paillettes.

OPPOSITE Underwear as outerwear became a mainstream trend in the early 90s, with Lagerfeld quick to interpret the idea by stamping his large 1950s-style pants with a Chanel logo on the waistband.

He was not a designer who spent time in the fitting salon, as Inès de la Fressange recalled. "He used to pop his head in at the end for four seconds!" That routine never changed, Lagerfeld himself explaining in 2013: "I never go to the salon. I am not a couturier from that school who goes downstairs to the salon to see if the dress fits. I only do collections."

Despite different methods of process, Lagerfeld and Chanel had much in common: they both maintained a disciplined working routine and were prolific in output. Initial worries about his vision for the company were quick to subside as the reputation of the house soared, sales boomed and he personally became increasingly famous, his flamboyant image as recognizable as the interlocking CCs he championed.

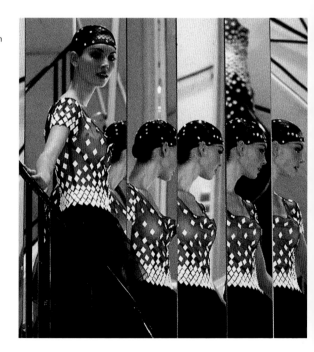

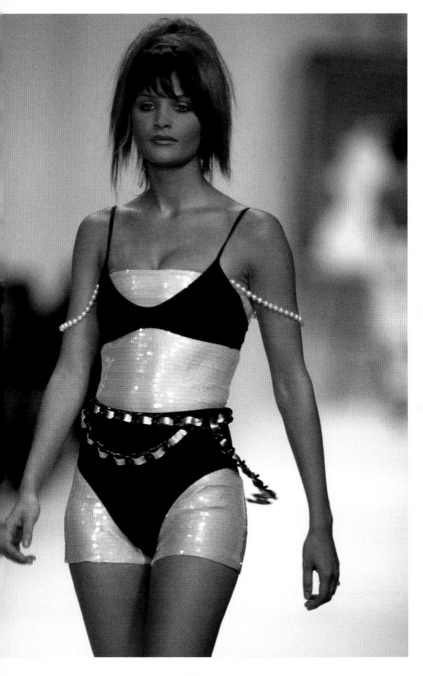

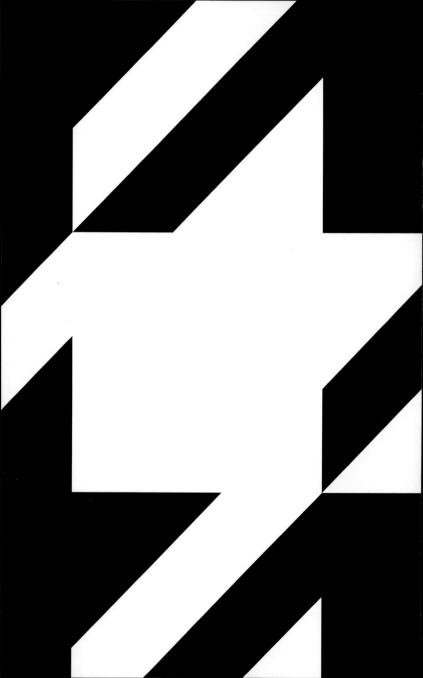

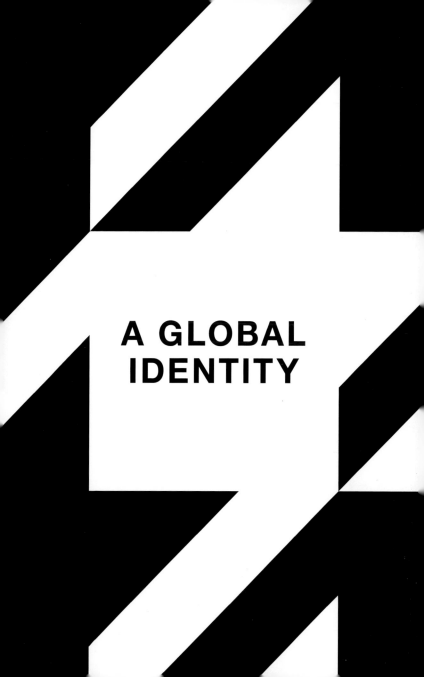

A GLOBAL
IDENTITY

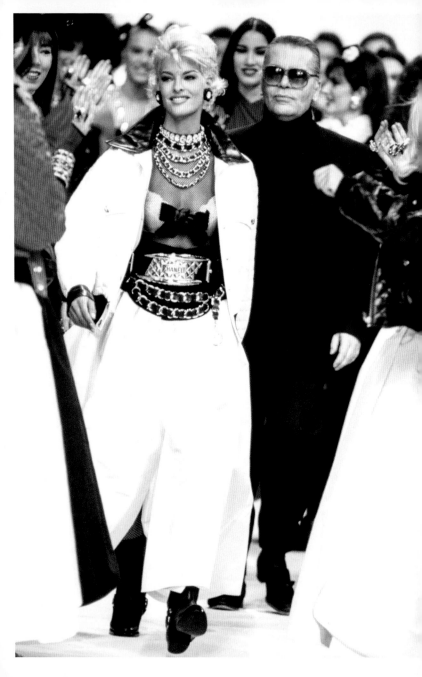

AN EXPLOSION
OF LOGOS

"The curiosity is ceaseless."
LADY AMANDA HARLECH

More than anyone, Lagerfeld was aware of the changing fashion landscape he found himself at the undisputed centre of. Ready-to-wear fashion shows had become big events, more like rock concerts than elegant, upper-class gatherings. The newly named supermodels were rewarded with sky-high fees for pouting provocatively on the runway (in 1990 Linda Evangelista famously said, "We don't wake up for less than $10,000 a day") and film stars, so often caught in the relentless glare of the paparazzi flashbulb, were styled as celebrities in a profusion of recently launched fashion magazines. Having negotiated with Alain Wertheimer a salary that was rumoured to be $1 million a year, Lagerfeld had a vision that would turn the House of Chanel into a global phenomenon and one of the most profitable luxury brands in the world. Astute to the power of publicity and the importance of brilliant advertising images, Lagerfeld told *WWD* at the time of his first collection, "I like to work only for big companies with big advertising power. I don't like anything small." He was perceptive in developing reciprocal relationships

OPPOSITE Karl Lagerfeld takes applause with Linda Evangelista at the finale of his rapper-influenced 1991 ready-to-wear show.

BELOW The famous
City Surfer collection
saw models walk
the runway with CC-
branded surfboards,
wearing lycra cycling
shorts and wetsuit-
shaped sequinned
jackets with sporty
zip-up fastenings.

OPPOSITE In
the studio at rue
Cambon, Lagerfeld
relied on a loyal team
of younger creatives
such as Gilles Dufour,
who worked with him
for over 15 years.

with dynamic media organizations, requested a budget of $100,000 worth of Chanel merchandise to give to high-profile actresses and influential friends in the industry, and was always a generous interviewee when dealing with the press. "Post-show he may have as many as 12 interviews lined up for television and more still for print. Blunt questions are met with remarkable humour, dignity and grace," noted fashion journalist Susannah Frankel in a detailed profile on the designer.

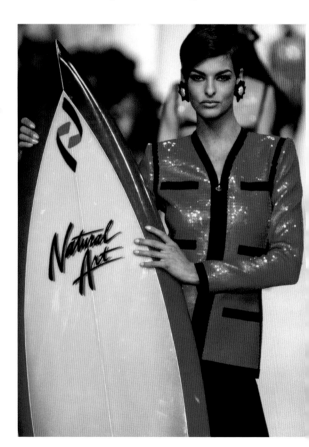

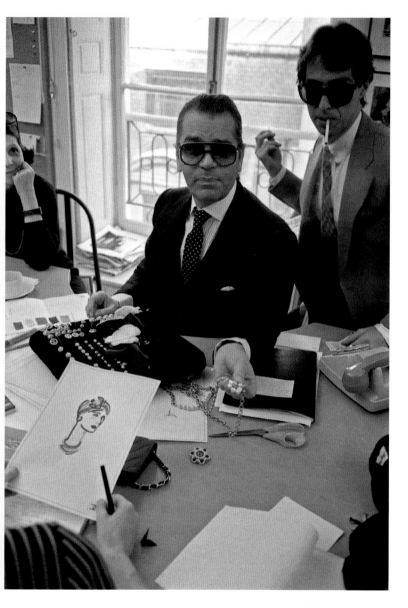

RIGHT Like Chanel,
Lagerfeld often took
inspiration from the
sporting arena, as in
this linen, baseball-
style, two-piece
pyjama suit, with
monogrammed gilt
buttons and a large
CC on the chest,
from 1984.

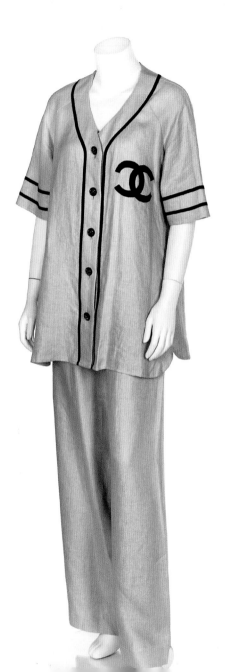

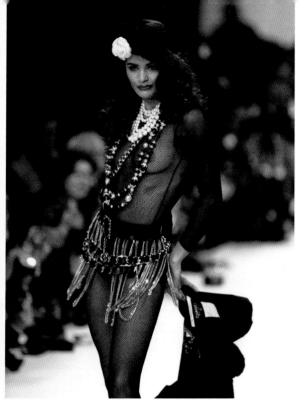

Highly intelligent, easily bored and obsessive about propelling the brand forwards, Lagerfeld consciously chose to break away from past traditions and live only in the present. "The designer must interpret the mood of the moment in clothes," he told *WWD* in 1988. A voracious consumer of books, newspapers and magazines, he had the ability to absorb vast amounts of information, simultaneously digesting current trends in music, films and popular culture before skilfully re-presenting the zeitgeist into desirable fashion items. Coco Chanel, he felt, had seriously misjudged the mood of the people with her outspoken derision of the 1960s miniskirt and blue

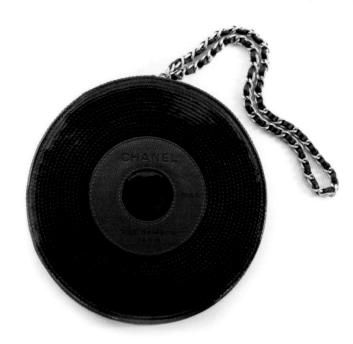

denim jeans. "The minute you think fashion everybody likes is horrible, you have to make an effort to understand why it is not. You have to like what is going on in the world to find a way to play with it," he explained to Anna Murphy from *The Times*. There was no definitive formula to the way Lagerfeld playfully reinvented each collection, but his constant quest for innovation coupled with a deeply held respect for superb tailoring and the exacting details of craftsmanship provided by the ateliers, proved to be a winning combination.

The studios at rue Cambon were constantly buzzing with music and chatter from an entourage of young creatives who helped Lagerfeld tap into the current mood on the streets. In the early days, Gilles Dufour, a good-looking Frenchman who was part of Paris's fashionable jet set, was a constant companion and integral part of the design team in the studio. Having first met Lagerfeld at Chloé, where he created fabric prints, Dufour started out as a studio director at Chanel and stayed as a loyal assistant for more than 15 years. He introduced Victoire de Castellane, his 22-year-old niece, to Lagerfeld, who immediately accepted the beautiful blonde aristocrat, known for her eclectic approach to fashion, into his inner sanctum. Castellane was both a model and muse for Lagerfeld, often walking on the catwalk for him as well as working in the studio. In the 1990s, she headed up the costume jewellery department and created some of the vibrant, surreal pieces that had become a signature of the Chanel lexicon, most memorably earrings that resembled mini quilted handbags, and miniature gilded birdcages with the interlocking-C insignia swinging freely inside.

"I learned how to play with the identities of the house," she says, "How to create without getting bored – without taking things too seriously." It was Gilles Dufour who hired

BELOW Victoire de Castellane was part of the Chanel team in the 1990s. She often walked the catwalk, but was also responsible for designing inventive pieces of jewellery.

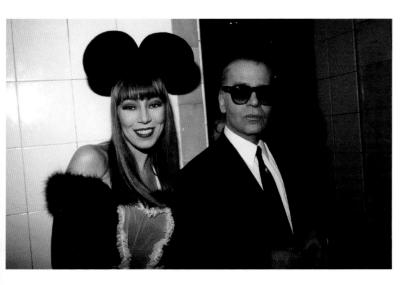

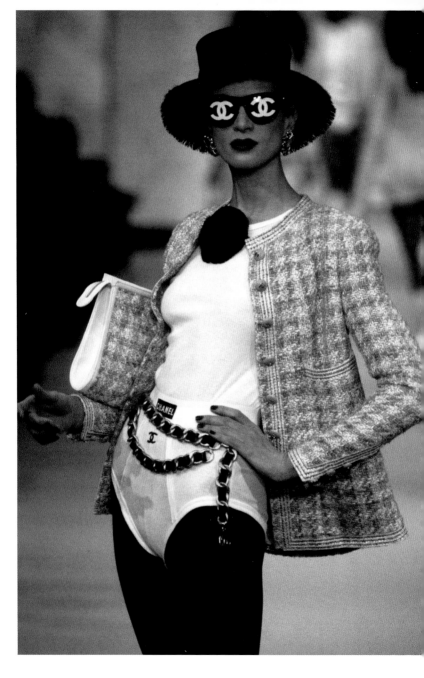

Virginie Viard, initially taking her on as an intern in the studios
in rue Cambon. Her outstanding talent and easy rapport
with Lagerfeld ensured she was quickly offered full-time
employment and became part of the team. With nobody in
charge of embroidery, Viard was chosen to work with François
Lesage, the legendary owner of La Maison Lesage, one of the
revered institutions of Parisian couture. It was an experience
that required great diplomacy to navigate the egos of Monsieur
Lagerfeld and Monsieur Lesage. Apart from a short spell at
Chloé in the 1990s (when Lagerfeld agreed to freelance for
them again), Viard worked exclusively for Chanel for over 30
years, working her way up from coordinator of haute couture to
overall director of Chanel's creative studio. Behind the scenes,
she was a trusted ally who could always be found at Lagerfeld's
shoulder, the designer acknowledging her contribution in the
2018 documentary *7 Days Out*: "Virginie Viard is the most
important person, not only for me, but also for the atelier. She
is my right arm, and even if I don't see her, we are on the phone
all the time."

With Inès de la Fressange on hand most days and Eric
Wright, a young American designer, also part of King Karl's
creative court, the designer unashamedly sucked up new ideas
from the whirlpool of energetic collaborators he employed,
eagerly taking on board their opinions and suggestions. He
called it "vampirizing" and it was a method he used throughout
his career, always surrounding himself with an entourage of
bright young things, celebrities and musicians as a means of
extracting the latest cultural trends, then later ruthlessly exiling
them from his orbit when he felt they had nothing useful to
impart. "I am a fashion vampire. I take what I want and leave,"
he told *The Cut*.

In the decades that followed, Lagerfeld succeeded in
producing a contemporary version of womenswear for Chanel,

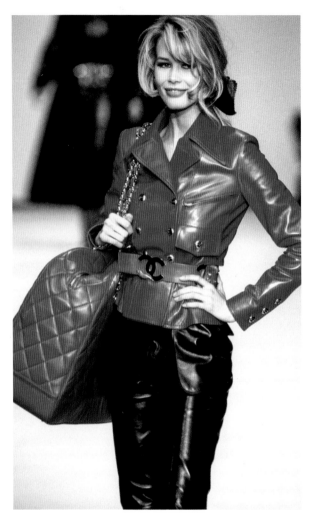

LEFT Claudia Schiffer stole the show wearing a reimagined motorbike jacket made in vibrant red leather and carrying a supersized quilted bag the size of a small suitcase over her shoulder.

OPPOSITE During the 1990s, the Chanel logo was emblazoned onto the most unlikely items of clothing and accessories, as here, with this acid-yellow and black, synthetic, furry muffler handbag taken from the 1994 Autumn/Winter collection.

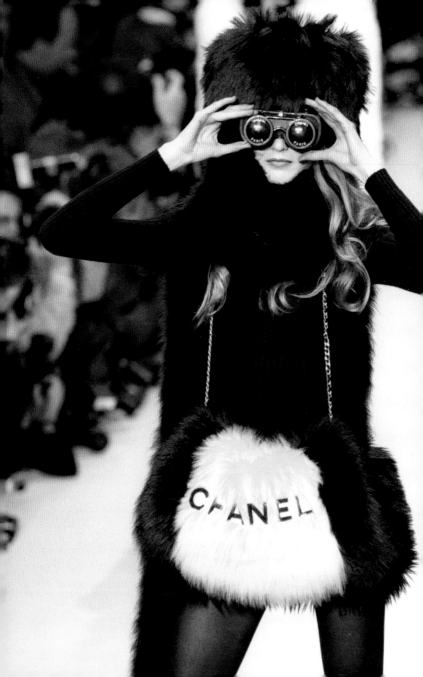

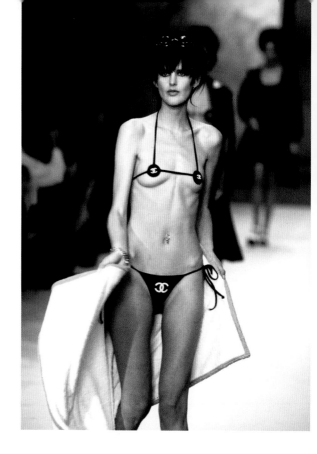

RIGHT Having exhausted themes of extravagant excess, Lagerfeld also explored minimalism, shown with this miniscule CC-branded bikini, modelled by Stella Tennant for the haute couture Autumn/Winter 1995 show.

taking many of her original themes of appropriation and re-presenting them with a post-modern twist of irony. Masterfully, he incorporated a connective thread that referenced the signature styles of Chanel herself: fluid pants and sailor collars in the late '80s reminiscent of 1920s Biarritz; sexier versions in the '90s of her famous tiered gypsy skirts, which were whipped off at the end of the catwalk to reveal fitted black leotards and leggings; exquisite evening jackets embroidered in the Coromandel patterns found on the screens in Coco's apartment; and endless reinvention of her trademark quilting, produced on a magnified scale for vest tops and dresses in 2000. Working instinctively, listening to his inner voice and designing what he felt was right for the time and the circumstances, Lagerfeld made imaginative use of the interlocking-C logo and helped the company to reach new levels of global recognition. His tasteful update of the original 2.55 handbag with a double-C twist lock in the late '80s provided the first clue of what was to come.

Glossy pictures from the catwalk shows from the 1990s onwards revealed a myriad of supersized logos emblazoned

BELOW Surrealism influenced the visually witty jewellery that Victoire de Castellane designed in the 1990s, such as these mini quilted Chanel handbag earrings, branded with the CC logo.

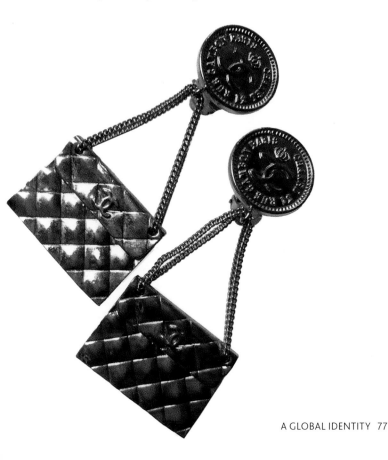

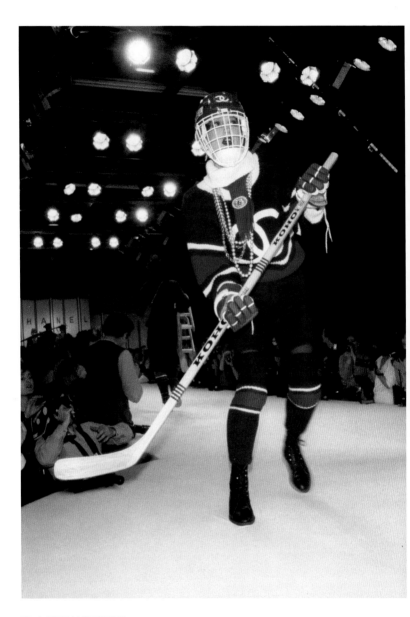

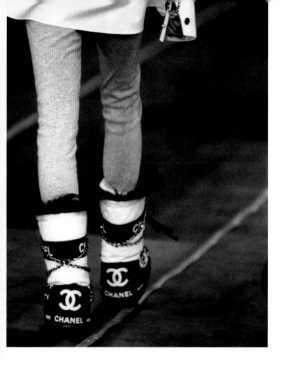

onto the most incongruous items of Chanel merchandise.
The double-C insignia could be found conspicuously stamped
onto moonboots, surfboards, sunglasses, trainers, braces, skis
and underwear – a genius touch of marketing for an audience
increasingly obsessed with luxury branding. For younger
consumers infatuated with fashion imagery, these attention-
grabbing tactics ensured that Chanel stayed modern and
relevant, but at the core of each collection the classic pieces
always remained. The little black dress freshly interpreted with
meticulous craftsmanship for every occasion; numerous versions
of the elegant suit remodelled with new proportions in a wide
range of unexpected materials – these are the essential items
that underpinned the ever-increasing success of Chanel, viewed
through the prism of Lagerfeld's genius.

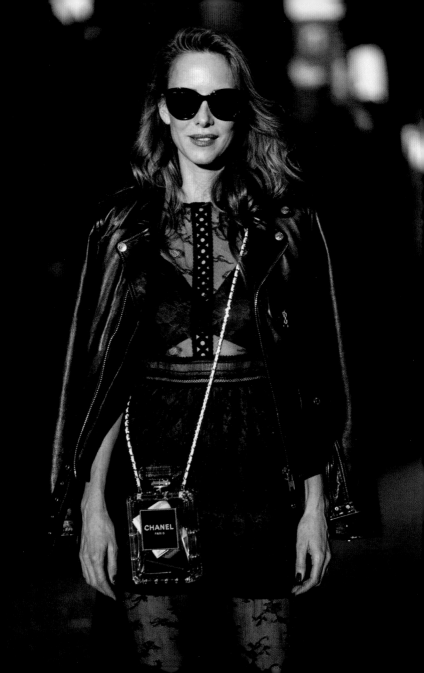

BELOW The blockbuster *hypermarché* show in 2014 saw many Chanel accessories reinvented as ordinary household goods, including this carton of milk handbag, emblazoned with seed-pearl script declaring "lait de COCO".

OPPOSITE Taking design inspiration from the most famous perfume in the world, Lagerfeld created a clear Perspex novelty bag modelled on Chanel N°5, complete with unique stopper and black and gold labelling.

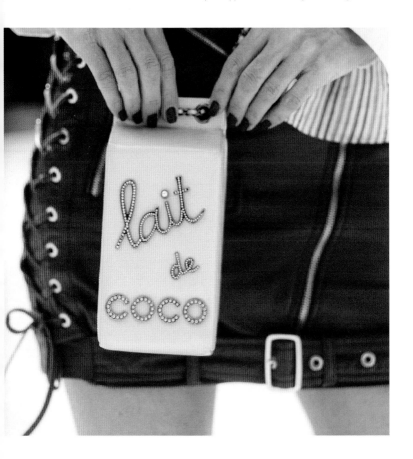

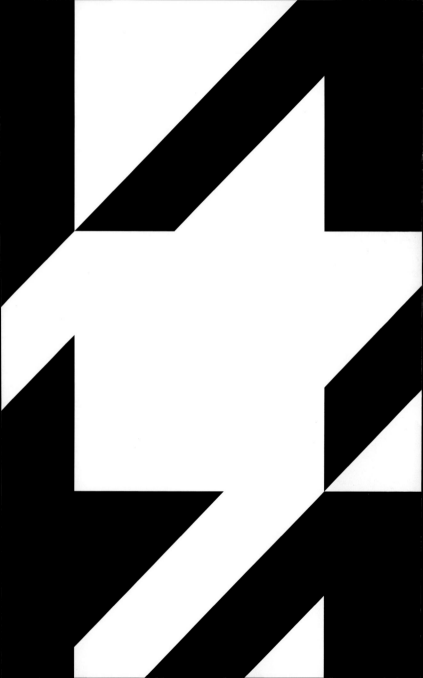

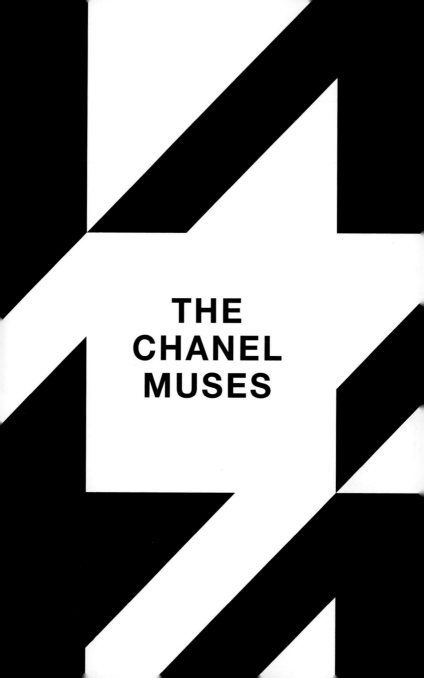

THE
CHANEL
MUSES

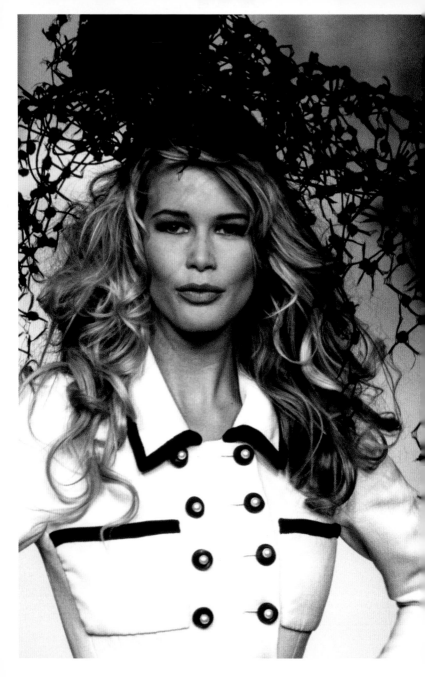

THE WOMEN WHO
MADE AN IMPACT

It was well documented that Lagerfeld adored his beautiful,
demanding mother, an accomplished violinist from Berlin
who treated him with disdain but remained
highly influential throughout his life.

A free-spirited individual who had little interest in the childhood years of her precocious only son, Elisabeth Lagerfeldt was mentioned reverentially in almost every interview he gave. The designer wore her wedding rings around his neck, explaining to Justine Picardie in 2018 that he sometimes felt his celebrated Birman cat Choupette was "my mother's reincarnation". A cultured and complicated woman, she was responsible, at least according to Lagerfeld, for his unique, rapid-fire style of speech, explaining that when his mother asked a question of him as a child, his response had to be fast and it had to be funny, or she would walk away, bored. "If I thought of something to say 10 minutes later, she would slap me," he told an audience at the Lincoln Centre in 2013. She encouraged his drawing, but was critical of his piano playing, banging the piano lid down on his hands when he was practising. She regularly mocked his appearance, teasing him about his wide nostrils and

OPPOSITE German-born Claudia Schiffer first walked for
Chanel when she was just 18 years old.

ugly hands, an insult that resulted in his daily ritual of wearing fingerless gloves to hide the shameful fingers. Lagerfeld's quick wit and acid tongue were inherited from Elisabeth, along with a steely determination to keep up appearances even to the end; his mother famously asked for the hairdresser to attend to her when she was dying, before the doctor was called. "Discipline is something that has to increase with age, I hate slobby people," he told Anna Murphy from *The Times*, after he had spectacularly lost more than six stone (38 kg) in 2001 and written an international bestseller detailing his punishing diet.

Not a fan of the term "muse", suggesting that the word itself can be "very limited", Lagerfeld made it clear from his eclectic choice of models throughout the years that attitude, spirit and approach to modern life were more important than the actual look of an individual woman. "In fashion you have to dress everyone, so you need all kinds of muses," he clarified to *Net-a-Porter* in 2012, and the roll call of visually disparate women who have represented Chanel during his tenure confirms this ethos.

One of the first things Lagerfeld did on his arrival at Chanel in 1983 was secure an exclusive contract for Inès de la Fressange, a long-limbed, upper-class French girl who perfectly encapsulated the face of Chanel in the 1980s. Already a successful catwalk model working for the hot Parisian designers of the time – Claude Montana, Thierry Mugler and Jean Paul Gaultier, as well as Lagerfeld at Chloé – she made the transition to Chanel and soared to international fame. Her rapport with Lagerfeld was immediate, and a long-term relationship that was both personal and professional ensued, with the giggly brunette a much-valued part of Lagerfeld's creative team at rue Cambon for several years. For a while the inseparable couple did everything together, with de la Fressange representing the brand as spokesperson on tour with Lagerfeld in the United

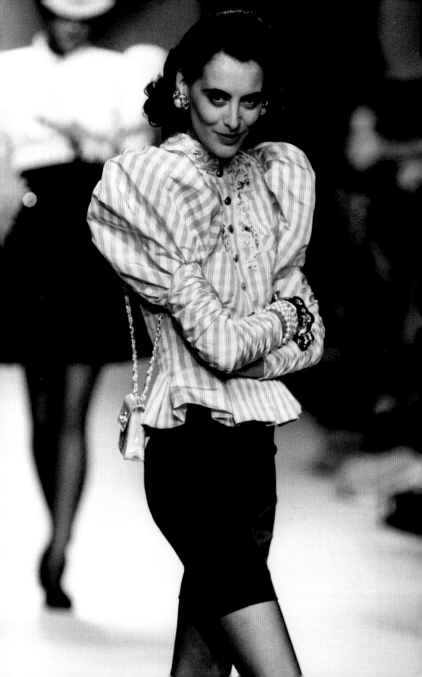

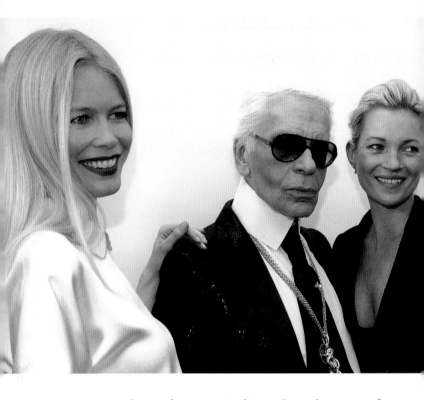

ABOVE Surrounded by supermodels: Lagerfeld flanked by Claudia Schiffer and Kate Moss, both of whom regularly appeared on the Chanel catwalk.

States and accompanying him on Concorde to see a performance of *Aida* at the Egyptian pyramids. Not surprisingly, their unexpected and much publicized falling-out in 1989 made front-page headlines throughout France. Her crime? Firstly, to have fallen in love with a new boyfriend Lagerfeld didn't like. Secondly, to have agreed (without his consent) to model as the face of Marianne, the symbol of the French Republic, an association he found distasteful, not least because a marble bust stands in every town hall in the country: "I do not dress public monuments." he quipped to the *Chicago Tribune*. Reconciled more than two decades later, de la Fressange agreed to walk the runway once again for her old friend and appeared in the ready-to-wear Spring/ Summer 2011 show at the Grand Palais. Even today, the spirited model remains one of the most recognizable brand ambassadors for Chanel.

At the tail end of the 1980s, Lagerfeld found a new muse who was in all respects the polar opposite to the slim "Coco style" he had previously championed. German-born Claudia Schiffer was a shy 18 year old hoping to become a lawyer when Lagerfeld saw her on the cover of British *Vogue* and asked her to come to see him at rue Cambon. His endorsement catapulted her to fame, starting with numerous photographic campaigns that Lagerfeld shot himself and continuing with her regular appearances by his side on the Chanel catwalk. Cool, blonde and curvaceously sexy, with piercingly blue eyes and a legendary pout, Schiffer was nervous about walking the runway for the first time in January 1989. The designer whom Schiffer called "a creative genius" asked her to imagine that she was just walking to school. "He wasn't looking for the coordinated catwalk moment, but rather something new," she told *Grazia* magazine. It was a pivotal moment for her, turning the timid young teenager into one of the best-loved supermodels in the world. "Karl was my magic dust," says Schiffer, who claims she will be eternally grateful to him for teaching her how to survive in the fashion industry.

A longstanding member of Lagerfeld's loyal creative retinue at Chanel was Lady Amanda Harlech, an elegant English eccentric who played the part of muse, right-hand woman and sounding board. For years she collaborated with the visionary concepts of John Galliano at Givenchy, but was lured to switch sides in 1997 for a huge pay rise and a permanent suite at the Paris Ritz. Discussing the importance of Harlech's role in creating a good atmosphere at the studios, Lagerfeld explained to *Observer* journalist John Colapinto: "She is an inspiration because she wears the clothes I make and mixes them with other things and is

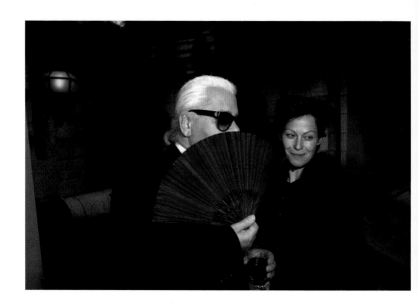

ABOVE English-born Lady Amanda Harlech worked alongside Karl Lagerfeld for over 20 years as a creative consultant whose opinion he trusted.

OPPOSITE Lagerfeld championed Cara Delevingne, whom he called "the 'It' girl of the moment".

very inventive herself." The official title for Harlech was Creative Consultant, her remit to come in several weeks before a show and sit alongside Lagerfeld for the final fittings, thoughtfully endorsing his opinions and ensuring every outfit that appears on the runway is sublime perfection. "Little details matter to Karl, and that makes the whole perfect," she explained to Tyler Brûlé after an haute couture presentation in 2018.

Committed to exploring new boundaries and fixated on youthful talent, Lagerfeld looked to Hollywood A-listers, titans of the modelling world, close friends such as the fashion editor Carine Roitfeld and indie music-makers in search of inspiration for Chanel. Top models Stella Tennant, Kristen McMenamy, Lara Stone and Cara Delevingne were not classical beauties, but refreshingly original, strikingly independent individuals who all played muse to the designer, while accomplished film stars who shunned blockbuster scripts in favour of unusual projects, such

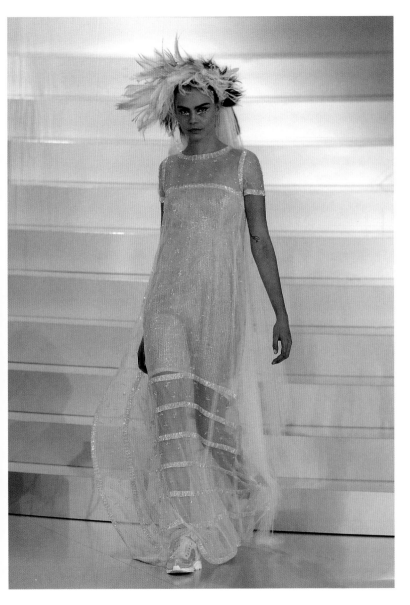

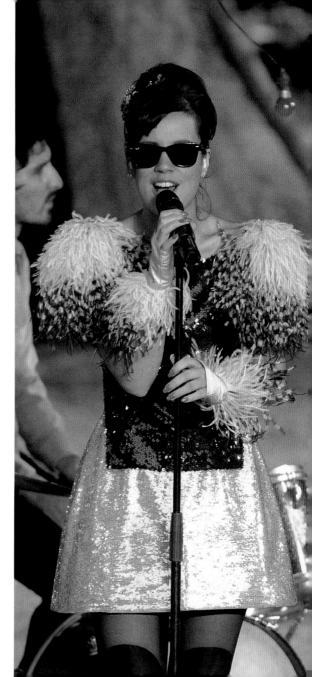

RIGHT In a campaign shot by Lagerfeld, Lily Allen became the face of the Coco Cocoon collection of bags, and later performed at the end of a 2010 rural-themed show in a CC-branded farm barn decorated with haystacks.

as Tilda Swinton, Kristen Stewart and Julianne Moore, stunned in Chanel creations on both the red carpet and the catwalk. Less obvious choices for house muse have included musicians Lily Allen, Rita Ora and Cat Power, and later the children of people who had been his collaborators in previous generations. Lily-Rose Depp, the sylphlike daughter of Vanessa Paradis and Johnny Depp; his godson Hudson Kroenig, cherubic offspring of one of his favourite male models Brad Kroenig; Kaia Gerber, Cindy Crawford's stunning lookalike daughter; and Violette d'Urso, youngest child of Inès de la Fressange, who at 17 appeared at the Chanel casino show in a

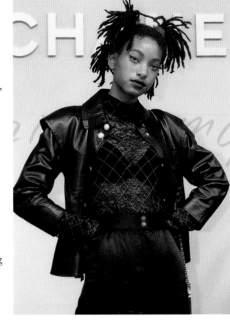

splendid couture dress and sneakers. A teenage Willow Smith became a Chanel brand ambassador in 2016. Not a fan of social media, vocally scathing of the need to post every personal detail of oneself online ("What I hate most in life is selfies," he told *WWD* in 2014), but aware that the company maintained a formidable Instagram presence with more than 30 million followers, Lagerfeld embraced the influential global reach of these young women. "I love Cara. She is the 'It' girl of the moment. Nobody has as many followers as she has," he gushed after sweeping through the multicoloured, Instagrammable supermarket aisles with her at the finale of the ready-to-wear show at the Grand Palais in 2014. His innate curiosity enabled him to recognize what lay ahead – and then keep one step ahead.

ABOVE At just 15 years old, Willow Smith was named as a new face for Chanel after appearing on the catwalk in 2016.

OVERLEAF Walking alongside Lily-Rose Depp, who was chosen to close the show as the couture bride in layers of frothy pink organza at the Spring/Summer 2017 collection.

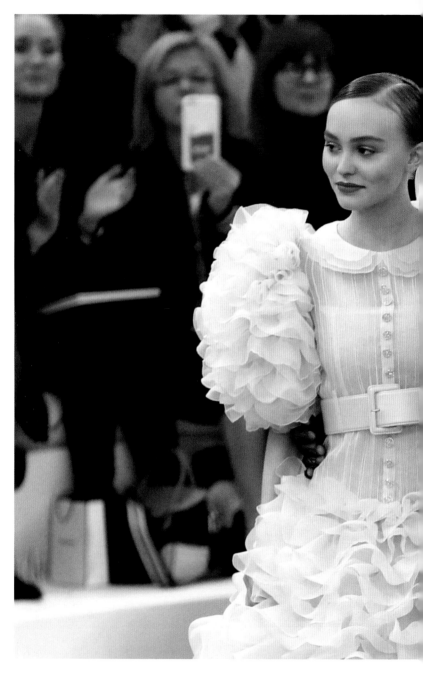

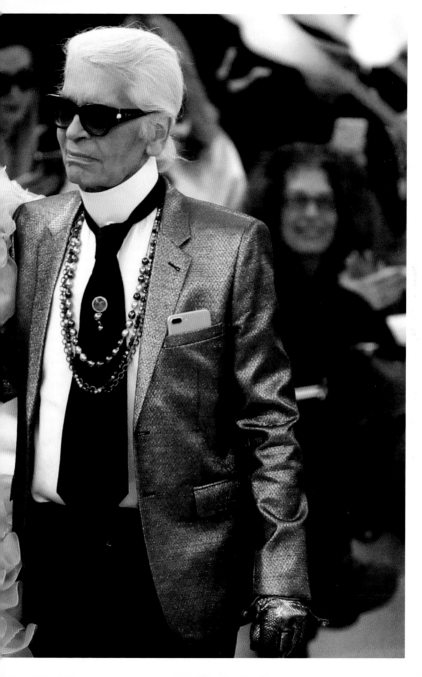

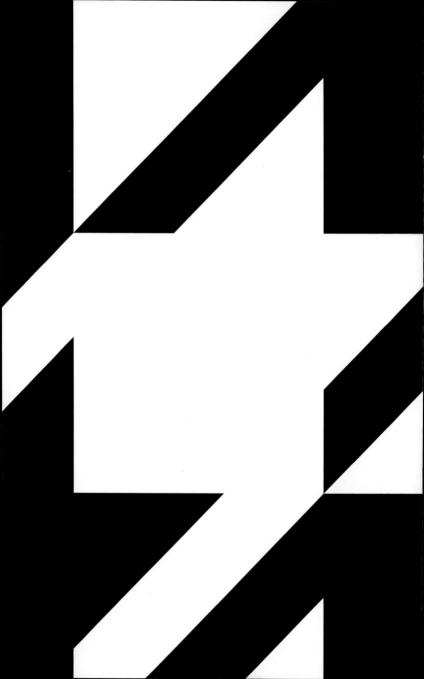

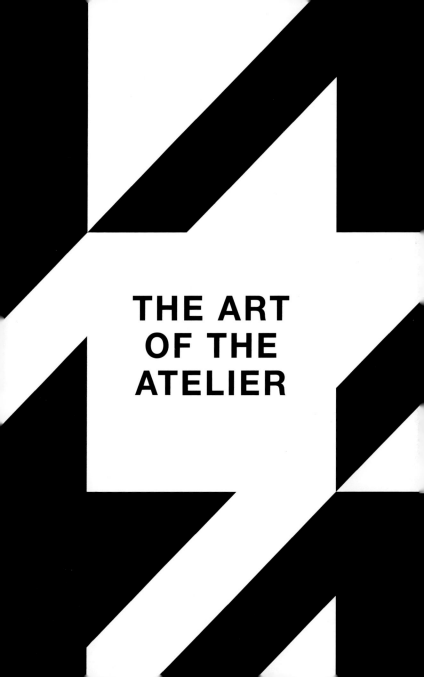

THE ART
OF THE
ATELIER

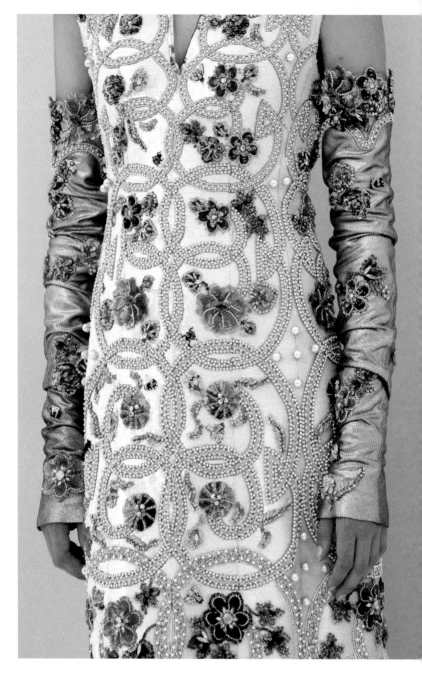

A TRADITION OF CRAFTSMANSHIP

Designed to celebrate the exquisite workmanship of the
traditional ateliers that worked with Mademoiselle Chanel,
the annual Métiers d'Art show succeeds in highlighting
the finest examples of technical expertise within
the fashion industry.

It showcases an array of artisanal skills, which includes luxury
tweeds, embroidery, beading, costume jewellery, hats, buttons
and leatherwork, all lovingly created by hand by teams of highly
proficient craftspeople. This spectacular event of theatrical
showmanship takes place in December and is a relatively new
addition to the fashion show calendar, instigated by Lagerfeld
in 2002 to show off the unique talents of the numerous Parisian
workshops that are now owned by Chanel. From his early days
with the company, Lagerfeld recognized that many of the family-
run businesses which had supplied Coco Chanel in the latter
part of her career now found themselves in a precarious position,
including Maison Lesage, Maison Goossens and Maison
Lemarié. With future generations unwilling to continue the

OPPOSITE Thousands of seed pearls lovingly hand-stitched in patterns
reminiscent of the intricate illustrations used to illuminate medieval
manuscripts, produced for Chanel in 2006 by the skilled craftspeople
at Maison Lesage.

BELOW Lagerfeld
continued Chanel's
legacy for bold
costume jewellery,
such as this mid-80s
gemstone brooch
made by Maison
Gripoix.

OPPOSITE Black
satin couture dress,
with bodice edged in
sable and decorated
with chess boards and
pieces, embroidered
in ivory and scarlet
bugle beads by
Maison Lesage.

in-house traditions, and with so much of fashion increasingly industrialized, there was a real chance that the slow production methods employed by the specialist artisan houses were in danger of extinction. Without Chanel's financial intervention, the artistry of these French-based businesses would have disappeared forever, resulting in a devastating impact on the entire business model of couture fashion.

Looking to secure their own future supply chain, as well as that of other luxury brands who have also supported these houses, Chanel invested in its first atelier, the jewellers Desrues, in 1985. In the intervening years the company has purposefully acquired a stable of 26 others (and further acquisitions are possible). All unite under the banner "Les Métiers d'Art de Chanel", each providing a unique craft that cannot be replicated by modern machinery.

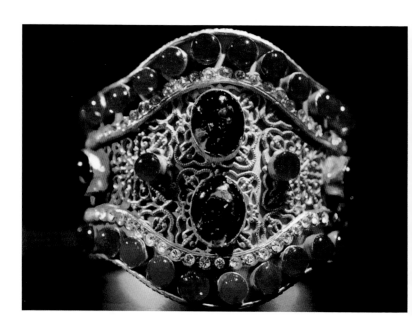

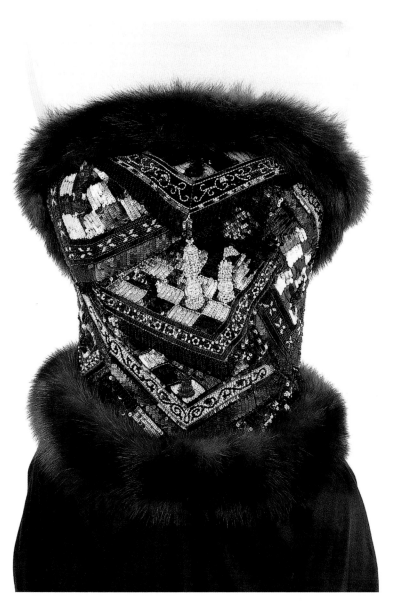

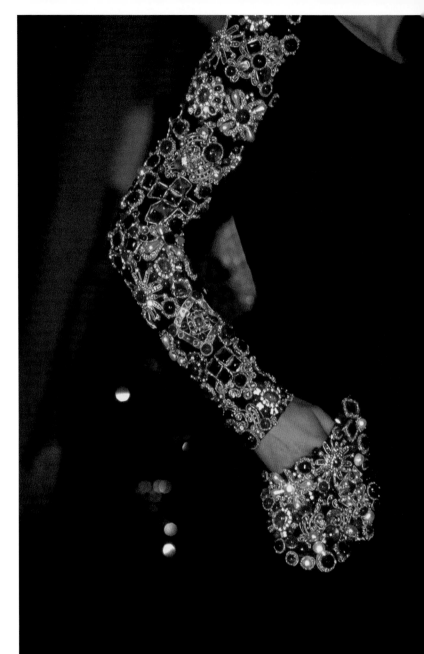

OPPOSITE Closely
aligned to the brightly
jewelled Maltese
cuffs that Chanel had
commissioned for
herself in 1937, the
heavily decorated
sleeves and pockets
of this slim black shift
dress are emblematic
of the finest
craftsmanship of
the ateliers.

The inaugural Métiers d'Art show was a small affair named Satellite Love, which featured 33 stunning looks presented in the Chanel haute couture salon in rue Cambon to an invited audience of clients and journalists. In subsequent years, Lagerfeld took his shows on the road, choosing a different location every year by tapping into the personal history of the company or its indomitable figurehead. From Dallas to Rome, Salzburg to New York, the Métier d'Art collections are presented using lavish sets in stunning locations, and Lagerfeld continually pushed the creative boundaries to ensure the global audience watching online did not get bored. Speaking to *WWD* in 2013 after the Métiers d'Art presentation held at Linlithgow Palace outside Edinburgh, Lagerfeld explained the rationale of choosing the international cities for his "magical" fashion extravaganzas. "I try to find a vague connection. It was her love of hunting in Scotland, and how she discovered tweeds there," he said of his decision to present the catwalk show against the backdrop of the spectacular castle ruins, birthplace of Mary Stuart. "With a little detail you can make a whole story," he elaborated. "She went a lot to Venice, which is why I did a show in Venice [2009]. She had a Russian lover, and loved Russian art, so I did it in Russia [2008]." Other venues included the Chanel building in Ginza, Tokyo (2004); the Casino at Monte Carlo in the principality of Monaco (2006); and the Elbphilharmonie concert hall designed by Herzog & de Meuron, in his hometown of Hamburg (2017).

Surrounded by the impressive ruins of the Temple of Dendur, now located in the Metropolitan Museum of Art in New York, the Métiers d'Art collection in 2018 was clearly inspired by the treasures of ancient Egypt. Golden camellias, scarab beetle handbags and hieroglyphic embroideries all featured, but it was musician Pharrell Williams who stole the show, in a gold lurex knit embellished with a neck adornment created

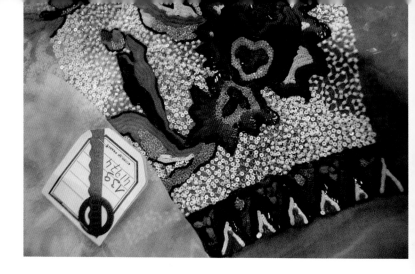

ABOVE Technology can never replace the unique skills of the Maison Lesage haute couture embroidery team, who hand stitch every sequin and bead for Chanel with a needle and thread.

OPPOSITE Spring/Summer 2000 was strong on colour and silhouette, with lavish embroidery and skilful appliqué work used to create decorative floral patterns echoed by hairstyles twisted neatly into chic camellia-flower shapes.

by Atelier Montex, and gold leather boots by the shoemaker Maison Massaro. "Luxury has to be luxury," said Lagerfeld after the event. "It means a beautifully made product." The task of turning dreams into reality requires passion and patience. The opulent clothes produced for the Métiers d'Art collections fall into the ready-to-wear category, although the exacting techniques used for each outfit ensure that they are closely aligned to couture levels of workmanship. With a myriad of revolutionary ideas constantly spilling out of Lagerfeld, all of which proffered exciting new directions to explore, the heads of the ateliers were eager to experiment, always searching for reinvention and ready to accept the most demanding challenges. Hubert Barrère, Artistic Director at Maison Lesage, spoke to Derek Blasberg in 2016 of his admiration for Lagerfeld, his long-time friend and collaborator: "Karl is unique because he is always looking to tomorrow. To always be yearning for other things is terribly stimulating. Fashion is not about making pretty things, it's about making things that are different, current and desirable." Respecting traditions but embracing

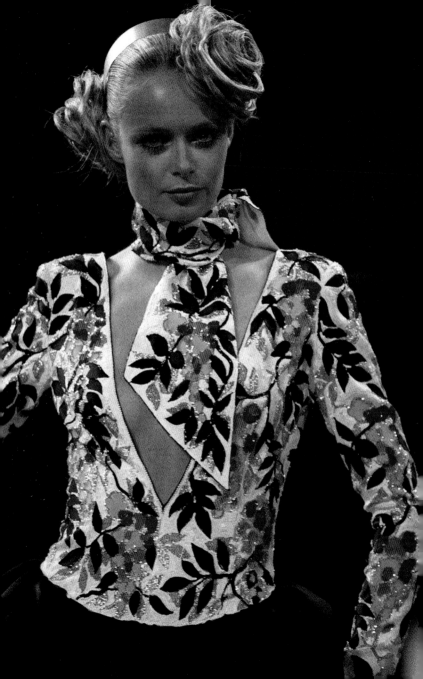

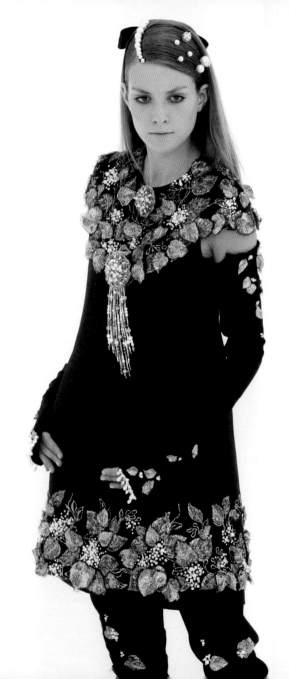

new technologies such as laser cutting and 3D printing has expanded the scope of possibilities for all the ateliers, and while Lagerfeld continued to play with the recognized iconography of the house – the quilting, the camellias, the tweeds – he cleverly introduced the most improbable materials into the mix to upend people's expectations. Delicate wooden shavings were magically embroidered onto outfits to embellish the Spring/Summer 2016 haute couture collection and mini paillettes made from cement by Atelier Montex (which Amanda Harlech recalled as "extraordinarily beautiful") were used for decoration in a show that paid homage to the modernist architect Le Corbusier in 2014. Updated tweeds were invented for Lagerfeld, interwoven with zip fasteners, feathers, nylon thread and even LED lights, in the quest for originality and creative merit.

In March 2021 Chanel announced the opening of a purpose-built, multidisciplinary artistic hub in Paris where all the ateliers are now based. The spacious new building provides more than 25,500 square metres (275,000 square feet) of space for workshops and is located beyond the busy Périphérique ring road in Porte d'Aubervilliers, the northeastern corner of the city. Designed by award-winning French architect Rudi Ricciotti, the triangular-shaped structure with a visual outer skeleton of cylindrical concrete spines is known as 19M; the number 19 is taken from both the day of Chanel's own birth and the arrondissement where it is located, and M represents the words *mains, mode et métier* (hands, fashion and craftsmanship). Bruno Pavlovsky, Chanel's President of Fashion who was instrumental in saving the original artisan houses, was also responsible for creating an umbrella subsidiary called Paraffection ("with love and affection"), now a thriving company that groups the network together. Within the bright and airy space, there is enough room to house decades' worth of archives, with hundreds of embroidery patterns, buttons, flower creations and

OPPOSITE Luxurious gold leaf embroidery and ornate beading embellished thigh-high boots and long evening gloves in a collection that paid homage to the medieval style of the Middle Ages.

BELOW Hand stitched with perfect precision, the instantly recognizable sixteen-petal Chanel camellia is produced in many different forms by the atelier Maison Lemarié.

fabric swatches all secured in perfect conditions for posterity. With every atelier recognized as the global expert in their specialist field, the talented teams who spend countless hours creating memorable details of beauty are fashion's unnamed geniuses, known only to those within the business who appreciate their art.

Established in 1880, Maison Lemarié originally produced extravagant creations for the fashionable attire of the Belle Époque, using every type of animal feather they could secure. In addition to feather work, the house is now responsible for making all of Chanel's signature 16 petal camellias, as well as couture pieces that require ruffles, pleats and smocking. Costume jeweller Desrues crafts high-quality buttons and jewellery by hand, employing the techniques of sculptors, engravers and chisellers to achieve the desired results, and producing a daily tally of 4,000 buttons.

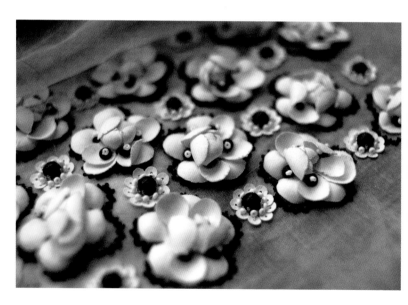

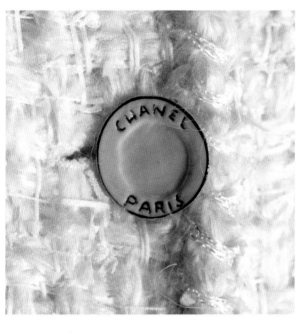

Recognized for the exceptional beaded embroidery it has produced for Schiaparelli, Yves Saint Laurent and, more recently, Christian Lacroix, Maison Lesage has been at the forefront of intricate hand stitching for nearly a hundred years, showcasing gold thread, crystal beads, diamanté and precious stones to produce the most impressive items of fashion decoration. Coco Chanel worked with Maison Goossens in the 1950s, asking the founder Robert Goossens to collaborate on ideas for costume jewellery that incorporated Byzantine influences. She also commissioned mirrors and chandeliers from him for her apartment at 31 rue Cambon. Today the house combines the talents of goldsmiths and craftspeople, producing pieces from metal, stone, leather, enamel and wood. Couture milliner Maison Michel joined Chanel's Métiers d'Art stable in 1997,

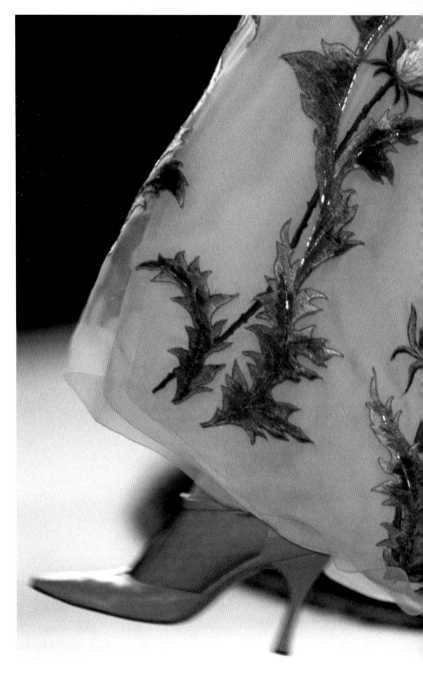

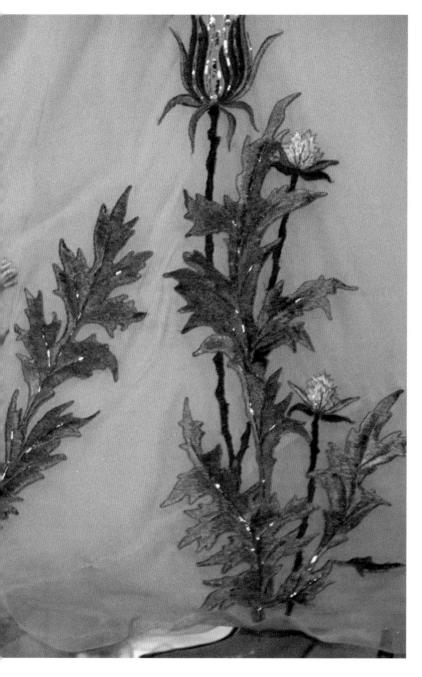

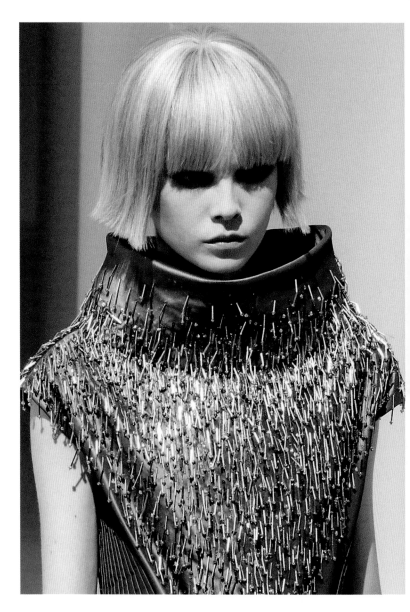

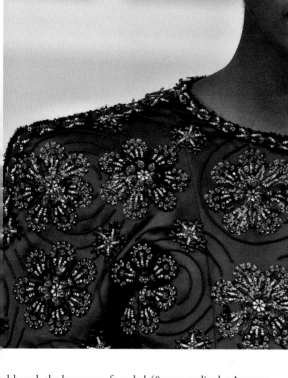

LEFT Ink-blue satin evening wear, embellished with embroidery produced by the atelier Maison Lesage, intricately shaped into floral motifs using matt sequins, stones, and tiny beadwork, part of the Autumn/Winter 2016 haute couture collection.

OPPOSITE Introducing a new neckline, the complex beading created from seed pearls and crystals produced a glistening raindrop effect for this ultra-modern silhouette in 2009.

although the house was founded 40 years earlier by Auguste Michel. With an archive of almost 4,000 wooden blocks of different shapes and sizes to choose from, the house artisans deftly use their hands to shape a variety of unusual materials into unexpected forms of millinery. Legendary footwear company Massaro was set up in 1894 by Raymonde Massaro's grandfather, and acquired by Chanel in 2002. It was Raymonde who, in 1957, helped Mademoiselle Chanel create the two-tone slingback that became one of the house's most iconic signature pieces, a design that immediately identifies it even today.

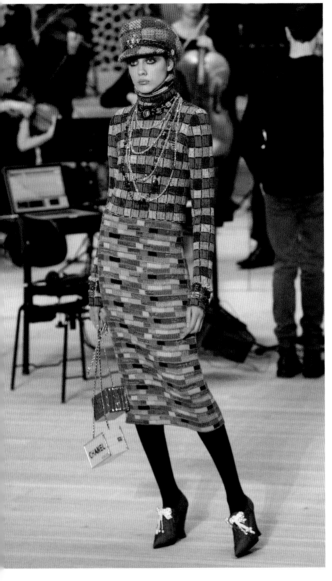

LEFT Returning to his hometown of Hamburg, the 2017 Métier d'Art collection showcased cashmere nautical caps from the millinery specialist Maison Michel, and stunning jewellery in the form of crystal brooches and cap pins made by Maison Goossens.

OPPOSITE The final Métier d'Art collection that Lagerfeld conceived took place in December 2018, showcasing a modern take on ancient Egypt. Vibrant graffiti doodles mixed with traditional hieroglyphics in a show laden with gold, found woven through tweeds, spun through the finest knits and gracing the distinctive boots crafted by Maison Massaro.

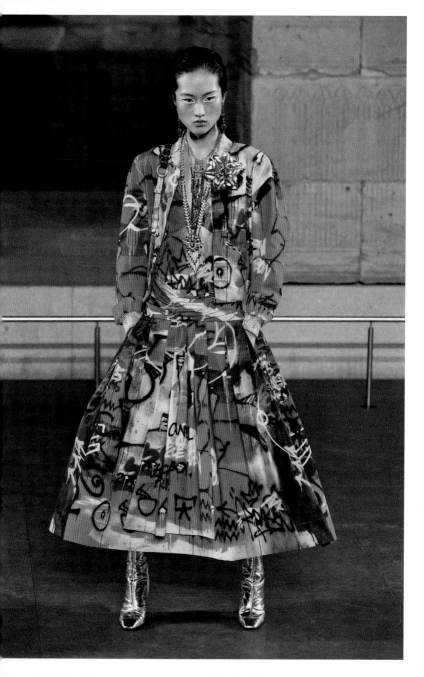

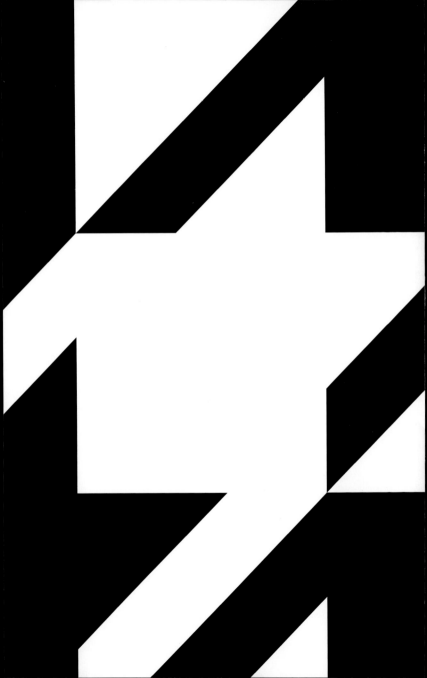

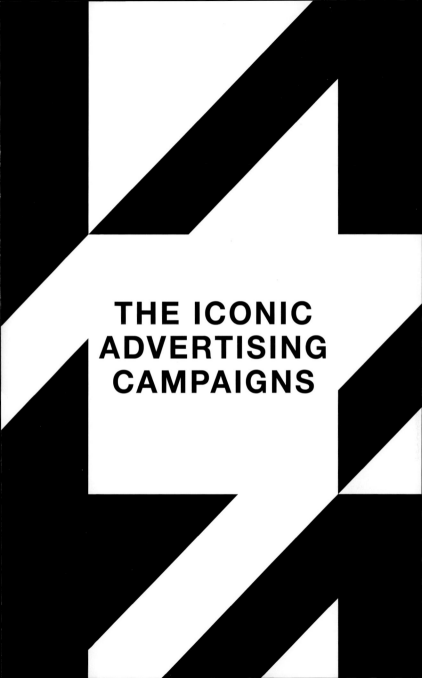

THE ICONIC ADVERTISING CAMPAIGNS

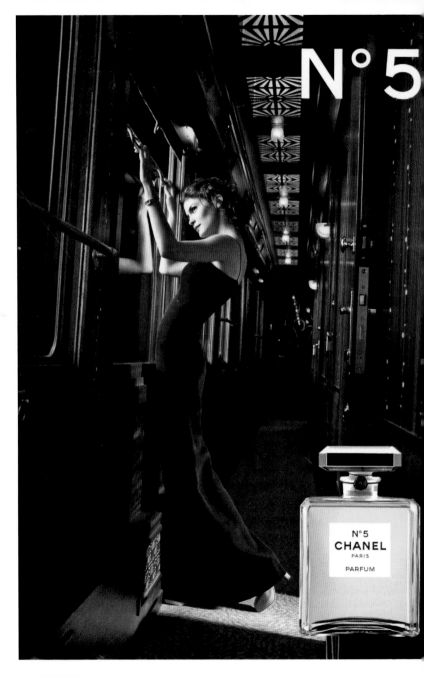

STORYTELLING WITH STYLE

"I don't think a woman is well dressed unless she is wearing perfume."
KARL LAGERFELD

For more than 40 years Jacques Helleu, in-house Artistic Director, was responsible for producing the outstanding advertising campaigns that helped to boost worldwide sales of Chanel's range of fragrances. He conceived the idea that N°5 (which was launched in 1922 and continues to be a global bestseller) should be promoted using film stars such as Catherine Deneuve, Ali MacGraw, Candice Bergen and, more recently, Nicole Kidman, Audrey Tautou and Marion Cotillard, as well as Keira Knightley (Coco Mademoiselle). Chanel was one of the first companies to tap into the aspirational appeal of choosing beautiful actresses to endorse the exclusivity of their fragrances. The campaigns they starred in were produced by some of the greatest creative talents of the era, in both photography and film-making, including Richard Avedon, Mario Testino, Jean-Paul Goude, Ridley Scott and Baz Luhrmann. The initial concept for the print campaigns relied not on witty slogans or hard-

OPPOSITE Evoking the glamour of a bygone age of travel, French actress Audrey Tautou represented the face of N°5 in a commercial loaded with *Brief Encounter* moments and shot on the Orient Express.

BELOW Continuing a well-established tradition of stylish understatement, with adverts that focused attention on an outsized bottle of perfume, Carole Bouquet was the face of Chanel throughout the 80s.

selling tag lines, but on a visual simplicity that created impact through clean-cut minimalism, focusing on the transparency of an outsized perfume bottle and the chic understatement of the elegant Chanel woman. The unique personality of each actress was paramount to the ongoing success of N°5, with the Chanel website clearly acknowledging the winning collaboration of these modern images: "French elegance and eternal femininity… embodied by the greatest celebrities." French actress Carole Bouquet, best known for her role as a Bond girl opposite Roger Moore in *For Your Eyes Only*, was the recognizable face of Chanel N°5 in the 1980s. She appeared in numerous print campaigns that adhered to the original concept, her role to represent a timeless vision of the Chanel woman alongside the iconic perfume bottle, with the product visually more prominent than the beauty who endorsed it. Bouquet also starred in a series of television commercials directed by Ridley Scott and based on the strapline "Share the Fantasy". These stylized 30-second cinematic films were shot in strong saturated colour and kick-

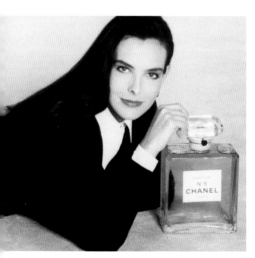

started the trend for a romantic storyline, played out in exotic locations using expensive props, with the obligatory presence of an attractive love interest and a powerful soundtrack. Notable for an absence of hard sell, these sophisticated adverts simply equated the dynamics of stylishly independent women with the allure of the fragrance.

French artist Jean-Paul Goude, one of the world's most unorthodox image-makers, was responsible for many of Chanel's

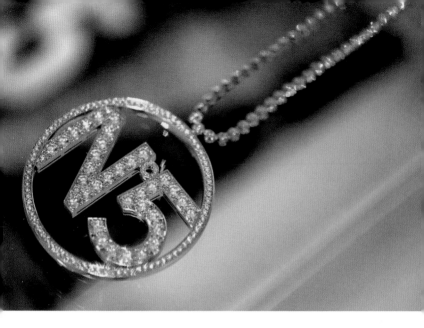

best-known commercials in the 1990s. Most memorably he created the campaign for the masculine fragrance Égoïste, which saw dozens of beautiful women throw open the shuttered windows of an impressive five-storey, turreted Riviera mansion (constructed and filmed in Rio de Janeiro) and yell "Égoïste! Égoïste!" to the dramatic soundtrack of Prokofiev's *Romeo and Juliet*. Later, taking inspiration from a small gold birdcage that was found in Coco Chanel's Paris apartment, he cast a whistling, 18-year-old Vanessa Paradis as an exotic bird of paradise. The 1993 "Tweety Pie" ad was conceived for the fragrance Coco, l'Esprit de Chanel, and saw Paradis dressed in a simple black leotard with fishnet tights and extravagant plumage trapped on a swinging trapeze in a giant metal cage, while being stalked from below by a mischievous, fluffy white feline prowling the cage perimeter.

An artistic collaboration between Andy Warhol, King of Pop Art, and the legendary French couturière Coco Chanel seemed

ABOVE Deliberately avoiding product placement, Baz Luhrmann's infamously expensive *Moulin Rouge* advert closed on the detail of a glittering necklace, made from 687 diamonds, fashioned into the Nº5 logo.

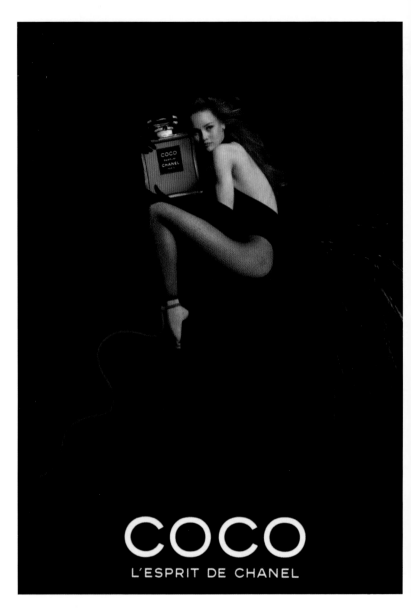

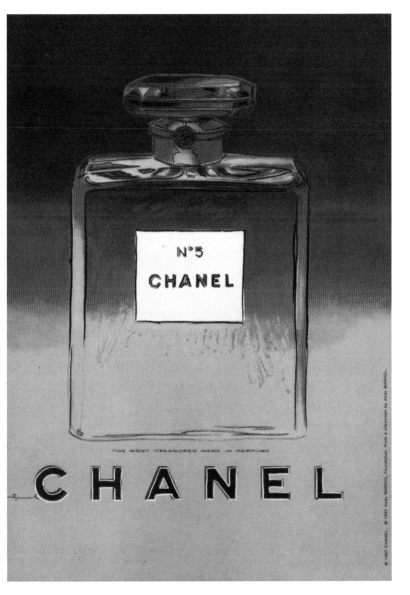

an ideal way to celebrate the 75th anniversary of N°5. Warhol's instantly recognizable silk-screen illustrations of the classic bottle consolidated "two works of art", according to Lyle Saunders, Vice President of Creative Services for Chanel in 1997, and the celebrated perfume is the first to enter New York's MoMA museum. Reproduced in a series of four vibrant colourways, including neon pink and acid yellow, this modern campaign was admired by everyone for the way it successfully aligned the talent of two twentieth-century icons.

Mega publicity about the astronomical costs of "the world's most expensive advert" circulated within the industry at the launch of Baz Luhrmann's cinematic creation for N°5, inspired by *Moulin Rouge*. Teased as more of a mini-feature than an explosive blast of corporate commercialism, and starring Oscar-winning actress Nicole Kidman as the leading lady, the cinematic advert, which played for a duration of three-and-a-half minutes, first aired in Britain on Channel 4 in 2004. Based loosely on the storyline of *Roman Holiday*, Kidman plays the part of an uber-famous cabaret dancer (stunningly dressed in a pink chiffon dress designed by Lagerfeld), who escapes a pursuing crowd of paparazzi by jumping into the nearest taxi, where she meets a devastatingly handsome, penniless young author on the back seat. After a brief romantic moment together on the rooftops of Paris, she is lured back to her high-pressured life, with the writer left only with his memories of her: "Her kiss, her smile, her perfume."

The advert never shows us the famous bottle, the final shot lingering on a dazzling necklace made from 687 diamonds formed into the N°5 logo. The production budget was rumoured to be around $18 million, and Kidman, who had previously always rejected commercial projects, received more than $2 million. The highly anticipated film and print campaign launched towards the end of November to capture the lucrative Christmas perfume market.

British actress Keira Knightley has represented the brand since 2007, when she was chosen as the coquettish face of a new fragrance called Coco Mademoiselle, created by Jacques Polge, Chanel's in-house perfumer for 37 years. Appearing in beautifully understated print adverts shot by Mario Testino, she exudes a smoky-eyed sexiness that is both playfully flirtatious and rebellious, somewhat reminiscent of Coco Chanel herself. In 2011 she starred in an action-packed commercial directed by her friend Joe Wright (*Pride and Prejudice, Atonement, Darkest Hour*), which saw her mysterious character posing seductively for

OVERLEAF In 2005, American actor Brad Pitt was chosen to front both print and television advertising campaigns to endorse Chanel's bestselling perfume N°5.

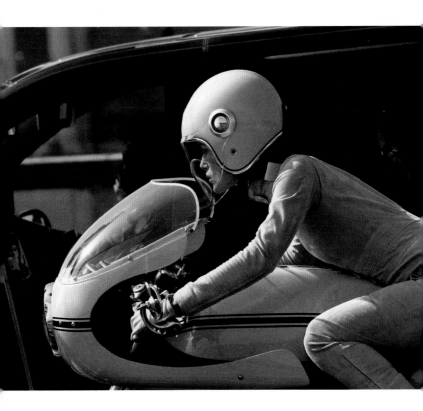

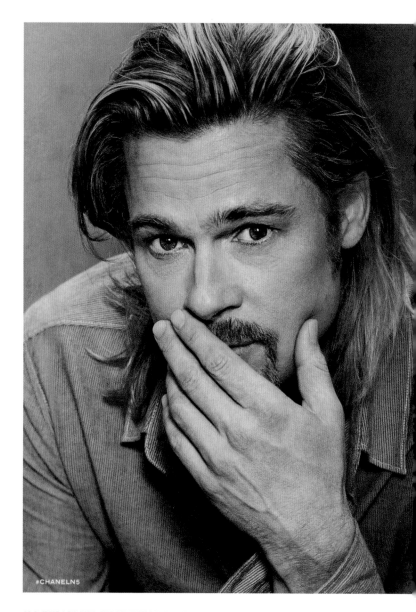

#CHANELN5

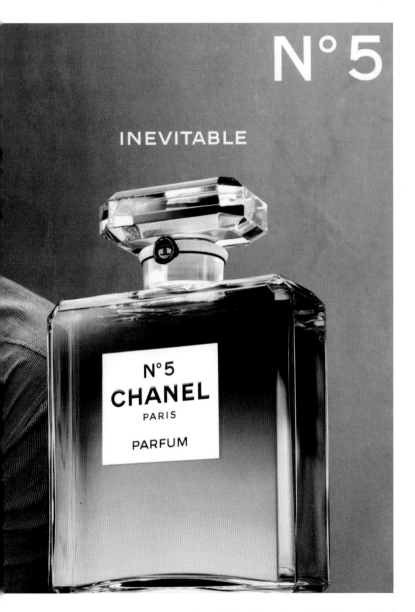

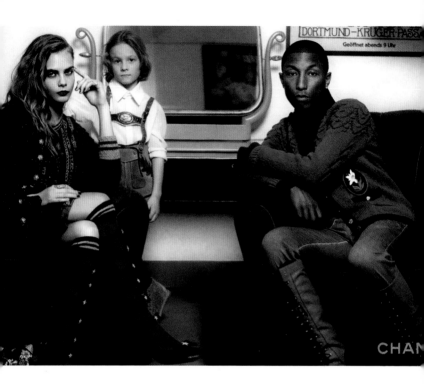

ABOVE To coincide with the Paris-Salzburg Métier d'Art show in 2015, Lagerfeld shot the Instagram campaign featuring then-favourites Cara Delevingne, Pharrell Williams and his godson Hudson Kroenig, wearing Chanel's interpretation of traditional Bavarian costumes.

a photographer on a fashion shoot, before the final frame cuts to her zooming off on a motorbike across the Place Vendôme, fabulously kitted out in a body-hugging catsuit. Featuring a Joss Stone cover of 'It's a Man's World', this unforgettably stylish advert has been seen over 14 million times on YouTube.

Intent on innovation and originality, the company enticed Brad Pitt to become the new face of Chanel N°5 in 2012, the first time a man had fronted the campaign for their bestselling perfume. A shaggy-haired, unshaven Pitt starred in a decidedly low-key, minimalist advert that was shot in black and white, in a nondescript studio location. Speaking directly to camera, in a voice loaded with sincerity, Pitt informed the viewer, "Wherever I go, there you are. My luck. My fate. My fortune. Chanel N°5." For the finale, the screen burst into full technicolour and showed a translucent bottle floating above a twinkling sky at night. Pitt wraps up his performance with a single heartfelt word: "Inevitable."

High production values, enviable locations, and the tried-and-tested cinematic skills of film director Baz Luhrmann were all utilized in 2014, when supermodel Gisele Bündchen became the new face of N°5 for the fantasy short film *The One That I Want*. It was shot on numerous locations around the world (the ocean around Fiji, The Box nightclub in New York, a beachside residence in Montauk) and follows a predictable narrative that captures the athletic Brazilian as she breezes through her enviable life, juggling the demands of motherhood, career and lover. From confidently navigating the roaring surf with a Chanel-branded surfboard in tow, to arriving beautifully dressed at the theatre to meet her tuxedo-clad love interest (Michiel Huisman from *Game of Thrones*), the aspirational images are familiar ones.

In the 1990s, Lagerfeld developed an interest in photography and subsequently started to shoot many of Chanel's press kits and advertising campaigns himself. Later turning to film, he directed several mini-features, starring Geraldine Chaplin, Rupert Everett, Kristen Stewart and Pharrell Williams, to satisfy social media's increasing demand for narrative content. Today, more than a hundred years after it launched, Chanel N°5 continues to dominate the fragrance market, helped in part by a succession of exceptional advertising campaigns which keep the brand contemporary. With each new launch, the creative team conceive an individual marketing campaign designed to ensure the Chanel legacy maintains its status as the ultimate house of luxury.

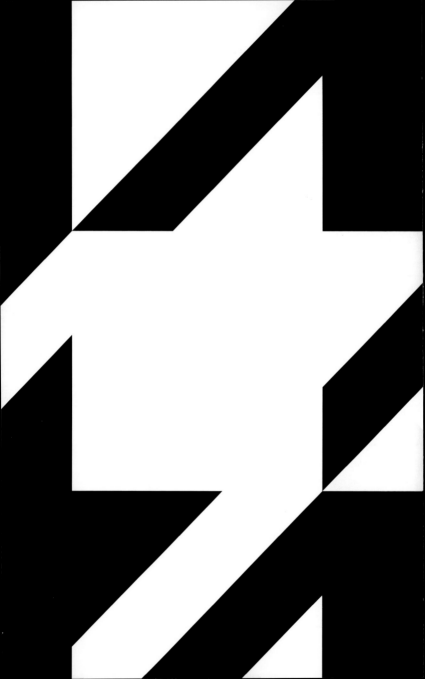

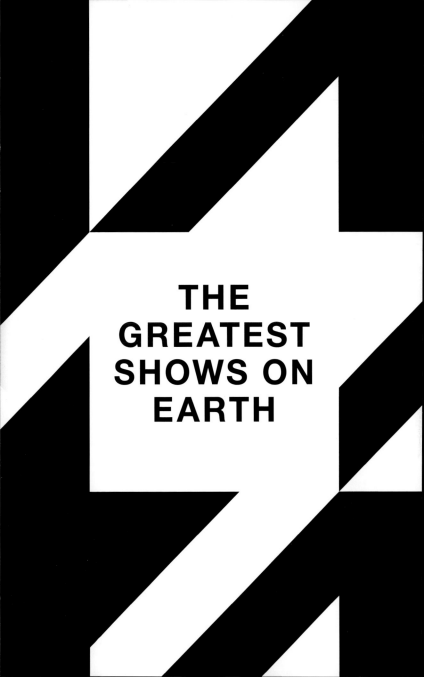

THE
GREATEST
SHOWS ON
EARTH

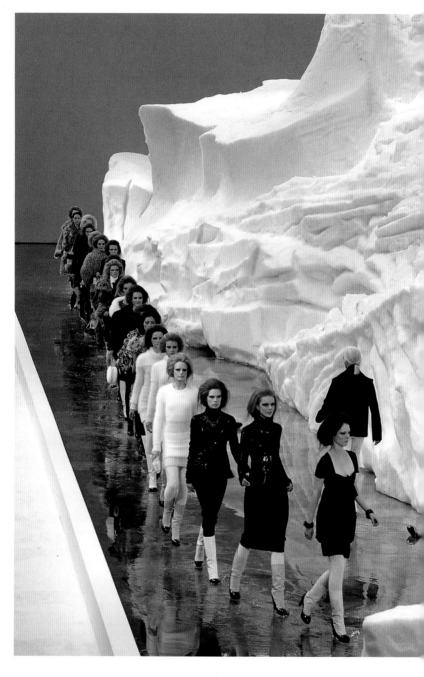

LUXURY FASHION AS THEATRE

"My job is to propose a fantasy."
KARL LAGERFELD

Astutely attuned to the globalization of the fashion industry and the dynamic impact of social-media imagery, Lagerfeld was the first creative director to consistently up the ante of the traditional catwalk show, turning them into showstopper extravaganzas of epic proportions – a successful idea that every other luxury house promptly copied. Combining theatricality with an experiential fashion event, Lagerfeld conceived an original theme for each show, and subsequently created an appropriate fantasy to showcase the collection. With clothes and accessories cleverly designed to mirror the concept, he regularly transformed the glass-domed Grand Palais in Paris into a 360-degree, immersive, other-worldly location, paying meticulous attention to every last detail. These legendary shows saw the Chanel team install formal French gardens with fragrant lemon and cypress trees; a surreal underwater world designed by revered architect Zaha Hadid; and an astronautical NASA-style space centre complete with CC-branded rocket launch. On other

OPPOSITE The Grand Palais venue needed to be kept at below-freezing temperatures for the chilly polar iceberg show, where Lagerfeld presented a collection that included an abundance of fake fur.

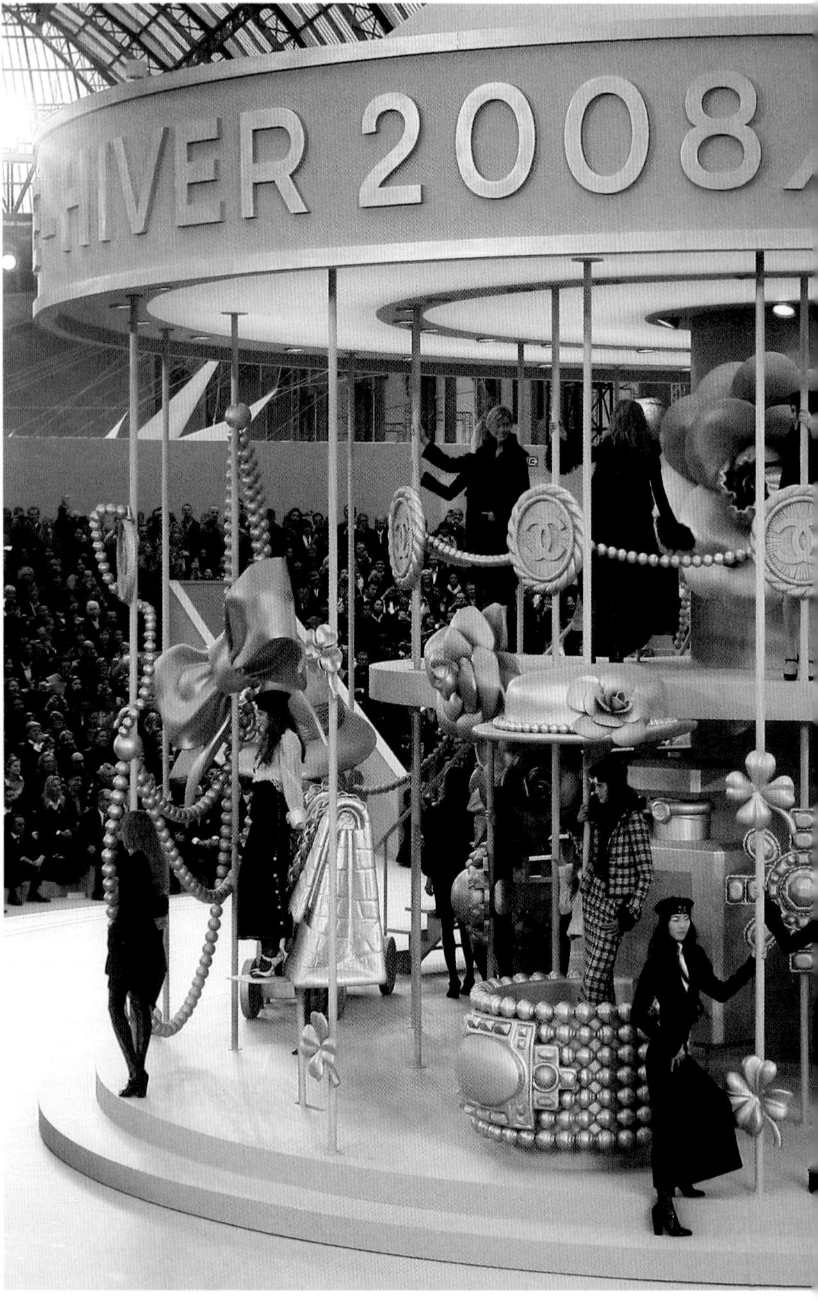
-HIVER 2008

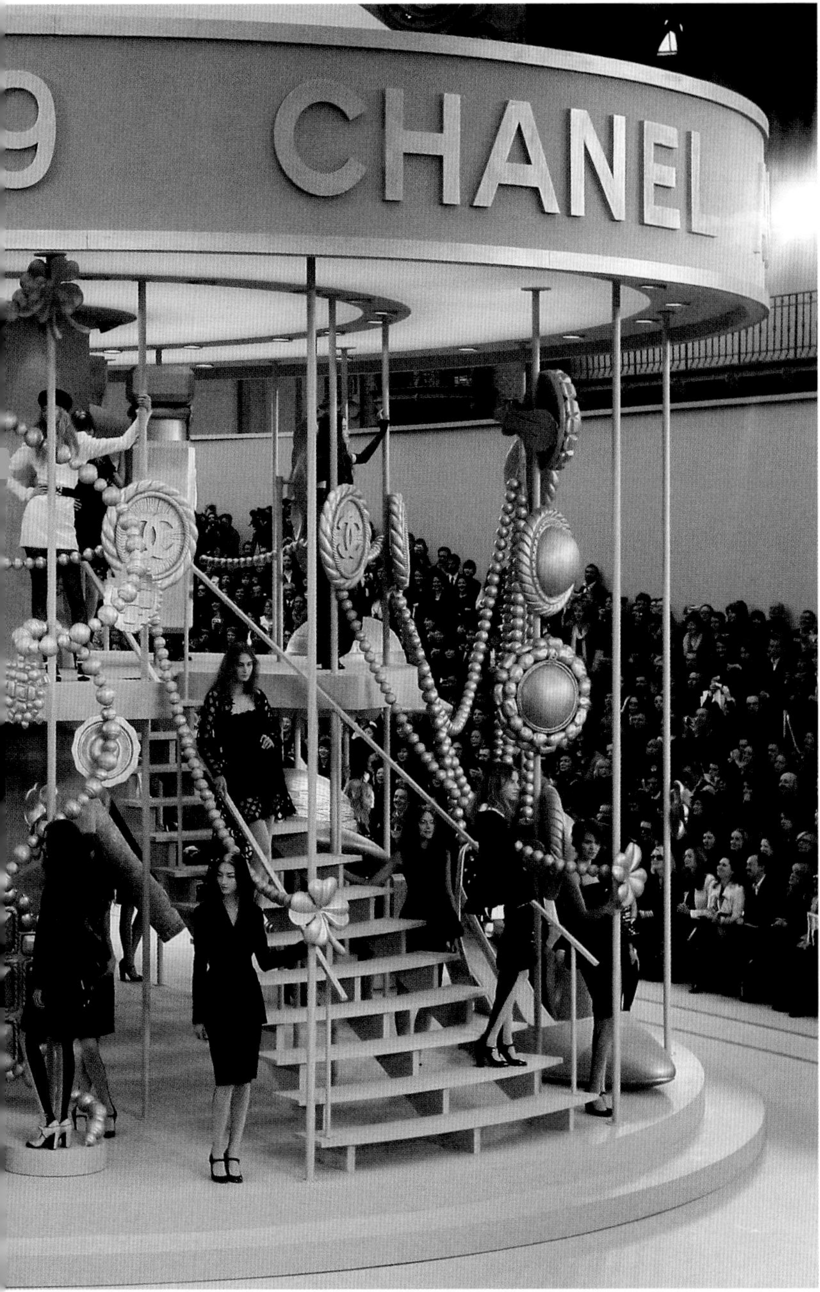
9 CHANEL

PREVIOUS PAGE
Supersized pearls, camellias, logo buttons and a quilted handbag took centre stage on a spectacular spinning carousel that replaced the catwalk in a collection that deliberately underplayed the iconic Chanel lexicon.

RIGHT
Acknowledging the importance of Coco Chanel's astrological sign – Leo, the fifth sign of the zodiac – a stupendous golden lion dominated the Grand Palais stage in 2010, its paw resting on a giant pearl for a a luxurious collection characterized by gold embellishment in all forms.

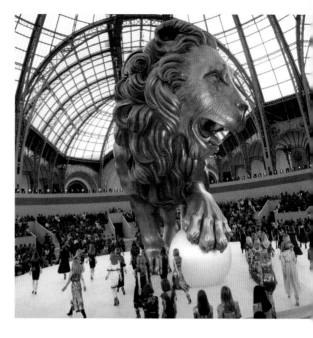

occasions he took his Cruise and Métiers d'Art shows on the road and utilized iconic locations that provided a scenic backdrop, taking over the picturesque quayside streets in Saint-Tropez, for example, for his 2010 Cruise collection. Blonde, tousle-haired models who looked strikingly similar to a young Brigitte Bardot arrived by speedboat to the Riviera location wearing hot pants and miniskirts, and guests watched the proceedings seated on the red wooden chairs of Sénéquier, the famous waterfront café. The showstopping finale saw Georgia May Jagger speeding along on the back of a Harley-Davidson motorbike, in a beaded shift dress and thigh-high leather boots, to the booming soundtrack of the Rolling Stones hit 'Let's Spend the Night Together'.

Coveted as the hottest ticket at Paris Fashion Week, Lagerfeld's imaginative sets and flawless presentations became

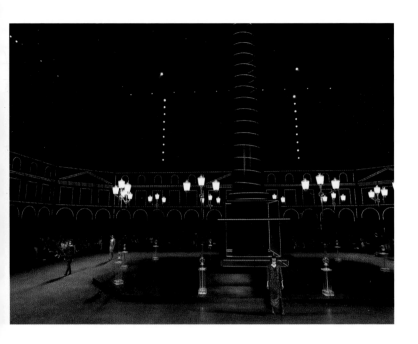

as much a talking point with the audience as did their appreciation of the actual clothes on the catwalk. "I just thought a basic show was boring, even for the journalists to look at a show, with mostly the same girls, it's not that exciting, so one has to make something more memorable," Lagerfeld told *WWD* in 2013. Without the constraints of working to a controlled budget, his outlandish ideas continually surprised the faithful Chanel devotees, most spectacularly when he shipped in a 265-tonne, melting iceberg from Scandinavia (which had to be returned intact) to provide the backdrop for a show of modern tweeds, woven through with fake fur, a collection dubbed by one journalist as "Shackleton Chic". As the creative director of the most financially successful fashion house in the world, Lagerfeld claimed never to consider the

ABOVE Recreating the familiar surroundings of Place Vendôme, Lagerfeld presented his romantic collection inspired by 1930s Parisian nightlife.

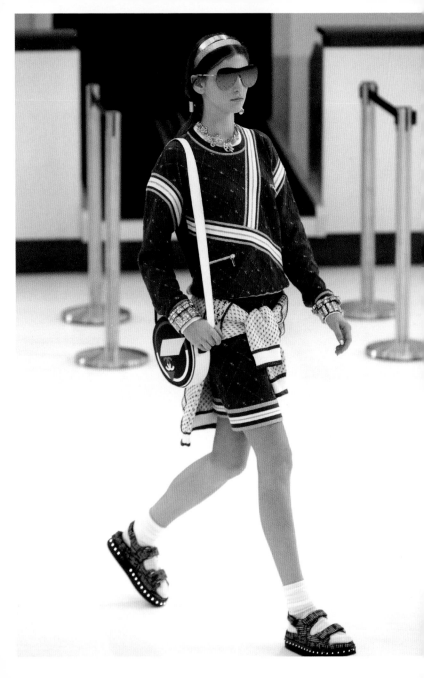

expense of such striking presentations, saying he didn't even know how much they cost. "If somebody would tell me: 'It's too expensive', I would say: 'I don't work for the poor', but I never had to say that," he explained to Bridget Foley in 2017.

At the beginning of his freelance contract with Chanel in 1982, the commercial expectations on Lagerfeld were far less demanding, with the designer required to produce only four fashion shows a year, two presentations for the haute couture market and two seasonal ready-to-wear collections. As the global appetite for fashion became increasingly voracious, and the number of boutiques around the world increased, Lagerfeld responded to customers' hunger for more merchandise and provided a solution by developing a faster seasonal turnaround. In addition to Spring and Autumn, he personally suggested pre-Spring and pre-Fall, with the Chanel boutiques renewing their stock and their windows every two months. Addicted to hard work, and vocally dismissive of other designers complaining about commercial pressures, Lagerfeld was the individual who expanded the fashion calendar, working tirelessly to produce eight spectacular annual collections – a decision guaranteed to preserve the Chanel fantasy and satisfy consumer demand. Overloaded with a brain that never stopped working, he claimed that most of his good ideas came to him in the small hours of the night. "The best things I've ever done have come from dreams, sometimes it's the whole show including the sets, I dreamed it all," he told Rodolphe Marconi, director of *Lagerfeld Confidential*. With an invited audience of around 450 guests, and later live-streamed to thousands of international fans of the brand, these Chanel blockbuster shows and their ambitious extravagance did much more than simply present a Disney-esque vision of aspirational fashion. With his fierce intelligence, acid wit and formidable capacity

OPPOSITE Set in a Chanel airport, the Spring/Summer 2016 collection featured comfortable clothes embellished with tiny aeroplane prints, including Velcro sandals with cabin strip-lights detailing the soles.

OVERLEAF The Grand Palais is transformed into a realistic Chanel airport terminal called Paris Cambon, with check-in desks, a departure board featuring previous show destinations and wheelie suitcases, all branded with the iconic double-C logo.

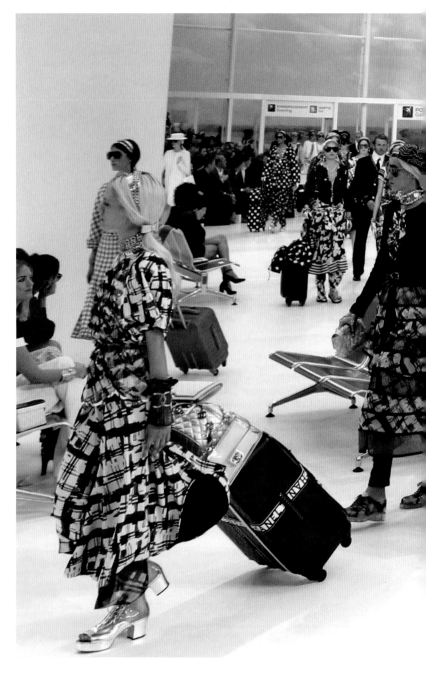

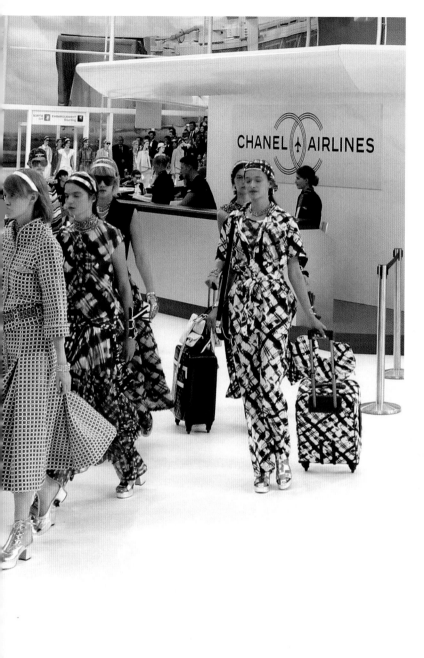

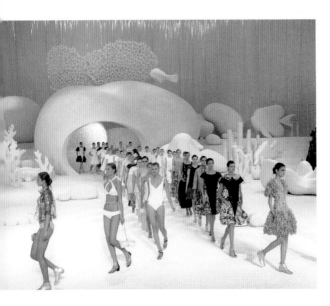

for humour, Lagerfeld often acknowledged that, "Fashion is a game that has to be played seriously," using the platform of his wildly decadent presentations to provide a social commentary on the shifting cultural landscapes of society.

For Autumn/Winter 2014, Lagerfeld installed a fully functioning Chanel *hypermarché* in the spectacular setting of the glass-domed Grand Palais, complete with supermarket shelves stacked with over 500 basic products that had been individually repackaged in fashion-savvy Chanel branding. Before the show, fashion journalists and guests mingled in the realistic set, browsing products such as Confiture de Gabrielle and Coco Chanel Coco Pops, amused at the sky-high prices ($12,500 for a Chanel shopping basket) and the lack of buy-one-get-one-free bargains. When the supermodels arrived to swagger though the aisles (Cara, Stella, Naomi) laden with candy-coloured sweetie necklaces, and carrying bespoke

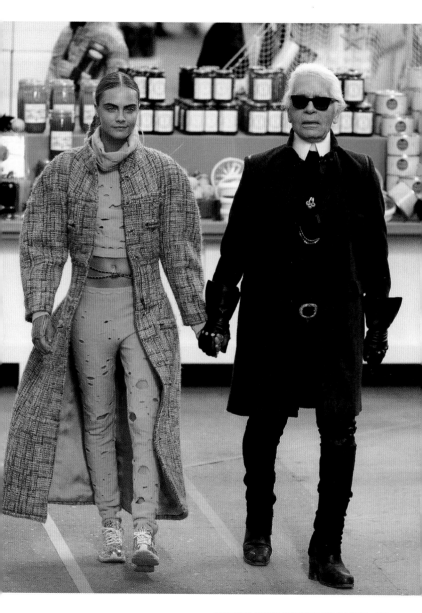

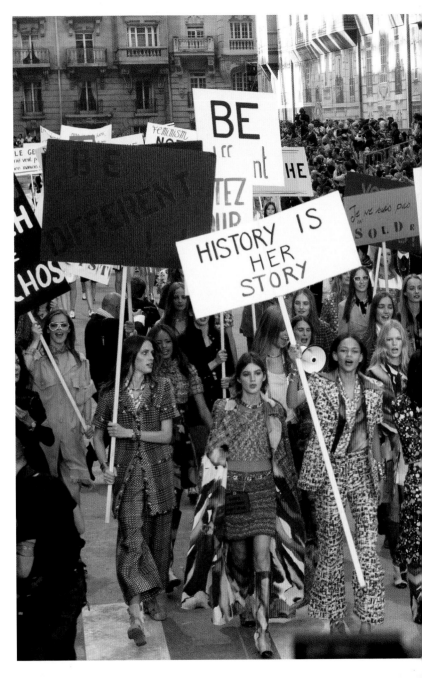

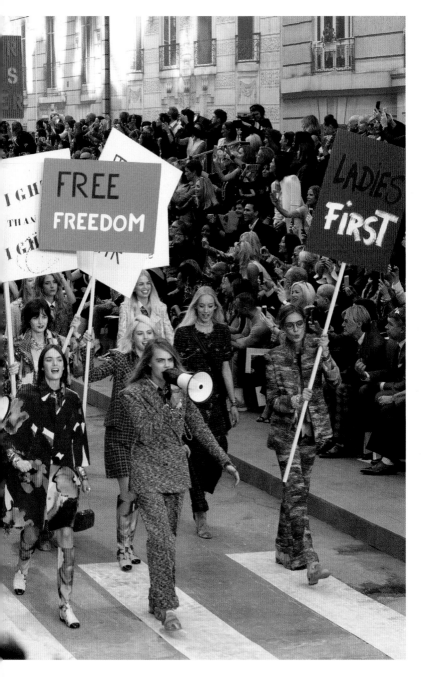

Chanel shopping baskets luxuriously crafted in black leather and trimmed with the signature flat chain, Lagerfeld's tongue-in-cheek critique on his own industry and a world dominated by consumerism was hard to miss.

Taking inspiration from leisure-influenced street fashion, models paraded in beautifully deconstructed tweed tracksuits, wearing psychedelic iridescent trainers in a spectrum of rainbow colours. Following on from Coco's legacy of functional

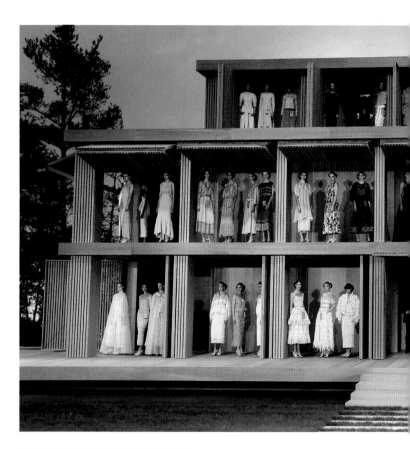

practicality, Lagerfeld explained to journalists after the show: "If you want to look really ridiculous, you go in stilettos in a supermarket."

Eloquent about his desire to keep the fashion wheels of reinvention firmly directed towards the future, Lagerfeld was quick to embrace the power of A-list celebrity, aligning the brand with prestigious global talent who could embody the international spirit of Chanel. With a packed front row of

BELOW With an emphasis on understated elegance, soft colours and pared-down silhouettes, Lagerfeld built a modern doll's house from recyclable materials, set among a Japanese-themed garden for Spring 2016.

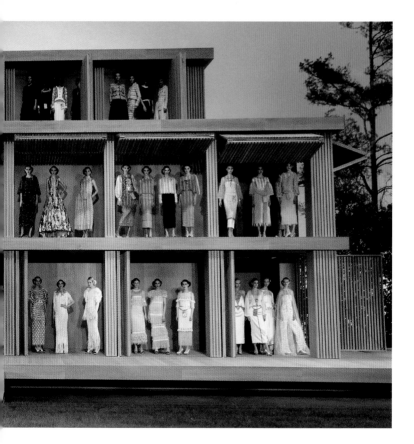

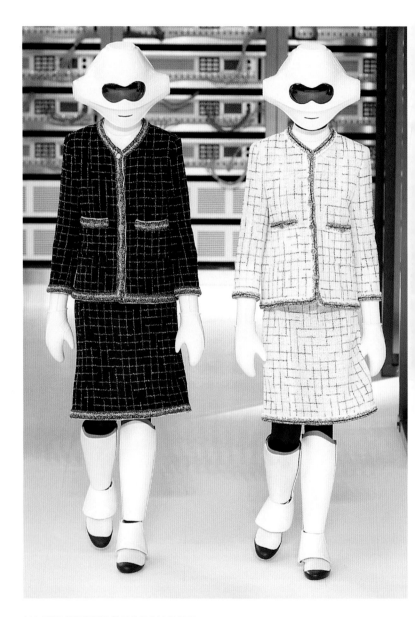

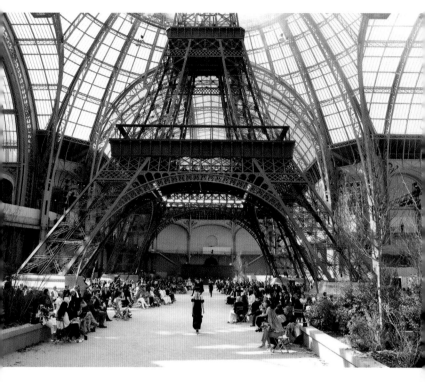

OPPOSITE Technology takes over, with Chanel-bot models in stormtrooper-style wellington boots, carrying handbags fitted with flashing LED displays, set against a giant futuristic data centre.

ABOVE Parisian chic, exemplified in the form of Chanel's famous boater hat reimagined in soft tweeds, supersized pearl earrings and a more exaggerated suit silhouette, walked the runway under the arched iron legs of an almost full-scale replica of the Eiffel Tower in 2017.

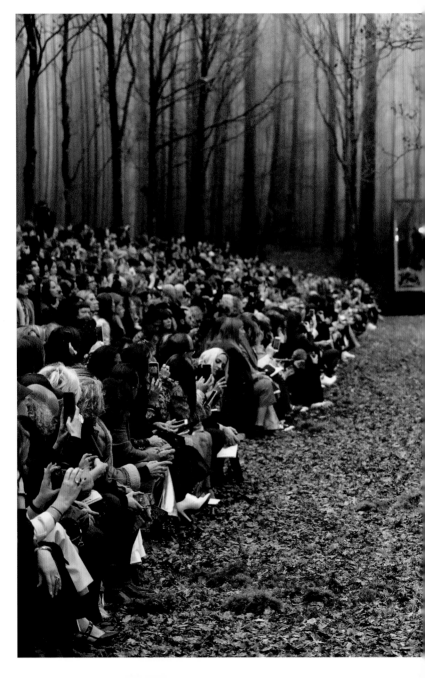

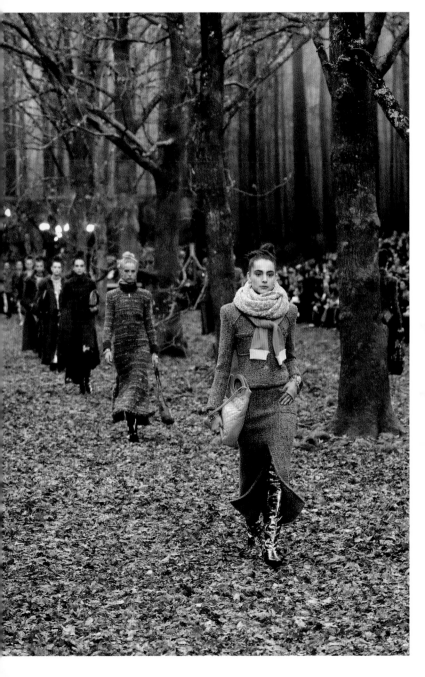

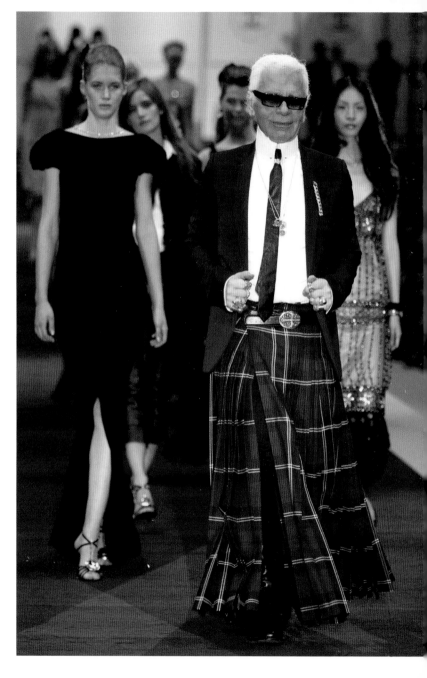

superstars that included regular supporters Julianne Moore, Kristen Stewart, Carla Bruni, Vanessa Paradis, Rita Ora and Penélope Cruz, the mega theatrics of a Chanel runway show provided nonstop visual glamour, beamed instantaneously around the world to promote sales of luxury fashion.

Though Lagerfeld himself had become one of the most famous fashion designers in the world, unable to walk down the street or take a commercial flight, and so instantly associated with Chanel branding that he joked to a German broadcasting company in 2018, "My name is no longer Lagerfeld, but Logofeld", he remained unimpressed by his own achievements. Constantly striving for the next great idea, with a complex mind perpetually whirring onto something bigger and better, he said, "I never look back at what I did because fashion is like show business today. You're as good as your last show." Talking to the *Observer* about her friend's lifelong pursuit of perfection, Amanda Harlech explained, "The thing about Karl is that he is never happy with what he's done." Lagerfeld himself endorsed her comment in an interview with *Monocle* magazine: "I am never pleased with myself, I always think I could do better." With boundless energy and utter contempt for designers who look back into their archives for inspiration, Lagerfeld was often quoted as saying, "Fashion is about change – and I like change." His desire to stay relevant, to push the boundaries of reinvention constantly and keep the surprise hits coming, remained unquenchable to the end.

"THE BEAT GOES ON." KARL LAGERFELD

Rumours that Lagerfeld was unwell began to circulate at the beginning of 2019, when for the first time in over 35 years he failed to appear at the finale of the Chanel haute couture show in Paris. At the October presentation three months

PREVIOUS PAGE Building a magical set that included mature trees and a catwalk covered in thousands of Chanel-branded autumn leaves, Lagerfeld created a fabulous scenic forest for a collection that included multiple mixes of tweed and eye-catching botanical prints.

OPPOSITE Always a great showman, Lagerfeld accepted applause at the finale of his 2004 show in a traditional full-length kilt, at the end of a collection that featured tartan as a major theme.

OPPOSITE With his right-hand woman Virginie Viard alongside him, Lagerfeld appeared frail at the finale of the Spring/Summer 2019 show in Paris.

earlier, he had looked frail as he navigated the catwalk, hand in hand with Virginie Viard, to receive the traditional post-show applause. Their appearance together was a clear indication, if one were needed, that Viard, who had worked behind the scenes alongside Lagerfeld for over 30 years, was his personal choice to continue his legacy as Creative Director at Chanel.

Lagerfeld died aged 85 on 19 February 2019, at the American Hospital in Paris, after a short illness. A statement from the House of Chanel read: "An extraordinary creative individual, Karl Lagerfeld reinvented the brand's codes invented by Gabrielle Chanel. The Chanel jacket and suit, the little black dress, the precious tweeds, the two-tone shoes, the quilted handbags, the pearls and costume jewellery." It ended with the words, "One cannot refer to Karl Lagerfeld without mentioning his innate sense of repartee and self-mockery."

In June a star-studded memorial, attended by close friends and the fashion elite, was held in his honour at the Grand Palais in Paris. Karl For Ever, a spectacularly lavish event, was a fitting final tribute to the legendary showman, with tearful contributions from many of his lifelong associates, including Anna Wintour, Nicolas Ghesquière, Alain Wertheimer and Cara Delevingne. Two thousand guests attended, with poignant memories, praise and affection heaped on the late designer, who had picked up the historical legacy of the House of Chanel and successfully transformed it into the most iconic brand of the twenty-first century.

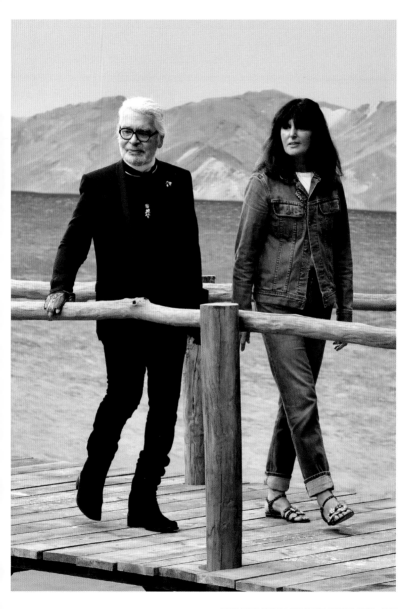

INDEX

Italic numbers refer to
photographs/captions

accessories 18, *24*, 29, 35,
  45, *70*, *74*, *81*, 133
  21–3
advertising 53, 65, 119–29,
  121, *121*, *125*, 129
aesthetic shift 43, *43*
Aghion, Gaby 18
Allen, Lily *92*, 93
Atelier Montex 103–7

Balmain, Pierre *13*, 16–17, 32
bamboo fan 23, *24*
boater hats *34*, *35*, 36, *149*
Bouquet, Carole 120, *120*
branding 8–9, 21, 24, 45–8,
  65–9, *66*, *73*, 76–9, *76*, *77*,
  79, 86–9, *92*, 100, 125,
  129, 133, 139–47, 153–4,
  153
Brûlé, Tyler 30, 90
Bündchen, Gisele 129

Campbell, Naomi 56, 142
Campocasso, Eva 32
Castellane, Victoire de 71, *71*
Cazaubon, Jean 29
CC branding, *see* double-C
  logo
celebrity culture 8, 32, 65,
  73, 90–3, 119, 120, *128*,
  129, 136, 147–53
Chanel:
  buttons *109*

camellias 36, 45, 103,
  104, *105*, 107, 108,
  108, *134–5*, *136*
denim 45, 70
founding 8, 154
house identity 71, *136*
Lagerfeld joins 24,
  29–32, 43
Lagerfeld's vision 8
legacy 43, 45–8, *48*,
  50–1, *54*, *55*, 56, *73*,
  76–7, 89, *100*, *102*,
  103, 109, *109*, *110–11*,
  113, 125, 128, 129,
  146–7, 154, *154*
logo, *see* double-C logo
model diversity 56
"more is more" zeitgeist
  45
multidisciplinary artistic
  hub 107–9
original designs *13*, *32*,
  34, 35, *35*, *36*
ready-to-wear 18–21,
  29–30, 64, 65, 93, 104,
  139
rue Cambon HQ 31–2,
  31, 65, *66*, 70–3, 86,
  89, 103, 109
Chanel-bot models *148*, *149*
Chanel, Gabrielle "Coco" 8,
  29, 30–1, *31*, *46*, *79*, 109,
  121, 154
  astrological sign *136*
  birth 107
  mood misjudged 69–70

Chanel N°5 29, 80, *81*, 118,
  119–29, *119*, *121*, *123*,
  124, *125*, *127*
  75th anniversary 124
Chloé *14*, *15*, 18, *20*, *21*, *22*,
  24, *25*, 71–3, 86
Choupette (cat) 8, 85
Christensen, Helena *69*
Cleveland, Pat 22, 56
Coco, l'Esprit de Chanel 121,
  122, *124*
Coco Mademoiselle 119,
  125, *125*
Colapinto, John 14, 45, 89
collections:
  Autumn/Winter 1983 *28*,
    29, 35
  Autumn/Winter 1985 *35*,
    78, 79
  Autumn/Winter 1994
    74, 75
  Autumn/Winter 1995 76
  Autumn/Winter 1998
    48, *50–1*
  Autumn/Winter 2014
    142
  Autumn/Winter 2015
    109
  Autumn/Winter 2016
    11, *113*
  City Surfer 1991 53, *66*
  Coco Cocoon *92*
  Cruise *136*
  inaugural 36, *37*
  Lagerfeld's early 32–5,
    32, *33*

medieval-style *106*, *107*
Nouveau Rapper *64*,
    65, *69*
"Paris-London" *56*, *57*
"Paris-Shanghai" *54*
reimagined 43–5, *43*
Spring 1991 *52*, *53*
Spring/Summer 1984 45
Spring/Summer 1985 48,
    48, *49*
Spring/ Summer 2000
    104, *105*
Spring/Summer 2011 89
Spring/Summer 2015
    142, 144–5
Spring/Summer 2016
    138, *139*, *140–1*,
    146–7
Spring/Summer 2019
    154
tartan 2004 *152*, *153*
colour palette 35, 48–53
costume jewellery 35, 53,
    71, *71*, *77*, 99, 100, *100*,
    102, *103*, 108–9, *114*, *121*,
    124, 154
Cotillard, Marion 119

d'Alessio, Kitty 30
Delevingne, Cara 90, *90*, *91*,
    93, *128*, 142, *142*, *143*, 154
Depp, Lili-Rose 93, *94–5*
Desrues 100, 108, *109*
DeWitt, Diane 35
Dior, Christian 14
double-C logo *44*, 45, *45*,
    60, *66*, *68*, *72*, *73*, *76*,
    77–9, *77*, *79*, *92*, 133, *139*,
    140–1
Dudel, Yvonne 29
Dufour, Gilles *66*, *67*, 70–1

d'Urso, Violette 93

Égoïste 121
Evangelista, Linda *58*, *59*,
    64, 65, *65*

Fendi 21, 59
finances 65–6, 100, 124, 142
fragrance, *see* perfume
Frankel, Susannah 17, 66
Fressange, Inès de la 35,
    36, *54*, *55*, 57, 86–9, *86*,
    87, 93
functional practicality 146–7

Galliano, John 89
Gaultier, Jean Paul 86
Gerber, Kaia 93
Ghauri, Yasmeen 53
Ghesquière, Nicolas 154
Givenchy 16, 89
Goossens 99, 109, *114*
Goude, Jean-Paul 119, 120–1
Grand Palais 89, 93, *132*,
    133, *133*, *134–5*, 136, *139*,
    140–1, 142, 154
Guibourge, Phillipe 30

Hadid, Zaha 133, *142*
Hall, Jerry 48, *48*, *49*, 56
Harlech, Lady Amanda 65,
    89, *90*, 107
Helleu, Jacques 119
hypermarché show 2014 *81*,
    142–7, *142*, *143*

"It" girl *90*, *91*, 93

Jagger, Georgia May 136
jewellery, *see* costume
    jewellery

Karl For Ever 154
Karl, Roland, *see* Lagerfeld,
    Karl-Otto
Karliatures 9
Kennedy, Jacqueline 36
Kidman, Nicole 119, 124
KL 59
Knightley, Keira 119–20,
    124, *125*
Krizia 18
Kroenig, Brad 93
Kroenig, Hudson 93, *128*

Lacroix, Christian 109
Lagerfeld Confidential 139
Lagerfeld, Karl *6*, *7*, *64*, *65*,
    95, *143*, *152*, *153*
    birth and early life 13–14,
        59, 85
    coat design *12*
    de la Fressange falling out
        and reconciliation 88–9
    flamboyant showmanship
        7, 8, *9*, 21–3, *23*, 60,
        85–6, 132–54
    freelance career 18
    homes *36*, *38–9*
    ill health and death
        153–4
    legacy 154
    "mirrored staircase" pose
        31
    own label 59
    photography/filming 129
    weight loss 86
    witty critique 142–7,
        142, 153
Lagerfeldt, Elizabeth
    (mother) 13–16, 85–6
Lagerfeldt, Karl-Otto, *see*
    Lagerfeld, Karl

Lagerfeldt, Martha "Christel" (sister) 13
Lagerfeldt, Otto (father) 13–16
Laurent, Yves Saint 17, 30–1, 109
Le Bon, Yasmin 56
Le Corbusier 107
legendary shows 132–54
Léger, Hervé 32
Lemarié 99, 108, *108*
Lesage *35*, 73, 99, *99*, *100*, 104, 109, *113*
Lopez, Antonio 22
Luhrmann, Baz 119, *121*, 129

McMenamy, Kristen 90
Mandelli, Mariuccia 18
Marconi, Rudolphe 7, 139
Marianne 88
Marie Antoinette 53–6
Massaro 104, 113, *114*
Memphis *36*
merchandising 29, 66, 79, 139, 142
Métiers d'Art *56*, *57*, 99–115, *114*, *115*, *128*, 136
Michel 109–13, *114*
Montana, Claude 86
Moore, Julianne 93, 153
Moss, Kate *88*
Mugler, Thierry 86
Murphy, Anna 70, 86

19M 107–9
1920s chic 17, *47*, *48*, 76
N°5, *see* Chanel N°5

Ora, Rita 93, 153

Paradis, Vanessa 93, 153
Paraffection 107
Paris Cambon *138*, *139*, *140–1*
Patou, Jean *16*, 17
Pavlovsky, Bruno 107
pearls 36, 45, *46*, *58*, *59*, *81*, *98*, *99*, *112*, *113*, *134–5*, *136*, *149*, 154
perfume 29, *80*, *81*, 119–29, *120*, *122*, *124*, *127*
Pitt, Brad *125*, *126*, 128–9
Place Vendôme 128, *137*
Polge, Jacques 125
Power, Cat 93
Prada 18
publicity, *see* advertising

Ramos, Juan 22
Robart, Anne 35
Robirosa, Mercedes 32
Rothschild, Marie-Hélène de 36

Sala, Paquito 32
Saunders, Lyle 124
Schiaparelli 109
Schiffer, Claudia *74*, *84*, *85*, *88*, 89
Scott, Ridley 119, 120
7 Days Out 73
Shu Uemura 59
signature pieces *6*, *7*, 8, *34*, *35*, 43, 48, *70*, 71, 76, 108, 113, 146
Sjöberg, Emma *52*, *53*
Smith, Willow 93, *93*
sporting attire 66, *68*, 79, *79*, 93, *142*, *143*, 146
Stewart, Kristen 93, 129, 153
Stone, Lara 90

supermodels *61*, *65*, *88*, 89, 129, 142 (*see also by model*)
supply chain 99–100

Tautou, Audrey *118*, 119, *119*
Tennant, Stella *76*, 90, 142
Testino, Mario 119, 125
Tippin, Corey 22
trademark 23, *25*, 77
tradition 8, *16*, 43, 69, *73*, 99–115, *120*, *128*, 133, *153*

understatement 36, 45, 53, 120, *120*, 125, *146–7*

vampirizing 73
Viard, Virginie 73, 154, *154*, *155*

Warhol, Andy 22–3, 121–4
Watteau, Jean-Antoine 48, *48*
Wertheimer, Alain 29, 30, 65, 154
Wertheimer, Pierre 29
Williams, Pharrell 103, *128*, 129
Wintour, Anna 154
women's liberation *18*
Wool Secretariat *13*, 16–17
work ethic 7, 59–60, 86
Wright, Eric 73

zeitgeist 7, 45, 69

RESOURCES

Bacqué, R. (2020) *Kaiser Karl: The Life of Karl Lagerfeld*. Woodbridge: ACC Art Books

Drake, A. (2006) *The Beautiful Fall: Fashion, Genius and Glorious Excess in 1970s Paris.* London: Bloomsbury

Gautier, J. (2011) *Chanel: The Vocabulary of Style*. London: Thames & Hudson

Jolliffe, K and Garnett, B. (2007) *The Cheap Date Guide to Style*. London: Transworld

Mauriès, P. (2020) *Maison Lesage: Haute Couture Embroidery*. London: Thames & Hudson

Mauriès, P. (introduction) (2016) *Chanel Catwalk: The Complete Karl Lagerfeld Collections*. London: Thames & Hudson

Napias, J. (ed) and Gulbenkian, S. (2011) *The World According to Karl*. London: Thames & Hudson

7 Days Out, Chanel Haute Couture Fashion Show (2018), directed by Andrew Rossi. Netflix

Lagerfeld Confidential (2007), directed by Rodolphe Marconi. Revolver Entertainment

The 3.55: Métier Class by CHANEL (2019), Karl Lagerfeld and Amanda Harlech. Apple Podcasts

anothermag.com
businessoffashion.com
chanel.com
cnn.com
dw.com
guardian.com
i-d.vice.com
lofficiel.com
nytimes.com
monocle.com
numero.com
observer.com
telegraph.co.uk
thelovemagazine.co.uk
thetimes.co.uk
standard.co.uk
youtube.com
vanityfair.com
vogue.com
wmagazine.com
wwd.com

ACKNOWLEDGEMENTS

For Mo and Sarah, constantly skating on thin ice together.

My very special thanks go to Issy Wilkinson, ever generous with her time, enthusiasm and wisdom, and to all of her exceptional team at Welbeck.

CREDITS

LITTLE BOOK OF

HERMÈS

Published in 2022 by Welbeck
An imprint of Welbeck Non-Fiction Limited,
part of Welbeck Publishing Group.

Based in London and Sydney
www.welbeckpublishing.com

Design and layout © Welbeck Non-Fiction Limited 2022
Text © Karen Homer 2022

A CIP catalogue record for this book is available from the British Library.

ISBN 978-1-80279-011-5

Printed in China

10 9 8 7 6 5 4

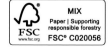

LITTLE BOOK OF

HERMÈS

The story of the iconic fashion house

KAREN HOMER

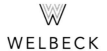

WELBECK

CONTENTS

INTRODUCTION 06

EARLY YEARS... 10

NEW GENERATION 18

CONSIDERED EXPANSION 36

BAGS 54

SCARVES 78

ARISTOCRACY AND

CELEBRITY CLIENTELE 94

THE EVOLUTION OF FASHION.................... 114

INDEX..158

CREDITS... 160

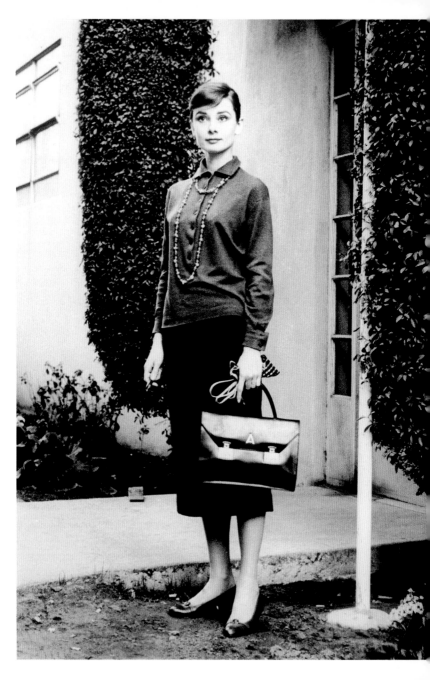

-○○○-

INTRODUCTION

"I think Hermès objects are desirable because they reconnect
people to their humanity… Our customer feels the presence
of the person who crafted the object, while at the same time
the object brings him back to his own sensitivity, because
it gives him pleasure through his senses."
PIERRE-ALEXIS DUMAS, businessoffashion.com

In 1837, when Thierry Hermès started making saddlery,
harnesses and bridles, he vowed that the Hermès name would
always be synonymous with the finest materials, crafted by the
most talented artisans. It is an ethos that has continued down
through six generations and to this day Hermès still uses the
rarest leathers, the most exquisite silks and the softest natural
fabrics in their clothes and accessories. Every bag is stitched by
hand, using the original saddle stitch; each scarf is meticulously
screen-printed, its edges hand-rolled; and the current family
incumbent and creative director, Pierre-Alexis Dumas,
personally signs off all Hermès products. This dedication to

OPPOSITE Audrey Hepburn with the leather brief-case style bag bearing
her initial which Hermès designed exclusively for the actress in several
colours in 1956.

OPPOSITE Hermès
is a name that
evokes the most
decadent clothes
and accessories.
For example this
flowing ensemble
in rich turquoise
silk, complete with
glamorous turban,
designed by Jean
Paul Gaultier for
Spring/Summer
2008.

quality and refusal to compromise has made Hermès a luxury fashion brand that stands in a league of its own.

It is impossible to talk about Hermès without considering their most iconic accessories. Not only the sought-after Birkin and Kelly bags, or the limited edition printed silk scarves, but the double-strapped watch and the Collier de Chien bracelet have all played their part in creating a mythology appropriate to a fashion house that carries the name of the Greek god associated with both travel and wealth.

In more recent years, ready-to-wear has become an increasingly prominent part of the label, especially since 1997, when first Martin Margiela and then Jean Paul Gaultier were tasked with upping Hermès's profile in the world of high fashion. Since Gaultier's departure in 2010, both Christophe Lemaire and the current head of womenswear, Nadège Vanhee-Cybulski, have continued the tradition of creating clothes that represent the pinnacle of luxury dressing, with price tags to match. And it is equally important to acknowledge the input of Véronique Nichanian, menswear designer for over three decades.

Unlike many of its competitors, Hermès remains under family control, having fought off acquisition bids by its rivals – something that remains key in maintaining its high production standards. Similarly, its many global stores are closely monitored to ensure they achieve the quality of design and presentation that Hermès stands for, while still remaining sensitive to local markets. And with a marketing strategy that beats all others, Hermès have made their products so exclusive that they do not need to gift them; instead celebrities plead to get their names on the list to be allowed to buy a made-to-order Birkin bag. Lesser mortals can only hope that one day they might possess an orange box of their own.

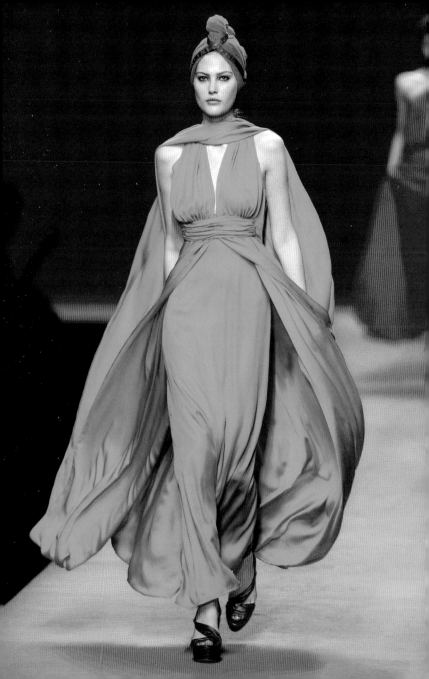

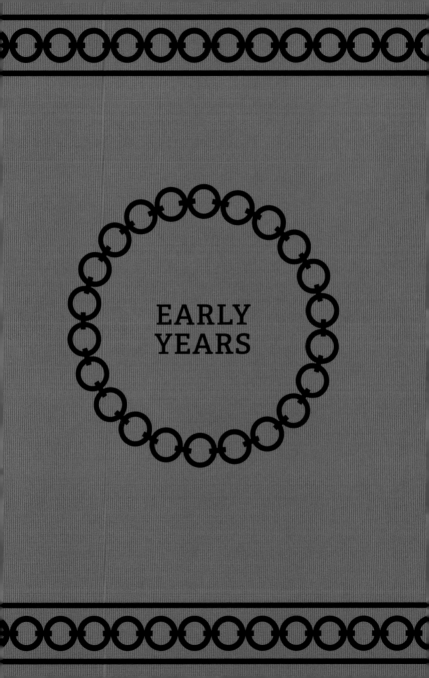

EARLY
YEARS

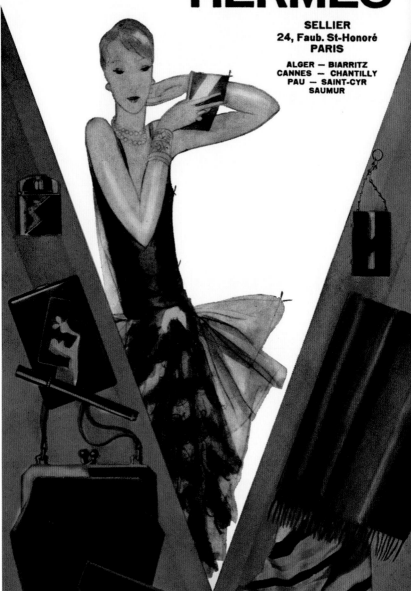

HERMÈS

SELLIER
24, Faub. St-Honoré
PARIS

ALGER — BIARRITZ
CANNES — CHANTILLY
PAU — SAINT-CYR
SAUMUR

-OOO-

HUMBLE BEGINNINGS

Thierry Hermès was born in 1801, in what is now the
German town of Krefeld. At the time it was under the control
of Napoléon Bonaparte, making him a French citizen. The
town was renowned for its textiles industry and known as
stadt wie samt und seide or the "city of velvet and silk".

In 1821, after the loss of much of his family to disease and
the Napoleonic wars, Thierry moved to Normandy where, in
the town of Pont-Audemer, he learned the art of the *sellier-
harnacheur*, or saddler and harness-maker, under the Pleumer
family, who employed him in their business.

In 1828, Thierry Hermès married Christine Pétronille Pierrat
and their first son Charles-Émile, who would later succeed
his father, was born in 1831. The family moved to Paris, and
in 1837 Thierry put his skills to good use, opening his own
equestrian supplies business on the Rue Basse-du-Rempart.
There he made bridles, harnesses and carriage fittings in both
leather and wrought iron. He became particularly famous for

OPPOSITE An early Hermès advertisement from the 1920s showing the
iconic flapper surrounded by her Hermès accessories, including bag, scarf
and vanity mirror.

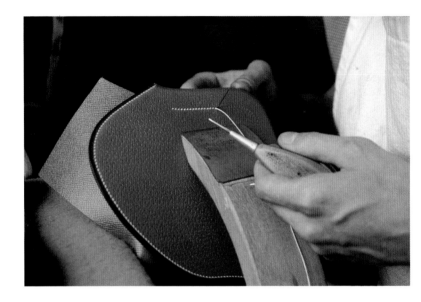

ABOVE An artisan craftsman works on a piece of Hermès luggage using the exceptionally strong saddle stitch, pioneered by Thierry Hermès and still used to this day.

OPPOSITE A contemporary Birkin bag from 2009 in canvas with tan leather trim and gold hardware.

his exceptionally strong saddle-stitch, which was done by hand, using two needles working two waxed linen threads in tensile opposition. With this unique method of stitching, one or more stitches might break, but the rest will hold firm, and it is still used by Hermès in the production of its bags today.

At a time when horses were still essential to all aspects of life, including work, sport and travel, the quality of Hermès craftsmanship attracted a wealthy clientele, including Empress Eugénie, the wife of Napoléon III. Thierry Hermès's skill was such that in 1855 he won the first of several medals for design at the Exposition Universelle in Paris. His reputation continued to grow, and in 1867 he won yet another series of medals for his technical ability, craftsmanship and innovative design.

Thierry Hermès died in 1878 but his son, Charles-Émile, who had been working for the company since 1859, was primed to take over. Like his father, Charles-Émile was dedicated to

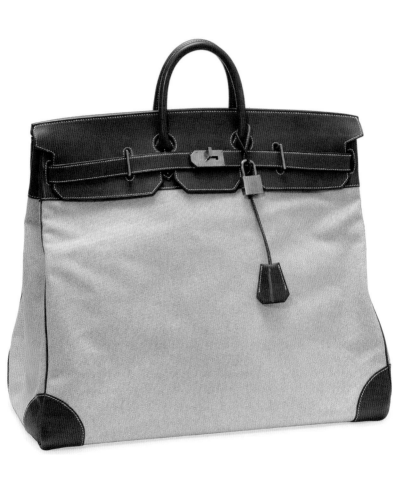

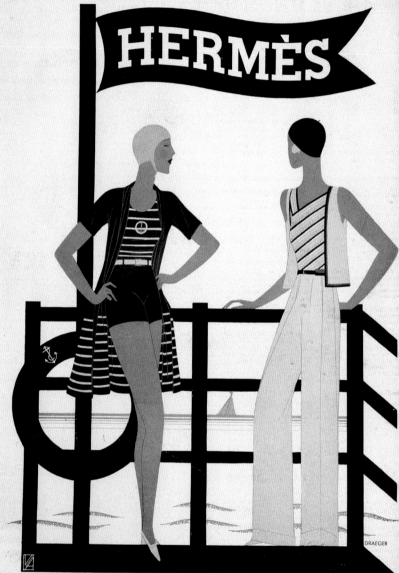

ensuring that Hermès's products were the finest on offer. He added saddlery to the company's offerings, thus widening its appeal and this, along with the expertly wrought, yet lightweight and functional harnesses and bridles helped the company to grow. Soon Hermès was attracting customers from all over Europe and as far as Russia, the United States and parts of Asia.

As the company expanded, extra space and a more prestigious retail spot were needed. In 1880, Charles-Émile Hermès moved the workshop and store to Rue du Faubourg Saint-Honoré, where it remains to this day. Charles-Émile worked alongside his two sons Adolphe and Émile until his retirement in 1902. One of his last creations, designed in collaboration with his sons, was the large and sturdy Haut à Courroies bag. Designed for riders who needed to carry their saddles and boots, it was the forerunner of the Hermès bags that are so coveted today.

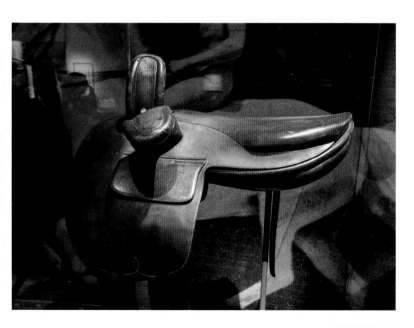

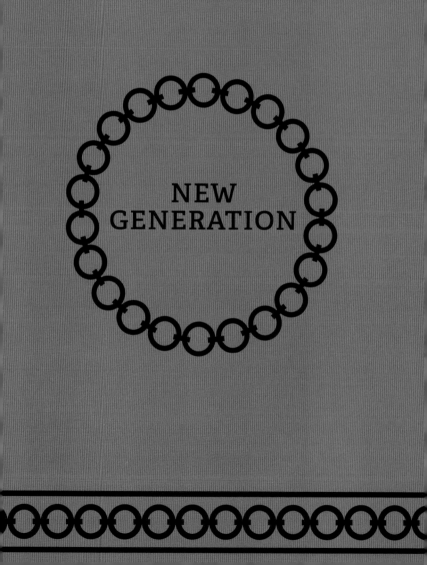

NEW
GENERATION

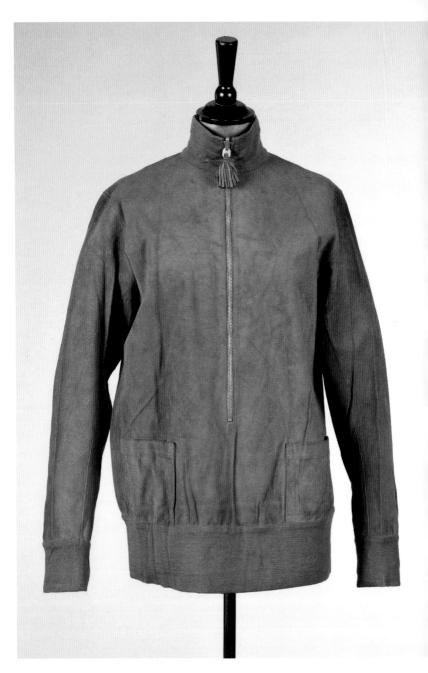

-OOO-

HERMÈS FRÈRES

One of the first things that Émile and his brother, Adolphe, did when they took over from their father was to rename the company Hermès Frères. The change coincided with the move to Paris's Rue du Faubourg Saint-Honoré, an impressive new premises in keeping with Hermès's reputation as an elite, artisan business.

Saddlery was still the mainstay of the business, with Hermès's client list now reaching across the globe. However, on a trip to the United States, Émile realized that the company needed to expand if it was to move into the modern era and truly thrive. On meeting automobile magnate Henry Ford, he was given a tour of his factory workshops. Hugely impressed by their efficiency, Émile took the model on board and by 1914 he had 80 craftsmen of his own in Hermès's saddlery workshop,

OPPOSITE On a tour of the United States and Canada in 1914 Émile Hermès, the third generation to take on the mantle at Hermès, discovered a new and exciting fastening mechanism, the zip. He brought the design back to France and was granted a unique patent allowing Hermès to be among the first to produce clothes such as this brown suede sporting blouson top from the 1930s.

allowing more orders to be fulfilled without compromising on quality.

On the next leg of his tour, to Canada, Émile discovered an intriguing zip-fastening mechanism being used on the canvas roof of his convertible Cadillac. Excited by the possibilities of using the zip in his own designs, Émile took the invention back to France and applied for a two-year patent for its exclusive use. He realized that modern, faster forms of travel would require leather accessories and clothes of all sorts and a far more efficient closing mechanism to keep luggage and jackets secure. Thus, the "Hermès Fastener", as it became known in France, was born, thanks to the company's exclusive rights to its use.

Unlike the flat zips we know today, this version was round and snake-like and the original is still kept in the Hermès Museum today. One of its first appearances was as part of a 1918 leather golfing jacket designed for Edward, Prince of Wales, the fashionable, playboy prince who would later, as Edward VIII, abdicate the throne of England for his beloved Wallis Simpson, herself a huge fan of Hermès. The zip was much admired and it is rumoured that the ingenious design impressed Gabrielle "Coco" Chanel so much that she sent her in-house makers to Hermès to learn how to use it.

By the end of the First World War, it was becoming clear that the world was changing. Horses were no longer as important as they had once been, and the era of the automobile had dawned. Adolphe Hermès was reluctant to expand the company's traditional production of equestrian goods, but Émile was determined to look forward to a new age. As a result, in 1919 Émile bought Adolphe out of the family firm. Hermès still catered to the needs of horse riders for luxurious, beautifully made saddlery, but new products were now on the horizon.

One collaboration was with French car-maker Ettore Bugatti. A client of Hermès before the war, from whom he bought

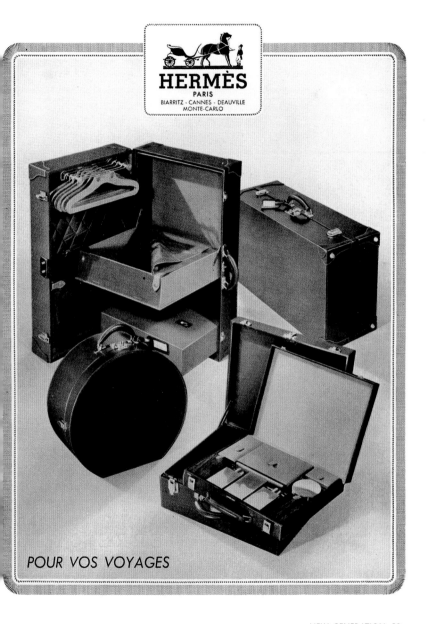

HERMÈS
PARIS
BIARRITZ - CANNES - DEAUVILLE
MONTE-CARLO

POUR VOS VOYAGES

saddlery and tack, in the 1920s Bugatti commissioned a trunk in yellow cowhide to match the first Bugatti Royale. Further commissions included a bag that was the forerunner to the Hermès Bolide. The century-long collaboration between Bugatti and Hermès continues to this day in the shape of some of the world's most exclusive cars, such as the Hermès Bugatti Chiron. Other famous names who patronized Hermès for their design expertise included legendary modernist designer and architect Le Corbusier, who admired the elegant simplicity of their new bags, and interior designer Jean-Michel Frank, who commissioned Hermès to line his walls with pale, beige leather to emulate stone.

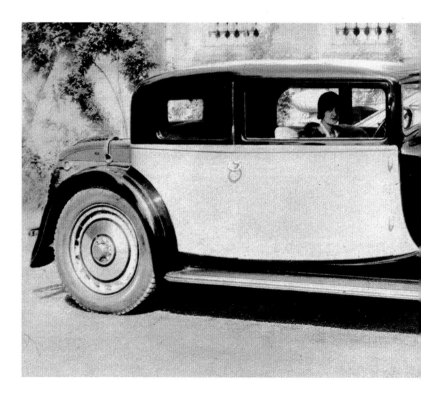

Over the ensuing years Émile, in partnership with his son-in-law Robert Dumas-Hermès (who added the Hermès to his name on joining the business), transformed Hermès from a small artisan Parisian business into a fledgling global luxury brand, and in 1922 the company started selling a range of handbags. Previously, the only bag the company had produced was the basic Haut-à-Courroies saddlebag, but when Émile's wife asked him to make a handbag for her, he designed a scaled-down, refined version which immediately became popular. Three years later, in 1925, Hermès launched a range of travel bags. Using the new zip mechanism, the collection was perfectly timed for

BELOW By the 1920s, Émile Hermès realized that horses would soon be usurped by automobiles as a means of transport. One of the earliest collaborations between Hermès and a car manufacturer was a series of trunks for the Bugatti Royale.

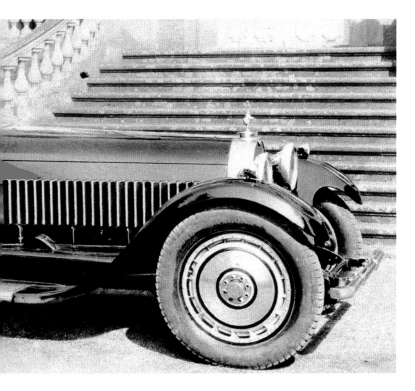

the explosion in travel among the social elite by both rail and transatlantic steamer. New stores were opened in the French resorts along the Côte d'Azur, popular holiday destinations for the rich and famous, and in 1929, Hermès launched a carefully considered range of clothes. By the 1930s an agreement with the Neiman Marcus department store in New York gave Hermès its first sales outlet in the United States.

Hermès's expert skill in working with leather led to other accessories which are still in production today, for example the Collier de Chien range. Translating as "dog collar", it was first made as a commission in 1923 for a customer's bulldog, but the Art-Deco style studded leather was so appealing that women started wearing them as belts. In 1927 Hermès officially produced the Collier de Chien belt and in the 1940s the bracelet, which still sells so well, was created. The cuff carries the

BELOW The interior of an Hermès store in Paris in the early 1940s.

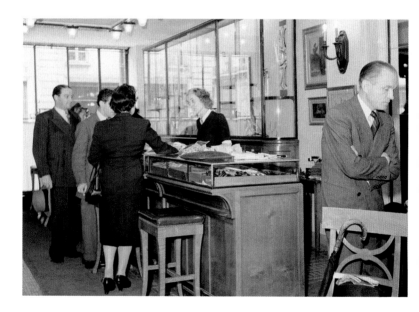

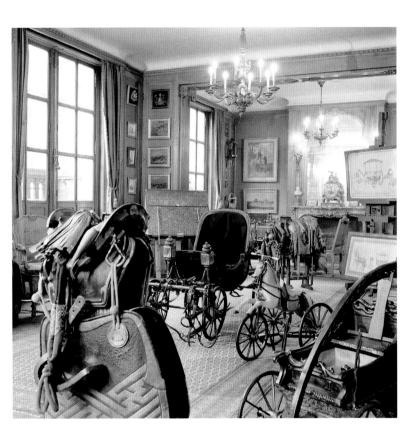

central "O" ring, surrounded by pyramid studs, that on a dog collar would have held its lead.

Wristwatches, too, appeared in the late 1920s, the first of which, according to Hermès family lore, was designed by Émile in 1912 for his daughter, whose pocket watch kept falling out of her pocket. For years, watches played only a small part in the accessories range by Hermès, usually featuring an equestrian motif such as a stirrup or a simple saddle-stitched strap. It was not until 50 years later that Hermès became a serious player in

ABOVE Hermès's elaborate store interiors, such as this one from the 1950s, reflected the wealthy and aristocratic clientele the house attracted.

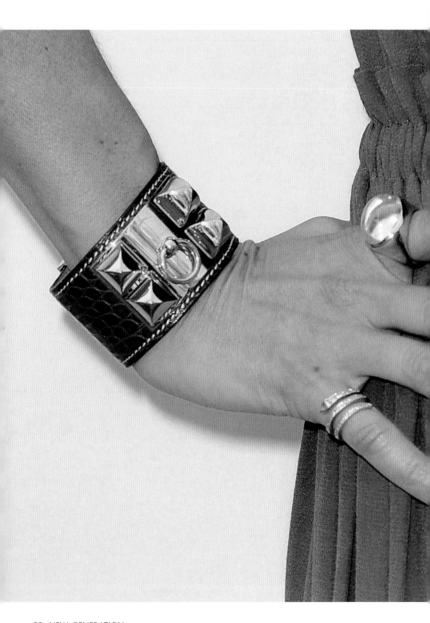

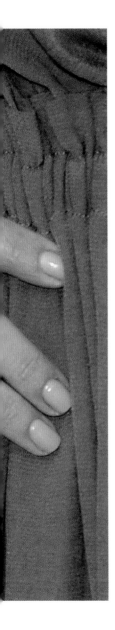

the luxury watch market when the company established its own Swiss watch-making operation.

Other now-iconic Hermès creations were also debuted during this time. In 1935 came the Sac à Dépêches, which would famously be renamed the Kelly bag in 1956, and remains one of Hermès's most coveted items to this day. And in 1937, under the creative eye of Robert Dumas-Hermès, the company began designing their own range of silk scarves or *carrés*, as they are known. Many of the scarf designs took their inspiration from a collection of interesting and sometimes odd artefacts and books that Robert's father-in-law, Émile, had been curating since his early teens, which eventually numbered in the thousands. Art and literature have always played a big part in Hermès's designs and, along with its heritage of equestrianism, are still frequently referenced in modern prints.

The Chaîne d'Ancre line of jewellery was another inspiration of Robert Dumas-Hermès. In the 1930s, he would sketch pictures as he wandered the seafront, and he seized on to the image of a ship's anchor to design a bracelet that has since expanded into a range including necklaces, rings, earrings and even sandals. Dumas-Hermès continued evolving the design aesthetic of the brand through accessories including ties and belts, as well as closely overseeing the expanding range of scarves for which he had a huge affection, creating many of the most popular designs of all time.

LEFT A modern version of the iconic Art-Deco style studded leather Collier de Chien cuff that carries a centre "O" ring, surrounded by pyramid studs, that on a dog collar would have held its lead.

THE ORANGE BOX

The Hermès distinctive orange box is a tremendously exciting gift to receive and one of the most instantly recognizable pieces of luxury wrapping in existence. Today, the folding box comes in approximately 188 sizes and in 1994 won a packaging Oscar. Its origins were, however, accidental. It was originally made in a cream cardboard with a grainy finish to imitate pigskin and early boxes had a gilt or brown edge. However, in 1942, during the Second World War, a shortage of the original cream led to Robert Dumas-Hermès having to accept the only colour that was available: orange. To this day, Hermès uses this trademark colour which is entirely exclusive to the fashion house and not listed by Pantone.

In the early 1950s, shortly after the box made its debut, Hermès decided to create a logo in keeping with the brand's heritage. The simple, elegant design features a Duc carriage with a horse and top-hatted rider, often appearing above the company name which uses the Memphis Bold font. It is widely accepted that inspiration for the logo was drawn from the painting Le *Duc Attelé, Groom à L'Attente*, which translates to "Hitched Carriage, Waiting Groom", by the nineteenth-century French painter Alfred de Dreux.

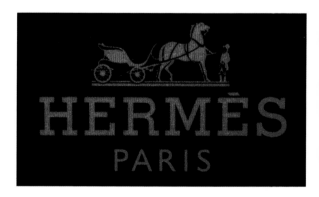

BELOW The iconic Hermès orange box, coveted by women around the world, is a unique colour only used by the fashion house.

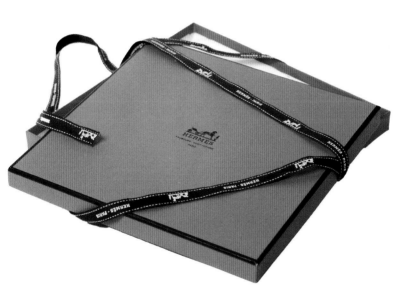

BELOW In 1950
Hermès launched its
first unisex scent, *Eau
d'Hermès*, designed
by French master
perfumer Edmond
Roudnitska.

OPPOSITE In 1961
Jean-René Guerrand,
Émile Hermès's
son-in-law and the
company's longtime
fragrance director,
collaborated with
perfumer Guy
Robert to create
Hermès's first
women's perfume,
Calèche.

PERFUME

During the early part of the twentieth century, Émile had
welcomed not only his son-in-law Robert Dumas-Hermès but
his daughter Aline's husband Jean-René Guerrand, a perfumer,
into the family business. Perfume was an obvious way to extend
the Hermès brand and, in 1950, Émile worked with French
master perfumer Edmond Roudnitska – the nose responsible for
many of the classic scents from the mid twentieth century – to
launch *Eau d'Hermès*. The complex unisex fragrance has base
notes of leather and sandalwood, redolent of a new Hermès
bag, but is softened by verdant top notes of bergamot, lavender,
lemon, petitgrain and sage. The scent was launched in 1951, the
same year that Émile passed away.

Guerrand assumed the role of fragrance director and in 1961
collaborated with perfumer Guy Robert to create Hermès's first
women's perfume, *Calèche*. Nine years later this was followed by
a scent for men, *Equipage*.

Hermès always enjoyed fruitful relationships with master
perfumers such as Edmond Roudnitska, and in 2004, unusually
for a fashion house, employed
their first in-house "nose". The
appointment of Jean-Claude
Ellena heralded a new era in
the success of the company's
fragrances. From 2004 to 2016,
Ellena, himself heavily influenced
by Roudnitska, who was his
mentor and friend, created 35
memorable scents for Hermès. His
first, *Un Jardin en Méditerranèe,*
was inspired by the garden of
Hermès's inimitable director of
window displays, Leïla Menchari,

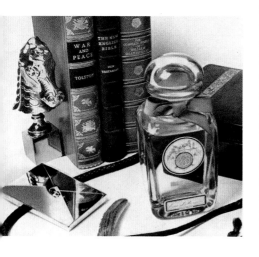

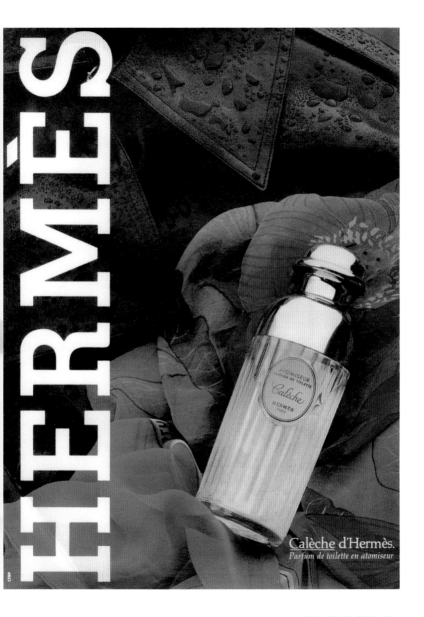

Calèche d'Hermès.
Parfum de toilette en atomiseur

and other fragrances regarded as modern classics include *Cuir d'Ange*, a unisex perfume, its title juxtaposing leather and angels, and *Terre d'Hermès*, the best-selling men's fragrance.

Hermès differs from other major fragrance brands by never testing new perfumes or undertaking market research on large numbers before release, preferring instead to trust the judgement of the in-house nose. As current "nose" Christine Nagel explained to perfumesociety.org:

"When you test a perfume, a lot of people smell it, and give their feedback, and after you remove any extremes that challenge people. You'll have a nice perfume – but in the middle ground, for mass market."

As with their accessories, the judgement of what is good enough to bear the name Hermès comes only from the handful of family members and experts at the heart of the company's leadership, a policy that has allowed Hermès to maintain the highest standards of artisan craftsmanship across all its products.

Hermès continued to open stores globally and has maintained steady sales across clothes and accessories and a loyal clientele, thanks to its excellent reputation. However, by the 1970s the company had begun to stagnate somewhat. Challenged by the growth of competitors using new and innovative man-made materials, Hermès still insisted on using only the finest natural materials and with long lead times on many of their accessories, their workshops were not always fully occupied. It took until 1978 when Robert Dumas-Hermès's son, Jean-Louis Dumas became chairman, to turn Hermès's fortunes back onto an upward trajectory.

OPPOSITE Jean-Claude Ellena, Hermès's in-house "nose" who between 2004 and 2016 created 35 fragrances for the luxury goods brand.

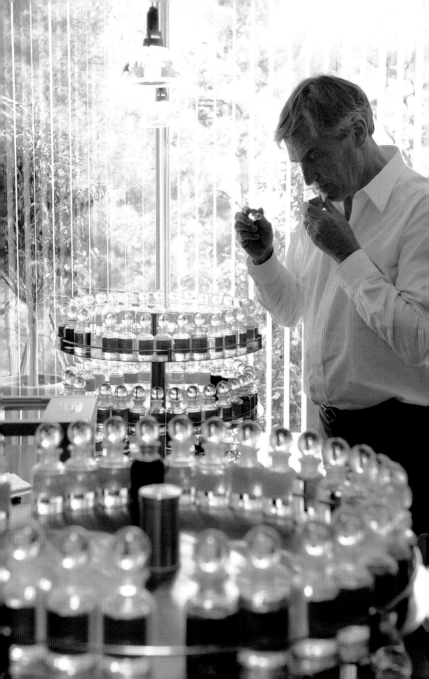

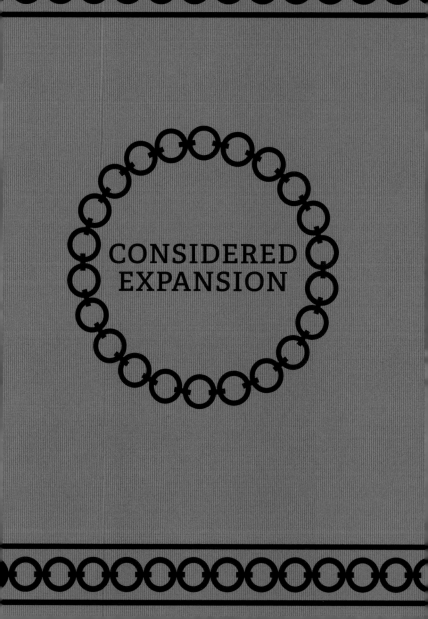
CONSIDERED
EXPANSION

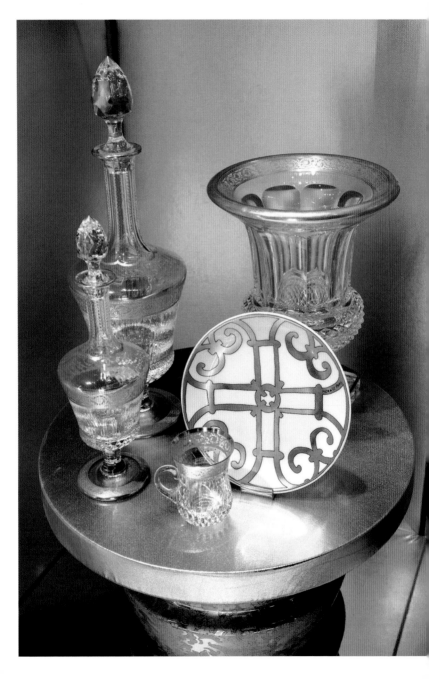

THE ART
OF LIVING

"We don't have a policy of image,
we have a policy of product."
JEAN-LOUIS DUMAS, Vanity Fair

In 1978 Jean-Louis Dumas, Thierry Hermès's great-great-grandson, took over as CEO of Hermès, re-establishing the family line of direct descendants at the head of the company. Over the next three decades, Dumas would steer Hermès into a new era of success, modernizing the label without sacrificing its traditional heritage or superlative production values.

When Dumas took the reins at Hermès, the company was stagnating. Loyal clients were placing orders but not enough to keep the in-house workshop busy. In fact, Dumas was advised that it would be financially advantageous to outsource the making of Hermès goods, something he flatly refused to do. Like his forebears, Dumas knew that keeping the production of goods under his watchful and meticulous eye was essential in ensuring quality was maintained.

OPPOSITE Luxury crystal and dinnerware from Hermès's
"Art of Living" range.

Dumas did, however, realize the need for a degree of modernization, particularly with regard to ready-to-wear fashion, and in 1979 he launched a revolutionary advertising campaign featuring edgy young Parisians wearing Hermès silk scarves, not with traditional elegant couture but with jeans. The image of high-society elegance represented by the iconic silk scarf teamed with jeans, which at the time were still considered inappropriate for many settings, was shocking, particularly to the extended Hermès family who still had roles within the company. But Dumas simply stated, as quoted in *Vanity Fair* in 2007, "The idea is always the same at Hermès, to make tradition live by shaking it up."

Whatever the views of some board members, within a few years Hermès started reaping rewards in the form of a new, young clientele. As he told the *New York Times* in an interview in 1986, "The young customers came to us more than we went to them. People saw again, but with a new eye, the beauty of materials worked by fine hands. They came. We followed."

The second strategy that Dumas took to grow the business was to invest in companies that he both admired and felt shared the artisan ethos of Hermès – a practice he had started two years earlier with the purchase of traditional British bootmaker John Lobb. This would continue throughout Dumas's tenure both with high-profile investments, such as buying a 35 per cent stake in Jean-Paul Gaultier in 1999, and with more strategic acquisitions within the luxury goods supply market, including stakes in Perrin & Fils, a specialist textile weaver, and Vaucher, a manufacturer of parts for high-end precision watches.

Dumas positioned Hermès as a brand that embodied an entire luxury lifestyle, encompassing homewares as well as fashion and accessories. This part of the business has thrived over the last few decades, and now offers a whole interior design concept including wallpaper and furniture. Dumas

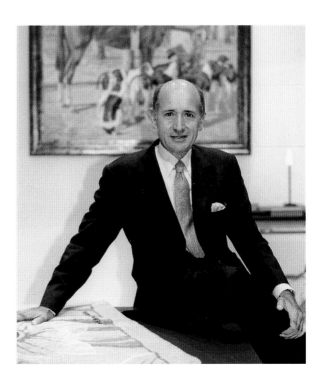

continued to invest in prestigious brands such as Puiforcat silver and Saint-Louis crystal, and since 1984 tableware has been produced in-house. The stunning dinnerware, still a mainstay of Hermès's "Art of Living" today, came about when Dumas formed a partnership with wildlife artist Robert Dallet. He first commissioned a series of silk scarf designs and later an exquisite range of painted porcelain featuring many creatures of the animal kingdom that inspired Dallet.

The early 1980s were also significant for the fortunes of Hermès when Jean-Louis Dumas had a chance meeting with actress Jane Birkin on a plane. The singer and actress was struggling with her open-topped basket bag as her possessions

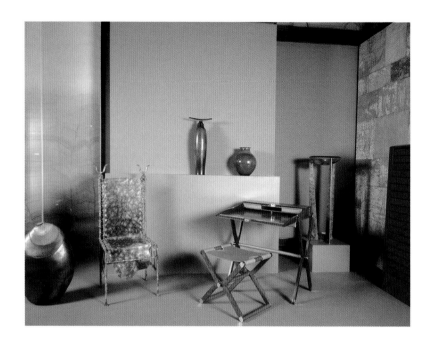

ABOVE Hermès "Art of Living" offered an entire design concept, shown here in exhibition at the Cooper Hewitt Museum in New York in 1989.

OPPOSITE Jane Birkin, for whom Jean-Louis Dumas designed the iconic Birkin bag.

fell from her overhead locker, and on hearing her complain that she couldn't find a suitable handbag Dumas offered to design one. The result was, of course, the legendary Birkin bag, launched in 1984, and the most iconic and coveted of Hermès accessories.

Dumas's strategy of expansion quickly paid off with sales growing from $82 million to $446.4 million between 1982 and 1989. In June 1993, Hermès took the decision to float on the Paris stock exchange, releasing 19 per cent of the company's shares for public sale. It was enough to generate excitement and income but without seriously endangering the control of Hermès from investors outside the family. The move was a great success, with stock prices rising sharply at a time when other luxury brands were barely moving.

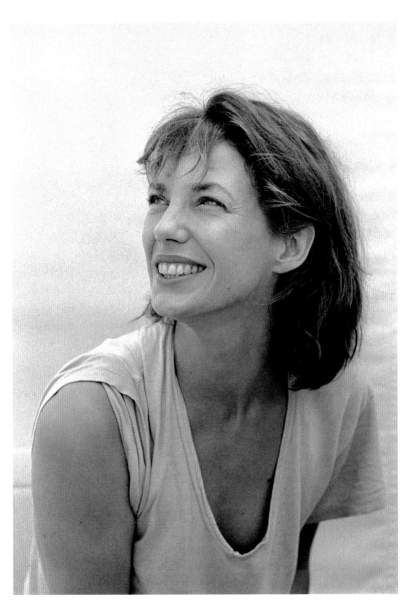

The Hermès family policy of keeping control of the company themselves has not always been easy, especially once sales started growing towards the late 1990s and into the 2000s. Inevitably, once the company went public, large luxury goods conglomerates eyed up what could be considered the ultimate headliner for their own stables. LVMH, the world's most powerful luxury group, controlled by businessman Bernard Arnault, was determined to own this prize. Knowing that the Hermès family would not allow large numbers of shares to be bought up by an outsider, he slyly built up a portfolio through a series of equity derivatives instead of straightforward share purchases. This effectively prevented LVMH from declaring them until 2010 when Hermès realized their biggest competitor was angling for a takeover bid. Four years of legal wrangling ensued, dubbed in the press "the handbag wars". LVMH was fined for failing to declare the stake building and Hermès launched legal proceedings of insider trading and stock price manipulation. LVMH retaliated with a libel case against Hermès. Unexpectedly, in 2014 the parties came to a truce, with LVMH agreeing to disperse the shares and not acquire any more.

Global store expansion was essential to the growth of Hermès and thrived under Dumas's careful stewardship. Initially this worked as a system of franchises, common to other luxury brands, but very closely overseen by Hermès. The company bought iconic buildings or built new, exciting spaces in cities across the world, especially in Asia. As well as offering their Paris designers work with local decorators to maintain the Hermès style, especially when it came to the legendary window displays, the company upped its profile by sponsoring local events such as art exhibitions. Eventually, however, towards the late 1990s Hermès reversed this policy, worried that the family was losing its tight control of the brand, buying back franchises to focus on company-run stores.

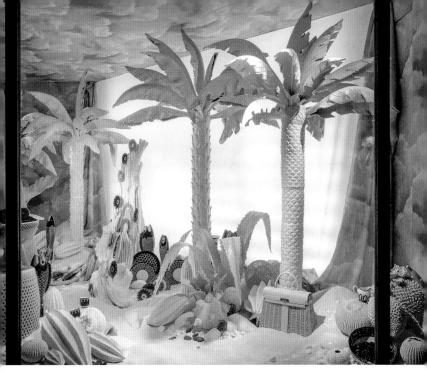

LEÏLA MENCHARI: WINDOW DISPLAYS

Since Robert Dumas-Hermès sketched out ideas for window displays in the 1930s, the face that Hermès presented to the world through its storefronts has been hugely important. During the 1950s the innovative displays by the then director of window dressing, Annie Beaumel, were much admired by Jean Cocteau and Christian Bérard, but it was Beaumel's protégée, Leïla Menchari, who made Hermès windows truly legendary.

Born in Tunis in 1927, Menchari was the first woman to attend her home city's Beaux-Arts Institute as well as the Beaux-Arts school in Paris. She was appointed by Annie Beaumel to the decoration team at Hermès in 1961, after impressing Beaumel with a selection of her drawings. In 1978, the same year that

ABOVE Beach or underwater sets were also a favourite of Menchari. This blue and white sandscape with porcelain palms, shells and urns full of blue glass pebbles and a draped, printed fabric sky, complements Hermès's printed china perfectly.

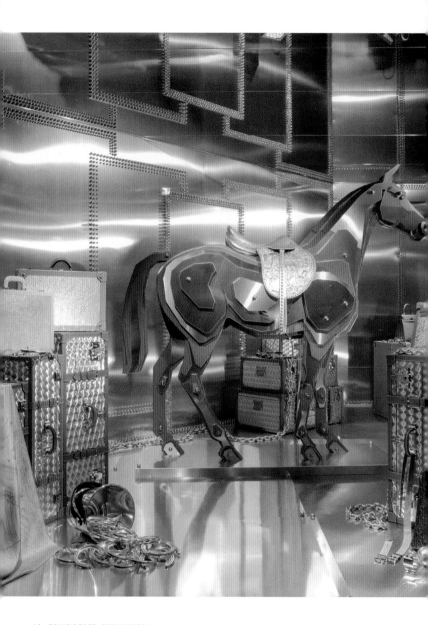

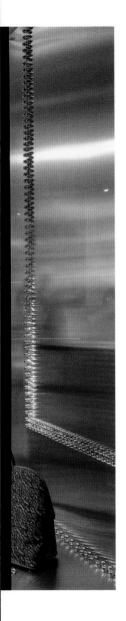

Jean-Louis Dumas took over leadership of the company, Menchari replaced Beaumel and was appointed director of window displays at Hermès's flagship store at 24 Rue du Faubourg Saint-Honoré. She stayed in the role until her retirement in 2013, creating a total of 136 magical designs, each telling its own story. Given her training in theatre set design, it is unsurprising that her windows were so dramatic and for half a century she wowed passers-by and critics alike. As she described in an interview with *Vogue Arabia* in 2017:

"When designing a scene, there must always be some mystery, because mystery is a springboard to dreams. Mystery is an invitation to fill in the gaps left by the imagination."

Her displays, in homage to Hermès's equestrian heritage, often featured horses, in particular Pegasus, the mythical winged divine horse from Greek mythology, but also elaborate beach scenes, opulent gilded palaces and even a meteorite rotating as if in space. She was a magpie for collecting unusual artefacts and favoured textural fabrics such as organza and tulle, which she wove into her displays. Her use of colour was extraordinary and she did not leave any of the senses unawakened, once famously creating a scene that included liberal amounts of the scent *Eau d'Orange Verte* sprayed onto

LEFT Reflecting Hermès's equestrian heritage, Leïla Menchari's displays often featured models of horses.

OVERLEAF Creating an opulent scene was Menchari's speciality and the designer frequently called to mind Greek myths in her window displays. This classical palace, full of decadent hanging fruits and lush foliage, is the perfect backdrop for Hermès bags and scarves in the same rich tones.

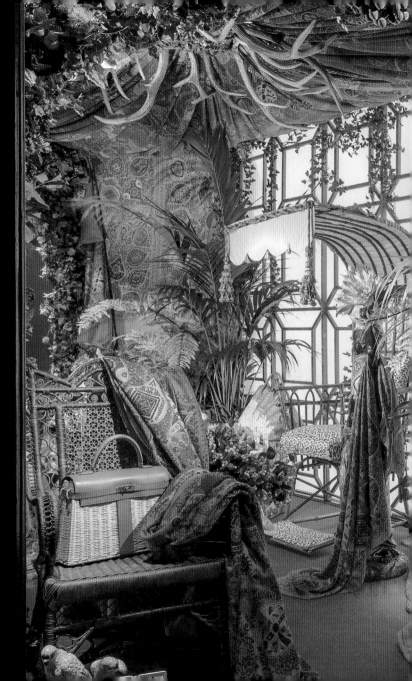

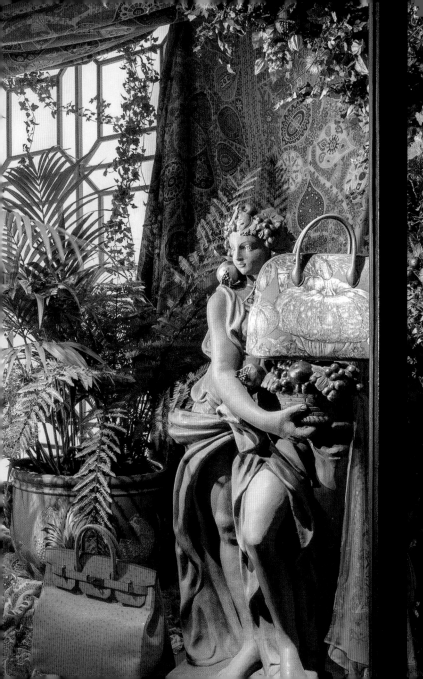

the street outside. On seeing this, Jean-Louis Dumas exclaimed: "But Leïla, there's nothing there!" until he saw a passer-by stop and breathe in the scent and all that it evoked. It is fitting that one of Hermès's most iconic scents, *Un Jardin en Méditerranée*, the first designed by master perfumer Jean-Claude Ellena, was inspired by Menchari's garden in Tunisia.

As with so many longtime employees of Hermès, who were more like family than members of staff, Menchari kept an office at the headquarters until she was in her eighties. Acknowledging the importance of her artistic creations, in 2017, an exhibition was held at the Grand Palais in Paris to showcase the windows of Leïla Menchari for Hermès. She died in April 2020, at the age of 93, from COVID-19.

Leïla Menchari always spoke fondly of Jean-Louis Dumas and his wife Rena, similarly considering them more like family than employers. Fittingly it was Rena Dumas, a renowned architect and interior designer, who created the look of the stores that Menchari so beautifully dressed.

RENA DUMAS: ARCHITECTURE AND INTERIORS.

Born Rena Gregoriades in Greece in 1937, Rena Dumas was inspired to become an architect after watching her brother who attended the technical school in Greece. After graduating with a degree in applied arts and crafts from the École Nationale Supérieure in Paris, where she met and married Jean-Louis Dumas in 1962, she spent time in the United States and in 1968 she met and was influenced by the architect André Wogenscky. In 1972 she founded her own interior design and architecture agency Rena Dumas Interior Architecture (RDIA) and started designing for Hermès in 1976. Her first commission was to design the interior of the newly doubled flagship store on Rue Faubourg when Hermès bought the building next door, and she subsequently took control of the design of all Hermès boutiques

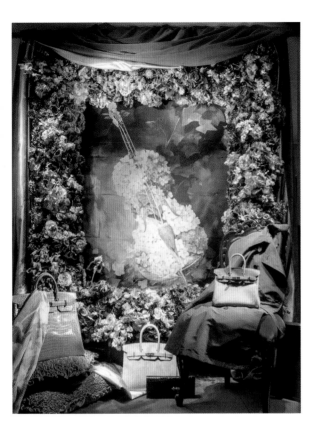

LEFT Leïla Menchari's floral display, with its centrepiece of a white and lilac floral cello, evokes summer concerts. The Birkin bags, crocodile clutch and trench coat thrown casually across a chair are suitably elegant accessories for such an event.

worldwide. She also designed furniture and other objects for Hermès, such as a beautiful, sculptural silver teapot with leather handles, all of which carried her unique aesthetic imprint.

The work Rena Dumas did in designing Hermès stores worldwide played a large part in the brand's global success, and her skill in juxtaposing Hermès's Parisian luxury with local features was expressed with great sensitivity. In an interview by Fashionnetwork.com with her design agency RDIA, following her death in 2009, she is quoted describing the way in which

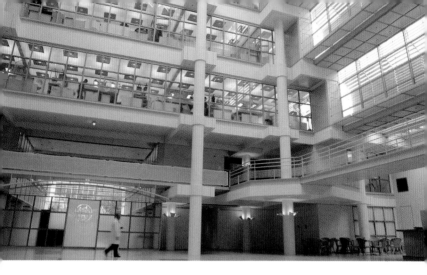

ABOVE Jean-Louis Dumas's wife Rena, a renowned architect, was responsible for designing many of the Hermès stores both as architect and interior designer.

she approached her global commissions: "Each project starts by studying the country, the city, the road and ends as a journey through the building and its interior."

PIERRE-ALEXIS DUMAS

Jean-Louis Dumas retired in 2006 due to his declining health and was succeeded as artistic director by his son, Pierre-Alexis Dumas. The business side of Hermès was taken over by Patrick Thomas, the first non-family CEO in the company's history. Most other senior roles were still filled by the extended Hermès family, including Axel Dumas, Pierre-Alexis's cousin, who managed first the jewellery and then the leather divisions of the company, and eventually took over from Patrick Thomas as CEO in 2014.

Pierre-Alexis Dumas began his journey at Hermès in 1992, working within the creative team at the company's subsidiary brands – Saint Louis crystal and Puiforcat silver – before moving to oversee Hermès's business in China. After five years in Asia, he moved to manage Hermès in the United Kingdom before becoming creative director of silks in 2002.

Like his ancestors before him, preserving the quality of Hermès products is of the utmost importance to Dumas. In an interview with the *Wall Street Journal* in 2011 he explained:

"My job is to keep the strong creativity of Hermès alive. To nourish the rigor and the vision… to make these values vibrate. This is the force of Hermès."

To this end, every product that leaves the Hermès workshop is personally signed off by Dumas, and bags that have even the slightest imperfections are destroyed. In this way he can maintain the exclusivity of the brand, even as its popularity soars. The long waiting lists for every hand-made item, if clients can even get their names on such a list, is part and parcel of the mythology of Hermès.

Pierre-Alexis Dumas's passion for his company's products is obvious, as is his recognition of the importance of sustainability. Hermès products have always been investment buys, not just because of their extremely high price point but because of the level of craftsmanship that means they will last a lifetime. In an interview with Vogue.com in 2020, during the first wave of the COVID-19 pandemic, Dumas talks of the importance of maintaining a balance with nature:

"An ecosystem is a sense of balance. It's like farming; if you exhaust the land, you will not be able to farm anymore. You need to anticipate, and rest, and tend, so that you will have a balanced and sustainable relationship. I think it will take time for our industry to really include that in its process."

He goes on to hope that consumers are changing their attitudes and embracing the philosophy that Hermès has had from the very beginning.

"I think today there is a desire for meaningful objects. You don't just buy anything on impulse anymore … You're buying a philosophy, that this is something that is going to be beneficial and not destructive."

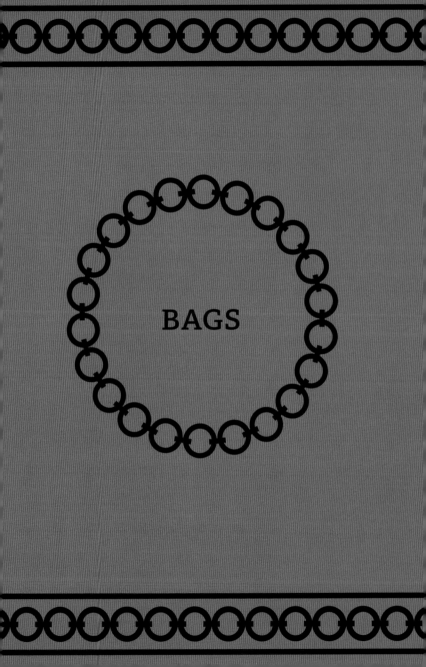

BAGS

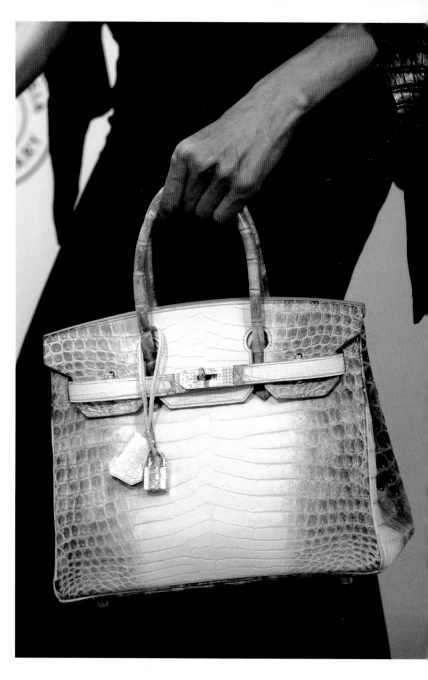

OBJECTS OF DESIRE

In 2017, Christie's in Hong Kong sold a white crocodile
Hermès Diamond Himalaya Birkin 30 bag
for £208,175 ($281,500).

At the time, the Niloticus Crocodile skin bag with 18k white gold hardware and encrusted with 10.23 carats of diamonds was the most expensive bag ever to have sold at auction. This rare bag, deemed the holy grail for serious collectors, epitomizes everything that Hermès stands for: exclusivity, craftsmanship and heritage.

The first incarnation of the trademark Hermès bags we know today was produced by Charles-Émile Hermès in the early 1900s. Labelled the Haut à Courroies (HAC) bag, which literally translates from the French as "tall with straps", this sturdy leather equestrian bag with a wide opening was designed for riders who needed to carry their saddles and boots. The HAC bag is still in production today, albeit in a more refined form. It retains the height and trapezoid shape with the

OPPOSITE The white crocodile Hermès Diamond Himalaya Birkin 30 bag.
Dyeing crocodile skin is time-consuming and becomes more difficult as the
colour lightens. The process calls for great skill.

trademark side straps, and is available not only in traditional leather but in a myriad of fabrics, including felt and canvas, or patterned with exotic designs.

It was not until 1922 that Hermès started seriously producing and marketing high quality handbags. The impetus came from Émile Hermès's wife who, complaining that she couldn't find a suitable handbag, turned to her husband who created a smaller version of the Haut à Courroies bag for her. The handbag proved a success and was followed up in 1925 with a range of travel bags. The expansion of Hermès into America, with its well-travelled elite, helped to increase the popularity of these bags. In 1935, the classic that we know today, the Sac à Dépêches, or Kelly bag as it was renamed in the 1950s, came into being. A redesign of Hermès's original simple leather bag by Émile's son-in-law, Robert Dumas, took the plain, well-crafted bag and refined it into an elegant, and timeless, classic.

THE HERMÈS KELLY BAG

In 1956, American actress Grace Kelly, who was a long-time client of Hermès and newly married to Prince Rainier of Monaco, was photographed by paparazzi – an image that would become iconic and lead to the renaming of the Sac à Dépêches. The actress-turned-princess was pregnant but not yet ready to reveal this fact to the world, so clutched her beloved handbag to her stomach. The photograph was sold worldwide, landing on the covers of many magazines, and the huge popularity of Grace Kelly led to the public nicknaming her trademark bag the "Kelly". The name stuck and Hermès benefited from the publicity, although it was not officially adopted by the company until 1977. Unlike modern celebrities who boast a whole wardrobe of handbags, Grace Kelly loved her brown Hermès so much that it became battered and worn

RIGHT Hermès earliest bags were as practical as they were beautiful. Designed for travel, this c.1920 gentleman's overnight bag included a lower compartment for shirts and was fastened by the then-unusual zip fastener along with Hermès's trademark lock.

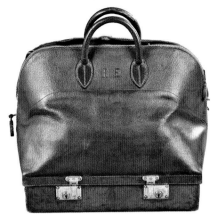

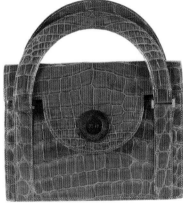

LEFT Although Hermès's instantly-recognizable orange hue did not come into common use until after the Second World War, there are rare early examples of bags in similar tones such as this golden tan crocodile 368 bag from the 1930s.

RIGHT This early example of the Hermès Malette bag from the 1930s is made from brown crocodile skin. It was designed for women who wished to carry their jewellery with them and has a separate compartment at the base of the bag secured by the iconic tumbler lock.

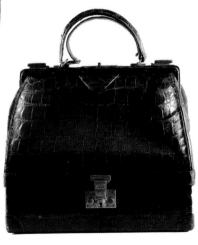

BELOW The famous paparazzi shot of Grace Kelly in 1956 clutching her Hermès Sac à Dépêches to her stomach to disguise the pregnancy bump that she was not yet ready to share with the world. The bag would soon be renamed the "Kelly".

OPPOSITE The princess was often photographed carrying an Hermès Kelly bag.

by use. In 2010, the Victoria and Albert Museum in London included it as part of an exhibition devoted to the style icon.

Kelly bags are the epitome of refinement. With a single handle and shoulder strap it is more formal than its two-handled sister, the Birkin, and can be carried in the hand or across the body. Today, Kelly bags, along with Hermès Birkin bags, are exclusively handmade to order with waiting lists of up to six years. With a ranking system in place where priority is given to previous clients, it is not even always possible to put your name down on the list. This not only keeps the cachet high but fuels the lively trade in second-hand Hermès bags at auction. These bags still command prices in the thousands and the most sought-after, such as the very limited number made from crocodile skin, sell for six-figure sums.

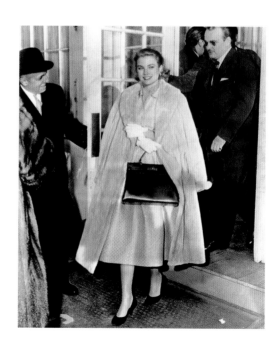

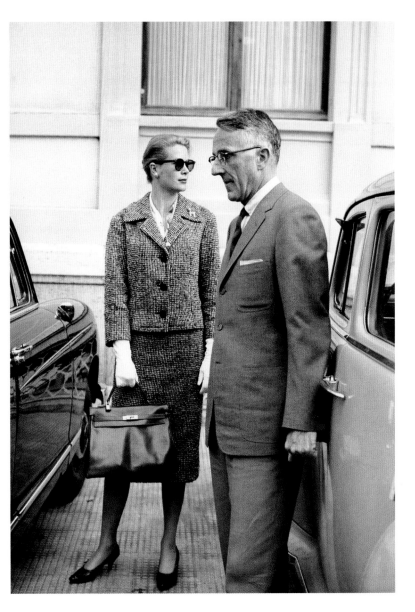

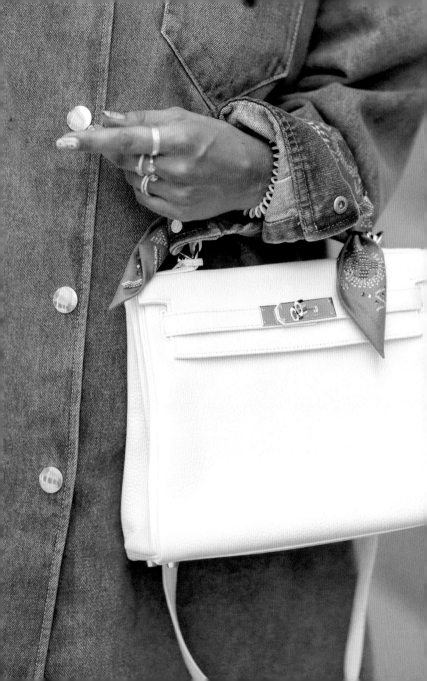

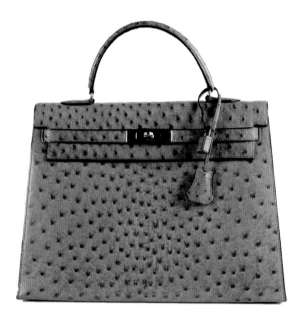

ABOVE Kelly bags are popularly made in a range of animal skins such as this grey-brown ostrich leather version from 1986.

OPPOSITE The Kelly bag has both a shoulder and wrist strap and comes in a wide range of colours, allowing it to be worn in a myriad of ways. This white version is given a street style look by blogger Karin Teigl in 2021, offset against a denim dress and tied silk Hermès printed scarf.

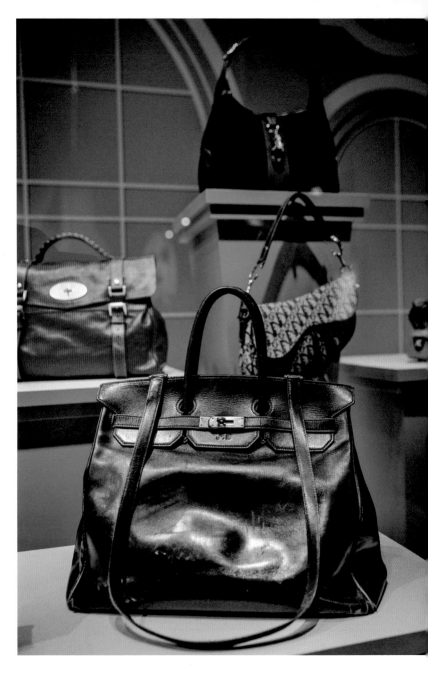

THE HERMÈS BIRKIN BAG

The more recent of Hermès's most iconic bags is, of course, the Birkin. It is perhaps even more coveted than the Kelly and popular among celebrities, including the Kardashians and Victoria Beckham, who reputedly owns more than 100 versions.

The story of its creation has gone down in fashion history. In the early 1980s, on a flight from Paris to London, actress Jane Birkin found herself deluged with the contents of her trademark wicker basket, which fell out everywhere as she tried to grapple it into the overhead compartment. As luck would have it, the seat next to her belonged to Hermès CEO Jean-Louis Dumas. The pair started chatting about handbags as Birkin bemoaned the lack of roomy versions suitable for young mothers with all they needed to carry. The actress even started sketching out her perfect design on the back of the airline sick bag.

Over the next year, Dumas, never one to resist a challenge, created a new Hermès bag, larger than the Kelly and more modern in feel. Launched in 1984, it is essentially a superior tote

BELOW Birkin bags come in a range of colours to suit every season and occasion, including a bright pink crocodile for those who prefer a bolder statement.

OPPOSITE Jane Birkin's original Birkin bag featured in the Victoria and Albert Museum's Bags Inside Out exhibition, 2021.

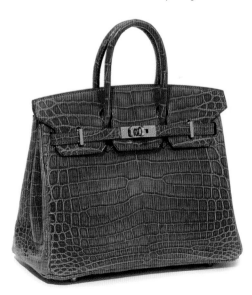

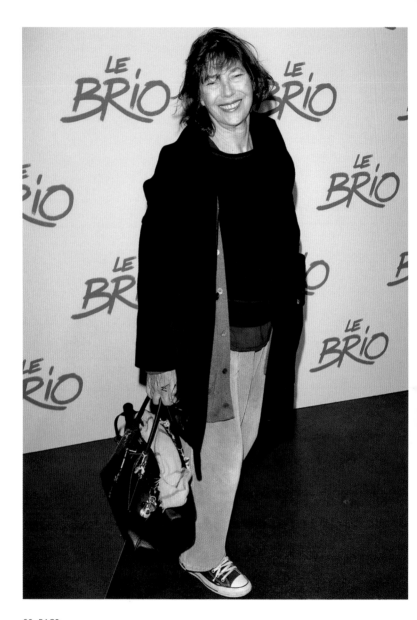

RIGHT Victoria Beckham is reputed to own over 100 Birkin bags, accessorizing each of her outfits with the perfect one. Pictured here in California in 2007 carrying a dark pink ostrich leather version to match her outfit.

OPPOSITE Jane Birkin often carries a version of the iconic Birkin, appropriately bulging with her belongings and more often than not individually customized by the activist. Photographed here in 2017 attending the Paris premiere of *Le Brio*.

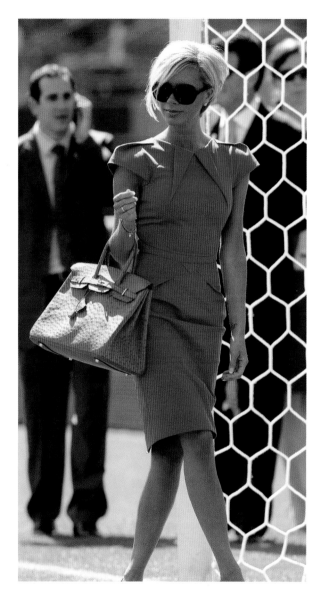

bag, created to be not only elegant but functional. In contrast to the Kelly, the Birkin has two handles and no shoulder strap, making it the perfect fit for the crook of the arm. The original 35cm version that Jean-Louis Dumas presented to Jane Birkin, a year after their flight, had space for the milk bottles she carried for her children, but also a spacious internal pocket for the actress's personal items. Like the Kelly, it has a flap and is secured by two straps. However, unlike the Kelly, which needs to be carried fastened shut so as not to strain the single handle, the Birkin can be worn half-open in a more casual style. And despite its stratospheric price tag, it looks as good paired with jeans and a T-shirt as it does with dressier outfits, making it the holy grail for handbag enthusiasts. Like the original Kelly bag, the original Birkin made for the British actress and singer went on display at London's Victoria and Albert Museum in 2021 as part of their Bags: Inside Out exhibition.

THE MAKING OF AN HERMÈS BAG

To this day, Kelly and Birkin bags are handmade by highly skilled artisans. First the tanned leather, already graded to the highest quality, is closely examined for the tiniest flaws, which are carefully cut away. Symmetrical pieces are meticulously cut and laid out before being stitched using the Hermès trademark double saddle-stitch. The stitching is done while the bag is held by a wooden clamp. The two-needle process, devised by founder Thierry Hermès, is remarkably strong and designed in such a way that in the unlikely scenario that one stitch becomes broken, the others are unaffected.

Once stitched together, the seams are gently tapped with a hammer to ensure that they don't stand out too much from the body of the bag. The seam is then sanded and shaved to create a perfectly smooth finish. Finally it is coated in beeswax, with the dual purpose of waterproofing the bag and making it beautifully smooth to the touch. The handles, made out of four or five layers of compressed leather, are laboriously hand-shaped: the artisan traditionally places it across their thigh to create the perfect shape.

The final stage is attaching the hardware, which is not done with screws that can loosen over time, but with a more secure process devised by Hermès known as "pearling". A clasp is placed on the front of the leather and a piece of metal at the back. A nail is then inserted from behind and clipped before being tapped with a special tool into a pearl-like shape, fastening the two pieces of metal together. Once the bag is finished, it is closely inspected for any defects before being sold. Bags that do have flaws are destroyed.

BELOW Hermès bags and accessories have traditionally been made by hand and the saddle stitch and "pearling" method of fastening leather together, both invented by Thierry Hermès, are still in use today.

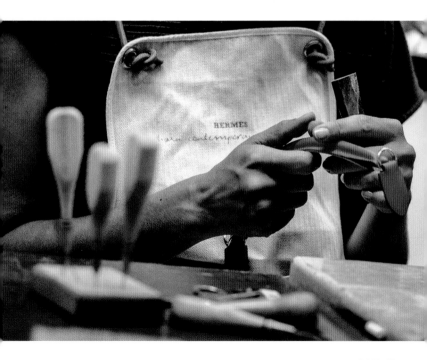

BELOW A black crocodile leather version of Hermès's Constance bag.

OPPOSITE Anna Schürrle gives a red leather Constance bag a streetwear vibe in Berlin in 2020.

OTHER ICONIC HERMÈS BAGS

Probably the third most recognizable of the Hermès handbags is the Constance. Designed in 1959 by in-house designer Catherine Chaillet, it was named after her fifth child, who was born on the same day that the first bag left the production line. A more modern, rectangular handbag with a long shoulder strap, it is instantly recognizable for its large "H"-shaped clasp. This elegant and versatile bag became a staple of Jackie Kennedy's wardrobe, instantly increasing its popularity.

The Evelyne, created in 1978, took Hermès back to its equestrian roots and was named after Evelyne Bertrand, the former head of Hermès's riding department. The roomy bag was originally designed to carry horse grooming equipment, hence the perforated "H" logo, which would allow the necessary ventilation for damp brushes to dry. Large, with an open top and a single leather fastening, it has a thick shoulder strap lending itself to crossbody wear, messenger-style. The versatility of this relatively casual bag has given it a more unisex appeal than many of Hermès's other designs.

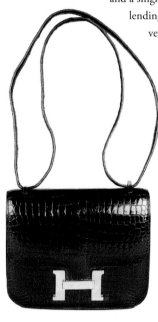

The Bolide is the discreet cousin of the famous Kelly and Birkin bags. Classically shaped, with a rounded top and double handle straps, as well as a removable shoulder strap, it has a zip closure which makes the fact that its forebear was designed in 1923 all the more remarkable. This unique mechanism, which we take for granted today, was not seen in Europe until Émile Hermès saw it used on automobiles on a trip to Canada. Émile patented the design for use in France and immediately added it to the fledgling Hermès bag. Nicknamed *le sac pour*

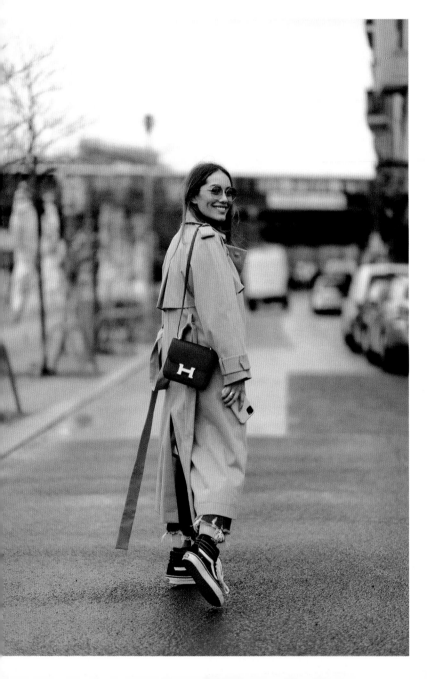

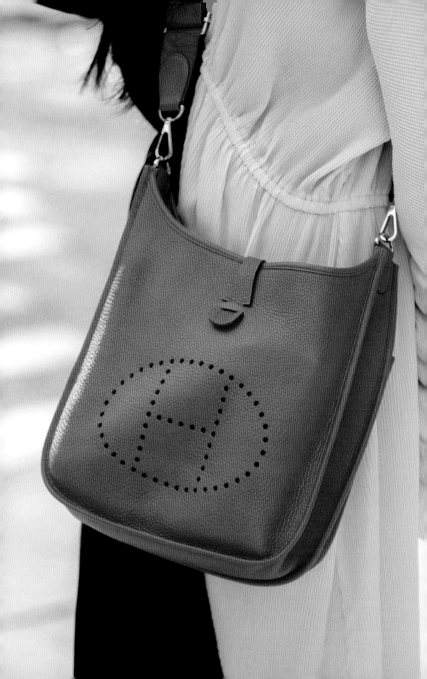

l'auto, it was redesigned in 1982 to become the classic that is still regularly used today as a travel bag, especially in its larger sizes.

The Hermès Herbag, a discontinued classic, was relaunched in 2009 as the Zip Herbag, and marketed as the affordable Kelly, although the price tag still landed in the low thousands! Extremely similar in shape and style to the Kelly, it differs in its closure mechanism and includes a padlock and an exterior zip pocket.

Hermès, true to its ethos as a company that created small quantities of bespoke artisan bags, rarely launches a new style, preferring to adapt its classics. But on the A/W 2014 catwalk, the Halzan made its debut. In keeping with Hermès designs, the Halzan has a classic shape, complete with a fastening fashioned to look like a leather stirrup. Its appeal is in its functionality, allowing the wearer to choose from using it as a classic shoulder bag, tote, cross-body bag or even a clutch.

BELOW The Hermès Bolide bag is similar in style to the Kelly and Birkin but smaller with a zip closure. The original version was designed as early as 1923.

OPPOSITE The Evelyne bag, named after Evelyne Bertrand, the former head of Hermes's riding department.

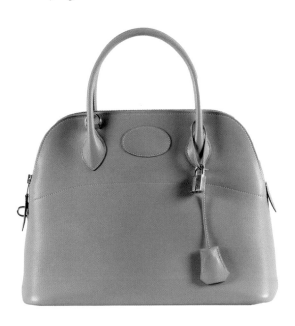

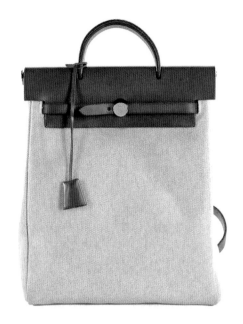

RIGHT The modern version of the Hermès Herbag was relaunched in 2009 and can be worn in several ways, including as a backpack.

OPPOSITE The Jige clutch is a the most classic of Hermès's smaller bags. It is carried here by Olivia Palermo at London Fashion week in 2012.

As a rule, almost all Hermès bags are structured in style, with the exception being the Lindy. Introduced in 2007, it is made from slouchy, soft leather and was given its name as a reference to the Lindy Hop – the American swing dance from the 1920s. Spacious, with two large, zipped interior pockets and two exterior pockets, like many Hermès bags it can be carried either as a tote or shoulder bag.

Finally, it is worth remembering that the Hermès woman needs a bag for every occasion and while the Kelly, Birkin and Bolide are perfect for daytime, for the evening a clutch is more suitable. The most famous of Hermès's clutch bags is the Jige. Designed in 1975 as a wedding gift from Jean Guerrand, Émile Hermès's son-in-law, to one of his future daughters-in-law, the Jige takes its name from his initials. A pared-down classic, it comes in several sizes and features the trademark "H" clasp.

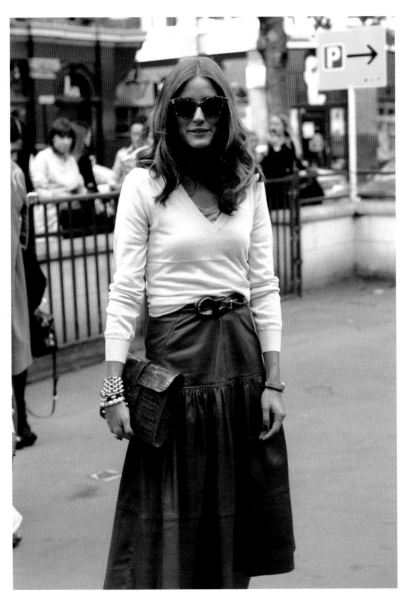

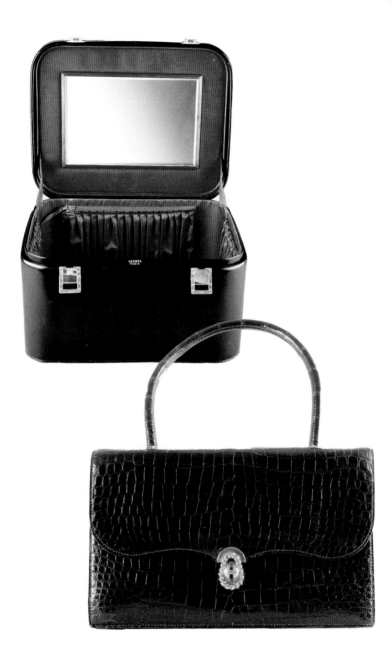

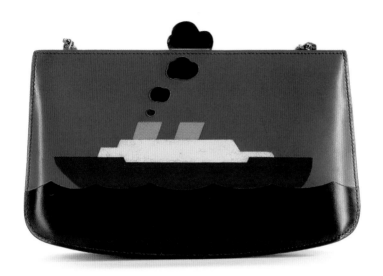

ABOVE Despite being renowned for their classic bags Hermès has also produced some individual and striking designs such as this Cruise shoulder bag from the 1980s.

OPPOSITE TOP Hermès has traditionally made leather goods that are both practical and stylish such as this black leather vanity case from the 1960s, lined in red leather with an inset mirror in the lid.

OPPOSITE BOTTOM A stunning Hermès wine-coloured crocodile leather Escale bag with a gilt rope-twist loop and button clasp from the late 1960s.

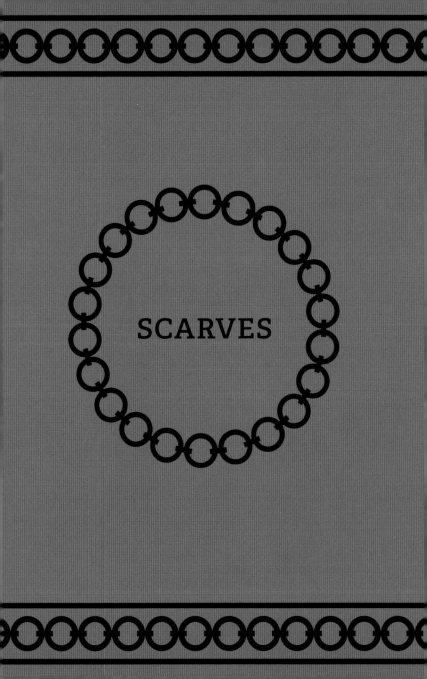

SCARVES

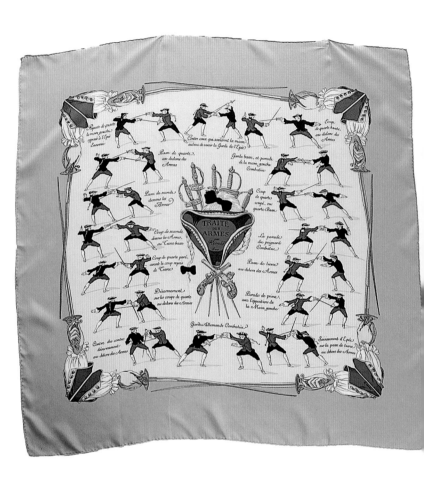

CARRÉS DE SOIE

There are few accessories as iconic or as redolent of luxury as
the Hermès silk carré, a word which simply translates
as "square". Worn by celebrities and aristocrats and
coveted by both young and old, tied over the head
to keep hair safe from the wind or looped through the handle
of a handbag, Hermès's striking colours and prints
are instantly recognizable.

There has always been a long tradition of using silk in the
equestrian world that Hermès catered to, with jockeys
traditionally sporting silk shirts in the colours of their horse
owners. During the 1920s, the company sold scarves from
Bianchini Férier, the quality silk house, alongside their own
products, but it was not until 1937, a full century after the
company was founded, that Hermès started making their own
silk scarves to sell. As Hermès's reputation for artisan excellence
grew, Robert Dumas, who had been working alongside his
father-in-law Émile Hermès, decided to commission exclusive

OPPOSITE Hugo Grygkar worked for Hermès throughout the 1940s and 50s,
creating iconic designs such as the *Traite des Armes* scarf from 1951, which
has subsequently been released in a number of different colourways.

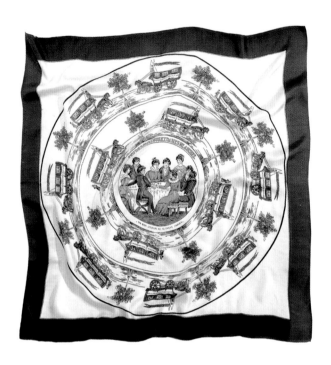

ABOVE In 1937 Hermès released its first scarf design. Named *Jeu des Omnibus et Dames Blanches*, it was based on a woodblock engraving by Robert Dumas and created by artist Hugo Grygkar.

prints, overseeing the process from design to execution. The production of the silk carré was to become a lifelong passion for Dumas, who helped evolve the scarf into the icon it is today.

The first design was created for Hermès by artist Hugo Grygkar and based on a woodblock engraving by Robert Dumas. Born in Germany in 1907 to Czech parents, Grygkar moved to France in 1914 and worked as an illustrator and commercial artist for magazines including *Vogue*. He was both a devoted artist and a keen reader, attributes that influenced his designs for Hermès. The debut scarf was named *Jeu des Omnibus et Dames Blanche*s, the inspiration coming from an 1830s board game belonging to Émile Hermès. The design depicted fashionable players seated at a table beneath the words: "A good player never loses his temper". It was both witty and a little bit frivolous, a perfect foil to soften the sharply tailored jackets favoured by women of the period. Working in close collaboration with Robert Dumas, Grygkar became one of Hermès's most prolific designers, creating many similarly playful scarves, often with ironic quotes or satirically harking back to historical French figures such as Napoleon Bonaparte.

Throughout the 1940s these scarves proved an excellent antidote to the harsh realities of war, and Grygkar's work at Hermès continued right up until his death in 1959. He created some of Hermès's most iconic prints including the 1946 *Ex Libris*, based on the famous 1923 bookplate created by Émile Hermès which formed the basis of the company logo, and *Brides de gala*, one of Hermès's most popular prints, which has

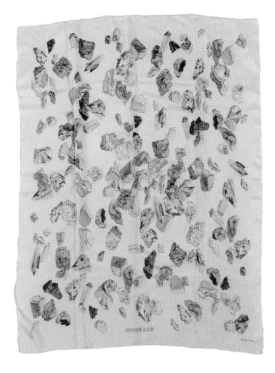

LEFT Hugo Grygkar continued to design for Hermès until his death in 1959. This *Mineraux* scarf was one of his final creations.

been reinvented many times. Grygkar and Dumas had a truly collaborative relationship born out of their obsessive attention to detail and quality of design with Dumas suggesting subjects including art, literature and the natural world. Grygkar would then incorporate these ideas into the drawings for his scarf templates as precisely as possible – for instance, finding a live rooster to inspire the 1954 design *Combats de Coqs*, and a genuine zebra skin for *La Chasse en Afrique* three years later.

The other artist who could be considered a founding father of the Hermès scarf is Philippe Ledoux. Born in Britain to French parents in 1903, Ledoux returned to France as a teenager and studied at Paris's Académie de Peinture. A long-time caricaturist

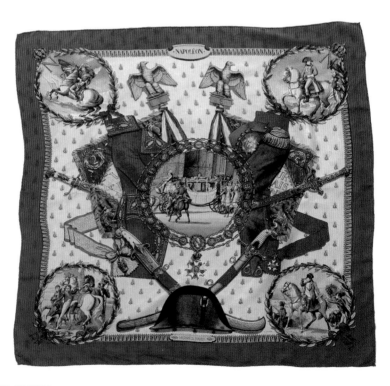

who enjoyed sketching scenes from local cafés, Ledoux was also a renowned book illustrator by the late 1940s, with an unusually keen and sensitive drawing style. In 1947, Robert Dumas first commissioned Ledoux who went on to design 90 *carrés*, many with equestrian or naval scenes, and his ability to draw horses particularly impressed Dumas. Some, including *Napoléon* (1963), *La Comédie Italienne* (1962) and *Cosmos* (1964) are among the most collectable of Hermès's scarves.

Over the years, Hermès has commissioned many designers, including some famous names such as A.M. Cassandre, the lauded Art Deco graphic artist whose unique style was a combination of cubism and surrealism. Along with his

BELOW The renowned Art Deco graphic artist A.M. Cassandre designed the *Perspective* scarf in 1951, which the house has reinvented many times since. This particular colour-way was released in 1995.

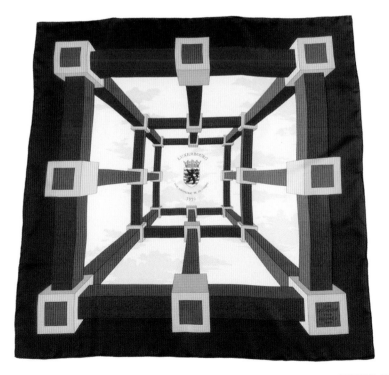

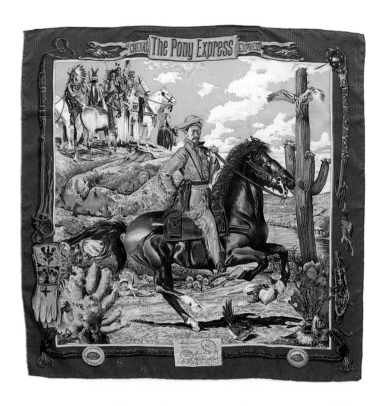

popular 1952 design *Littérature,* his geometric optical illusion *Perspective* (1951) has since been reissued in various colours and is sometimes known just as the "Cassandre" scarf. Other contributors were experts in hunting and equestrianism as well as naval history, themes that hark back to the company's history and constantly recur in the Hermès catalogue.

When Jean-Louis Dumas took over from his father in 1978, his determination to bring Hermès to a younger generation hinged on the silk carré, this time marketed to edgy young Parisians. Dumas was a modernizer and this, combined with his passion for travel and photography, greatly influenced the scarf designs that he commissioned. A turning point came in 1989 when the controversial exhibition Magiciens de la Terre (Magicians of the Earth) was staged at Paris's Centre Georges Pompidou and the Grande halle de la Villette. The exhibition showcased over 100 global artists, half of whom came from non-Western countries, and examined not only the aesthetic history of art but its social impact too. The exhibition inspired Jean-Louis Dumas to broaden the artistic reach of Hermès's scarves as he sought to depict a global kaleidoscope using a range of design techniques and motifs. Artists who were commissioned to this end include the only American to ever design for Hermès: African American painter Kermit Oliver. Since 1986, he has produced 20 opulent and colourful designs, drawing on his experience of Native American people and wildlife. One of his early creations, *Flores et Faune du Texas*, depicts the wide-ranging local flowers and wildlife of Texas, with a border detailing more than 50 native animals.

In total there are over 2,000 scarves in the Hermès archives, with popular vintage designs highly sought after by collectors. Some more recent designers are equally recognizable, their first editions quickly selling out. One example is that of French artist Annie Faivre, who has produced 40 designs since 1979, with a colourful, abstract style that often includes animals such as her trademark monkey. More recent collaborations have included commissions from Paris-born artist and illustrator Ugo Gattoni and multi-media artist Zoè Pauwels with new, young artists, such as Londoner Alice Shirley, welcomed into the ever-evolving Hermès stable of designers. In 1986, the company introduced an annual theme beginning with *Chasse en Inde* (Hunting in India). Within this brief approximately a dozen scarves are designed along with regular reprints of older patterns. Despite wide-reaching global themes, the brand frequently harks back to its equestrian heritage, often with a modern twist.

OPPOSITE African-American painter Kermit Oliver is the only American ever to design for Hermès and his depictions of the flora and fauna of Texas as well as Native American way of life has resulted in some of Hermès's most creative scarfs. A typical example is *The Pony Express* from 1993.

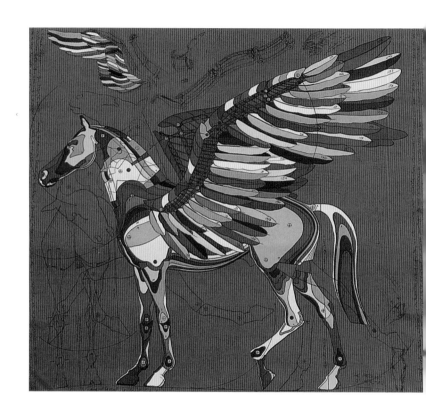

ABOVE Vibrant colours such as this *Le Pégase d'Hèrmes* silk
scarf designed by Christian Renonciat in 2011 have become
a hallmark of Hermès scarves in more recent years but the
references to Greek mythology and of course, the horse
motif, look back to the heritage of the label.

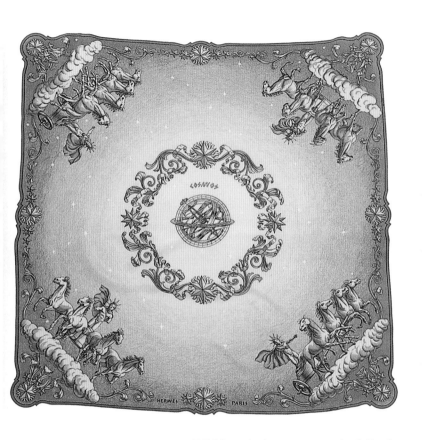

ABOVE Equestrian themes are commonplace in Hermès scarves and the iconic *Cosmos*, designed by Phillipe Ledoux in 1966, includes figures on horse-drawn chariots in each of its four corners.

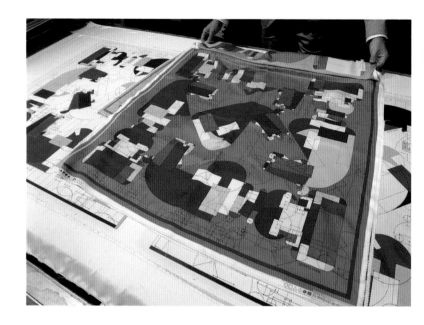

THE MAKING OF AN HERMÈS SILK *CARRÉ*

The very first Hermès scarves were made from imported Chinese silk and were twice as strong as any other silk scarves. Today, the scarves are just as robust thanks to the 450,000 metres of raw silk that are required for a single 90cm × 90cm square. The silk comes from Hermès's own eco-friendly silk farm in the southern Brazilian state of Paraná, where *Bombyx mori* silk moths feast on mulberry leaves, their cocoons each producing a single 1,500m strand of silk. Therefore, 300 cocoons are required for each scarf. Only silk certified as grade 6A, the finest available, is used by Hermès. Creating the finished product, from design to printing, can take as long as 18 months – an artisan process that more than justifies its hefty price tag.

The scarves themselves are woven in Lyon in France, which has been the centre of Europe's silk industry since the

RIGHT Hermès scarves have often been put to inventive uses, as in this iconic image of Grace Kelly who. After injuring her arm, she used her silk scarf as a makeshift sling, shown here as she prepared to board the yacht belonging to Aristotle Onassis.

OPPOSITE The "Lyonnaise" silkscreen printing method of making a Hermès scarf is complex and lengthy. After a design is meticulously finished, colour is carefully built up in layers. Although Hermès moved from entirely hand-printing to a mechanized model in 2014, each stage is closely monitored by trained artisans before the scarves are cut and hand-rolled.

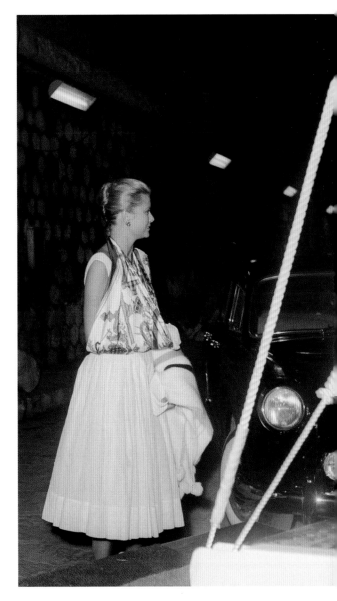

Renaissance. The collaboration between Hermès and Ateliers AS, who print their scarves, began in 1948 when Émile Hermès and Robert Dumas started using the "Lyonnaise" silkscreen printing method developed by engraver Marcel Gandit, chemist Auguste Arnaud and colour specialist Aimé Savy. The technical expertise offered by this new print method gave an extraordinarily precise representation of the original drawings, depicted in rich and vibrant colour. Today, a team of colour specialists draw up charts and mix exact shades, all blended in-house.

The process of screen printing is done in layers. A stretched piece of silk is dyed one colour at a time using laboriously hand-engraved screens, originally taking as many as 750 hours to create. However, since the advent of computer technology, photo-engraving using digital files has made the engraver's work somewhat easier. It is an extremely precise operation: each mesh-covered metal frame must be perfectly aligned to avoid colour leakage.

While many screen printers will use fewer than 10 layers, Hermès scarves typically use 20 to 30 individual screens, with some designs demanding up to 46 layers. Each layer takes around 20 hours to print, so a whole design can take up to 700 hours. Although Hermès mechanized its production process around 2014, the printing process is closely monitored by artisans who train for up to 3 years and are allowed to actually work with the scarves only in the final one. Tables 150 metres long allow for enormous rolls of silk to be unfurled in preparation for the flatbed screens. An artisan is stationed every 40 metres, monitoring the speed, regulating the colour and checking the printing markers are carefully adhered to. The dyes are fixed with steam, washed, rinsed and dried and finally hand-rolled, when the scarves are then hemmed with silk thread. Each scarf is meticulously examined to ensure that it is flawless before being released for sale.

OPPOSITE A more topical use for the Hermès scarf is adopted by Olivia Palermo who, in New York in July 2020, protects herself by using her silk as a makeshift mask.

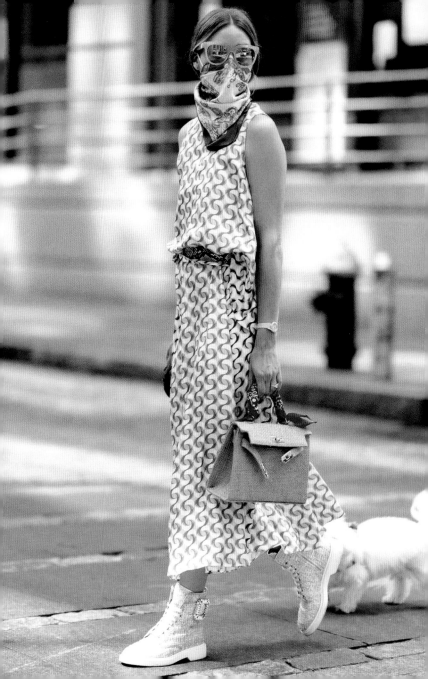

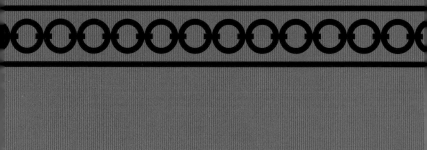

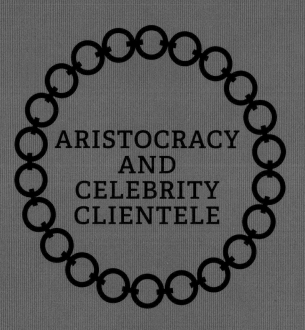

ARISTOCRACY
AND
CELEBRITY
CLIENTELE

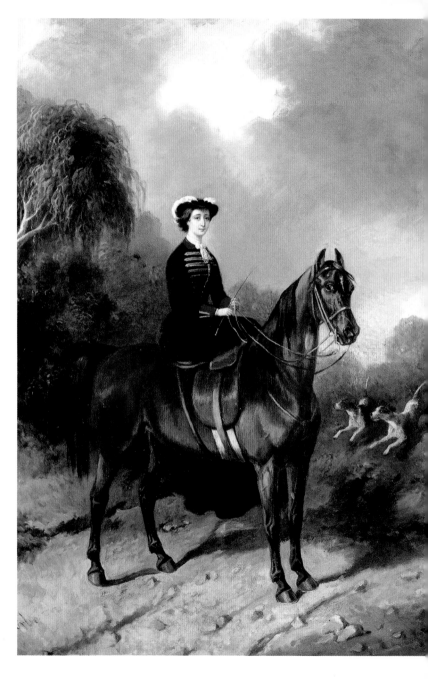

-OOO-

PRINCESSES, PATRONS AND PERSONALITIES

Since Thierry Hermès founded his saddlery business in 1837, Hermès has attracted the most prestigious of customers. Empress Eugénie, wife of Napoleon III, was an early patron of his equestrian goods and other European noblemen quickly followed suit.

By the 1880s, when Charles-Émile Hermès took over the business, opening the flagship store on Paris's Rue du Faubourg Saint-Honoré, socialites and aristocrats were ordering Hermès's prize-winning harnesses and bridles from as far away as North Africa, Asia and the Americas.

The tradition of supplying royalty continued after the turn of the twentieth century, and the patronage of the Tsar of Russia

OPPOSITE Empress Eugénie, wife of Napoleon III, was an early patron of Thierry Hermès's equestrian supplies.

in 1914 required an 80-strong workforce to supply the saddles
that he ordered. British royals have also had a longstanding
relationship with Hermès. A leather golf jacket, designed
in 1918 for Edward, Prince of Wales, was remarkable in its
feature of a zip-closure, then exclusively patented in Europe to
Hermès. The Duke of Windsor, as he became after abdicating
the British throne, and his wife, Wallis Simpson, were both
great fans of Hermès.

Simpson was well-known for her dedication to high
fashion, famously remarking, "I'm not a beautiful woman. I'm
nothing to look at, so the only thing I can do is dress better
than anyone else."

For the Duke of Windsor, it was a challenge to buy gifts
for his wife who had so much already, but in 1947, a visit to
Hermès resulted in a most unusual present. The story was told
by a Hermès spokesperson to the *Independent* in 2012: "He was

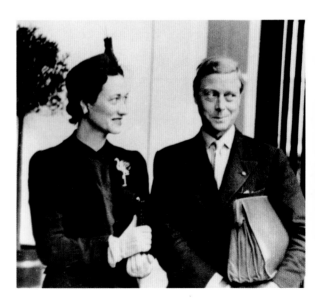

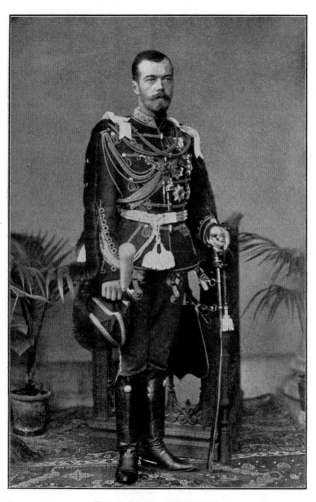

THE EMPEROR NICHOLAS II.

OPPOSITE The Queen of England's trademark headscarf is often made by Hermès, including this yellow, navy and grey version that she wore to the Royal Windsor Horse Show in 2017.

asking advice from one of the salespeople and they said, 'What about fragrances?' and he said she had wheelbarrows of them. The salesperson said, 'What about the gloves then?' He said, 'It's just same thing: she has wheelbarrows of them.'"

Legend has it that window designer Annie Beaumel, overhearing this conversation, suggested making the Duchess an actual wheelbarrow and filling it with perfume and gloves. Hermès did just that, crafting the most unique wheelbarrow out of black patent cow skin, complete with brass handles, drawers and leather-upholstered wheels. The piece went on display at the 2012 Hermès exhibition, Leather Forever, at London's Royal Academy of Arts. Also included were a Royal Stuart tartan blotter imprinted with Edward's initial "E", a sporran and a green leather belt with a silver-plated buckle engraved with the badge of the Prince of Wales from the 1940s, and several handbags, including an "H" bag and a Chaîne d'Ancre belonging to the Duchess, all personalized with her initials.

The Queen of England, famous for her headscarves, started wearing Hermès silk *carrés* when she attended the Royal Windsor Horse Show in the 1940s. A staple of the royal wardrobe, the Queen's collection is extensive, and in 2016, in honour of Her Majesty's 90th birthday, Hermès released a collectible tribute design with £100 from the sale of each scarf going to the Queen's Trust. The silk, featuring four horses surrounding the Hermès logo, nodding to both the company's heritage and the Queen's love of horses, is a reworking of the Tatersale print, originally created by Henri d'Origny in 1980.

Royalty and Hollywood came together in the figure of actress Grace Kelly, later Princess of Monaco, and the 1957 paparazzi shot of her shielding her growing pregnancy bump with her Hermès Sac à Dépêches. Both Grace Kelly and fellow actress and style icon Audrey Hepburn were fans of

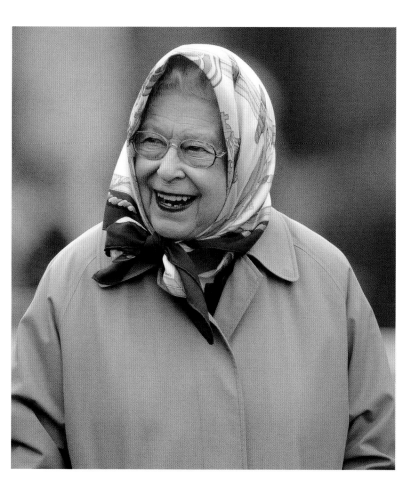

Hermès's headscarves, as was Jackie Kennedy who teamed her
silk carré with oversized dark glasses. Kennedy favoured the
Hermès Constance bag, launched in 1959, and Audrey Hepburn
also had a collection of favourite Hermès bags. One of these,
a leather briefcase-style bag, was designed exclusively for the
actress in 1956 in several colours.

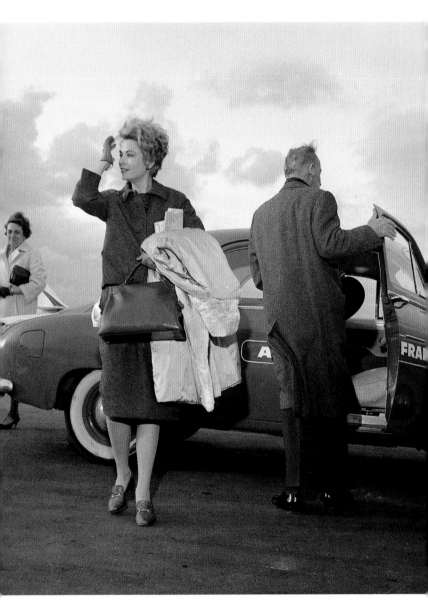

The star that has influenced Hermès the most of course, must be singer and actress Jane Birkin. Since its launch in 1984, after Jean-Louis Dumas designed it especially for her, the Birkin has become the most coveted of all Hermès bags. As Jérôme Lalande, an antique dealer specializing in twentieth-century leather goods told the BBC in 2015, "It opened Hermès up to new markets and customers, but it also changed the typical Hermès client."

Ironically, Birkin herself has sold the four bags she was given by Hermès, preferring to use the money for her charities. As she told *Women's Wear Daily* in 2011, "I sold one of my Birkin bags for $163,000 to help the Japanese Red Cross. So that rather trivial piece of heavy luggage has done a lot of good in the world."

She has also used her influence to ensure that selected charities are supported by Hermès themselves, who give a direct annual payment to her preferred causes in order

OPPOSITE Grace Kelly was rarely photographed without her iconic Kelly bag. The princess is photographed here in Orly in 1961.

BELOW A luxurious red leather Hermès Malette handbag reputed to have belonged to Grace Kelly. The bag was a favourite during the 1950s and 60s for its separate jewellery compartment that had its own unique lock and key, separate to that of the main bag.

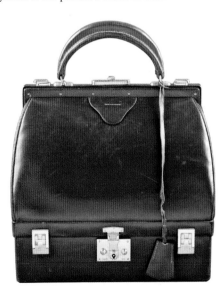

to continue using the Birkin name. Despite the friendly relationship between Hermès and its greatest muse, controversy arose in 2015 when Birkin took issue with Hermès after animal rights activists PETA claimed that the leather house were treating crocodiles and alligators – the source of the leather for the Birkin Croco – with extreme cruelty. Birkin asked for her name to be removed from that version of the iconic bag until ethical practices were established. Hermès immediately issued a statement reassuring not only Birkin, but their many devoted fans, that they were similarly shocked at the images and would investigate thoroughly. The name stayed.

In general, Hermès does not use celebrity endorsements, unlike many of their luxury goods competitors. The fact is, they don't need to since so many celebrities are eager to own a Hermès bag. As a result, high-profile names are among the few who Hermès allow to buy new Birkin and Kelly bags, and these celebrities are happy to pay the price required, thus giving the brand an even higher level of authentic endorsement. This, combined with the limited edition policy, the time it takes to produce a Hermès bag and the refusal to ever discount them means that Hermès doesn't need to actively promote their bags.

The strategy is clearly working, and many celebrities seem to own at least a couple of Hermès bags – the Birkin being the stand-out favourite. For some, like Victoria Beckham, whose collection stretches into triple figures, the classic Birkin appears in a multitude of colours and leathers to perfectly match her every elegant outfit. Jennifer Lopez teams hers with sweatpants, Ashley Olsen prefers a classic tan Birkin 35 and Kate Moss used hers as a nappy bag – following in Jane Birkin's footsteps, since part of the design brief of the original bag was to accommodate everything a busy mother needed.

For other celebrities, something a little more unusual appeals. The most extravagant handbag a husband has ever given a wife

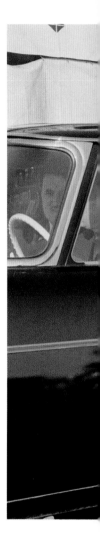

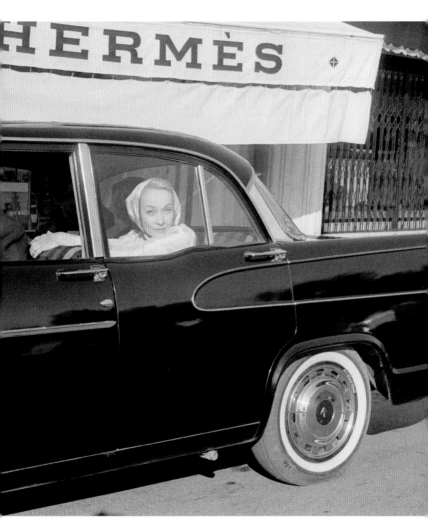

ABOVE German actress and singer Marlene
Dietrich in front of the Hermès boutique in Monte
Carlo in 1963.

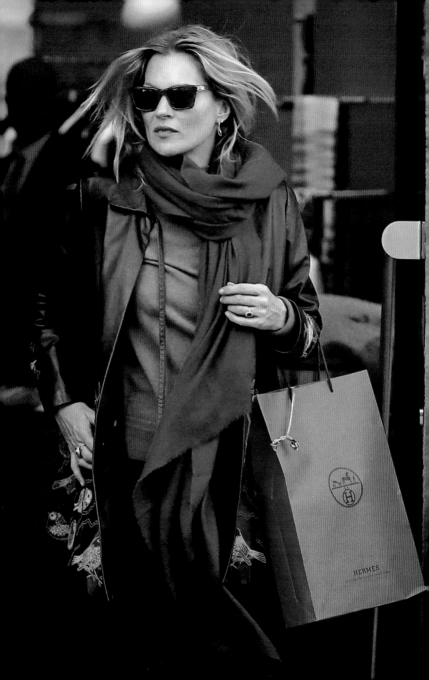

RIGHT Ashley and
Mary-Kate Olsen,
both carrying
Hermès bags, arrive
at the Metropolitan
Museum of Art in
2009.

OPPOSITE Kate
Moss remains a
long-time fan of the
label and is shown
here departing the
Hermès store on
London's Bond Street
in 2018.

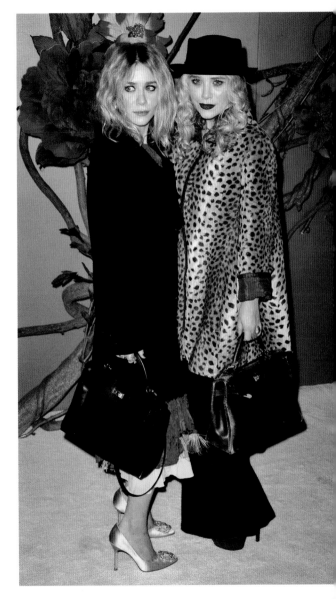

must have come from Kanye West, who for Christmas 2013 gave his wife at the time, Kim Kardashian, a £29,500 ($40,000) Birkin bag emblazoned with a hand-painted image of three nudes and a monster by contemporary American artist George Condo. With Condo's art selling for hundreds of thousands of dollars, Kim's bag is priceless.

The reaction to the luxury bag, which Condo had apparently done at Kanye West's request in 15 minutes, was decidedly mixed. Fans and the press alike wondered whether it was art or defacement, leaving one to wonder if it was another typical West-Kardashian publicity stunt. As Condo told *W* magazine at the time:

"Kanye and I both knew immediately that people who knew our collaboration would think it was fun but that Kim's fan base would go berserk."

Turning Birkin bags into art has become something of a phenomenon. Khloe Kardashian is a fan of graffiti artist Alec Monopoly, who has recently turned his unique style, a commentary on capitalism and luxury lifestyles in modern society, to the customization of high-end goods. His Hermès collection has become highly sought-after, featuring the character Rich Uncle Pennybags with a dollar sign. Khloe Kardashian's neon green bag also displays a tag of her nickname "KHLOMONEY".

Miley Cyrus is also the proud owner of an Alec Monopoly Birkin, but Monopoly is not the first to succumb to the temptation of superimposing street art onto the world's most expensive leather bag. In 2014, singer Rita Ora commissioned American artist Al-Baseer Holly to cover her black Birkin in a jumble of symbols and colourful paint drips.

Commissioning a well-known artist to decorate your Birkin is probably only going to increase its value, but a more home-grown approach was taken by Lady Gaga who in 2010 customized her black Birkin by covering it in spiked metal

OPPOSITE Kim Kardashian carrying the Birkin decorated by contemporary American artist George Condo during Paris Fashion week in 2020. The striking bag with its image of three nudes and a monster was a gift from Kanye West.

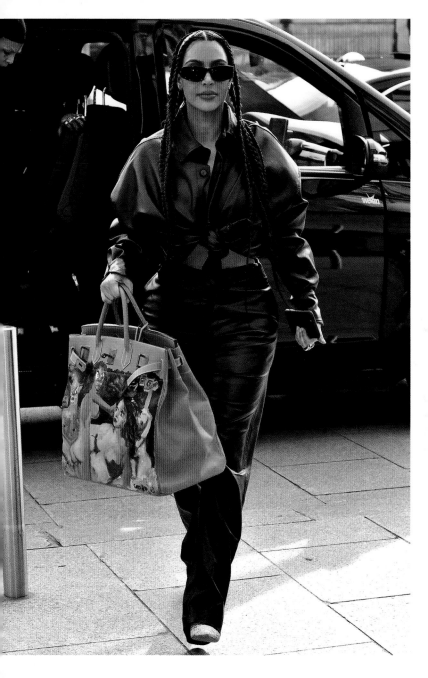

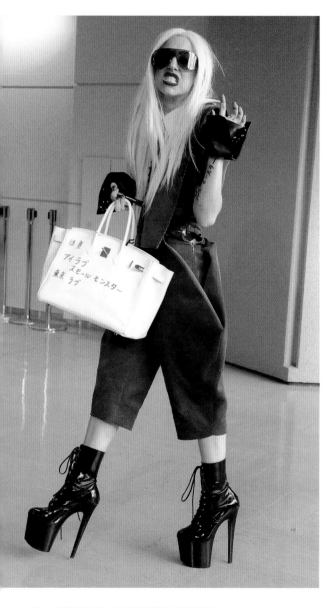

LEFT Lady Gaga carrying her self-customized white Birkin bag at Japan's Narita Airport in 2012. The bag bears Japanese text which translates as: "I Love Little Monsters, Tokyo Love," scrawled in black Sharpie

OPPOSITE Chrissy Teigen, dressed down but still carrying her rare Hermès Ostrich HAC 40 Birkin bag in New York in 2021.

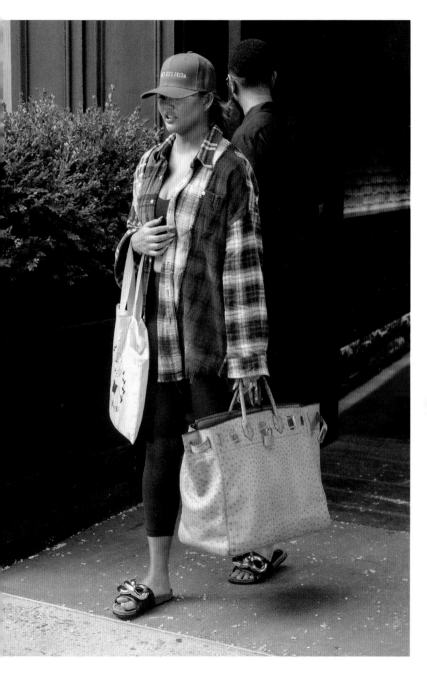

studs. A decade later, the singer and actress horrified Hermès aficionados by flaunting a white Birkin on which she had scrawled with a Sharpie pen the words "I Love Little Monsters, Tokyo Love", in Japanese.

In fact, the art of customizing a Birkin goes back to Jane herself: she frequently plastered her bags with typically hippy accessories such as political stickers and worry beads. Actor Kelly Osbourne followed suit in 2014 when she was photographed at Heathrow Airport with her Birkin covered in patches featuring emojis. Perhaps spotting a trend, Hermès has also legitimately produced limited-edition customized versions of its Birkin bag, such as an embroidered range by Jay Ahr, designer Jonathan Riss's label, another favourite of the Kardashian clan.

Hermès has also become a luxury label, like Gucci and Louis Vuitton, to be embraced by rappers. Rapper Cardi B is a big fan of the Birkin – even her toddler daughter has a small pink version – and to celebrate the huge success of her single 'WAP' she presented collaborator Megan Thee Stallion with a customized Birkin as a gift. The bag, featuring a painting of a scene from the music video of Megan dressed in a black and white tiger outfit next to the real animal, and the words "Be Someone" on the back, was revealed in a live unboxing on Instagram to the rapper's 22.5 million followers.

With fans like these generating publicity in the press and across social media, it seems that Hermès's policy of exclusivity has paid off. The words of Megan Thee Stallion as she opened her orange box might not have been quite what Thierry Hermès, or even modernizer Jean-Louis Dumas, imagined when he sought to create the world's most perfect leather goods, but they certainly sum up what it means to be given a Hermès bag:

"I know you fuckin' lyin', girl! Bitch! Not the Birkin! Not the Houston Birkin! Wow, I'm dead."

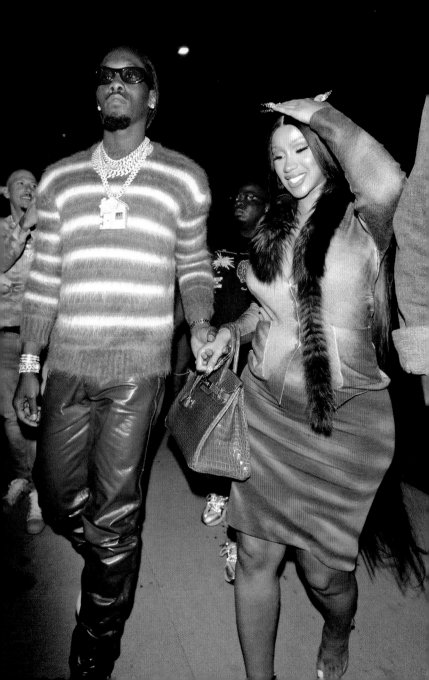

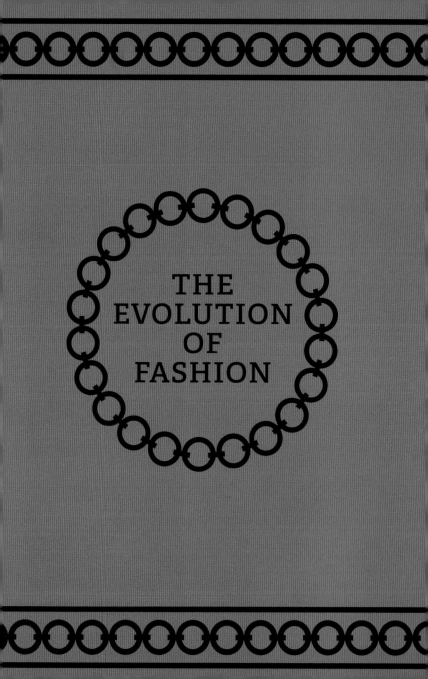

THE
EVOLUTION
OF
FASHION

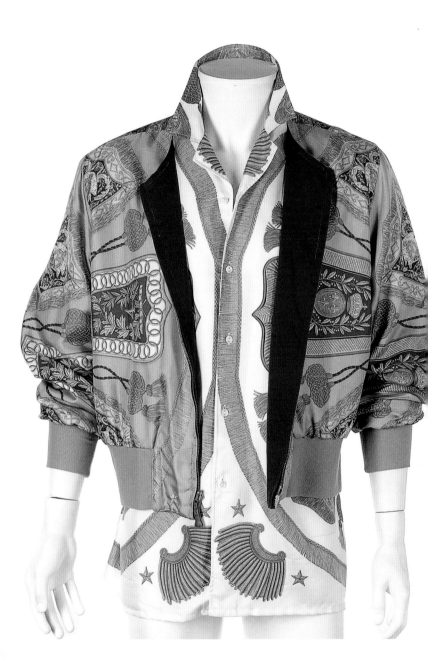

TURNING
THE PAGE

In an interview with the *New York Times* in 1986, as Hermès's
ready-to-wear range started to be taken seriously, the
company's press representative Flavie Chaillet told a story of
how Hermès came to start producing clothes:
"At the beginning of the century, a woman came in and said:
'I'm fed up seeing my horse better dressed than me.
When will you dress ladies?'"

Thus, the equestrian suppliers started producing clothes,
all exquisitely made in the same vein as their accessories
and handbags, and by 1922 outfits were being sold alongside
watches and gloves. By the 1960s and 1970s, however, the
popularity of man-made fabrics including nylon, and the earliest
incarnations of fast fashion, began to threaten Hermès, which

OPPOSITE In 1980 designers Eric Bergère and Bernard Sanz were employed
to overhaul Hermès's outdated ready-to-wear collections. This printed silk
blouson men's bomber jacket is characteristic of the period.

was still devoted to using only the finest and most exclusive materials and designing clothes that were intended to last years, rather than for just one season. Style was also an issue with the clothes: they were still being beautifully made and were what might be termed "classic", but they had an unappealing, even old-fashioned quality to the modern eye.

When Jean-Louis Dumas, or Dumas-Hermès as he sometimes styled himself, took over in 1978 he was determined to overhaul the fashion side of Hermès, making it enticing to a younger customer. One of his early advertising campaigns featured Hermès scarves worn by cool, streetwise Parisians. Photographed by Bill King, it was playful and adventurous. For example, one image pictured upside-down models trailing colourful silks from their tongues.

The images foreshadowed what would become a trend among the young and beautiful: wearing Hermès scarves in all manner of creative ways. Ever more creative ways to tie them were invented and soon brightly coloured silks in exotic prints were transformed into a bandeau, a mini skirt or a belt. Scarves were slipped around the handles of bags or even fashioned into one, Japanese Furoshiki style. And in an emergency, a carré makes an excellent sling for an injured arm, as demonstrated by the original Hermès muse, Grace Kelly.

But accessories aside, it was the ready-to-wear part of the business that most needed updating. As a result, in 1980, Jean-Louis Dumas employed Eric Bergère to take control of womenswear alongside Bernard Sanz, who designed for menswear. As Bergère commented, quoted in the *New York Times* when he took on the role at Hermès, the clothes appeared to be intended for "…a very, very, very old woman."

Bergère stayed at Hermès until 1986, modernizing the brand without sacrificing Hermès's commitment to fine craftsmanship in the most luxurious fabrics. The fashion house became known

Exquisite fabrics in sophisticated styles have always been a mainstay of Hermès and during the 1980s womenswear included classics such as this cream cashmere coat, brown tweed jacket and black crepe skirt outfit.

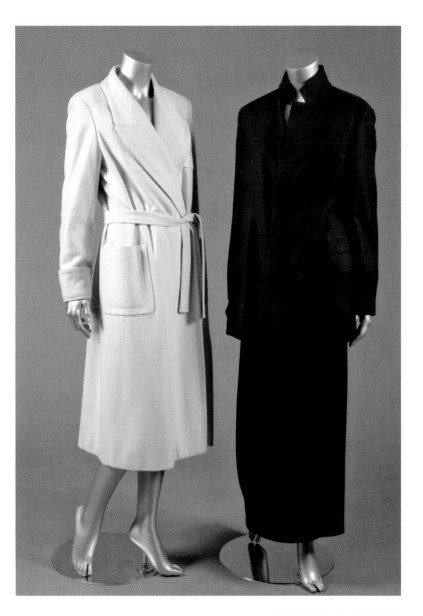

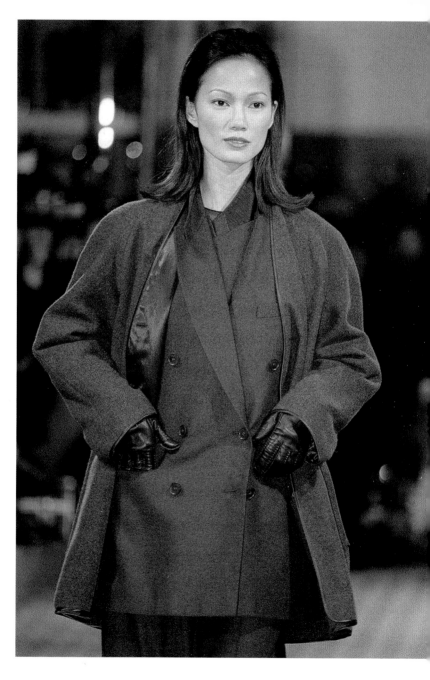

for using exotic animal skins, creating statement pieces such as python motorcycle jackets and ostrich-skin jeans as well as embracing a thoroughly upper-class 1980s country aesthetic complete with pussy-bow blouses and nods to the British "Sloane Ranger". Most importantly, though, while attracting younger customers Bergère remained true to the central tenet of Hermès – that the best made clothes and accessories have longevity. As Dumas summed up, "A page is being turned … I think people want to be more in style than in fashion."

MARTIN MARGIELA

During the 1990s, Hermès womenswear had been overseen by a collective of designers including Marc Audibet and Thomas Maier, but in April 1997, at a time when the label's ready-to-wear lines accounted for only 13 per cent of its turnover, Jean-Louis Dumas announced that Belgian designer, Martin Margiela would take up the role of creative director of womenswear. It was a controversial appointment since the designer seemed to be the antithesis of everything the traditional fashion house represented. While Hermès was all about perfect construction, the avant-garde Margiela made his name with deconstruction, finding discarded garments to take apart and reinvent. His landmark first show, staged in a derelict playground on the outskirts of Paris, featured unfinished clothes with ragged hems and tops made out of old carrier bags. In contrast, Hermès's clothes and accessories were made from the finest fabrics and were the epitome of refinement.

Dumas obviously saw something in Margiela that others didn't. During his six years at Hermès the designer showed that despite the differences between the designs for his eponymous label and the clothes he created for Hermès, the impetus was the same – to challenge the fashion system.

In 2017, an exhibition entitled Margiela: The Hermès Years was held at the MoMu Fashion Museum in Antwerp, Belgium.

OPPOSITE Belgian designer Martin Margiela joined Hermès in 1997 and during his six years at the label presented a continuum of beautifully-cut, eminently wearable luxury clothes which women could keep in their wardrobe for decades. This Autumn/Winter 1998 catwalk outfit of a double-breasted, loosely structured suit and transformable charcoal camel jacket, sums up Margiela's understated style perfectly.

Curator Kaat Debo, who cleverly displayed clothes from both Maison Martin Margiela and Margiela for Hermès side by side, explained how the two related in an interview with *Vogue:*

"These are not entirely divergent worlds … I think also of the overall vision of Martin, resisting the fashion system, resisting some of the obsessions like the ideal body, eternal youth, constant innovation and renewal. At Maison Martin Margiela he resisted in a very conceptual way. And at Hermès, it was this slowly evolving wardrobe … For me it is 'slow' fashion before the concept even existed."

Margiela certainly showed prescience regarding sustainability. The designer constantly challenged conspicuous consumption, creating clothes intended to last a lifetime, and in this he was perfectly aligned with the ethos of Hermès. His intention

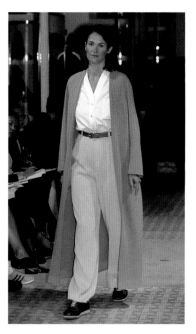

obviously worked, neatly illustrated by the fact that many of the women who were asked to loan Hermès clothes for the 2017 exhibition did so reluctantly because they still regularly wore them some 15 or 20 years later.

Margiela had a talent for creating garments which could be worn in multiple ways. Take for example a luxurious camel hair coat that could double as a cape if you put your arms through cleverly-placed holes, a form of deconstruction not dissimilar to what he did with his own label. Similarly, he designed sweaters that could be worn inside out and a peacoat that had a removable collar and leather fastenings.

With hindsight, Margiela's collections for Hermès delivered far more than was

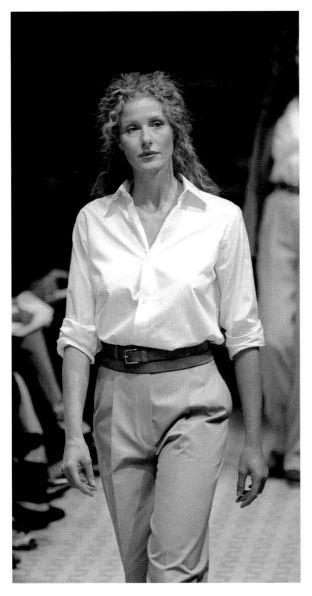

LEFT The double leather accessory was much used by Margiela, here shown in the form of a belt but most famously as the double-tour watch strap which has become a house icon.

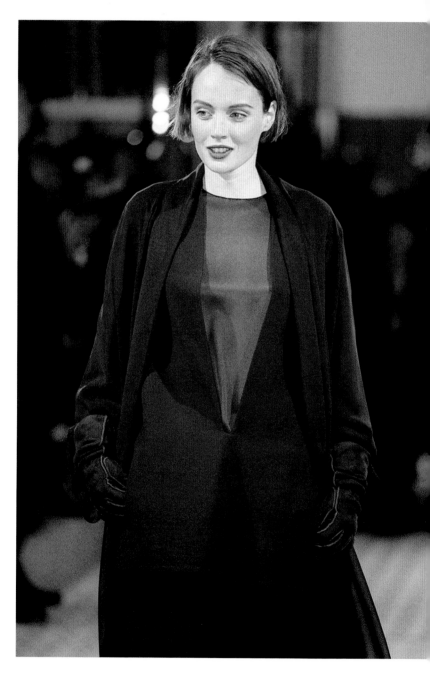

recognized at the time when the press often wrote them off as dull, a judgment that many major fashion commentators have since retracted. In fact, the unstructured coats and jackets, perfectly cut trousers and luxury sweaters – all in a tasteful, sophisticated palette ranging from white, through grey to black, warmed up by tan, caramel and brown – were brilliantly pitched towards modern, elegant Parisian women. His flattering trademark tunic with a deep-V neckline, called the *vareuse*, was a great success, the silhouette also appearing on coats and blazers. This devotion to creating designs that flattered the women who wore them, combined with his brilliance as a technician, was Margiela's real triumph at Hermès.

As always at Hermès, luxury fabrics were key, but Margiela offered longevity by tempering the world of indulgence with designs that verged on utilitarian at times. This was, of course, a fashion house where customers expected to invest considerable sums in its clothes – take a lambskin-lined crocodile skin skirt from Autumn/Winter 2000 which, *Vogue* reported, demanded a £22,600 ($31,000) sum. One might hope it would last more than a single season at that price.

Perhaps the most lasting contribution that Martin Margiela made to Hermès was the double-tour watch strap, a reincarnation of the iconic Cape Cod watch which had originally been designed by Henri D'Origny in 1991. The design wraps twice round the wearer's wrist, and has become a modern classic.

During his 12-season tenure at Hermès, both Martin Margiela and his clothes shunned the limelight. At a time when the personality of designers was as important as their collections – think Tom Ford at Gucci, Alexander McQueen at Givenchy and John Galliano at Dior – Margiela communicated only by fax and kept a remarkably low profile. Yet the Hermès customer was happy and, as the Antwerp Fashion Museum retrospective of his work showed, Margiela was a designer ahead of his time.

OPPOSITE One of Margiela's most successful designs was his flattering tunic with a deep-V neckline called the *vareuse*.

OVERLEAF In 2017 the exhibition Margiela: The Hermès Years was held at the MoMu Fashion Museum in Antwerp. By displaying pieces from the designer's own label, Maison Martin Margiela, the curator cleverly highlighted the continuation of the designer's radical ethos: whether deconstructed grunge or high-end luxury, these were clothes that embodied sustainability and "slow fashion".

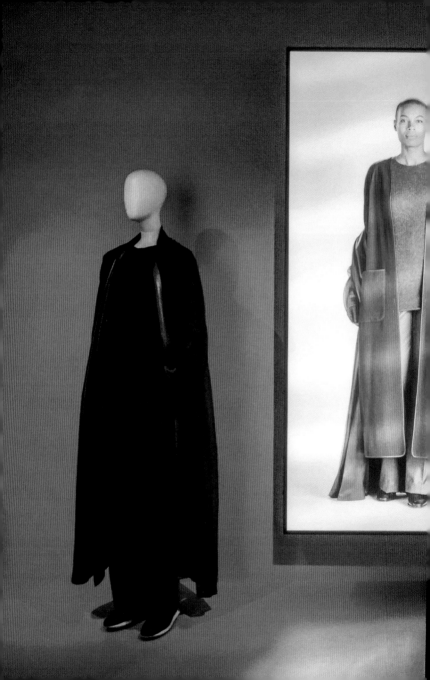

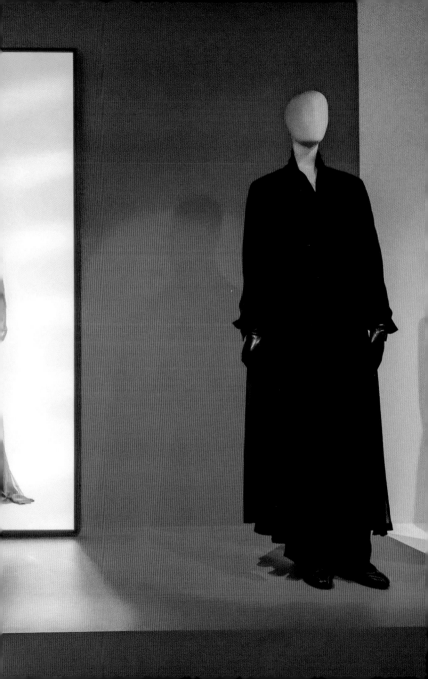

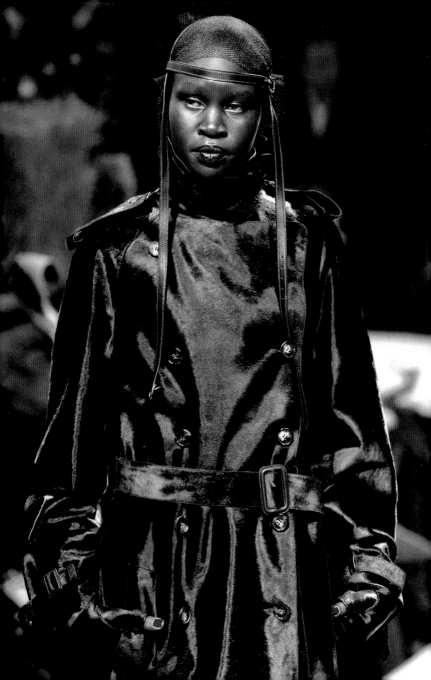

OPPOSITE Alek Wek
walks the catwalk
in a glossy black
pony skin double-
breasted coat.

JEAN PAUL GAULTIER

In 2003, Margiela left to concentrate on his own label and
Hermès confirmed his successor as Jean Paul Gaultier. The
fashion house had long had a relationship with Gaultier, having
secured a 35 per cent stake in his business in 1999, so in many
ways the appointment was an obvious one. However, in terms of
fashion design, Gaultier's flamboyance could not have been more
of a contrast to Margiela's understated style, but perhaps Hermès
felt they needed an injection of theatre after the somewhat
lukewarm reception Margiela had received.

Accepting the role at Hermès was the first time that the
51-year-old Gaultier had designed for a label other than his own,
and his first collection for Autumn/Winter 2004 was eagerly
awaited. Fittingly, given Hermès's heritage, the new creative
director staged the show at the École Militaire cavalry training
ground before an audience perched on bales of hay. Equestrian
was a major trend that season and Gaultier fully embraced it
with an opening ensemble of a riding habit, complete with top
hat and whip, following up with outfits featuring skirts flaring at
the thighs – jodhpur style – and riding boots.

For a designer with a reputation for risqué outfits, the
collection was not as naughty as it might have been, though
models wearing harness-style head straps subtly referenced the
notorious Helmut Newton shoot for *Vogue Paris* where the
photographer (who famously commented that he considered
Hermès to be "…the world's greatest sex shop – with its whips,
saddles, spurs") used Hermès saddlery in a bedroom scene.
Gaultier's penchant for corsetry also appeared in the form of a
tooled leather tan version, worn over jodhpur trousers, with a
flowing cape coat and riding boots.

Even so, the collection was reasonably pared down, showing
great respect for the Hermès traditions of luxury fabrics, elegant,
flowing silhouettes and plenty of leather. Colours were in the

OPPOSITE
Equestrianism
will always be the
mainstay of Hermès
heritage and Jean
Paul Gaultier
immediately gave
it his unique brand
of dominatrix style
by sending Linda
Evangelista down
the catwalk in an
elegant double-
breasted coat with
a veiled top hat,
leather collar and
gloves, riding whip
in hand.

wearable and sophisticated palette that Hermès clients had come to love, with accents of the house orange and regal purple in the form of a tailored crocodile skin jacket. And among supermodels including Linda Evangelista and Nadja Auermann, Gaultier had cleverly arranged a cameo by Lou Doillon, the daughter of Jane Birkin, wearing a full leather outfit accessorized with a riding crop and thigh-high boots.

With a background as a couturier, Jean Paul Gaultier was the perfect designer to carry on the Hermès tradition of expert craftsmanship, and his next collections for the house illustrated this beautifully. For Autumn/Winter 2005 he offered plenty of chic tailored jackets, pleated grey flannel skirts and wide, elegant trousers set off by sumptuous fabrics in rich, lush tones of red, burgundy and ochre that shone from the catwalk. Show-stopping coats and jackets in caramel-hued shearling summed up the luxe lifestyle associated with Hermès.

Clever tailoring, especially of Hermès's trademark soft leathers, remained key throughout Gaultier's tenure. In 2007 he offered a range of immaculate peacoats, tailcoats and swing coats along with a more casual crocodile skin bomber. A year later, it was the turn of blazers in a combination of suede and crocodile as well as perfectly cut belted shearing coats. His skill and attention to detail continued right through to his penultimate collection for Autumn/Winter 2010 when he sent a 1960s homage to *The Avengers* character Emma Peel in the form of a black leather catsuit, followed up by an array of skintight black leather outfits for his final presentation for Spring/Summer 2011.

The challenge for Gaultier at Hermès was to retain the traditionalism that customers wanted while still giving each collection enough of a fashion edge. In the main, he achieved this, mixing up collections by switching from warm colours to a more black and white palette, all full of exquisitely crafted clothes without any of the ostentation or shouty labels he

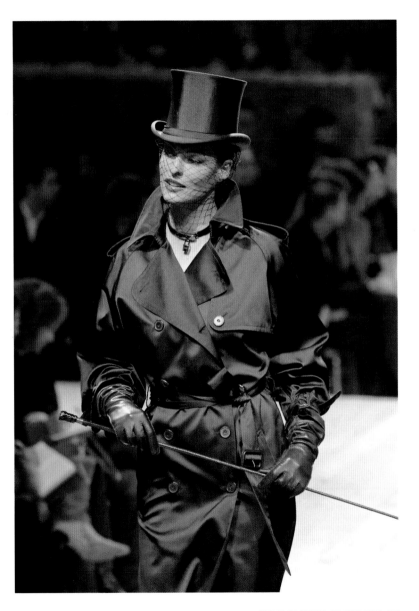

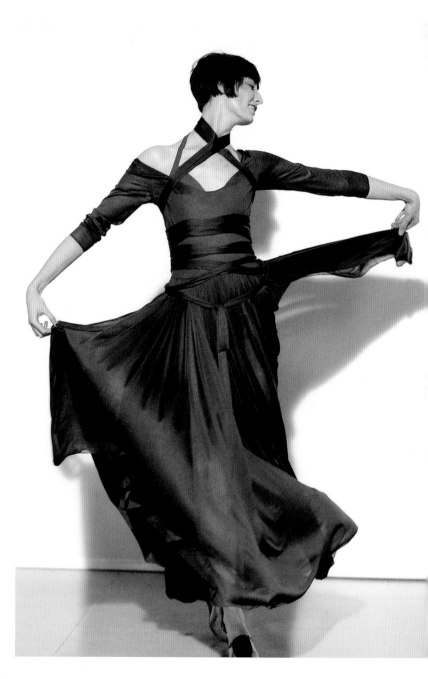

RIGHT This equestrian outfit from Autumn/ Winter 2007 reflects the Hermès heritage in both style and colour palette, featuring a tan double-breasted frock coat teamed with stretch satin jodhpurs, riding boots and matching suede cap and gloves.

OPPOSITE Gaultier's notorious love of bondage themes when it comes to his fashion designs is tempered for Hermès into an elegant beribboned dress worn by Erin O'Connor for Spring/Summer 2005.

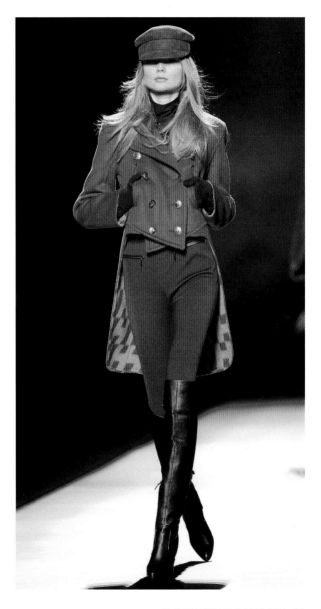

OPPOSITE
Hermès's instantly
recognizable orange
hue is crafted in
suede and leather in
this sumptuous coat,
teamed with paisley
scarf and matching
bag for Autumn/
Winter 2008.

has been tempted by in his eponymous collections. Such is the reputation of Hermès and what it stands for that when Gaultier did branch out, the fashion press called him out on it. For example, for Spring/Summer 2007 Nicole Phelps for *Vogue* complained that "…it didn't all convey the elegance long associated with the brand."

The success of Hermès's fashion collections rests mainly on its appeal to the house's rich clientele, and as he approached his later years at Hermès, Gaultier's collections started to increasingly reflect the international shopper that the brand was attracting. First came a nod to India with Nehru jackets and embroidered suede tunics, along with a reinterpretation of an evening sari. A year later, he headed to the Wild West. The common theme in all of these collections was the equestrian accent in the form of riding boots, horseshoe motifs and jaunty hats with riding crops, a regular catwalk prop.

It's important to remember that Hermès's clothes are also a backdrop for the accessories the brand is so renowned for. Gaultier played with these too, changing proportions right from his first show when he featured an elongated Birkin and creating everything from miniature crocodile Kelly bags to an oversized carryall version, which he proudly carried down the catwalk himself. He also adapted the house's iconic bags seasonally, even adding fringing for his Wild West collection. Scarves too got the Gaultier treatment, often in the form of iconic prints metamorphosing into clothes or draped over a classic bag.

Jean Paul Gaultier left Hermès to concentrate on his own ready-to-wear and couture lines but the parting was a cordial one. Hermès released a statement at the time that read: "Hermes is deeply grateful to Jean Paul Gaultier for his outstanding creative contribution during these past seven years." The relationship remained strong, with Hermès holding a 45 per cent stake in Gaultier's eponymous label.

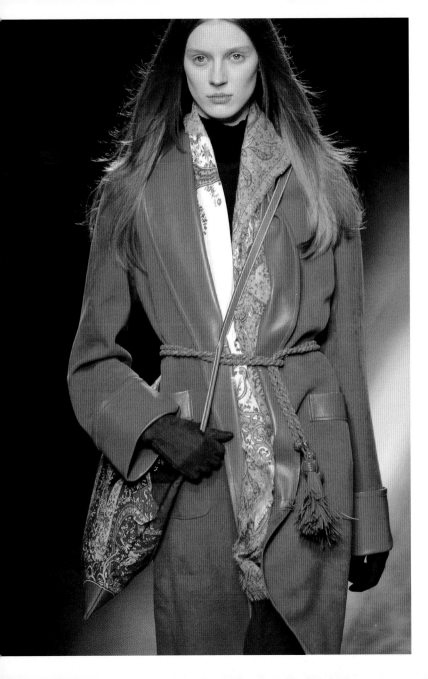

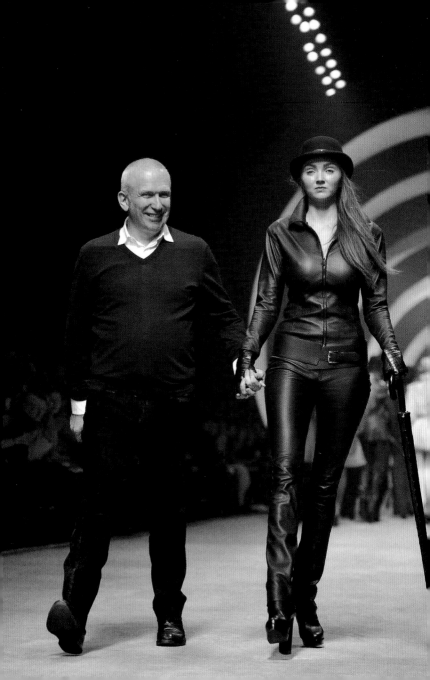

RIGHT Gaultier's skill at corsetry translated into a tan tailored leather waistcoat and mini-skirt teamed with multiple wrist stripes and matching hat for his final show, Spring/Summer 2011.

OPPOSITE Gaultier's background as a couturier meant that his designs for Hermès were beautifully tailored, especially in his use of leather and other animal skins. Here the designer walks out to take applause with model Lily Cole who wears an *Avengers*-style black leather catsuit after his penultimate show for Hermès Autumn/Winter 2010.

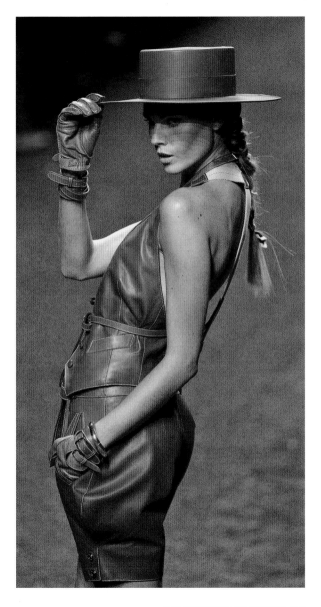

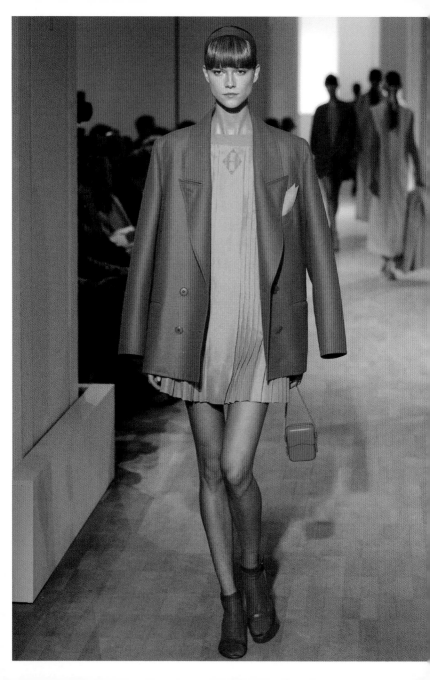

CHRISTOPHE LEMAIRE

Christophe Lemaire took over as artistic director at Hermès in June 2010, leaving his leading role at Lacoste. The appointment of a less than high profile designer from a very different fashion brand, especially after someone like Jean Paul Gaultier, was surprising, with Lemaire commenting to the *New York Times* at the time: "It was a recognition when Hermès came to ask me to design for them."

Despite initial scepticism, Lemaire's debut collection for Hermès was well enough received, with Tim Blanks at *Vogue* commenting that the designer seemed to possess a "fundamental compatibility" with the elite fashion house. The collection referenced Eastern silhouettes, with long, draped shapes reminiscent of kaftans and kimonos, and luxurious Hermès skins shaped into tunics. All-white outfits were offset by the familiar Hermès rich browns, tans and mustard yellow with a sprinkling of its house orange.

For Lemaire's second collection he continued the travel theme – which was appropriate for a fashion house that had started out by making luggage – venturing across the Mediterranean to Morocco in the form of djellabas and finishing with Native American-inspired prints. Again, the clothes were mostly minimalist and elegantly draped, colourblocked in white with the Hermès orange offset by dynamic electric blues and purples. This confident use of bold colour and print became a hallmark of Lemaire's time at Hermès, especially for his lighter Spring/Summer collections.

If anything, Lemaire had more in common with Martin Margiela than his immediate predecessor, Jean Paul Gaultier. Both designers understood that Hermès catered to the world of the chic Frenchwoman and created clothes accordingly. Their pieces were aimed at an independent and proud woman, well-versed in travel and culture.

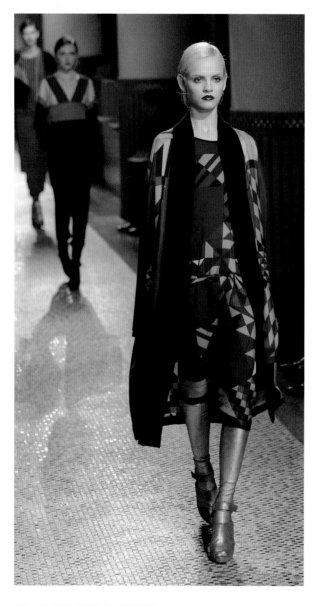

LEFT Geometric prints on draped silk such as this dress and matching coat offered a twist of modernism whilst still retaining the classic heritage of Hermès.

OPPOSITE This outfit by Lemaire from Autumn/ Winter 2011 comprised of rich tan polo neck and matching cashmere trousers tucked into ruched leather boots topped by a flowing trench coat and luxurious fur hat, sums up everything Hermès stands for: discreet elegance, finest-quality fabrics and a sophisticated yet subtle colour palette.

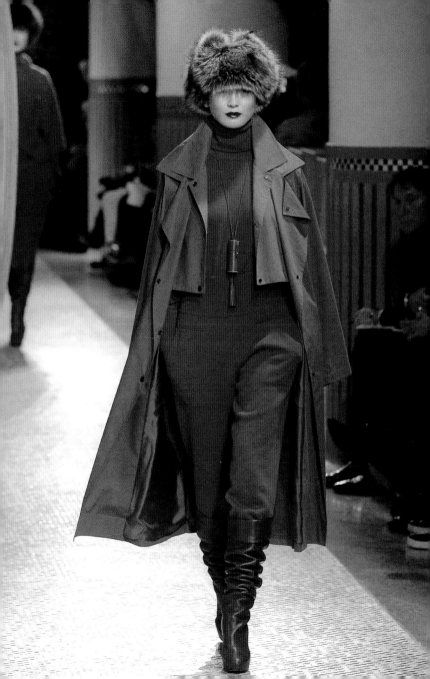

The clothes that both Margiela and Lemaire designed for Hermès blurred the gender lines just a little in the form of oversized jackets, tuxedos and even in accessories. In his first show, Lemaire gave his models scaled down briefcases to carry rather than Birkins.

By Autumn/Winter 2012, Lemaire had come into his own. Androgyny was still a big driver of his designs, and this season featured masculine jackets, suits and coats, all, as expected, beautifully tailored alongside oversized knitwear in the form of a brown grandad-style cardigan over a white shirt and tie and baggy flannel trousers, topped by a black fedora. Combined with the almost indecent luxury of the fabrics, the effect was sensual in the kind of understated way that only the Hermès woman truly appreciates.

Lemaire's love of print is most evident in the silks he used in his Spring/Summer collections, turning Hermès's iconic scarf designs into dresses and tops. The slippery elegance of these clothes offered the perfect foil to the more structured leathers that still had a role to play in the form of neat jackets and tailored shorts and skirts. This appreciation for the painterly quality of Hermès's silk *carrès* is most evident in Lemaire's Spring/Summer 2014 collection where bold, floral Rousseau-esque patterns flowed across dresses and skirts. Complemented by a colour palette of teal and orange, he presented the perfect holiday wardrobe.

Christophe Lemaire's final cycle of collections for Autumn/Winter 2014 and Spring/Summer 2015 saw the designer fully embrace the Hermès tenet of stealth wealth. On the surface, the clothes were far from ostentatious, and yet when examined closely fabrics like chiffon crocodile, pale python, shaggy goatskin and embroidered silks revealed new heights of luxury. Lemaire left Hermès having achieved an almost perfect pitch while still injecting enough of his own personality.

OPPOSITE This outfit from Autumn/Winter 2012 shows a model in a fine leather trousers, snakeskin printed blouse, an oversized fur coat and leather riding-style cap, carrying a bird falconry style in a nod to Hermès' heritage as a supplier for all aristocratic sports.

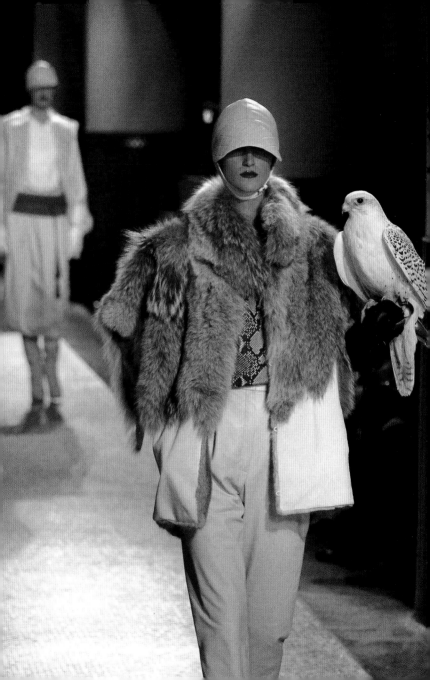

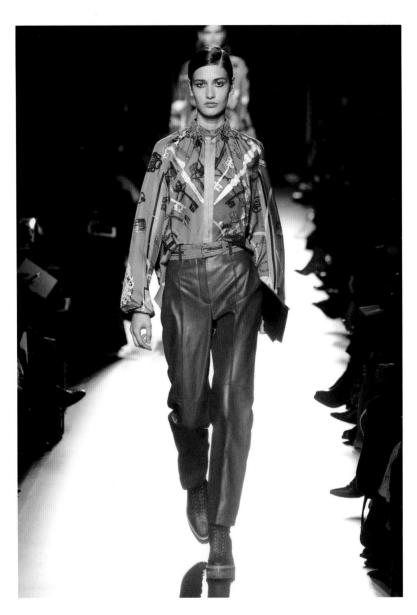

OPPOSITE An acknowledgment of androgyny within catwalk collections is virtually essential in the modern fashion landscape and Vanhee-Cybulski captures the mood perfectly with outfits such as this combination of mannish blue leather trousers and sturdy boots teamed with a classic Hermès print on a high-neck silk blouse. The leather clutch is almost an attaché case and appropriately finishes the look.

In June 2014, the role of womenswear designer at Hermès was taken on by Nadège Vanhee-Cybulski, who remains there to this day. Despite a low public profile, Vanhee-Cybulski has an impeccable fashion heritage. Her most recent role, as design director at The Row, Mary-Kate and Ashley Olsen's fashion label, came after key positions at both Céline and Maison Martin Margiela – all labels that embraced the same attention to detail and craftsmanship on which Hermès also prides itself.

Commenting on her first collection, as quoted by visual-therapy.com, the French-born designer immediately acknowledged the importance of Hermès's heritage: "Hermès is a very generous house and they really respect creativity. In return, you have to respect their roots, and those roots are equestrian."

The second driving force behind her debut collection was the acknowledgement to Vogue.com that, if you work for Hermès, "You have to work with leather."

Like Martin Margiela before her, Vanhee-Cybulski immediately embraced all of Hermès's understated sophistication while still imbuing the collection with her own flair. Her offerings included seductive midnight-blue leather in the form of jackets and coats, as well as the same dusky tone in cashmere, with nods to equestrianism in the details. Silk appeared too, in homage to the iconic scarves, but as a print on a silk dress or a panel on a skirt rather than as an accessory. Accents of vivid red immediately announced that she was not a designer afraid of colour.

Unlike other luxury fashion labels, the essence of Hermès is discretion, not showiness. Those choosing Hermès know that they are dressed in the finest fabrics, made to the highest artisan standards, without looking like they are trying too hard. As Sarah Mower at *Vogue* commented in the show appraisal of Vanhee-Cybulski's Spring/Summer 2016 collection, what

OPPPOSITE Unlike
her predecessors,
Vanhee-Cybulski
is not afraid to use
bold colour. The
construction of her
clothes, however,
is as detailed as
anything the fashion
house ever produced.
Here, for Spring/
Summer 2017, luxe
lightweight leather
is drawn into a
ruched waistline, the
stitching referencing
the label's saddlery
background and
giving texture and
form to her outfits.

Hermès is offering is "…a carefully calibrated sense of a lifestyle which consciously rises above trendiness."

And even in this sportier collection, full of graphic checks in both black and white and head-to-toe colour – including electric blue, mustard yellow and more vivid red – the sense of casual elegance shines through.

As Vanhee-Cybulski's tenure at Hermès has progressed, she has moved towards adding more of a fashionable twist to her collections. For Spring/Summer 2017 she gave a nod to the 1980s revival trend and the following season it was the turn of 1960s and 1970s, most obvious in the appearance of scarf prints resurrected from the archives. Over the last couple of years she has varied her collections considerably, pushing her penchant for colours and checks; creating an airy series of horse-blanket inspired capes and jackets for Spring/Summer 2018; and doing a U-turn a season later where models strode down the catwalk in a selection of powerful all-black leather outfits.

A new baby and a pandemic later, the designer is still offering a mix of heritage and wearability, always showcasing the prowess of the Hermès workshops. From taking the apron worn by the original Hermès artisans as inspiration for exquisite leather tunics, to her favourite horse-blanket coats, polo shirts and colourful jockey sweaters, she ensures that the brand's equestrian heritage is never forgotten.

As Hermès continues to sit at the summit of luxury French fashion, there is an ongoing conversation among its upper echelons about how to balance tradition with trend in a way that will appeal to the elite who can afford their clothes. Vanhee-Cybulski, working alongside Véronique Nichanian for menswear, has continued to manage this feat nicely, quoted by Vogue.com as firmly believing that there is a way of embracing "…classicism as a modern way of seeing life."

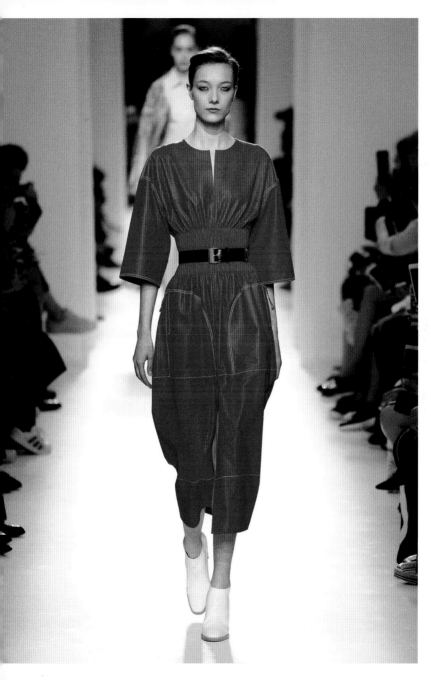

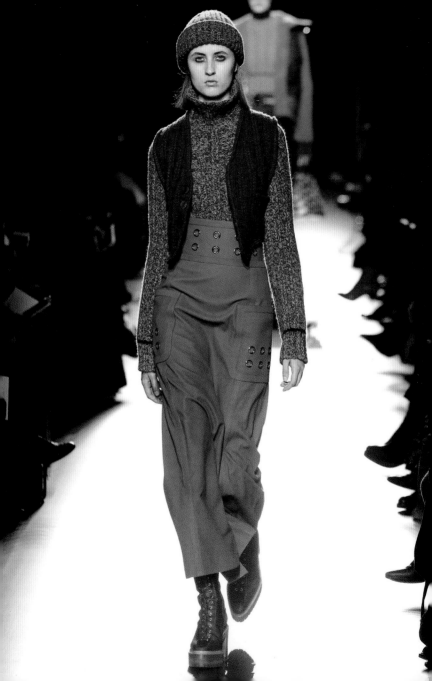

RIGHT Despite the ubiquitous heavy-duty footwear worn by the models during the Autumn/Winter 2017 show, there was no shortage of classy Hermès prints such as this blue on red handprint design column dress.

OPPOSITE Over the last few years Hermès has moved in a more fashion-focused direction, with references to 1980s and 90s grunge, albeit a high-end version. For example this look from Autumn/Winter 2017 featuring a long teal skirt with oversized eyelet motif, teamed with a marled cashmere jumper and matching beanie hat. The dress-down vibe is finished with a knitted waistcoat and heavy boots.

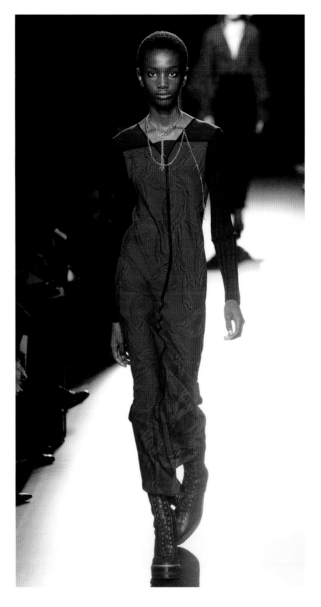

VÉRONIQUE NICHANIAN: MENSWEAR

When considering ready-to-wear at the house of Hermès, there is one designer who has perhaps shaped the evolution of its fashion more than any other: Véronique Nichanian, head of menswear for more than three decades.

In 1988, Nichanian took over menswear design at Hermès. Still in residence more than three decades later, she is currently the longest serving non-founding designer at a Paris fashion house, a status she achieved on the death of Karl Lagerfeld.

BELOW Hermès is a classic label, positioned towards customers who are happy to spend thousands on clothes that last a lifetime, so the heritage aspect of design is important to Nichanian. This smart casual combination of check tailored jacket, printed shirt, navy velvet trousers and wool flat cap juxtaposes the city and country lifestyle of the Hermès man.

OPPOSITE As a foil to the structured tailoring and animal skins so often used in her menswear collections, Nichanian also includes less traditional colours and prints as well as looser silhouettes for her Spring/Summer collections.

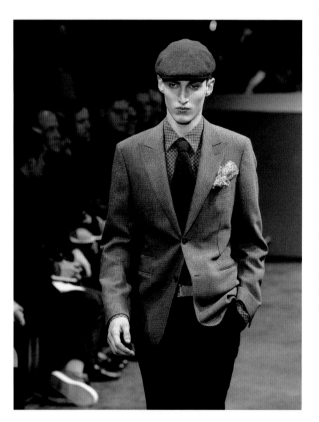

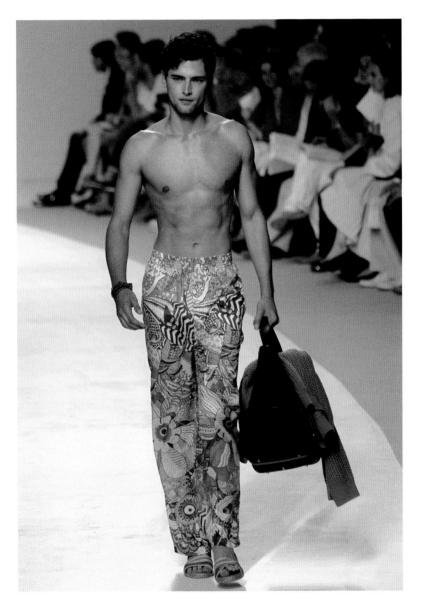

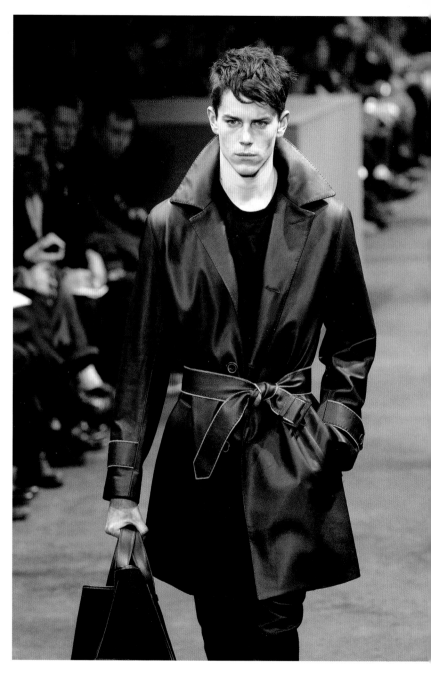

Before joining Hermès she had worked for Italian designer Nino Cerruti, a designer passionate about fine fabrics, an obsession which Nichanian still shares. "Some people like big diamonds – for me, it's fabrics," she laughed in a 2020 interview with the *Financial Times*.

Fabrics, most notably animal skins, are a huge point of pride for Hermès, and the fashion house has worked hard to address sustainability and animal rights issues in their sourcing. Nichanian has made leather, and other luxury fabrics, staples of her menswear collections in myriad ways. Recurring examples include immaculately crafted minimal blazers or belted leather trench coats, often made from butter-soft, brown Barenia calfskin. Each season Nichanian presents casual jackets in styles ranging from blouson to biker, often in that Hermès signature crocodile skin. Reversing the leather into shearling is another way in which Nichanian showcases Hermès finery, even crafting a bronze jumpsuit for Autumn/Winter 2011.

Designing clothes that stand up to her customers' lifestyles is extremely important to Nichanian and is exemplified in the tailoring that is Hermès's other great strength. Her designs, including leather suits, and tuxedos in glazed wools, lean towards a subtle sexiness. However, she isn't all about structure, and softer shapes have appeared over the last decade. In 2013, for example, navy crocodile skin assumed the form of a cardigan, and if that wasn't luxurious enough the collection also included a mink jumper that could be reversed to reveal cashmere flannel.

OPPOSITE AND BELOW Exqusitely crafted leather is a point of pride for Hermès and a fabric that Nichanian has made a staple of her menswear collections. This belted dark brown short trench and double-breasted sheepskin trimmed black jacket from Autumn/Winter 2010 are perfect examples.

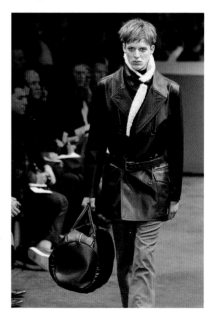

As both the fashion industry and clients' needs have evolved, Nichanian has experimented by juxtaposing traditionally indulgent fabrics such as silk and cashmere with modern, functional cloths including nylon, even nodding towards athleisure on occasion. The driving force for the diminutive French designer is always her customer's lifestyle, as she explains in a 2019 interview with men's magazine *GQ*:

"Like everybody, I have many lives. I want clothes that are modern and intelligent. So I play a lot on functionality to appeal to the different lifestyles of the clients. But I never lose the sensuality and also the construction, the way things are made."

Looking at the collections Nichanian has presented over her tenure at Hermès, this meticulous attention to accommodating the Hermès man is obvious. Most importantly, the clothes are

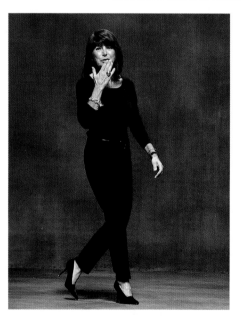

eminently wearable. Take her Autumn/Winter collections, which again and again feature immaculately tailored suits, overcoats and jackets in sophisticated palettes of blacks and greys, or a perfectly pitched spectrum of browns and caramels. Spring/Summer collections lighten things up with whites and pale greys, with this tentative neutral palette evolving over her career into bolder colours.

The early accent colours, including pops of Hermès red and bold, acidic yellows and greens, have lengthened into

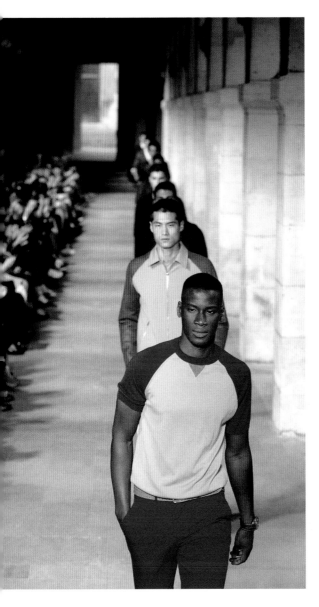

LEFT Nichanian
has introduced an
element of athleisure
into her mostly
classic tailored
collections over the
last decade, shown
here in these outfits
for Spring/Summer
2013.

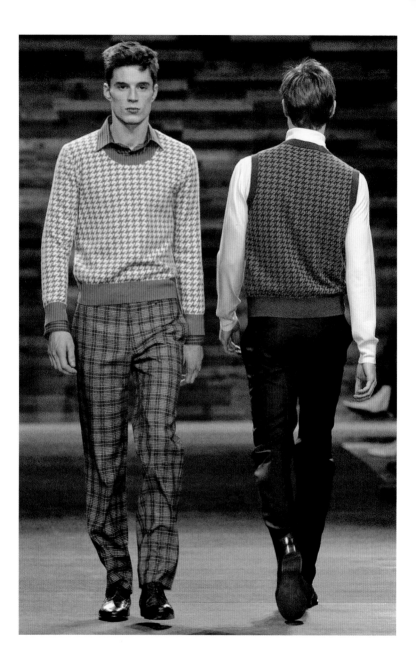

head-to-toe colour, with Nichanian presenting suits in myriad tones of blue and colour-blocking with burgundy, orange and pink. Prints play a part too. The equestrian theme that is so intrinsic to Hermès appears in the form of horses galloping across a silk shirt or on the scarves that often accessorize her outfits, and, more recently, candy-striped shirts in pretty pastels and summer checks which provide the elegant traveller with perfect holiday wear. There is no threat to masculinity in wearing pink here.

Since the beginning, when Jean-Louis Dumas gave her carte blanche to make menswear her own, Nichanian has disdained the moniker of "luxury brand" so often used when referring to Hermès. She told the *Financial Times*, "For many years, I hate this word of luxury, because it does not mean anything…This word is too much. We are doing quality things and beautiful things. What is luxury today? It is just to be deeply honest in what you're doing."

Similarly, she doesn't look back into the Hermès archives, disliking the concept of classic clothes and always preferring to design for today. Like her womenswear contemporaries, however, Nichanian does acknowledge that her clothes must strike a balance between the longevity for which Hermès is renowned while remaining current in the high fashion world the brand inhabits. Her words to *GQ* eloquently sum up Hermès's continued appeal: "When you buy something expensive, it's important that these are long-lasting things. And that's the quality of Hermès. It becomes a part of your life. It's not classical or traditional, it's modern and relevant to the way you are living."

OPPOSITE Sporting imagery is a huge part of the Hermès story illustrated here with this golfing-style knitwear and trousers in traditional house colours.

INDEX

Numbers in italics are pages of captions.

accessories 8, *13*
Ahr, Jay 112
androgyny 142, *145*
architecture 50–52, *52*
Arnaud, Auguste 92
Arnault, Bernard 44
"Art of Living" *42*
athleisure *157*

B, Cardi 112, *112*
bags 7, 14, *15*, 18, 24, 25,
   57, 58, *59*, *60*, 68–9, *69*
   Birkin bag 8, 42, 60,
      65–8, *65*, *67*, 3, *103*, 108,
      108, *110*, 112, *112*, 134
   Bolide 70, *73*
   Constance 70, *70*, 101
   Croco 104
   Cruise shoulder *77*
   Diamond Himalaya 57,
      57
   Escale *77*
   Evelyne 70, *73*
   Halzan 73
   Haut à courroies 57, 58
   Herbag 73, *74*
   Jige 74, *74*
   Kelly bag 8, 29, 58–60,
      60, *63*, 68, 134
   Lindy 74
   Sac à dépêches 100
Beaumel, Annie 45, 47, 100
Beckham, Victoria 65, *67*,
   104

Bergère, Eric *117*, 118, 121
Bertrand, Evelyne 70, *73*
Birkin, Jane 8, 41–2, *42*, 65,
   67, 68, 103, 104, 112
Blanks, Tim 139
bold colour *146*
bracelet, Collier de Chien 8,
   26–7, *29*
Brides de Gala print 83
Brio, Le 67
Bugatti Royale 24, *25*

Calèche 32, *32*
Cape Cod watch 125
carrés 29, 81, 85
Cassandre, A.M. 85, *85*, 86
Chaillet, Catherine 70
Chaîne d'ancre range 29
Chanel, Gabrielle 22
Cole, Lily *137*
Condo, George 108
Cooper Hewitt Museum *42*
Corbusier, Le 24
corsetry *137*
crystal *39*, 41, 52
Cuir d'Ange 34
Cyrus, Miley 108

D'Origny, Henri 100, 125
Dallet, Robert 41
Debo, Kaat 122
Dietrich, Marlene *105*
dinnerware *39*
Dreux, Alfred de 30
*Duc Attelé, Groom a L'Attente,
   Le* 30
Dumas-Hermès, Robert

   (Émile's son-in-law) 25,
      29, 32, 45
Dumas, Axel 52
Dumas, Jean-Louis (great-
   great-grandson) 34, 39–
   42, *41*, 47, 50, 65, 68, 86,
   87, 103, 118, 121, 157
Dumas, Pierre-Alexis 7, 52–3
Dumas, Rena 50–52, *51*, *52*
Dumas, Robert 58, 81, *82*,
   83, 84, 85, 92

Eau d'Orange Verte 47, 50
Eau d'Hermès 32, *32*
Elizabeth II, Queen *100*
Ellena, Jean-Claude 32,
   34, 50
equestrianism 129, 130, *130*,
   133
Eugénie, Empress 14, 97, *97*
Evangelista, Linda 130, *130*
Ex Libris print 83

fabrics 7, 47, 58, 117, 118,
   118, 121, 125, 129, 130,
   140, 142, *145*, 153, 154
Faivre, Annie 87
Financial Times 153, 157
Frank, Jean-Michel 24

Gaga, Lady 108, *1110*, 112
Gaultier, Jean Paul 8, *8*, 40,
   129–34, *130*, *137*, 139
geometric prints *140*
GQ 154, 157
grunge *149*
Grygkar, Hugo *81*, 82, *82*,

83, *83*, 84
Guerrand, Jean-René *32*, 32

Hepburn, Audrey *7*, 100, 101
Hermès, Adolphe (grandson) 17, 21, 22
Hermès, Charles-Émile (son) 13, 14, 17, 57, 97
Hermès, Christine (wife) 13
Hermès, Émile (grandson) 17, 21–2, *21*, 22, 27, 29, 70, 81, 92
Hermès, Thierry *7*, 13, 14, *14*, 68, 97
Holly, Al-Baseer 108

Independent, The 98–100
interiors 50–52, *52*

jacket, leather golfing 22

Kardashian, Kim 108, *108*
Kelly, Grace 58, 60, *60*, *91*, 100, *103*, 118
Kennedy, Jackie 70, 101
King, Bill 118
Krefeld 13

leather 26
Ledoux, Philippe 84–5, *84*, *89*
Lemaire, Christophe 8, 139–42, *139*, *140*
Lobb, John 40
logo 30, *30*
luggage *17*
LVMH 44

Margiela, Martin 8, 121, *121*, 122, *122*, 125, *125*, 129, 139, 142
Margiela: The Hermès Years exhibition 121, *125*
Menchari, Leïla 32, 34,

45–50, *45*, *47*
menswear 150, *150*, 153, *153*, 154, *154*
MoMu Fashion Museum 121–2, *125*
Monte Carlo 105
Moss, Kate 104, *107*
Mower, Sarah 145–6

New York Times 40, 117, 118, 139
Nichanian, Véronique 8, 146, 150–57, *153*, *154*, *155*
Nicholas II, Tsar of Russia (Emperor) 98

O'Connor, Erin *133*
Oliver, Kermit 87, *87*
Olsen, Ashley 104, *107*
Olsen, Mary-Kate *107*
Osbourne, Kelly 112

Palermo, Olivia *74*, *92*
perfume 32–4, *32*
Phelps, Nicole 134
Pont-Audemer 13
prints 157

Riss, Jonathan 112
Robert, Guy 32, *32*
Roudnitska, Edmond 32, *32*
Royal Windsor Horse Show 100, *100*
Rue Basse-du-Rempart 13
Rue du Faubourg Saint-Honoré 17, 47, 50, 97

saddle *17*, 22
saddle stitch 14, *14*
Sanz, Bernard *117*, 118
Savy, Aimé 92
scarves 118, 134, 142
    Chasse en Afrique, La 84
    Cheyennes, Les 87
    Combats des Coqs 84

Comédie Italienne, La 85
Cosmos 85, *89*
Faune et Flore du Texas, La 87
Littérature 86
making 90–92, *91*
Mineraux 83
Napoléon 84, 85
Pégase d'Hermès, Le silk *88*
Perspective 86
Pony Express 87
Traite des Armes 81
Schürrle, Anna 70
Shirley, Alice 87
silver, Puiforcat 41, 52
stores 26, *26*, 27

tablewear 41
tartan blotter 100
Tatersale 100
Teigen, Chrissy *110*
Teigl, Karin *63*
Terre d'Hermès 34
Thee Stallion, Megan 112
Thomas, Patrick 52

trunks *22*, 24

Vanhee-Cybulski, Nadège 8, 145–6, *145*, *146*
vanity case *77*
Vanity Fair 39, 40
vareuse 125, *125*
Vogue 47, 82, 122, 125, 129, 134, 139, 145–6
vogue.com 145, 146

Wall Street Journal, The 53
Wek, Alek 129
West, Kanye (Ye) 108, *108*

Windsor, Duke & Duchess of (King Edward VIII) 22, 98–100, *98*
womenswear 118, 121, *121*

CREDITS

The publishers would like to thank the following sources for their kind permission to reproduce the pictures in this book.

Image Courtesy of The Advertising Archives: 23

Alamy: Everett Collection Inc 60, 107; Peter Horree 38; incamerastock 96; John Frost Newspapers 99; PictureLux/The Hollywood Archive 6; Pictorial Press Ltd 98; Vladyslav Yushynov 30; Zuma Press Inc 17

Bridgeman Images: PVDE 33; © Christie's Images 15, 65; Leonard de Selva 16, 24-25; Lebrecht History 12

Getty Images: MEGA 113; Archivo Cameraphoto Epoche 43; Robyn Beck 67; Bettmann 91; Thomas Coex 123; Jean-Claude Deutsch 42; Marc Deville 14; Francois Durand 136; Estrop 144, 147, 148, 149; James Eyser 31; Tristan Fewings 64; Gotham 93, 111; Francois Guillot/AFP 128, 131, 151, 154, 155; Keystone-France 26; Jason LaVeris 28-29; Isaac Lawrence/AFP 56; Neil Mockford 106; Jeremy Moeller 62, 71; Max Mumby/Indigo 101; Jeff Pachoud 69; Eric Piermont 90; Marc Piasecki 66; Popperfoto 61; Anne-Christine Poujoulat/

AFP 35; Ben Pruchnie 75; Reporters Associes 104-105; Roger Viollet Collection 102; Joel Saget 120, 124; Jun Sato 110; Pierre Suu 109; ullstein bild 41; Pierre Vauthey 122; Pierre Verdy/AFP 9, 132, 133, 135, 137, 138, 140, 141, 150, 152, 153; Christian Vierig 72; Kasia Wandycz 52

© Guillaume de Laubier: 45, 46-47, 48-49, 51

Kerry Taylor Auctions: 20, 59t, 59c, 59b, 63, 70, 73, 74, 76t, 76b, 78, 80, 83, 84, 85, 86, 88, 89, 103, 116, 119

Mary Evans: © Illustrated London News Ltd 32

Shutterstock: Nat Farbman/The LIFE Picture Collection 27; Claude Paris/AP 156; Yannis Vlamos/Sipa 126-127

Topfoto: Roger-Viollet 82

Every effort has been made to acknowledge correctly and contact the source and/or copyright holder of each picture and Welbeck Publishing Group apologises for any unintentional errors or omissions, which will be corrected in future editions of this book.

LITTLE BOOK OF

BALENCIAGA

Emmanuelle Dirix is a cultural theorist who specializes in fashion studies. She has over 20 years of lecturing experience at institutions including Central Saint Martins, London College of Fashion and the Royal College of Art, and has been leading historic and contextual studies at the Antwerp Fashion Academy since 2009. She has published widely on fashion in both academic and popular publications. Her most recent book is *Dressing the Decades* (Yale University Press). In addition, she works as a freelance curator and fashion branding and communications consultant for the luxury industry. Recently she has joined the Institute of Global Health Innovation at Imperial College, as a senior teaching fellow.

Published in 2022 by Welbeck
An imprint of Welbeck Non-Fiction Limited,
part of Welbeck Publishing Group.
Based in London and Sydney
www.welbeckpublishing.com

Text, design and layout © Welbeck Non-Fiction Limited 2022

A CIP catalogue record for this book is available from the British Library.

ISBN 978-1-78739-830-6

Printed in China

10 9 8 7

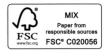

LITTLE BOOK OF

BALENCIAGA

The story of the iconic fashion house

EMMANUELLE DIRIX

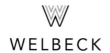

WELBECK

CONTENTS

EARLY YEARS........................... 06

A SPANIARD IN PARIS.............. 16

THE WAR YEARS 34

DESIGN INFLUENCES 52

THE ROAD TO ABSTRACTION..... 68

SPANISH INFLUENCES............. 88

RELIGION 104

THE MASTER OF MODERNITY ...124

A LABEL REBORN 140

INDEX.....................................156

BIBLIOGRAPHY........................159

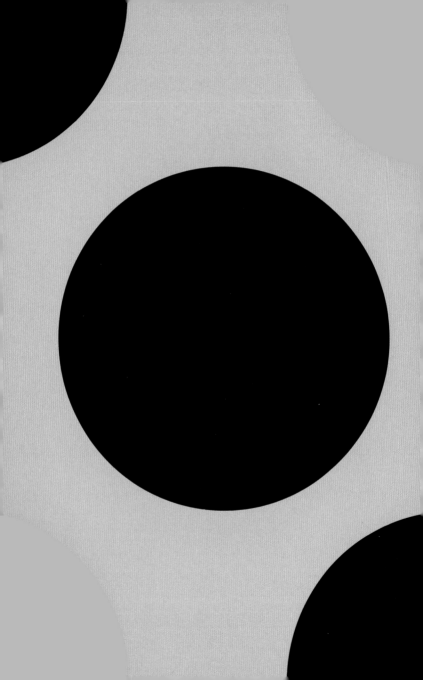

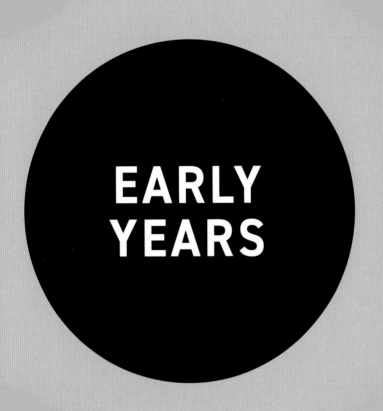

EARLY
YEARS

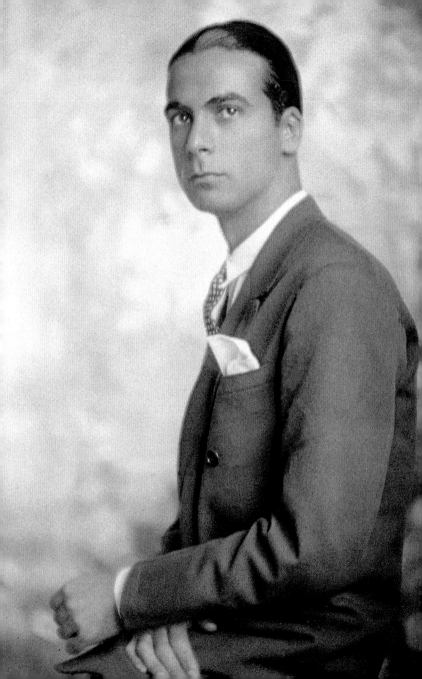

THE YOUNG VIRTUOSO

Cristóbal Balenciaga was born on 21 January 1895 to a seafaring father and a seamstress mother in the coastal town of Getaria in the Basque Country, Northern Spain. He came from a modest background, but his family were not impecunious by any means, as some biographies have implied. His father was the local mayor when Balenciaga was born and a state employee up until his demise in 1906, skippering boats for the Customs fleet.

After her husband's death, Balenciaga's mother, Martina Eizaguirre, took sole responsibility for supporting the family and set up a small workshop where she taught local girls to sew. In addition, she undertook private sewing commissions, most importantly for the Marquesa de Casa Torres, who in years to come would encourage, support and later act as the patron of the young Balenciaga. The story goes that Balenciaga made his first garment, a coat for his cat, at the age of six, but became frustrated as the animal kept running away and moving during "fittings". Another story, often recounted to illustrate his early interest in fashion, involves him audaciously asking the Marquesa de Casa Torres (to whom he had access through his mother) if he could copy her walking costume. She was apparently so amused by his request that she agreed and is even said to have worn his version.

OPPOSITE Cristóbal Balenciaga, c.1927

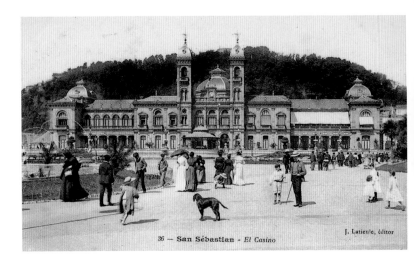

36 — San Sébastian - El Casino

J. Latieule, éditor

The occupation of Balenciaga's mother goes a long way to explain his passion for sewing, and he started on the road to a professional career in tailoring proper at the tender age of 12. Having completed his elementary schooling, he began a tailoring apprenticeship at Casa Gómez in the neighbouring town of San Sebastián. This illustrious establishment was a favourite of the aristocracy (many of whom owned holiday homes in and around San Sebastián). Indeed, Casa Gómez advertised in local newspapers and magazines, calling themselves "the most important tailors, preferred by the distinguished public". After a year the young Balenciaga decided to continue his training at the newly established New England tailor's shop. It was founded by Messrs Romeo, Quemada and Villar, three of the best tailors from Casa Gómez, who were very happy to take on the promising young apprentice at their new business venture.

After completing his apprenticeship, Balenciaga moved to the newly opened San Sebastián branch of the Parisian department store Les Grands Magasins du Louvre, which, like every large department store, had its own dressmaking salon and sewing ateliers. He started as a tailor in the women's workshop but within two years rose to become the head of the dressmaking department, which was no small achievement given he was only 18 years old. During his time at Les Grands Magazins du Louvre he also experienced the Parisian haute couture industry firsthand. Attending couture "shows", specifically organized for the department store trade, allowed Balenciaga not only to come into contact with the most prominent couture houses, buyers, suppliers and clients of the day, but also provided him with a thorough understanding of the business side of the fashion industry, which would put him in good stead in the years to come.

In 1917 Balenciaga opened his first solo business venture in San Sebastián, under the simple name: C. Balenciaga. He had chosen a most opportune moment to establish himself as a couturier in the region since many aristocrats, wealthy businessmen and members of the *beau monde* had fled to their summer residences and the lavish hotels of San Sebastián and neighbouring Biarritz to sit out the First World War in comfort and style. The region quickly saw a surge in luxury consumption. Not only did these wartime residents widen the market, but they also elicited a fashion shift from Paris to the Basque Country, as many of the couture houses were quick to move their collection presentations from their Parisian houses to the luxurious dining rooms and ballrooms of the region's upmarket hotels. Indeed, Callot Soeurs, Maison Worth, Paquin and Chanel all showed in Spain to a receptive audience. Not only did this shift bolster the business of local couturiers, but also allowed the likes of Balenciaga to attend the wartime shows and so stay abreast of design innovations in Paris. This in turn helped to shape his own designs, and in September 1918 he showed his first collection.

Creating and showing collections required a significant financial investment, so, given his humble background, Balenciaga was forced to find investors to fund his venture. The sisters Benita and Daniela Lizaso, both traders, provided him with the necessary funds. Less than a year later, Balenciaga and the Lizaso sisters established the company Balenciaga y Compañía, which suggests the first collection had been a resounding success. Balenciaga's association with the sisters would last six years, during which time he cemented his reputation for exquisite craftsmanship and indeed as a leading Spanish couturier.

In 1925, after a year spent securing financial backing and sourcing staff, Balenciaga presented his new collection under his full name: "Cristóbal Balenciaga". This attracted the attention of a distinguished clientele, not least Queen María Cristina de Borbón and several other women of the Spanish Royal Family, including her granddaughter the Infanta Isabel Alfonsa. Few of Balenciaga's designs from this period survive, but those that do provide some valuable insights into his design processes. Like most foreign couturiers he travelled twice a year to Paris – then regarded as the epicentre of fashion and taste – to attend the fashion presentations of the leading haute couturiers (Callot Soeurs, Doucet, Paquin, Chéruit and Redfern, to name but a few) and to find out where fashion was going next. He would then build his own collection, combining Parisian models (to stay relevant) and his own creations (often tailored to his established clientele's preferences), all executed meticulously with impeccable cut and great attention to detail. Interestingly, year on year his creative independence grew, almost in parallel to his success.

Two years later, in 1927, he created "Martina Robes et Manteaux" (Martina had been his mother's name) as a second

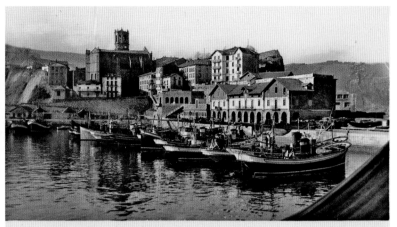

ABOVE The harbour in Getaria, the town of Balenciaga's birth, early twentieth century

brand in a diversification strategy. The brand was soon renamed EISA Costura in another clear link to his beloved mother whose surname was Eizaguirre. This was an ingenious business move that was in many ways well ahead of its time. EISA – unlike his eponymous couture house – offered models in line with the needs and preferences of his local San Sebastián clientele. Customers had a degree of agency and could choose the design and fabrics used, "adjusting" the silhouettes on offer to their personal preference.

While the association with its creator implicitly linked EISA to the world of high fashion and thus made it very desirable, the use of less lavish fabrics reduced the price significantly. As a result, more clients, most importantly the San Sebastián upper middle classes, patronized EISA. This business model resulted in a greater number of garments being sold (albeit at lower cost) and increased returns, which were in turn used to finance the presentation of Balenciaga's biannual couture collections. Balenciaga successfully managed his two businesses from San Sebastián, and while in many ways they worked in tandem (they presented their collections simultaneously, for example), they always advertised separately in the local media.

However, in spite of a well-polished business strategy, commercial success would soon be hindered by circumstances beyond Balenciaga's control. The proclamation of the Second Republic in Spain, in April 1931, and the subsequent exile of the Royal Family had dramatic consequences for his business. Many of his aristocratic clients, whose patronage was central to his success, were forced to leave, which proved to be a not inconsiderable blow to Balenciaga's business.

Balenciaga, by now a canny businessman as well as a highly accomplished designer, reacted with speed and commercial creativity. In 1932, he requested permission from the city to open a new establishment called B.E. Costura. Given the precarious situation, his new establishment continued the business concept pioneered by EISA Costura, as now more than ever he had to cater for the demands of the local upper middle classes in order to survive financially. It has been called "an emergency solution for an exceptional situation", but once things stabilized he turned these "emergency" measures to his advantage.

In 1933, after a year of simultaneously running EISA Costura and B.E. Costura, Balenciaga consolidated his business and opened a new establishment called EISA B.E. Costura in Madrid. The success of this venture led in turn to the opening of a third couture house in 1935, this time in Barcelona.

Balenciaga managed to keep his fashion businesses operational through innovative business decisions married with exceptional design until 1937. Given Spain's political situation in the 1930s, this was no mean feat. It was in this year, however, undeniably prompted by the outbreak of the Spanish Civil War the previous year, that Balenciaga finally moved his operation to 10 Avenue George V in Paris and so joined the Parisian couture world.

OPPOSITE Balenciaga black lace evening gown, c.1938

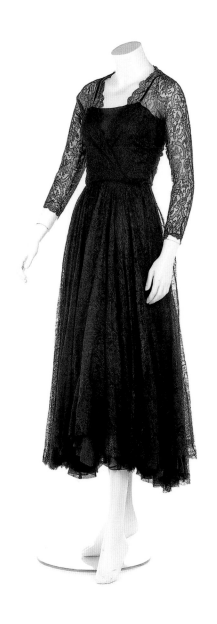

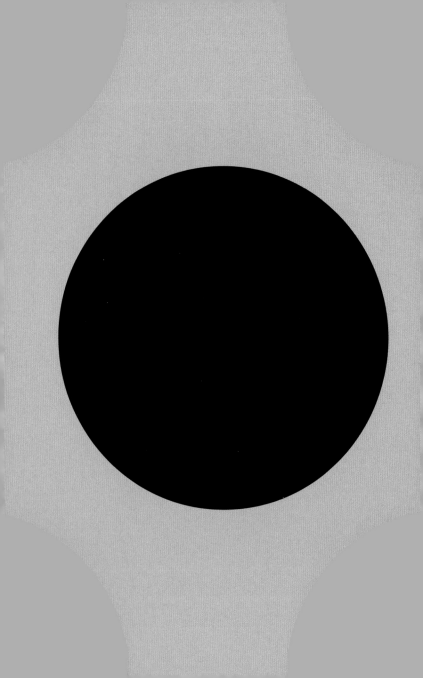

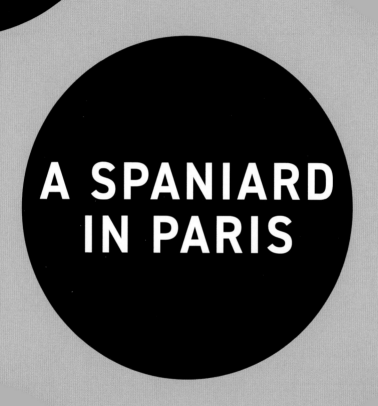

A SPANIARD
IN PARIS

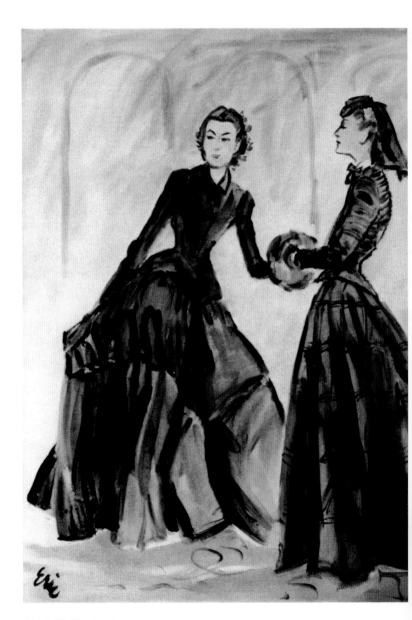

EXILE ON
AVENUE GEORGE V

In July 1936 the Spanish Civil War broke out and once again brought insecurity and disruption to Spanish life. It has been suggested that this latest fractious development in a decade marked by instability was the final straw for Balenciaga. Having already lost many of his wealthiest patrons after the proclamation of the Second Spanish Republic in 1931, and the subsequent exile of the Spanish Royal Family and the Court, he knew what lay in store and understood implicitly that in the immediate future there would be little demand for expensive couture in Spain.

Contemporary events combined with his longstanding connection to haute couture made his 1937 move to Paris not altogether surprising. On 7 July 1937, Balenciaga founded his couture house in Paris with his Franco-Polish life partner, Wladzio Jaworowski d'Attainville, and Nicolás Bizcarrondo, an exile from San Sebastián, at 10 Avenue George V. Less than two months later, Balenciaga presented his first Parisian couture collection.

From the moment he opened his Parisian house Balenciaga received considerable French press coverage and praise. By December 1937 he received his first mention in *Vogue* and by the following year they were regularly featuring his designs. The magazine even dedicated a whole page to his work in

OPPOSITE Balenciaga nineteenth-century style silk velvet dress and jacket in black and brown (left), *Vogue*, October 1939 their July issue, entitled "French Newcomers", which showed their American readership that he was one of the "new" haute couturiers to watch. Within a year Balenciaga also featured in adverts for Bergdorf Goodman and Marshall Fields & Company who retailed licensed copies of his clothes in New York and Chicago, respectively, indicating his immediate artistic acclaim and commercial success on both sides of the Atlantic.

In his first few years in Paris Balenciaga was often referred to by the press as "the Spanish designer", and his Spanish-ness was often regarded as central to his designs. In October 1938, *Harper's Bazaar* said that his whole first collection had "a flavour of Spain", while in September 1939, *Women's Journal* declared: "His beautiful clothes have the warm colourful drama of his country."

While much of Balenciaga's oeuvre is indebted to his Spanish roots and many of his designs feature Spanish influences (as later chapters in this book will show), it is interesting to note that many of the early parallels drawn by the press were often more to do with a focus on his nationality as a novelty – he was the only Spanish designer in Paris – than on genuine, indisputable Spanish influences. More accurately, Balenciaga's use of historic references in his designs was often related to Spanish costume and/or the work of the seventeenth-century Spanish artist Diego Velázquez. He did propose some overtly Spanish garments in the late 1930s – most famously his 1939 "Infanta" dress – but it is, in fact, his post-war output that features the most explicit Spanish references.

Often, when Balenciaga's work was referred to as Spanish, perhaps the press were really saying that his designs were restrained, modest or demure, features that were often incorrectly conflated with Spanish Catholicism. In 1939 alone, *Vogue* described his creations as "modest" on at least four separate occasions, despite being no more or less so than many other designs featured alongside them. This confusion between the historic and

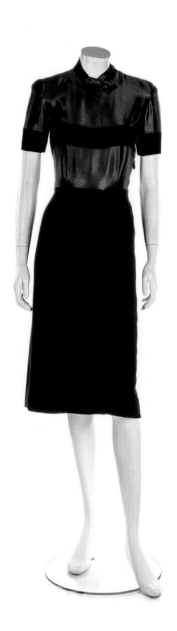

RIGHT Balenciaga
couture black wool
and satin dinner dress,
possibly from his first
Parisian collection,
c.1937

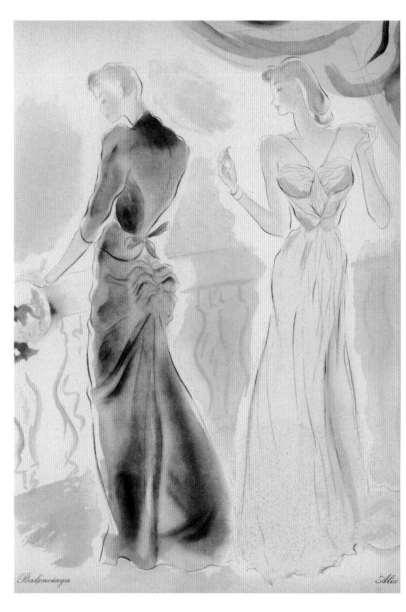

Balenciaga   Alix

Spanish-ness meant that these "identifying" elements of his work as Spanish not only made for easy journalism but all too often became conflated with the "unmodern".

It's true that much of Balenciaga's early Parisian evening wear referenced historic styles, but so did that of his contemporaries. In fact, the final years of the 1930s are marked by historicism in high fashion – most likely driven by a collective romantic nostalgia for better, safer days in a Europe that was once again on the brink of war. So, Balenciaga's adoption or reworking of older styles was actually more about fashion than it was about national identity. When viewed in isolation his use, for example, of white lace during this period could easily be ascribed to his heritage. However, this would be a truism and ignores the popularity of white lace and its abundant use in couture creations at the time.

It might be more useful to focus on how fashion publications often drew attention to the fact that Balenciaga's use of historic references was more innovative than many of his contemporaries. More than once he was credited with "re-introducing" old new elements, such as exaggerated 1850s triangular yokes, an eighteenth-century reticule dress or a "wedding dress that's as demure as a Mid-Victorian's". His use of, or playfulness with, history was often found in innovative details and interpretations, an approach praised at the time and one that would mature and become emblematic of his post-war work.

A link that was repeatedly made in the late 1930s was to the artist Velázquez. As we will see in later chapters, Balenciaga was heavily influenced by his work, but once again these aesthetic links became much more explicit in the years to come. The reason why Velázquez (and less often Francisco Goya) are repeatedly cited when discussing Balenciaga's output during this period was, in fact, down to the staging of the 1939 exhibition of Spanish art that took place in Geneva, Switzerland, which was extensively

OPPOSITE Balenciaga brown evening gown with bustle (left), *Vértice*, May 1939

covered in the same upmarket fashion publications that made those links to Velázquez. As *Vogue* noted in September 1939: "Perhaps this exhibition is what Balenciaga was waiting for, dreaming of. His Spanish mind was quick to respond to the dignity and beauty of Velázquez canvasses: the elaborate fabrics, covered arms, tiny waists, broad head-dresses…"

Fashion has, in fact, always liked to compare itself to art as a means of raising its status, and the comment in *Vogue* was just one example of this. In the same issue a caption accompanying one of Balenciaga's low-backed evening dresses reads: "Balenciaga borrows again from the earlier Spaniard – there's a Velázquez look about this dress which Mona Marie wears like a sixteenth-century [sic] court beauty." This clearly shows that the copy-writer was not familiar with the Spanish aristocracy, their wardrobe nor indeed with Velázquez's work. In the July 1939 issue of *Vogue* a caption accompanying an illustration of a pink satin evening gown makes an equally tentative link: "Balenciaga…draws on Goya's richness of fabric and colour, and round-hipped, tiny-waisted court belles" – this is misleading to say the least given Goya's rare use of the colour pink. Similarly, an illustration of the Balenciaga "Velázquez hat" made of violet felt flanked with fox tails, which featured in the September 1939 issue, is not immediately reminiscent of anything worn at the seventeenth-century Spanish court.

This focus on Spanish references, and especially on Velázquez, can easily overshadow the diversity of Balenciaga's actual output and, indeed, the rich and wide historic costume he drew on as sources in his early Parisian years. His range extends to 1860s-style wedding dresses, eighteenth-century evening coats, tightly fitted Polonaise gowns from the 1880s, seventeenth-century lace collars straight out of a Flemish painting, and nineteenth-century bustles and panniers. As *Vogue* commented in March 1939: "Balenciaga tops chiffon skirts with basket-like hip drapery of satin or taffeta,

OPPOSITE Balenciaga "Andalusian Dancer" dress with black ottoman silk bodice and a three-tiered Spanish lace skirt (right). *The Sketch,* June 1939

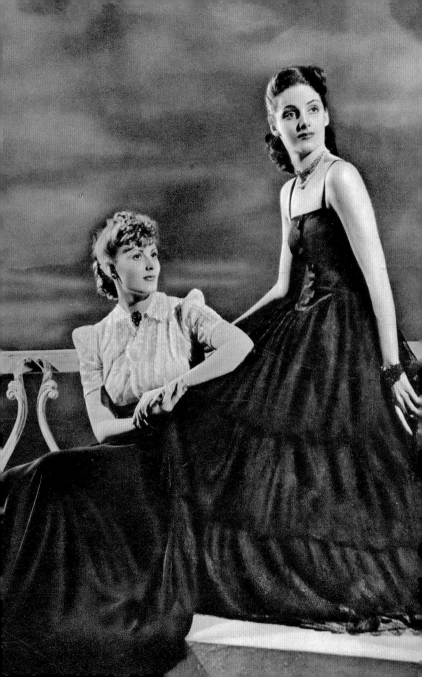

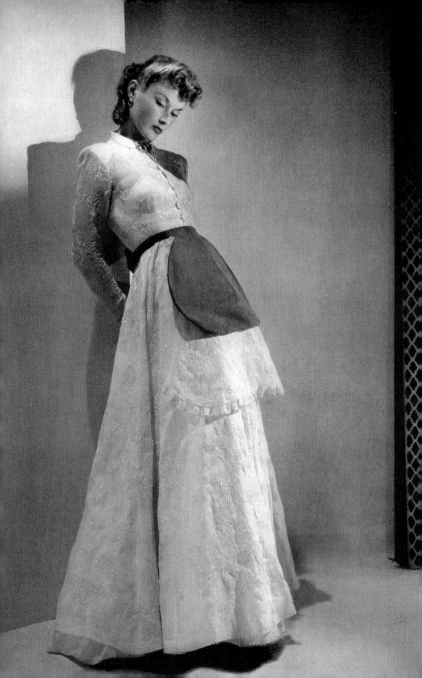

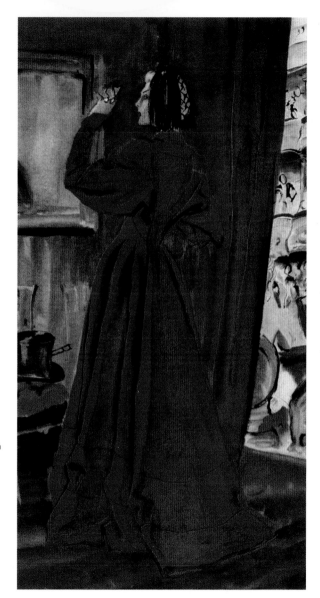

OPPOSITE Balenciaga
embroidered
handkerchief linen
dress with two
aprons, *Vogue*, 1939

RIGHT Balenciaga
red broadcloth coat
with dolman sleeves
and corseted bodice,
Vogue, June 1939

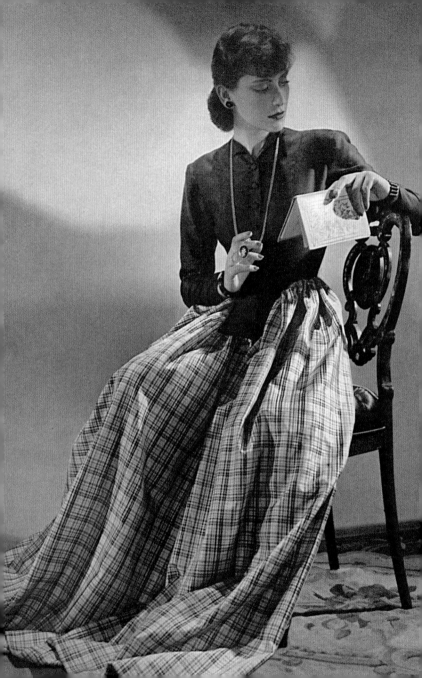

very Vigée Lebrun." Balenciaga's designs were all reinterpreted in such a way that they were both historic and modern, and they are evidence of their creator's extensive and in-depth knowledge and understanding of costume and art history.

Yet while Balenciaga's evening wear and occasion dresses were exquisite examples of the historicist and escapist tendencies that dominated fashion design in the late 1930s, his daywear was also a clear product of its period. It was typified by elegant practicality and versatility, and also combined a good dose of realism about what was to come with its innovative pattern cutting and draping. His calf-length day dresses and suits with peplums, his pleated skirts and exquisitely tailored, moulded jackets were particularly coveted by the press, and this marks the point at which his designs started to be described as sculptural, a term that would sum up many of his silhouettes in the 1950s and demonstrate his evolution in fashion.

While Balenciaga's Parisian business enjoyed considerable success and his move had clearly paid off, he longed for home. He kept a close eye on the situation in Spain, waiting for the right moment to restart his involvement with the three establishments that he had been forced to leave behind. He had asked his staff in Spain to keep all the fashion houses open, but what he really wanted was to be closely involved with the creation of collections once more. In 1938, he changed the name of his San Sebastián establishment back to its original name of EISA, and once the other two establishments were able to resume normal activity, they too adopted it. From 1942 until his retirement in 1968 Balenciaga was once again closely involved with EISA and supervised its collections – and in doing so maintained close links with his country of birth.

OPPOSITE Balenciaga plaid surah skirted dress and navy surah jacket, *Vogue*, March 1939

For now, though, his Spanish establishments were soon to become his only available fashion "link" to the rest of the world.

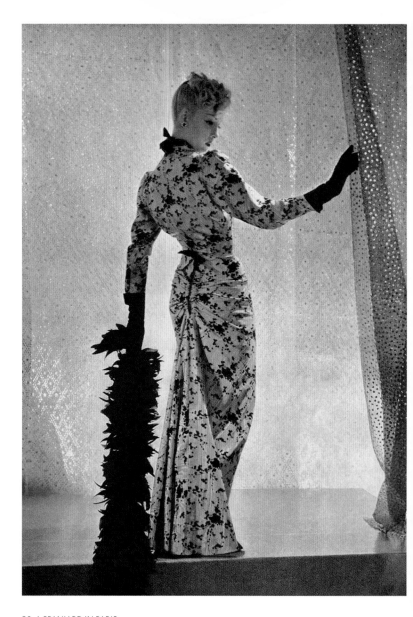

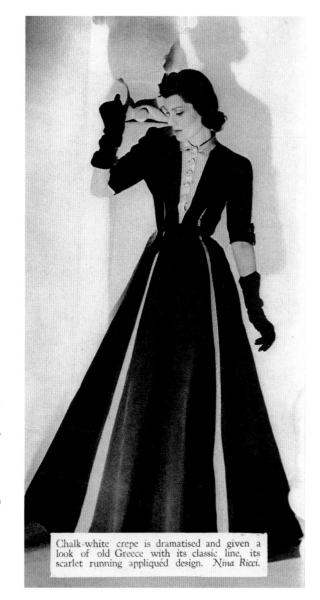

OPPOSITE Balenciaga pale blue printed moire Polonaise dress, *Vogue*, April 1939

RIGHT Balenciaga dinner dress of black faille, highlighted with pink and tied-bow waist, *Britannia and Eve*, August 1939. The dress is incorrectly captioned as being by Nina Ricci

Chalk-white crepe is dramatised and given a look of old Greece with its classic line, its scarlet running appliquéd design. *Nina Ricci.*

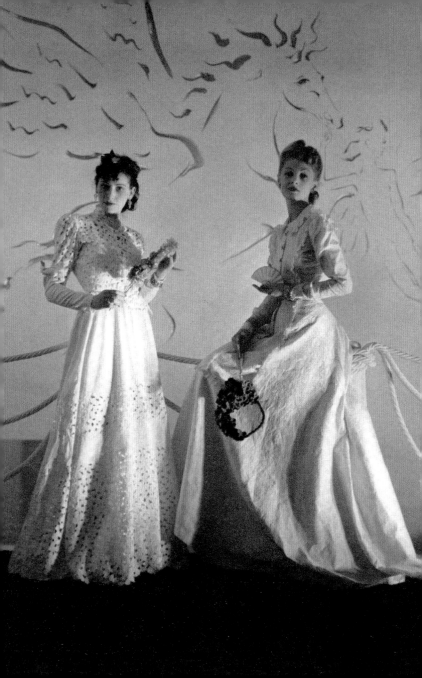

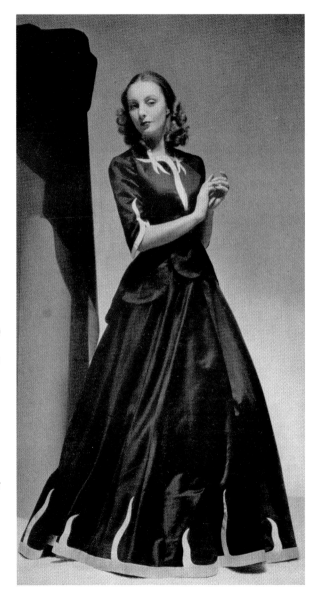

OPPOSITE Balenciaga (left) embroidered white lawn dress with peplum jacket and (right) embroidered white glazed chintz dress. *Vogue*, April 1939

RIGHT Balenciaga Victorian-style, strapless black slipper satin dress worn over a hooped taffeta petticoat and with a matching jacket with a petalled basque. *The Sphere*, December 1938

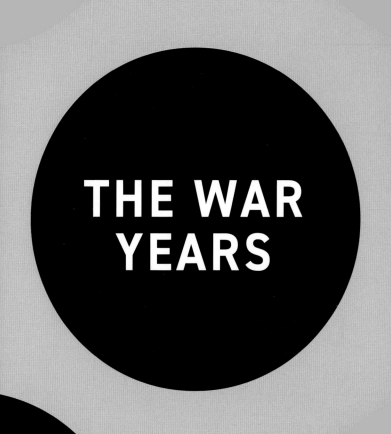

THE WAR
YEARS

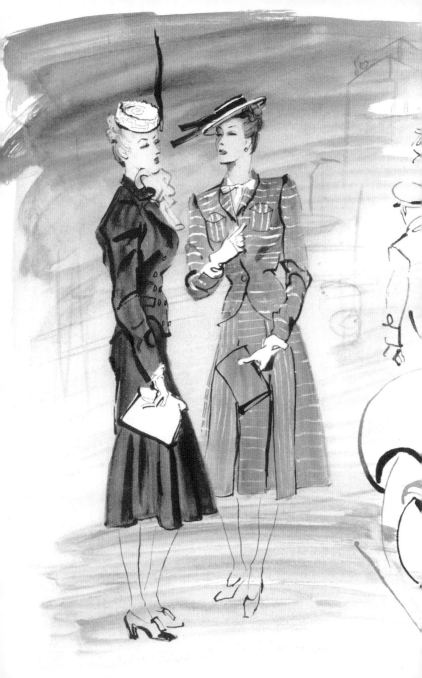

PRACTICAL LUXURY

Germany's invasion of Poland on 1 September 1939 came as
no great surprise. Most European powers had been quietly
preparing for war since the late 1930s, while nevertheless
hoping that another major conflict on European soil could
be avoided. This misplaced hope, combined with a good
dose of realism, was reflected in the Autumn collections that
were shown only days earlier: daywear was characterized by
increasing practicality whereas evening wear was romantic,
escapist and historicist in nature.

Piguet showed a reversible, wool "air-raid" outfit, the cape
of which doubled as a blanket; Hermès presented versatile,
plaid hooded capes and all manner of practical bags; Creed an
"Alerte Plaid" blanket that could be worn as a cape or overskirt;
Schiaparelli featured a one-piece zippered jumpsuit (available in
blue or shocking pink); and Lanvin made her own tweed gas-mask
case decorated with silver studs. Chic pyjamas by Molyneux were
suitable for use in both the home and air-raid shelter, while at
Lanvin there were practical day dresses. Box coats, an abundance
of fur, knitwear and hooded jersey dresses for keeping warm also
featured in most collections, and all this was mixed with a good
degree of patriotism and militarism. Colours such as aeroplane

OPPOSITE Balenciaga grey and white sheer wool suit (right),
Vogue, April 1939

grey and French soil beige were used to create military-style jackets and even scarves printed with French regimental flags became de rigueur. *Harper's Bazaar* summed up the mood: "The French have decreed that fashion shall go on…everyone makes an effort to be as elegant as possible."

As few items from this period survive, we are mostly reliant on their representation in magazines to establish what designers were doing. Interestingly, Balenciaga does not appear to have produced "special" wartime or bomb shelter items, and is never mentioned in articles that discussed these wartime sartorial "inventions". Arguably, this is reflective of both his clientele and his temperament, which was never suited to novelty. His designs were, however, still regularly featured in fashion publications and his daywear in particular was both a continuation of the increasing practicality suggested throughout the second part of the decade and in line with the rationality and practicality permeating all couture collections. Expertly tailored day ensembles and dresses, often combining masculine elements with more romantic detailing, in dark-coloured wool and velvet became his signature styles, and were often praised by the fashion press as "triumphantly wearable".

Upon the declaration of war several couture houses temporarily shut their doors, and eligible heads of houses reported for military duty; Balenciaga was exempt owing to his age and because he was a foreign national. Very quickly, though, special dispensations were granted to couturiers, so they could reopen and return to work: fashion was after all of vital importance to the French economy. In October 1939 *Vogue* was reporting how Parisian life was getting back to normal and how most salons had reopened and were busy preparing for the new collections. These 1940 Spring collections would become known as "Les Collections des Permissionaires", the name derived from

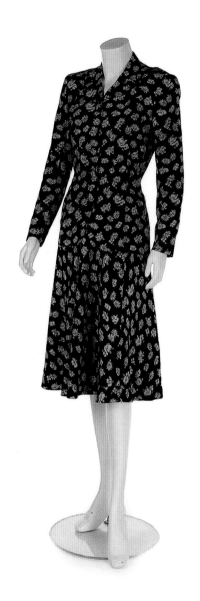

RIGHT Balenciaga
printed silk crepe
summer suit, c.1940

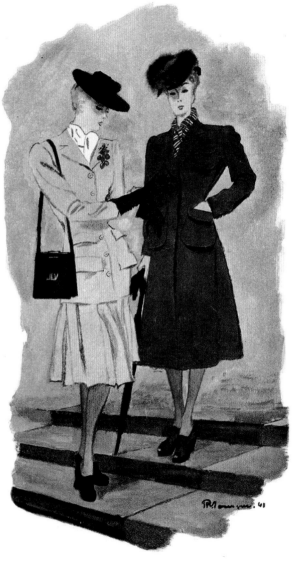

BALENCIAGA   ROBERT PIGUET

LEFT Balenciaga suit
in grey with double
flat pockets (left).
Accessorized with a
bag, gloves, hat and a
white satin scarf, 1941

OPPOSITE Balenciaga
lace, butterfly print,
white silk crepe
evening dress, *Vogue*,
April 1940

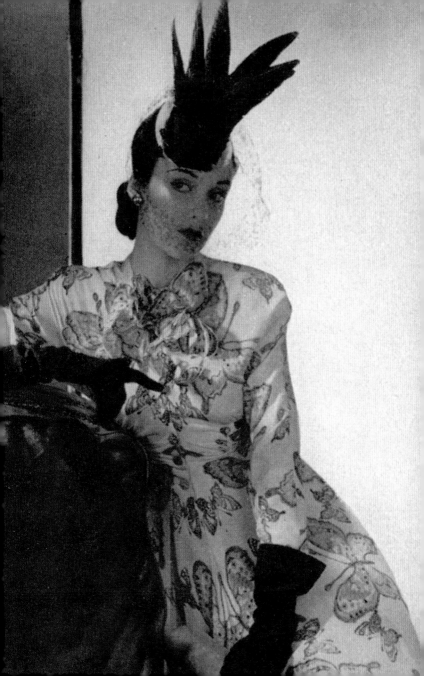

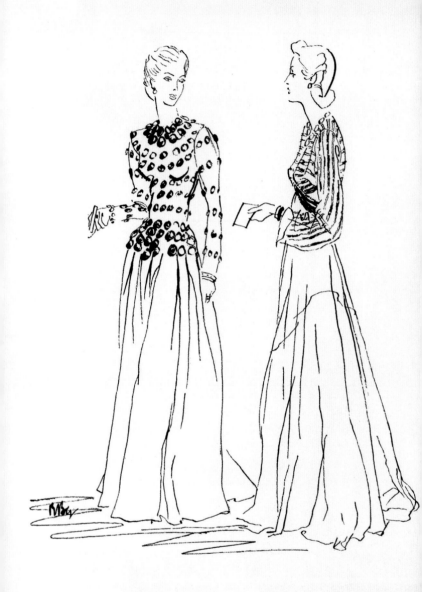

the aforementioned special permission granted to couturiers.

During the spring of 1940 France was engaged in the "phoney war" and while no actual fighting was yet taking place on French soil, the impact of the war was clearly noticeable in the Spring collections. The first collections shown after war was declared swung in favour of realism: increasingly practical, warm and versatile fashions were presented, especially for the domestic market. Luxury was still a feature of evening wear, but even luxury became pragmatic with long-sleeved gowns to keep out night chills in the event of an unexpected trip to the bomb shelter during a night out. Several Balenciaga evening dresses in this style were featured in both French and international fashion magazines and whereas they had previously been called "modest", they were now described as "practical luxury" and "versatile", which only goes to show how context is everything. Evening wear was still very much in the historicist style, and Balenciaga's offerings featured 1880s fitted cuts with bustle draping, large bustle bows and sashes, as well as exaggerated 1860s silhouettes with full skirts topped with bolero jackets.

On the morning of 14 June 1940 the first German troops entered and occupied Paris: the northern half of France was now under German administration. They entered a city that had shut up shop: theatres, cafés, restaurants and the couture salons were all closed for business; some were even boarded up. Many who were able had already fled the capital and one contemporary observer noted that these "refugees" were so overdressed it was as if they were attending a garden party rather than fleeing a war. Within days, however, many couture salons, including Balenciaga, reopened for business, not least to avoid having their business assets seized by the occupier. Balenciaga was no stranger to extreme situations and was probably better equipped than most for adjusting to the new regime in the city.

OPPOSITE Balenciaga blue crepe dress with pendant-sequinned bodice (left), *Vogue*, April 1940

The German occupation meant that France's borders were now closed, and crossing from the Northern occupied area into the unoccupied Southern zone was exceptionally difficult. With the country in turmoil, and with a lack of communications, the rest of the world assumed Paris had wound down its fashion operation. International *Vogue* closed its offices, which were located in Paris, and very little reporting emerged from the city after June 1940. In January 1941, *Vogue* ran one article entitled "Germans over Paris" written by an anonymous "eye witness" who detailed life in the occupied city. Of fashion she observed: "Many of the Paris dressmaking houses are open – Lanvin, Balenciaga, Molyneux, Patou… the collections are shown at 3 in the afternoon, and consist of wearable clothes – wearable clothes for an undertoned life. No real evening dresses…those simple woollen day dresses so rightly inspired by present circumstances, yet so varied, so beautifully made…The new fashions are real, that is why they are so good. They have carefully discarded any abstract, silly, or false proposition."

These remarks regarding the absence of evening wear were not completely correct. The entire war couture output continued to feature extravagant evening wear, albeit fewer models, but there are ample examples, including Balenciaga designs, that show it did not disappear entirely. In fact, an article in the *Tampa Bay Times* on 27 April 1941 describes evening gowns from Paris, including Balenciaga's, as "magnificent and of extreme elegance". Equally, daywear was hardly understated, especially when compared with what other nations were wearing. Balenciaga's day ensembles were often featured in French fashion publications and were a tour de force of his design skills, as he time and again reinvented the simple black day dress. His jackets and coats showed innovative cutting and tailoring and exuded a timeless luxury.

OPPOSITE Balenciaga black crepe afternoon dress with white dots (second from right), 1941

s du Succès?..

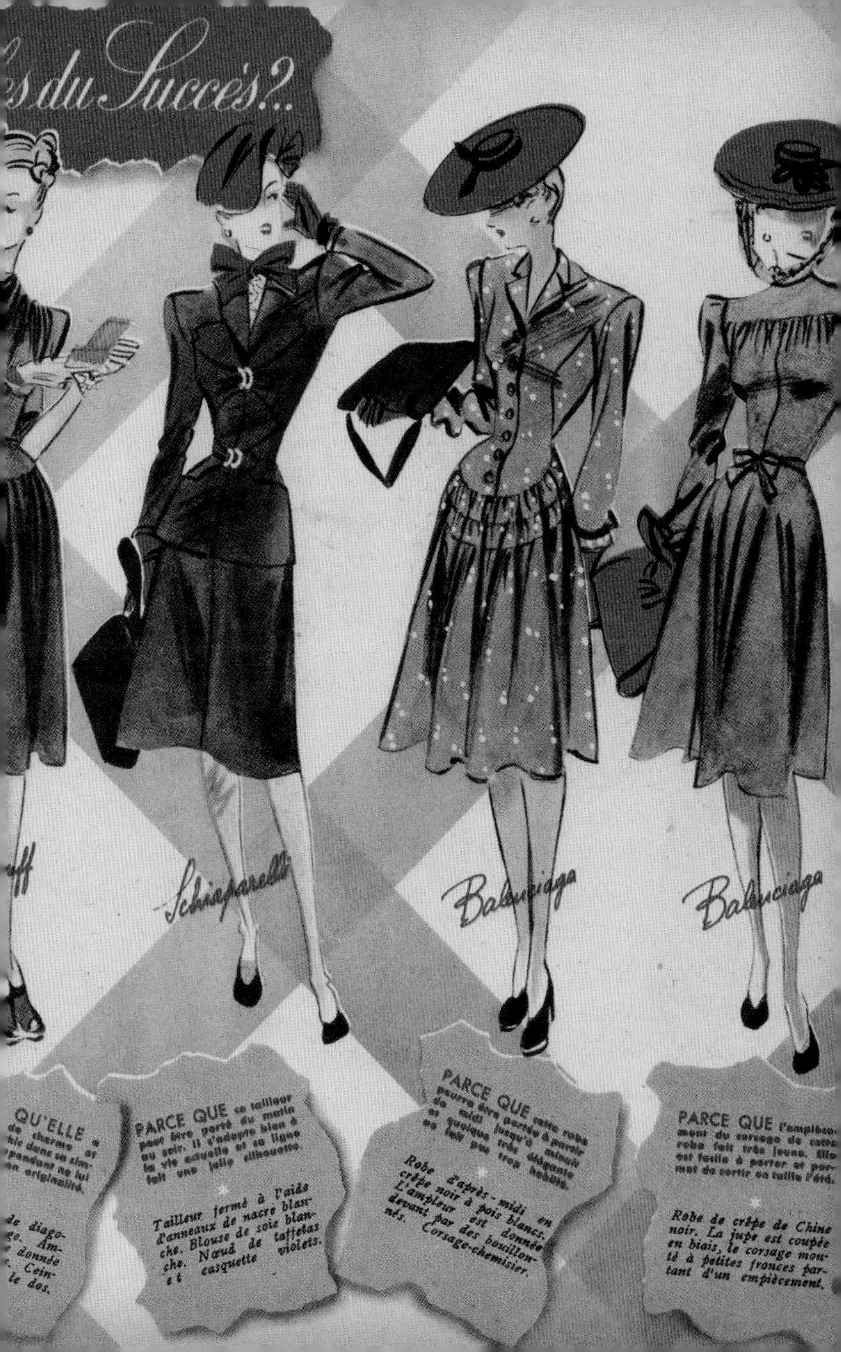

Schiaparelli

Balenciaga

Balenciaga

QU'ELLE a
de charme et
de ... dans ce sim-
... répondant ne lui
... originalité.

... de diago-
... An-
... donne
... Cein-
... dos.

PARCE QUE ce tailleur
peut être porté du matin
au soir. Il s'adapte bien à
la vie actuelle et sa ligne
fait une jolie silhouette.

Tailleur fermé à l'aide
d'anneaux de nacre blan-
che. Blouse de soie blan-
che. Nœud de taffetas
et casquette violets.

PARCE QUE cette robe
pourra être portée à partir
de midi jusqu'à minuit
et quoique très élégante
n'a pas trop habillée.

Robe d'après-midi en
crêpe noir à pois blancs.
L'ampleur est donnée
devant par des bouillon-
nés. Corsage-chemisier.

PARCE QUE l'emplace-
ment du corsage de cette
robe fait très jeune. Elle
est facile à porter et per-
met de sortir en taille l'été.

Robe de crêpe de Chine
noir. La jupe est coupée
en biais, le corsage mon-
té à petites fronces par-
tant d'un empiècement.

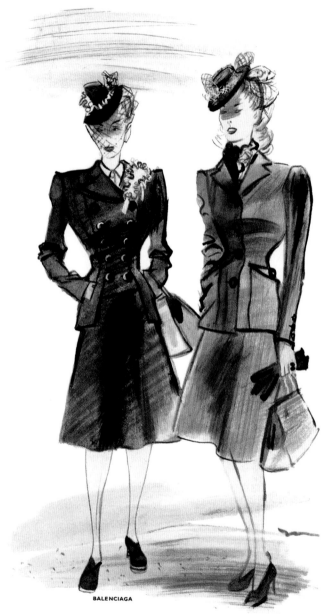

BALENCIAGA

ROBERT PIGUET

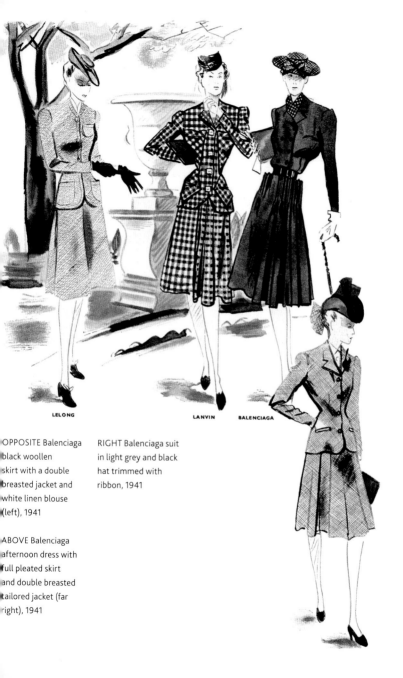

LELONG

LANVIN

BALENCIAGA

OPPOSITE Balenciaga
black woollen
skirt with a double
breasted jacket and
white linen blouse
(left), 1941

ABOVE Balenciaga
afternoon dress with
full pleated skirt
and double breasted
tailored jacket (far
right), 1941

RIGHT Balenciaga suit
in light grey and black
hat trimmed with
ribbon, 1941

While Balenciaga's designs were in line with the fashions his contemporaries were producing, in the sense that they were original but not radically different, it is worth noting that one of his dress designs from 1943, black with a fitted body but very voluminous long sleeves, was picked up by the French fashion press and described as "Très Nouvelles". Not only was this dress radically different from the rest of the silhouettes featured, but Balenciaga's play with form could also be regarded as an early example of his sartorial experiments with shape and volume which would come to define the later years of his career.

The same year also saw the first veritable incarnations of what would become another staple of his work: the matador jacket. This explicit Spanish reference to the traditional bullfighting costume can be explained in a variety of ways. Since the late 1930s there had been an increased interest in "regional" costume and many designers had incorporated elements from these traditional outfits in their fashions. This, paired with a revival in nationalism and regionalism, which was encouraged by many European nations during the war, might explain its appearance. Another more personal reason could be that the uncertainty of war elicited a nostalgic need in Balenciaga for a closer connection with his home nation. However, it could simply be that Balenciaga recognized the similarities in cut between the fashionable bolero of the early 1940s and the matador jacket, and hence embellishing the former to resemble the latter represented only a small leap in design. Regardless of the reason, we will see in later chapters that these matador jackets became a classic post-war Balenciaga item.

Until the Liberation of France, beginning in September 1944, the rest of the world had very little knowledge of what many of the couturiers of Paris were doing, though there were a few exceptions, and Balenciaga was one of them. Due to his Spanish

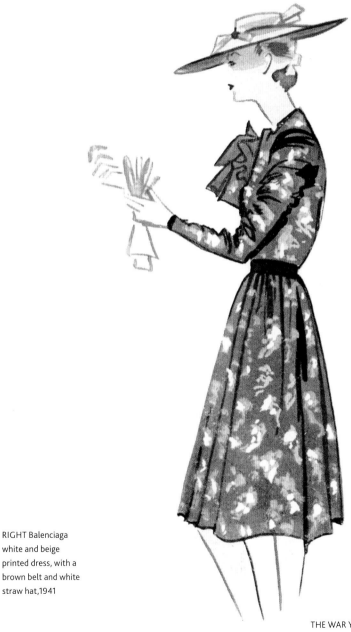

RIGHT Balenciaga
white and beige
printed dress, with a
brown belt and white
straw hat, 1941

nationality and Spain's neutrality in the war, he was able to travel back and forth between Paris and San Sebastián and so keep his Spanish EISA establishments open. It was through these that his work was able to travel to New York in the summer of 1941 to be included in a show of Spanish fashion designers. In July 1941, *Vogue* reported on the show and made the very astute observation that "almost the only Continental designers still free to express themselves are the Spanish modistas". The article included five illustrations of Balenciaga silhouettes, one an historically styled evening gown with a nipped-in waist, exaggerated hips and a fitted beaded redingote jacket and day ensembles with bustle pleat skirts and innovatively cut jackets. This international loophole also meant he was able to maintain his ties with American and Italian hat and footwear companies who advertised Balenciaga models throughout the war.

The first post-liberation *Vogue* report from Paris in October 1944 featured a Balenciaga deep amber, wool tailored coat, alongside designs by Lanvin and Mad Carpentier. Balenciaga's first post-Liberation collection was described by *The Province* newspaper on 9 December 1944 as "Spanish" and "not...very interesting, there being a monotonous sameness". The article complained in particular about the plain day dresses, the sombre colours and dull fabric choices. This "dulling" down was more about politics than design: upon its liberation, the world had been shocked to discover just how extravagant Paris couture had been throughout the war, especially when compared to countries that had endured strict rationing and governmental interference in fashion production. To heal their damaged reputations and to make their work internationally saleable, Parisian couturiers, including Balenciaga, deliberately toned down their 1944 collections. For now, Balenciaga's work still followed and complemented that of his contemporaries, but that was soon set to change.

OPPOSITE
EISA red and white shirt-waister style cotton summer dress, c.1944

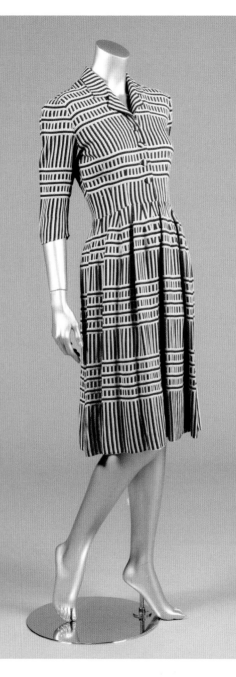

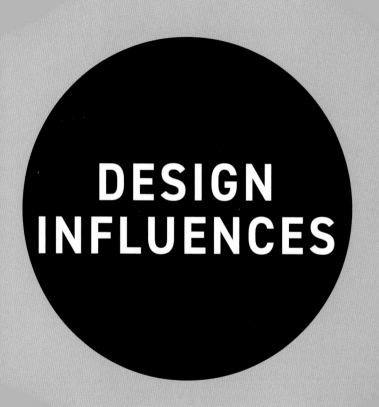

DESIGN INFLUENCES

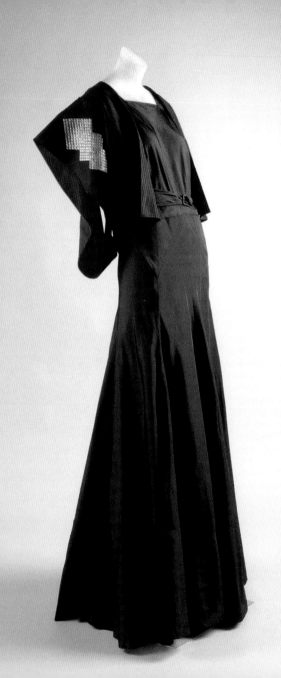

SOURCES OF INSPIRATION

To understand designers that are hailed as innovators or game changers, it is important not only to place them within their time frame and compare their work with that of their contemporaries, but also to consider those who paved the way for their radical sartorial experiments, who directly or indirectly influenced their design development, and who shaped both their aesthetics and/or design ethos.

The romantic notion that "pioneers" of fashion are genius mavericks is an attractive one, but it is essential to stress that they do not operate in an ivory tower and that their ideas, however "original" they may seem, have more often than not been shaped by the reinterpretation of both design concepts and cutting and sewing techniques which have been around for decades, if not centuries. Equally, for such innovations to occur, take root and make a genuine impact, one cannot ignore the need for the right sociopolitical time frame.

Balenciaga was a great innovator and created some truly original silhouettes. He experimented with cutting and tailoring techniques, and introduced several new fashions into

OPPOSITE Lanvin Kimono-style ensemble with
Japanese-inspired embellishment, c.1934

the mainstream, but it would be an oversight to ignore the designers who he himself admired and, indeed, cited as his own sources of inspiration.

This book has set out to emphasize that Balenciaga's truly original work, which constituted a radical departure from his peers, did not start until the post-war period. However, many of those who inspired and preceded him in taking an alternative path to that of the mainstream pre-date this time. Equally, while it is his post-war work that is mostly regarded as truly different, the ideas that were fundamental to these strikingly original silhouettes – namely, his treatment of the female body and his belief that fashion should not impede it – had been part of his work for much longer. Balenciaga's emphasis on the freedom of the female body is not altogether surprising, as his training as a designer coincided with important developments in fashion in the 1920s and '30s, not least the reconceptualization of the female body, the emergence of the New Woman, the new relationship between comfort and luxury, and indeed the liberation of the female form.

During his apprentice years Balenciaga was able to attend couture presentations, firstly in the resorts of Biarritz and San Sebastián. Later, while working at Les Grands Magasins du Louvre, he would travel to Paris to visit the trade couture shows since he was responsible for selecting and buying models that the department stores would interpret. As a result, although Balenciaga was not located in Paris, his knowledge of contemporary haute couture was up to date and extensive. Even after he opened his own establishment in San Sebastián, he continued to travel to Paris and attend the shows of his favourite couturiers, and he would incorporate their designs in his collections. Like many of

OPPOSITE Illustration from *Les Soieries Illustrées,* a fashion brochure for Parisian department store A Pygmalion, featuring a selection of ladies elegant house coats with kimono-style sleeves, Paris, 1909

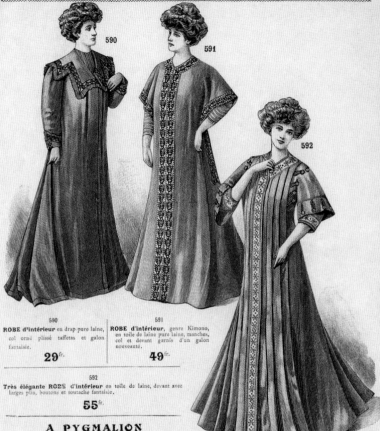

590
ROBE d'intérieur en drap pure laine,
col orné plissé taffetas et galon
fantaisie.

29fr.

591
ROBE d'intérieur, genre Kimono,
en toile de laine pure laine, manches,
col et devant garnis d'un galon
nouveauté.

49fr.

592
Très élégante ROBE d'intérieur en toile de laine, devant avec
larges plis, boutons et soutache fantaisie.

55fr.

A PYGMALION

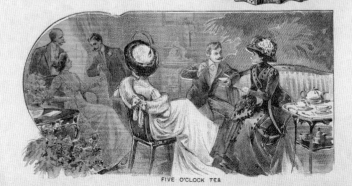

FIVE O'CLOCK TEA

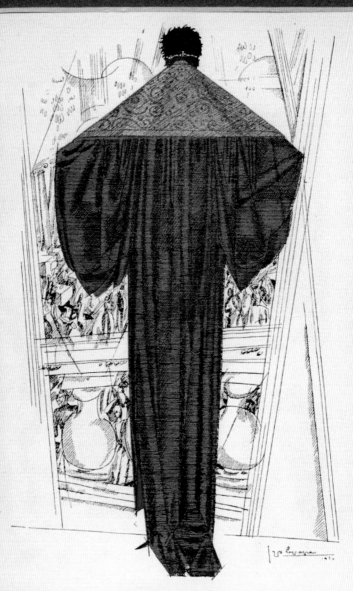

DANCING

Manteau du soir, de Paul Poiret

his contemporaries, Balenciaga attended a wide variety of couture shows and took inspiration from a cross-section, but the designers he most admired, and whose work he interpreted in his own collections, were female – specifically, Coco Chanel, Madeleine Vionnet, Louise Boulanger, Jeanne Lanvin and the Callot Soeurs.

All these designers were involved in redefining the fashionable female form. They were especially interested in liberating the female body from restrictive under- and outer garments. Their innovative pattern cutting was a great inspiration for Balenciaga and while his post-war work might not aesthetically resemble the work of these women, the ethos embodied by their oeuvre did.

The Callot Soeurs and Vionnet were particularly knowledgeable about non-Western patterns and techniques – including Arabic Moorish cutting, ancient Greek pleating and folding, and, possibly most influential of all, the Japanese kimono – and they incorporated and interpreted these extensively in their designs. Indeed, the T-shaped kimono (and the vogue for Japonisme) was instrumental in modernizing the fashionable wardrobe of the early twentieth century. Its shape was interpreted by all the most progressive haute couturiers of the time – Poiret, Paquin, Lanvin, Beer, Fortuny, Vionnet and Callot Soeurs – and it was instrumental in defining the flat silhouette of the early 1920s.

Balenciaga proposed his own interpretations of the kimono, albeit several decades later, and its influence can be discerned in several of his most innovative shapes: his 1947 barrel line and later his 1955 tunic silhouette, for example, were clearly indebted to the T-shape of the kimono. Its influence did not end there. Indeed, his cocoon coats featured the kimono's arched back; from 1939 onwards, he

OPPOSITE Paul Poiret "Dancing" evening coat illustrated by Georges Lepape, *La Gazette du Bon Ton*, 1920

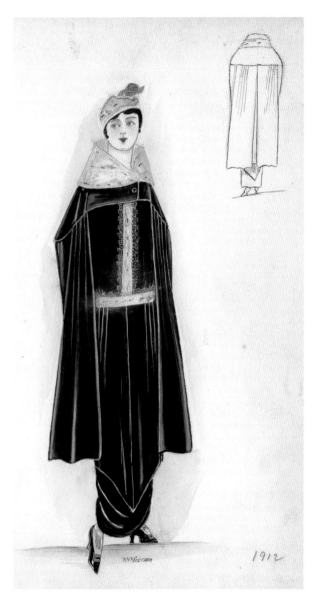

LEFT Callot Soeurs
black day dress with
matching cape, 1912

OPPOSITE
Mainbocher dresses
with Japanese
influences, *Vogue*,
1934

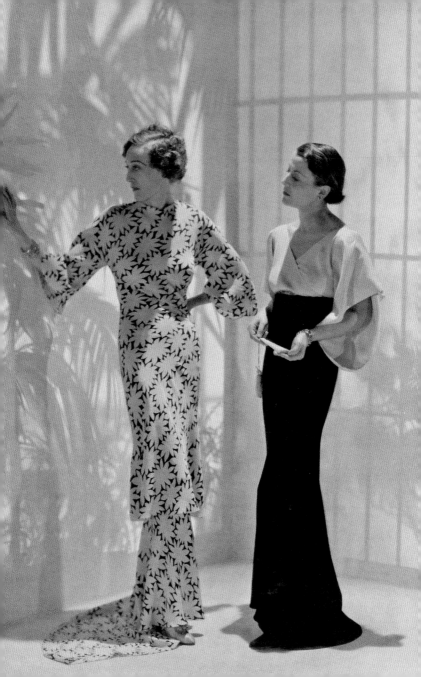

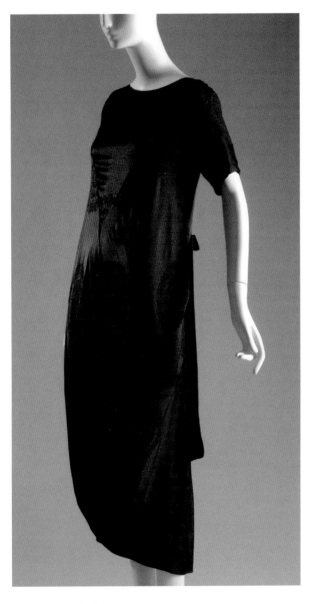

LEFT Callot Soeurs silk
jacquard afternoon
dress, c.1917

OPPOSITE Paul Poiret
"Sorbet" evening
dress in silk satin and
chiffon with glass
beads

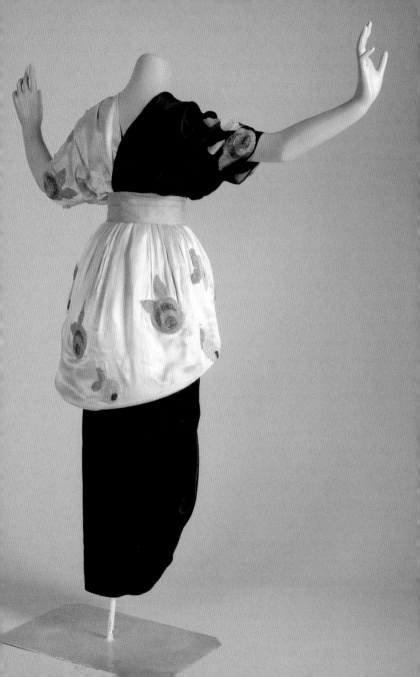

repeatedly interpreted kimono sleeves; his asymmetrical hems were shorter at the front than the back; and his haneri-like collars falling back to reveal the nape are all features of this traditional garment. Moreover, the way in which Balenciaga played with folds and volume, as in his spectacular 1967 chou wrap, referenced both the kimono and the early-twentieth-century designers who had championed Japonisme and incorporated it into their collections.

Thus, Japonisme and the kimono were arguably fundamental to Balenciaga's post-war work, but the other non-Western influences in his work, such as Moorish dress and Indian wrapping garments, should not be overlooked: their play with volume might not have translated literally into his creations, but the approach and relationship to space and the body suggested by them were a constant in his career. It should be noted, however, that Balenciaga's own design relationship with volume evolved significantly throughout his Parisian years, in yet another example of how he loved to take his time to develop and explore ideas at his own pace so he could test their limits. It could be contended that his Velázquez dresses of the late 1930s represented his first foray into experimentation with volume; that his voluminous silhouettes of the 1950s had a weightlessness, were more exaggerated and experimental, and moved away from their literal references; and that his designs during the 1960s arguably approached volume in an even more conceptual and rigid manner. So, although these periods have a clear aesthetic identity, the underlying idea remained the same: an exploration of the relationship between the body and space, influenced by history and multiple cultures.

OPPOSITE *Girl in a White Kimono* by George Hendrik Breitner, 1894

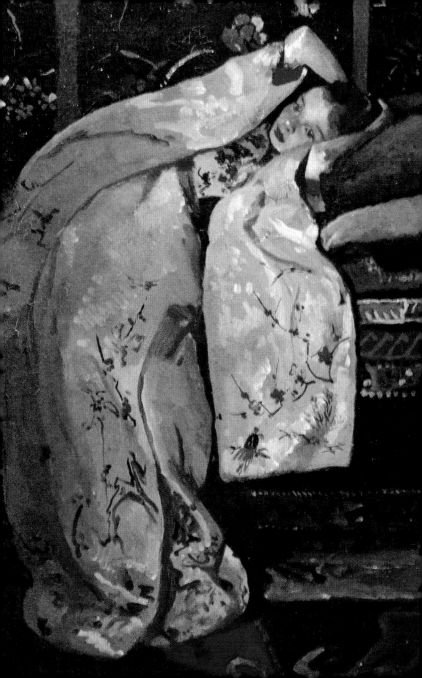

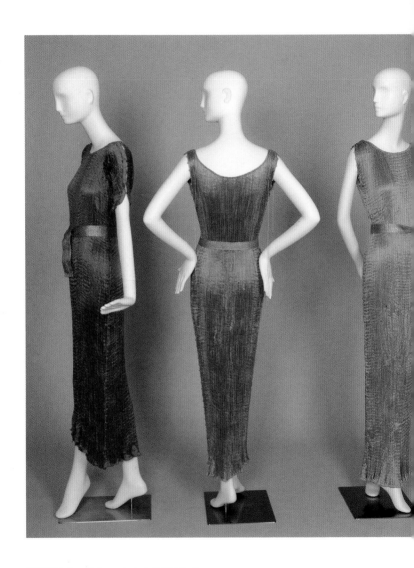

ABOVE Mariano Fortuny, pleated silk "Delphos"
dresses, c.1930s–1940s

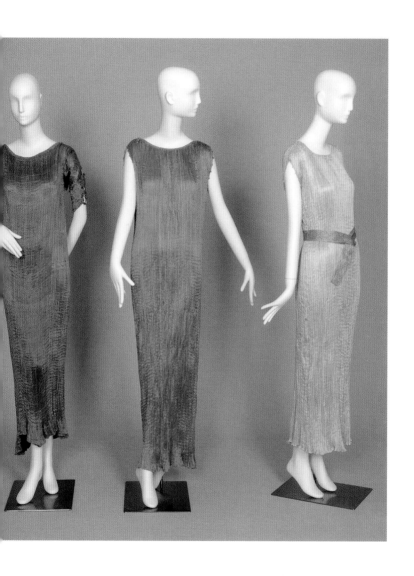

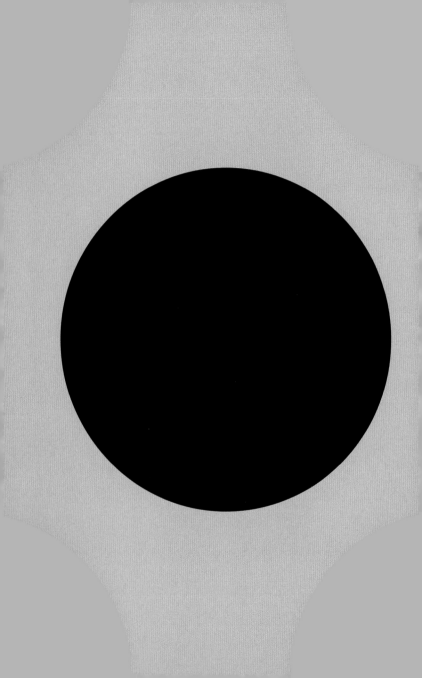

THE ROAD TO
ABSTRACTION

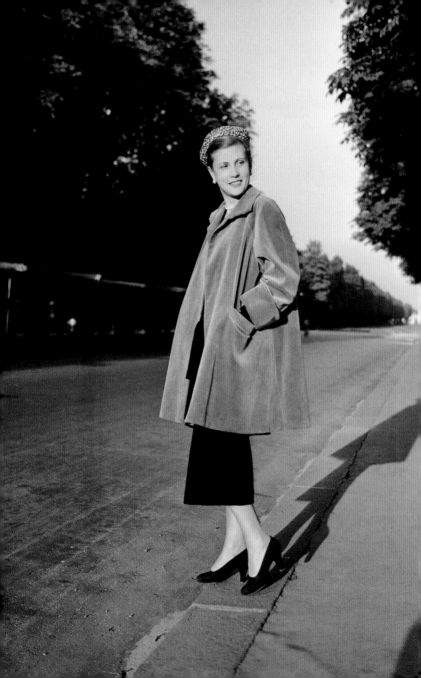

PLAYFUL
INNOVATION

Balenciaga's best-known pieces of work – and indeed the part of his oeuvre that has seen him referred to as a "great Modernist", the "high priest of haute couture" (*The Jewish Chronicle*, 1964), the "Shape master" (*Los Angeles Times*, 1957) and the "only true couturier" – are the designs he started producing after the Second World War.

O ver the next two decades he would slowly pare down his designs and strip away all superfluous detailing to achieve his iconic, sculptural, quasi-architectural and at times austere shapes of the 1960s. It is useful to trace his aesthetic development because it reveals the master's modus operandi: a near-obsessive perfecting of ideas through the meticulous exploration of their possibilities and limits.

Although there had been hints in his earlier work of things to come and how his aesthetic might evolve, it was Balenciaga's desire to offer an alternative to the dominant post-war silhouette that saw him move in a different direction to "the mainstream" by playing innovatively with shape, line and volume. What supported or lay at the base of these sartorial innovations was a profoundly different design approach to, and relationship with, the female body compared with that of his contemporaries.

OPPOSITE Balenciaga unfitted coat, 1947

The year 1947 witnessed the fashion bomb that was Dior's "New Look", which in many ways was the culmination of where Parisian fashion had been heading since 1939. It combined an 1850s rounded silhouette, full skirt and nipped-in waist to create the perfect hourglass shape. The word "create" is consciously used here, as Dior's garments necessitated a return to structuring undergarments and/or garment integral boning. For many, this full and luxurious silhouette marked a return to luxury and normality, although many others considered it regressive and outdated. Regardless of its detractors, this ultra-feminine line very quickly became the dominant post-war fashionable shape.

Dior was far from being the only couturier to put forward this vision of femininity. Several of his contemporary male colleagues – most notably Jacques Fath and Pierre Balmain – also took a sartorial approach which suggested through its structure that female bodies needed moulding and shaping, thus implying that the female body is flawed or lacking in some way and in need of enhancing.

Instead of wanting to restrict and accentuate the female body (and shackle it within the confines of an ideal shape), Balenciaga went the other way and started to play around with the space that exists between the body and the garment. In doing so, he started altering natural shapes and proportions rather than binding them into place. He preferred garments to move naturally with the body rather than restricting it and forcing unnatural movement.

While Dior was turning women into upside-down flowers, Balenciaga presented his cocoon coat, which had volume at the back and no defined waist, its rounded cutting presenting soft, sloping shapes and curves that only touched the body at the hem. It became an immediate success, hailed by the fashion press for its wearability, and was quickly copied by ready-to-wear

OPPOSITE Balenciaga striped wool coat, 1950

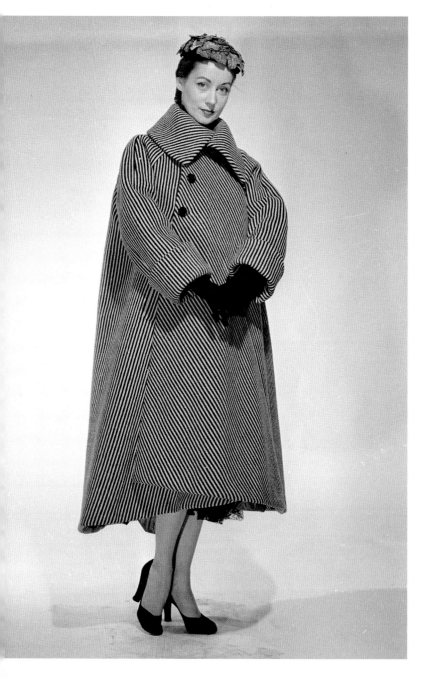

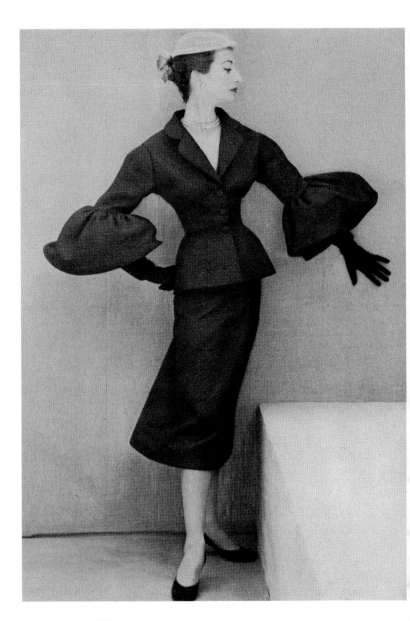

companies. This cocoon shape did not appear overnight but was instead a progression of a line Balenciaga had first proposed in 1942 when he designed a curve-shaped, three-quarter-length jacket that arched around the shoulders. This reworking and perfecting of cut and shape was a hallmark of Balenciaga's design methodology and his stylistic development and output.

The design also lays bare the other clear difference between the two post-war camps: the rapid change and heightened commercialism of Dior and his followers versus Balenciaga's preference for creating and introducing change and innovation at his own pace, showing that he was more concerned with creating classic styles than "Fashion" with a capital F. This approach meant his impact on the mainstream fashion world through replication by the ready-to-wear industry remained limited (with a few notable exceptions). Nevertheless Balenciaga quickly attracted a loyal and devoted set of customers and fans who appreciated his innovation and different method of working.

Very quickly Balenciaga's playing with space and volume developed into a bolder approach, and his dresses, suits and coats now started to take on increasingly large proportions through exaggerated draping and complex pattern cutting. The result was visually arresting and while very different from his contemporaries, it nevertheless had serious fashion gravitas, not least evidenced by the amount of coverage (and indeed covers) dedicated to his creations in upmarket magazines. In 1950, his mantle coat, an impressive yet wearable garment, presented a modern take on classic draping, while his now iconic bouffant, taffeta balloon dress which resembled two clouds was a striking play with volume. A year later the balloon motif was applied to the sleeves of an afternoon suit, again showing how Balenciaga took his time to explore and develop the full potential of shapes.

OPPOSITE Balenciaga tailored afternoon suit with balloon cuffs, *Vogue*, September 1951

Balenciaga's 1951 collection is considered by many a fashion historian to be the defining turning point in his aesthetic trajectory, as they argue that it presented models which would evolve and lead to future fashion revolutions. Most notable among these were his midi or Middy line – this would become "the tunic" – and his demi-fit which was the basis for his later sack dress. The "Middy", with its dropped waistline silhouette, was described by fashion editor Carmel Snow in *The Courier-Journal*, on 23 September 1951, as a line that "will bear watching". But it was near universally condemned by the mainstream press who (unjustly so) saw it as a return to the 1920s. Here are just two unfavourable comments from the press of the time, the first from *The New Yorker*, 22 September 1951, and the second from the *Indianapolis Times*, 15 October 1951:

> *"Balenciaga launched his long middy line with authority... We launch this objection with authority, too – we have behind us the authority of many millions of middle-aged, paunchy American males...It was one thing for us to cope with baggy, malformed women when Scott Fitzgerald was around to cheer us on...it's too much to ask us to accept girls whose pelvis appears to start just below the chin and look as though they had been hacked out of an old elm stump."*

> *"Mr. Balenciaga…is attempting to bring back the middy, the abominable style that made every woman look like a scarecrow in the Roaring Twenties…is preparing to get milady's hips slimmer, her derrière slimmer; well, just everything that has been built up over the years."*

OPPOSITE Balenciaga Middy blouse top in tartan over a matching full-pleated skirt, *Vogue*, September 1951

While it was not a great success commercially, the importance of Balenciaga's 1951 collection lies, as noted above, in the fact

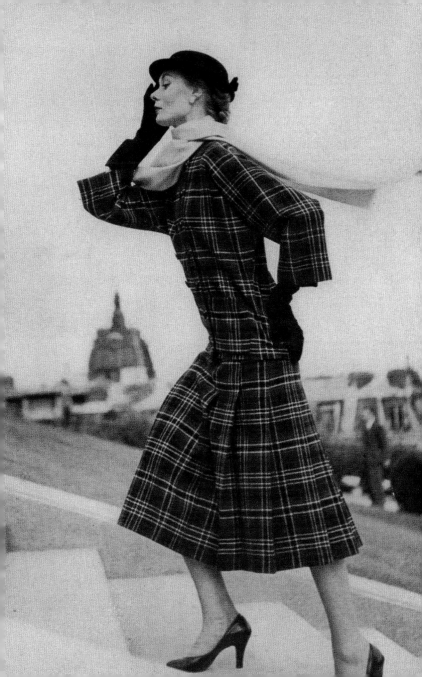

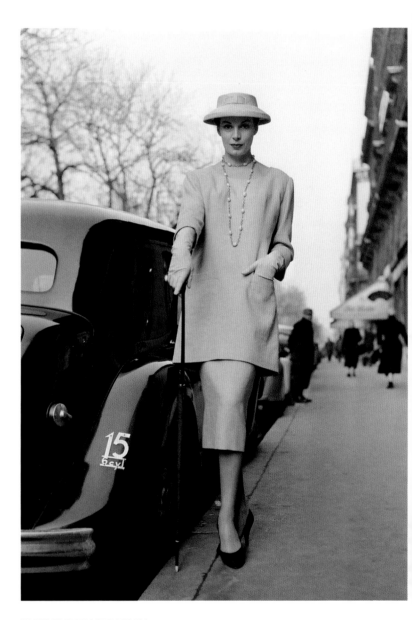

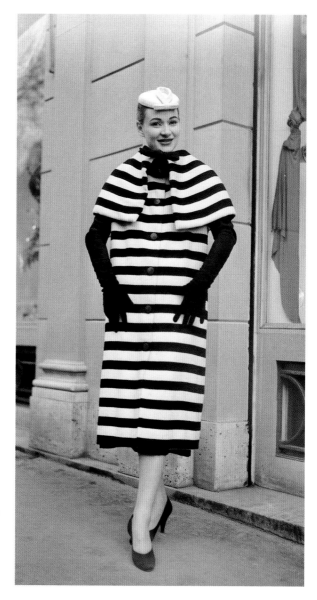

OPPOSITE Balenciaga
tunic silhouette, 1955

RIGHT Balenciaga
striped cape-coat,
1955

that it evolved into his tunic silhouette of 1955 and his sack/chemise dress of 1957.

Balenciaga's Tunic line, with its straight, slender cut that barely skimmed the body "represented a divorce between body and the dress" (*The Charlotte Observer*, 1 September 1955). It was initially met with mixed feelings: some journalists called the style a "shocker" (*The Philadelphia Inquirer*, 4 August 1955) and "deflated" (*The Morning Call*, 4 August 1955), but others praised its "wonderful newness" (*San Francisco Examiner*, 9 March 1955). On the one hand, the simplicity and linearity of the tunic dress drew emphasis away from the waist and, on the other, its skimming sheath nature proposed a different appreciation or celebration of femininity. More importantly, it set the tone for things to come, and was a clear precursor to the youth fashions of the 1960s.

However, it was Balenciaga's 1956–57 sack dress (also referred to as his chemise dress) – which had evolved out of his earlier barrel-, cocoon- and demi-fit lines – that took his level of abstraction to new heights and would consequently divide both the press and the public. Voluminous from the shoulders right to the tapered hem on the legs, the garment made no reference to the body within, which was completely de-emphasized. Its seemingly simple cut belied a technically complex structure. The waist, which had been such a focal point of Western fashion, was completely obliterated.

Traditionalists cried "infantalization" and deemed the sack dress a style only appropriate for children. These objections revealed more about prevailing ideas around femininity than they did about the sack, which, in fact, was the perfect symbiosis of dress and the female body and which had to be seen in motion to be fully appreciated.

A year later, Balenciaga's baby-doll dress, with its full, flaring trapezoidal design, once more played with volume and the

OPPOSITE Balenciaga black silk tunic with bow below the bosom, *Vogue*, October 1956

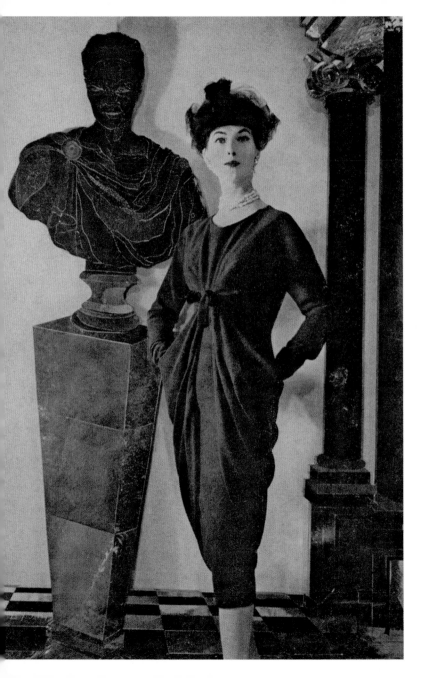

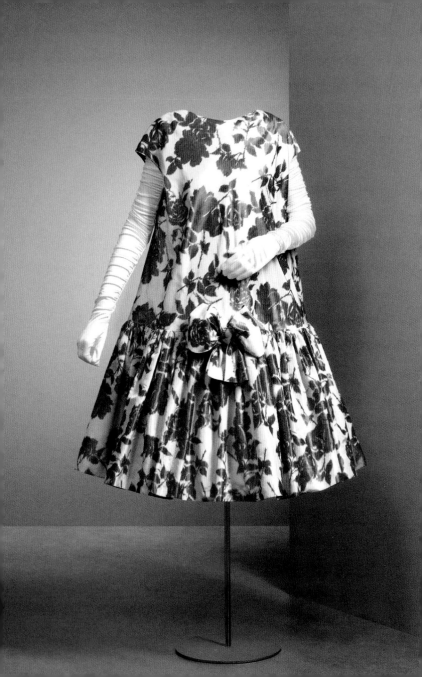

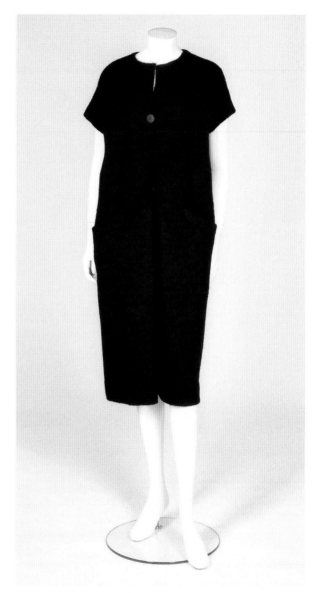

OPPOSITE Balenciaga
pink and white floral
baby-doll dress, 1958

RIGHT Balenciaga
black wool sack dress,
c.1962

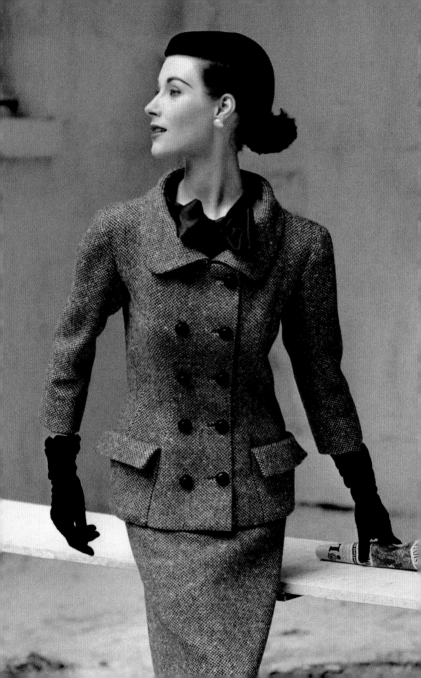

space between the garment and the body. The accusation of infantalization reared its head yet again, with some journalists describing the dresses – especially those executed in white and pastel-coloured cotton – as having "the look of a child's birthday party" (*The Philadelphia Enquirer*, 28 February 1958), while others compared them to a tea cosy (*The Salt Lake Tribune*, 29 August 1958). However, the aura of the baby-doll dress and its use depended on the fabric and colour in which it was executed. The transparent black lace versions, in particular, which were worn over a tight, black crêpe de Chine underdress, most certainly did not belong at a child's birthday party. Regardless of the more negative reactions, the trapezium-shaped baby-doll dress became a success and was quickly subsumed in other couturiers' collections.

It would be incorrect to think that these unfitted and increasingly experimental silhouettes meant Balenciaga completely renounced fitted clothing, as all his collections included tailored jackets and suits which were, in fact, his greatest successes from a commercial point of view. Indeed, many early businesswomen were great fans of his boxy jackets with slightly shorter sleeves that did not impede their hands in any way. A Balenciaga suit quickly became a symbol of success.

Aside from the baby-doll dress, the year 1958 also saw the introduction of the peacock-tail dress, which was based on the Spanish flamenco dress: short in the front and long in the back with a bunched, balloon skirt. An actual balloon-shaped dress from Balenciaga's Autumn/Winter presentation was arguably another step closer to abstraction and an almost outright denial of the body that it enveloped, but it still had an airy, almost weightless, appearance. This airiness would soon be replaced with a clean-cut rigidity, and his work with space would become less playful and more architectural – and come to define the final phase of his design career.

OPPOSITE Balenciaga double-breasted tweed suit, *Vogue*, September 1952

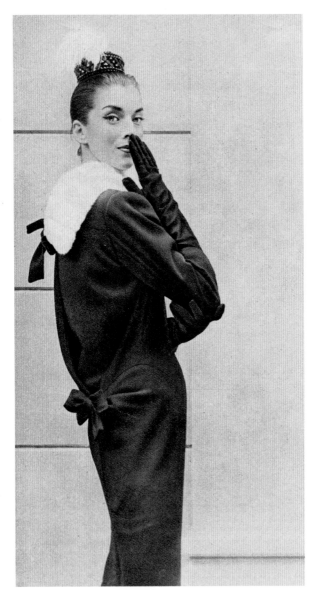

LEFT Balenciaga
black tunic gown
with back bow detail
and statement
hat, *Frankfurter
Illustrierte*,
September 1955

OPPOSITE Balenciaga
tiered balloon evening
gown, 1965

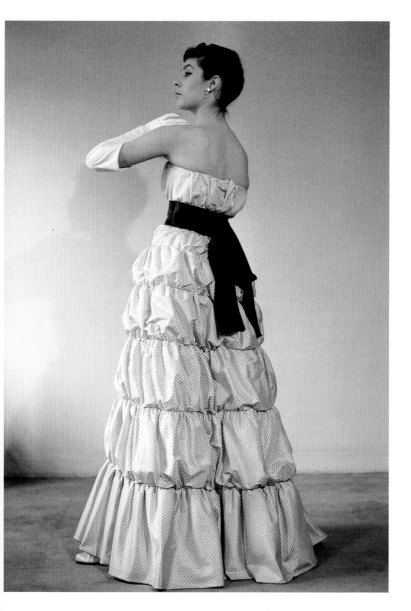

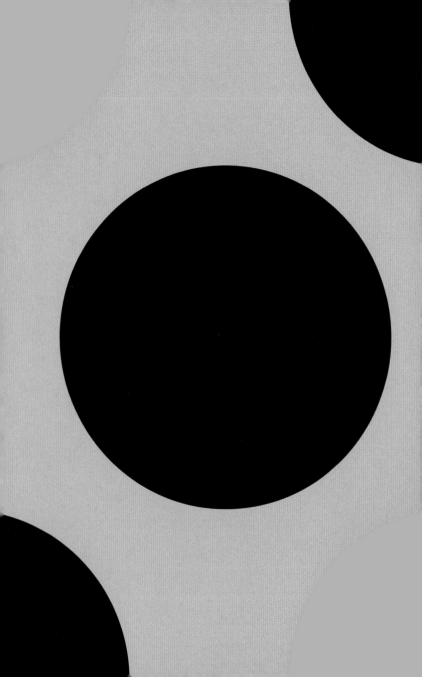

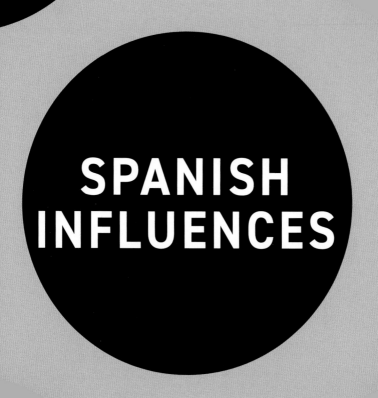

SPANISH INFLUENCES

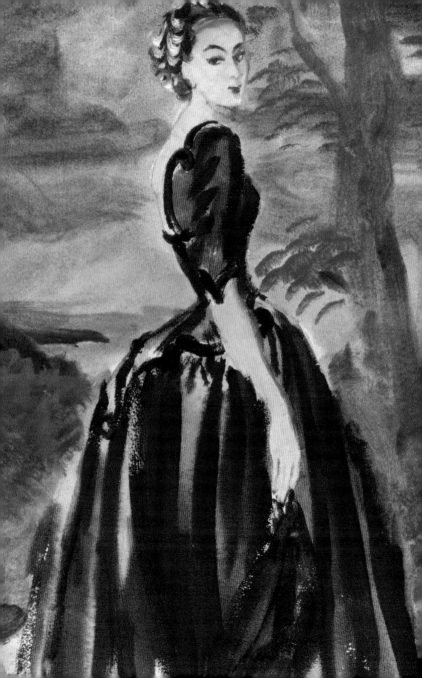

HOMELAND ECHOES

"[Balenciaga's] inspiration came from the bullrings, the flamenco
dancers, the fishermen in their boots and loose blouses,
the glories of the church and the cool of the cloisters and
monasteries. He took their colour, their cuts then festooned
them to his own taste." — Diana Vreeland, fashion editor

Fashion designers draw inspiration from different sources
from one collection to the next, but many tend to have
certain themes – leitmotifs, if you will – to which they
return time and again, and Balenciaga was no exception. His
overarching leitmotif is best described as Spanish-ness.

Even though Balenciaga moved to Paris in 1937 and worked
out his career in this city, it needs to be remembered that he
already had a near two-decade career under his belt in Spain.
Indeed, his formative years and experiences were exclusively
rooted in his native country. Even after settling in France and
climbing to the top of the haute couture industry, Balenciaga
always remained the "Spaniard in Paris" and maintained strong
links with his homeland, his family and his Spanish businesses.
He kept several flats and houses in Spain, where he would often
travel for work and where he spent his holidays surrounded by
family and a few chosen close friends.

OPPOSITE Balenciaga Velázquez or Infanta dress,
Vogue, September 1939

In Paris Balenciaga ran his couture house by bringing over the best staff from his Madrid and San Sebastián ateliers, and in turn he would send his most talented French staff to train at his Spanish enterprises. He never fully mastered French and it is no coincidence that many of the principal positions at his fashion house were occupied by Spanish speakers and that workroom conversations were mostly conducted in Spanish.

The press picked up on Balenciaga's close ties to his native country and many an article focused on the Spanish motifs and themes in his designs. In 1948, *Harper's Bazaar* asserted that "in his collection there is always an echo of his native land, an evocation of the Spain of brilliant colours, beads and paillettes, pompoms and the little matador jacket". While claiming that this was true of all his collections might be somewhat exaggerated, nevertheless many of these elements did indeed recur in his oeuvre. Even in his later, more austere and "clean" silhouettes the references to Spain were still there, albeit executed in a less explicit, more abstract and conceptual manner compared to the more literal translations in his earlier work.

Balenciaga's Spanish influences can roughly be divided into two categories (which we look at in this chapter and the next): traditional, historic and folk dress, and religious dress, although in reality the division is less clear-cut since religion had permeated all aspects of Spanish life over the centuries and inevitably filtered through into folk costume. While it is impossible to explore all the elements and details in Balenciaga's work in this volume, the major themes and references that led to important innovations will be addressed, so as to identify not only where his ideas came from but also how they were used.

The matador jacket, or *traje de luces*, was a favourite source of inspiration, and lavishly embellished and beaded bolero jackets were found in several of his pre-1950s collections. As noted by

OPPOSITE Balenciaga "Infanta" dress, 1939

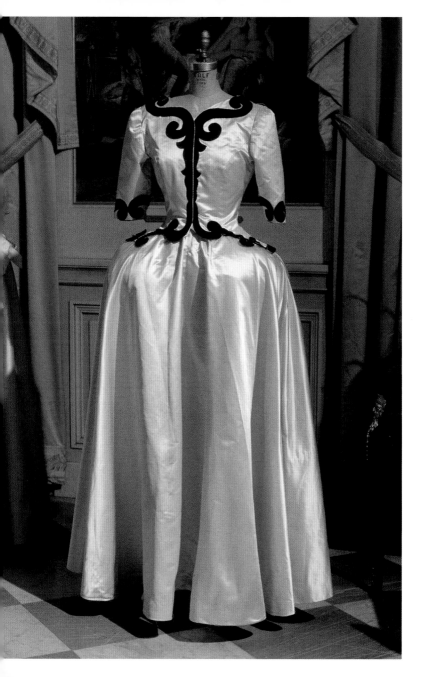

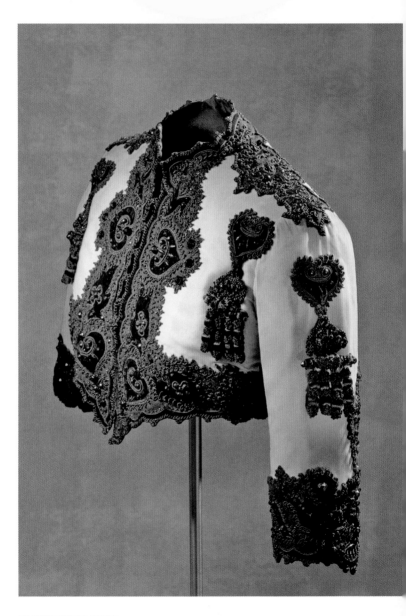

Miren Allurez – whose research features in Hamish Bowles's 2011 book *Balenciaga and Spain* – San Sebastián was the first Spanish city to advertise bullfights, with posters often featuring renditions of the glamorous matadors, so it is very likely Balenciaga grew up surrounded by this imagery. He is said to have hated real bullfights, but since the late nineteenth century the imagery of the bullfighter had been closely associated with Spanish national identity and public imagination – so Balenciaga's use of this as a reference is neither contradictory nor surprising.

One of the first mentions by the international press of a matador reference appeared in 1939 when *Harper's Bazaar* featured Balenciaga's "bullfighter snoods" (1 September 1939), but the first actual bullfighter-inspired jacket did not appear until 1943 and was illustrated for the French fashion press by Raymond Brenot. A year later, in his first post-Liberation collection, which was described as including "all Spanish ideas" (*The Province*, 9 December 1944), Balenciaga presented afternoon dresses worn with sequinned, crocheted, knitted and embroidered boleros, but his most spectacular versions, those most closely modelled on the matador jacket, were executed between 1946 and 1949. Aside from the matador jacket, and specifically its traditionally rich embellishments, the colour palette of the bullfighter costume can also be discerned in several of his creations, specifically his use of brilliant yellow and bright pink, which were two colours traditionally used for the matador cape. The matador hat – the *montera* – also appeared in various incarnations; these often tended to be paired with almost austere silhouettes as if to add an element of playfulness, but also to avoid a result that too closely resembled costume or looked old-fashioned – Balenciaga may have referenced tradition and the past, but the outcome was always resolutely fashion that presented new ways of using these ideas.

OPPOSITE EISA blue matador bolero, 1947

Spanish dance dresses, and the flamenco dress in particular, were another source of inspiration to which Balenciaga returned on several occasions. Flamenco dancers had captured the imagination and attention of artists since the nineteenth century, when *café cantantas* (cabarets) had started introducing flamenco to popular culture – artists such as Gustave Doré and John Singer Sergeant, and others, were all captivated by this fierce gypsy dance. The 1920s saw a revival of flamenco and, indeed, gitano (gypsy) culture in an effort to preserve their traditions, and this was therefore another aspect of Spanish-ness that was part of Balenciaga's formative years. Flamenco dancers such as Carmen Amaya and La Argentina, and later Lola Flores, became international sensations and introduced new audiences to the dance and its costume: the *bata de cola*.

The *bata de cola* dress was designed so as to extend the line of the flamenco dancer and exaggerate and dramatize the rapid flips of the flounced train. Balenciaga repeatedly used the *bata de cola* in his creations, both literally and in more abstract evocations. Sometimes the inspiration was found in the shape, sometimes in the fabric choice, at times in both. From the black velvet evening gowns with pink silk taffeta or white tulle ruffles from 1951 which closely mimicked the lines and effect of the flamenco dress, via his 1960s black-and-white, polka-dot creations, to his more abstract peacock dresses with ruffled hems of the late 1950s, or their pared-down successors from the 1960s, the austere, silk gazar versions… all found their origin in the flamenco dress.

Aside from these two iconic costumes that were so aligned with Spanish national identity, Balenciaga also explored Spanish regional costumes that were less familiar (particularly to non-natives) but which also regularly found their way into his aesthetic language. Prior to his move to Paris, he had travelled extensively in Spain, which at the time was going through a renaissance of

OPPOSITE Balenciaga flamenco-style evening gown with shocking pink taffeta on the graduated skirt, c.1958

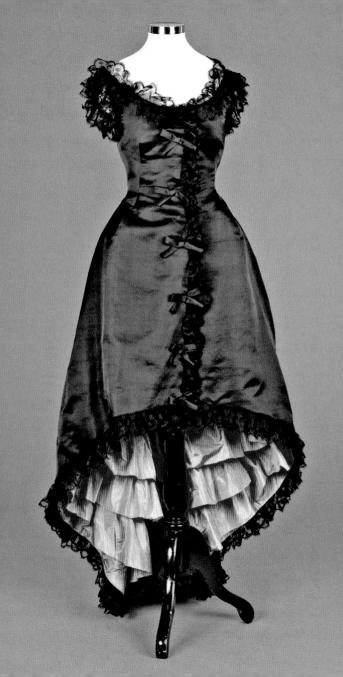

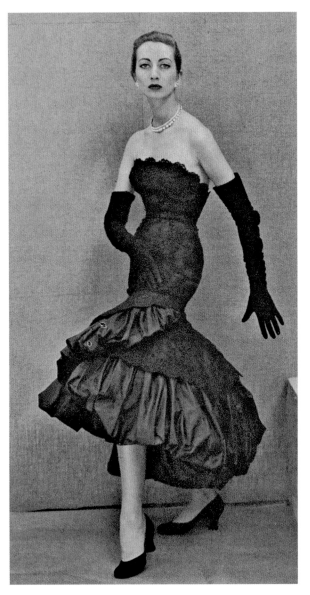

OPPOSITE Balenciaga polka dot evening dress, 1959

LEFT Balenciaga black lace-over-taffeta sheath with a double frill fan skirt, *Vogue*, September 1951

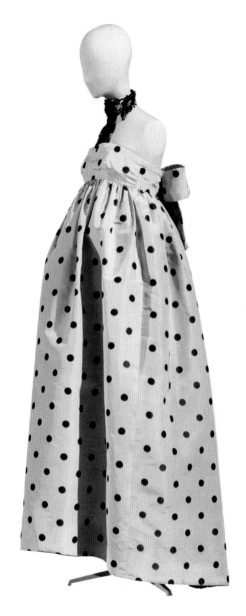

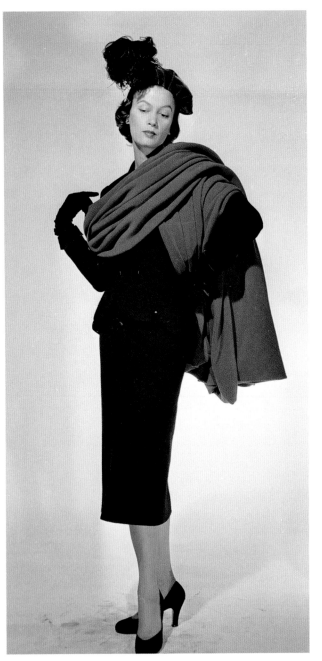

LEFT Balenciaga wool
suit with large draped
scarf, 1950

local and folk culture, so his exposure to this heritage was natural and inevitable. He is said to have collected folk and regional costume, and printed sources on Spanish dress history, and taken all together this goes a long way to explain the references that would crop up throughout his career: the pleated skirts of Cáceres, the rich appliqué work of Salamanca and the headdresses of Navarre…these were all reflected later in his creations.

One item of dress that needs specific mention is the cloak or cape. These were found in many regional dress styles across Spain, and it is no surprise that they were also a near constant in Balenciaga's work. Throughout his career he showed, as Hamish Bowles observes, "capes and cloaks in the manner they were worn in Spain" – that is, often voluminous and/or expertly pleated. His cape from 1956, which could also be worn as an overskirt or apron, finds close parallels in the folk dress of several regions – although Ruth Anderson notes in her book *Spanish Costume: Extremadura* that "the habit of using the upper skirt as a cloak is common". His 1950 pleated and draped cape coats also owed a clear debt to the cloaks of Northern Spain.

Balenciaga did not limit his referencing to traditional costume (which was often used for special occasions such as weddings or religious festivals); he also looked towards Basque everyday workwear. The beret, worn by Basque shepherds, can be repeatedly found in his 1960s' output, but it was the traditional shepherd's loose-fitting shirt jacket that would have the most profound fashion impact through its translation into his post-war suits and revolutionary blouses and tunics.

Through his creative reworking of the traditional and folk elements of Spanish costume in his couture creations, Balenciaga not only introduced his country's sartorial heritage to a global audience, but more importantly his conceptual play within workwear revolutionized the post-war female wardrobe.

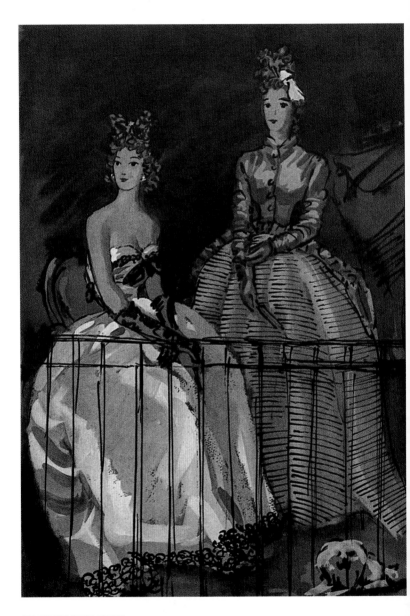

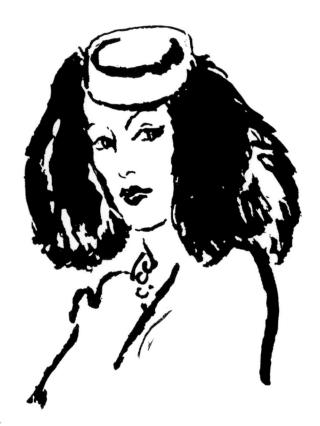

OPPOSITE Two
Balenciaga Goya-
inspired pannier
dresses, *Vogue*,
July 1939

RIGHT Balenciaga
"Velázquez" hat made
of violet felt flanked
with fox tails, *Vogue*,
September 1939

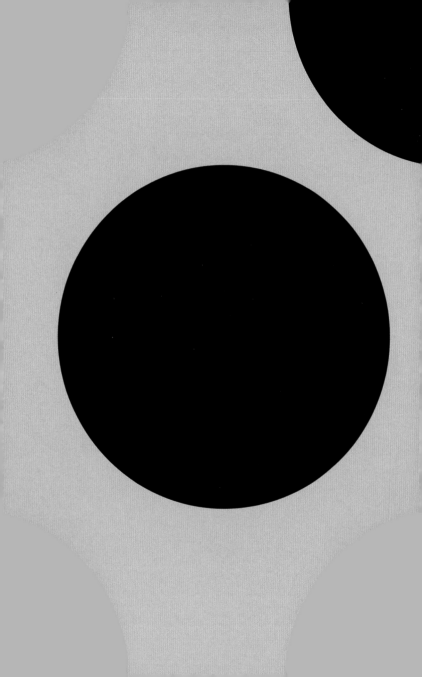

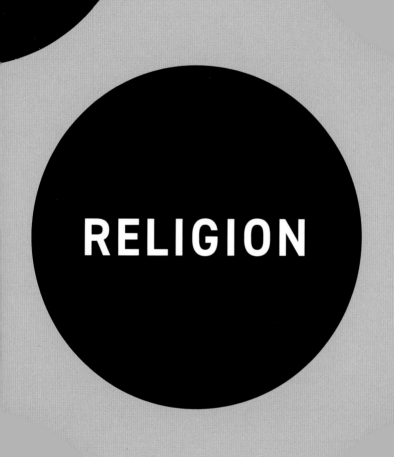

RELIGION

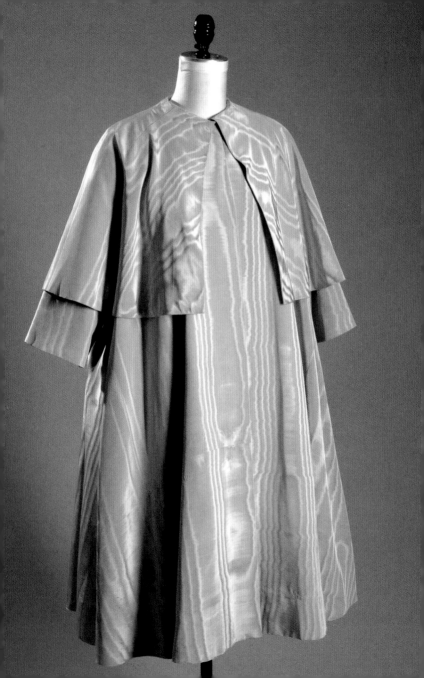

TAKING THE CLOTH

"The simple and minimalist lines of religious habits and the architectural volume of the fabrics were a constant in his pieces."
— Eloy Martínez de la Pera Celada, curator

As we saw in earlier chapters, both Spain and Spanish-ness shaped and became a strong thread throughout Balenciaga's career. The previous chapter identified some of the major themes that linked his designs aesthetically to his home nation but one specific subset, as it were, of the Spanish influences that shaped his work, and indeed his life, more profoundly than any other, was religion. As Hamish Bowles, writer and curator, explains: the "profound and pervasive influence of the Catholic church on the Spanish psyche and on its culture and its art was abundantly manifest in Balenciaga's work".

Balenciaga was a devout Catholic his entire life. A committed altar boy from an early age, he toyed with the idea of following his uncle into the priesthood, but even though he changed course to embark on a career in fashion, his commitment to the Church remained strong. Indeed, on several occasions he applied his expertise to executing religious vestments – most notably the cassock worn by the priest who gave Christian Dior's eulogy at his funeral in 1957 – and choral gowns. The couturier André Courrèges, who

OPPOSITE Balenciaga silk moire evening coat inspired by a cassock and cape, 1950 trained under him, remembered the opening and closing of his mentor's office door at least once a day as he went off to pray in a nearby church.

Balenciaga's commitment to Catholicism can be discerned in creations throughout his career, but his later designs in particular owed much to the austere yet imposing nature of religious dress. His designs reinterpreted elements from nuns' habits, priests' chasubles and cassocks, monks' hooded robes, religious head coverings and even the embellished robes that clad the statues of the Madonna carried through the streets during Holy Week.

The inspiration he drew from religion can be roughly attributed to two sources: he was inspired both by its practice and role in Spanish life and by its historic representation in Spanish art history. Once again it would be impossible to address every single instance of inspiration or reference in this book, but by examining a few choice examples it will become clear just how Balenciaga incorporated religious tradition and art into his designs.

The relationship between fashion and religion might appear to be one of opposites, but Catholicism in fact has a close and longstanding relationship to cloth and material: not merely through the religious vestments worn by men of the cloth, but also through its historic modesty diktats and sumptuary laws, its ceremonial use of fabrics and garments and the importance of materials in transubstantiation and relics. The shift in focus of the young Balenciaga from a life dedicated to the Church to one dedicated to fashion is therefore not as dramatic as it may at first appear. Neither was his continued use of religion in his oeuvre, especially as he always aimed to respectfully translate tradition into something original and modern – while the references were there, they were never easy, literal or derivative.

As with all his techniques and influences, once Balenciaga had settled on "something", he took his time to explore, test and

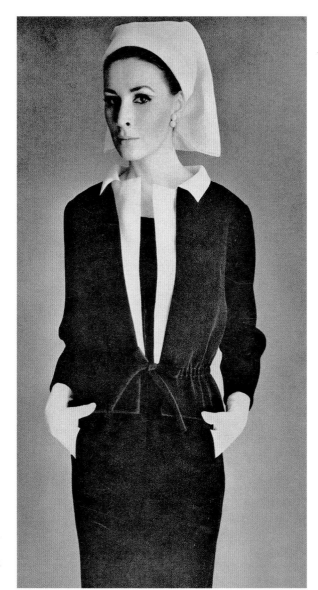

RIGHT Balenciaga
sleeveless black
alpaca dress and
short, tie-waisted
jacket with white
organdie, styled with
a hat resembling
a nun's wimple to
highlight Balenciaga's
use of religious
influences, *The Tatler*,
24 March 1965

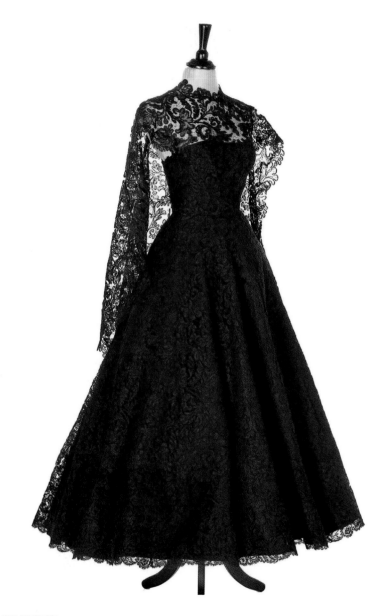

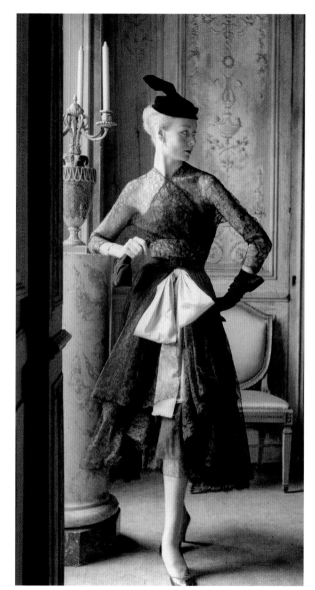

OPPOSITE Balenciaga
black lace evening
gown, inspired by the
mantilla, 1951

RIGHT A Balenciaga
licensed copy – a
black lace dress with
a pink sash, *Vogue*,
October 1951

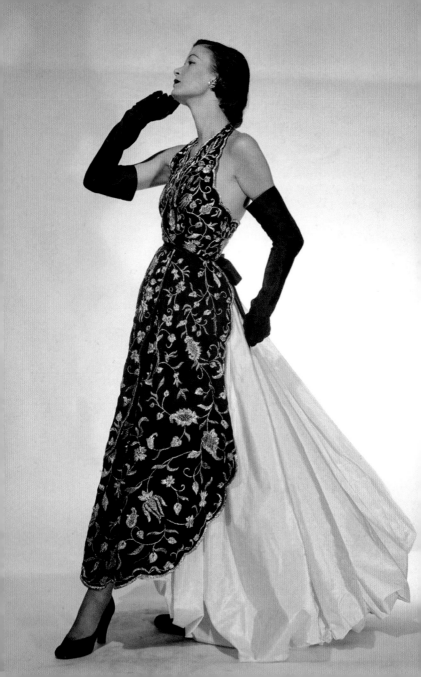

develop it to its limits. His religious influences were no different. Owing to this approach, the mantilla, a delicate Spanish lace scarf worn over the head and shoulders, was reinterpreted as fashion on numerous occasions. White mantillas often accompanied Balenciaga's wedding dresses and his 1950 collection featured a black mantilla embroidered with gold thread paired with a flamenco-inspired, tiered, tulle dress. On other occasions, he bunched the mantilla into bodices, capelets or puff sleeves, or layered the delicate black lace over brightly coloured silks; his most famous use of black lace was in his iconic 1958 baby-doll dress.

Another potent source of inspiration were the lavish embroideries on chasubles and those on the brilliantly coloured robes created for Madonna figures. Writer, biographer and journalist Judith Thurman observes that Balenciaga "adapted the vestments of his parish church…for the wardrobe of the worldly woman" and, indeed, the influence of the embellishments of these robes can be clearly discerned in some of his most spectacular evening gowns. Not only did he interpret the traditional metallic gold and silver designs, but their placement on his creations – with the focus on the bodice and hem or all-over scattered motifs – also referenced their originals. Further examples include an exquisite purple, silk velvet coat from 1951, evoking the robes of popes and cardinals through both its cut and colour, and the billowing drapery of much of his early 1950s work that bears a striking resemblance to Spanish religious art from the seventeenth and eighteenth centuries – which, incidentally, he collected.

A black evening cape and gown from 1967 resemble both a friar's habit and a cardinal's mozzetta and the austerity of the cut, set off by the luxurious fabric, embodies the "excessive restraint" that is central to Catholic art. Balenciaga's iconic one-seam wedding dress from the same year has a stiff, structured veil modelled on a nun's wimple and is a triumph of construction,

OPPOSITE Balenciaga embroidered organza apron dress with taffeta train, 1950

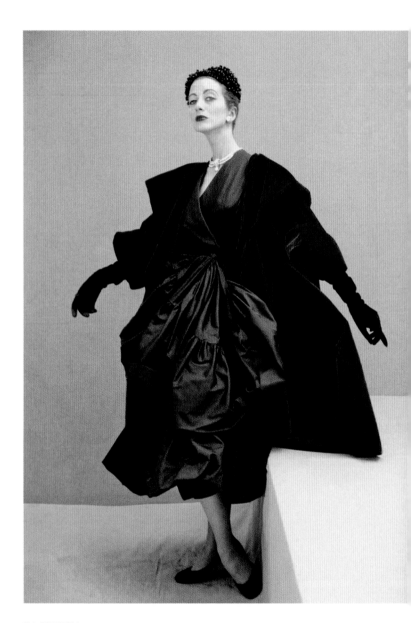

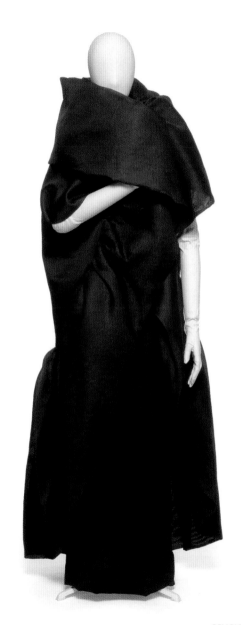

OPPOSITE Balenciaga
black taffeta wrap
dress with a balloon-
frill hemline under a
wide-sleeved cape-
collared purple silk
velvet coat, 1951

RIGHT Balenciaga
evening wrap coat,
1962

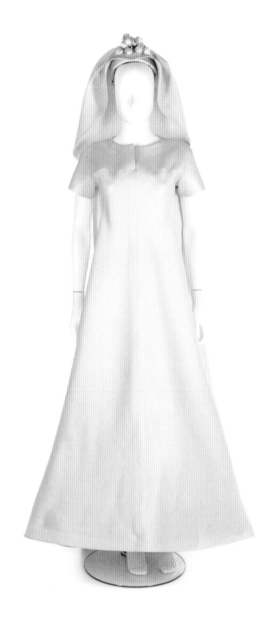

LEFT AND OPPOSITE
Balenciaga ivory
slubbed silk gazar
bridal gown and
matching EISA veil,
1968

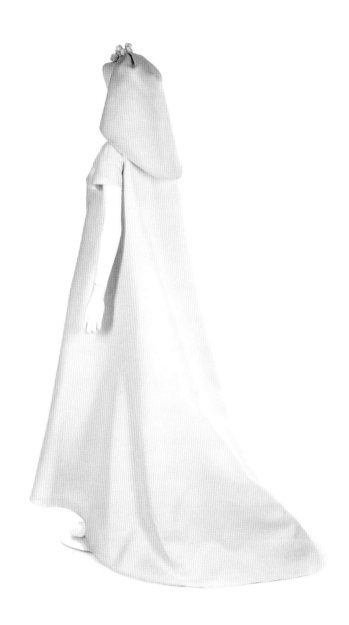

restraint and modesty. Even his love for and prolific use of deep black can be understood in the context of Catholic asceticism.

Balenciaga's engagement with Catholicism extended beyond the lived culture he had known since he was a young boy and encompassed its representation in Spanish art – references to Spanish art, and specifically religious art, were always highly present in his work. The direct relationship between his work and painting first became explicit in 1939 through his Infanta dress, but it's his post-war garments that were more conceptually related to religious art. Many of Balenciaga's wedding dresses resembled the cut and draping of the garments worn in Francisco de Zurbarán's seventeenth-century paintings of monks and saints; his early 1960s evening dress and jacket combinations bore more than a striking resemblance to Goya's painting of Cardinal Luis María de Borbón y Vallabriga; his choice of deep blues, crimson reds and mustard golds…all are straight out of El Greco's colour palette for his religious paintings.

It's worth noting that the influence of religion was seen not just in his creations but also in their making, his Parisian workrooms and salon being described by various parties as monastic. There was near total silence – any minimal conversation was conducted in hushed tones. The atmosphere was not unlike that of a church, and its seriousness and severity were felt by all visitors. Balenciaga's all-consuming focus and concentration during the making process could be described as akin to praying, and some of his closest co-workers testified that when he was trying to perfect the cut of a dress or figure out a pattern, he would pass a small piece of fabric between his fingers just as one would a rosary. Catholicism was a constant in Balenciaga's life, proving an enduring source of inspiration and reference, and indeed he worked at his craft with a near-religious devotion throughout his career to reimagine historic, religious costume in a modern and relevant way.

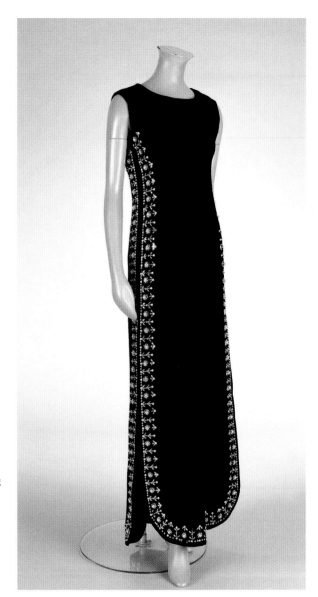

RIGHT
EISA black velvet
evening gown bearing
black EISA label,
curved front and
back panels edged in
dramatic gold beads,
silver leaf-shaped
sequins, pearls and
rhinestones, 1967

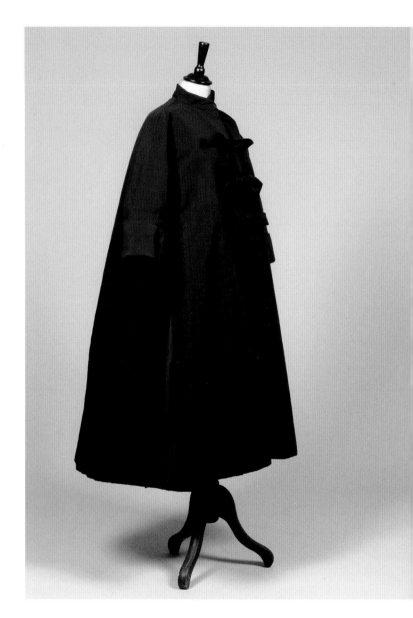

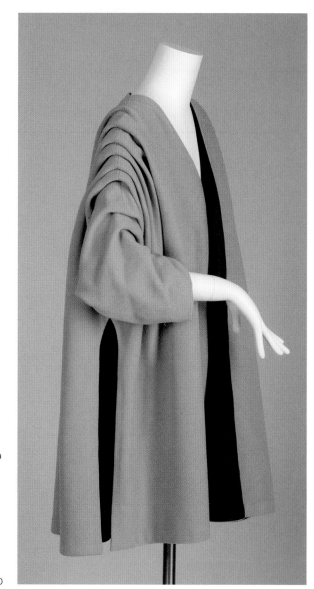

OPPOSITE Balenciaga
black silk faille coat
with short stand
collar in the style of a
cassock, c.1957

RIGHT Balenciaga
wool gabardine and
silk taffeta pleated
and draped coat, 1950

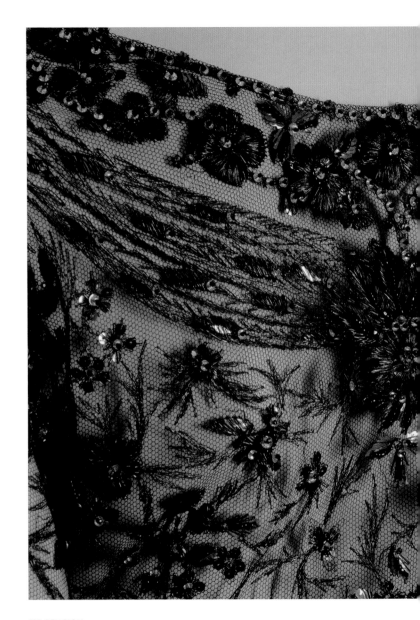

LEFT Back detailing on a Balenciaga evening jacket made up of silk faille, net, glass beads and sequins, 1955

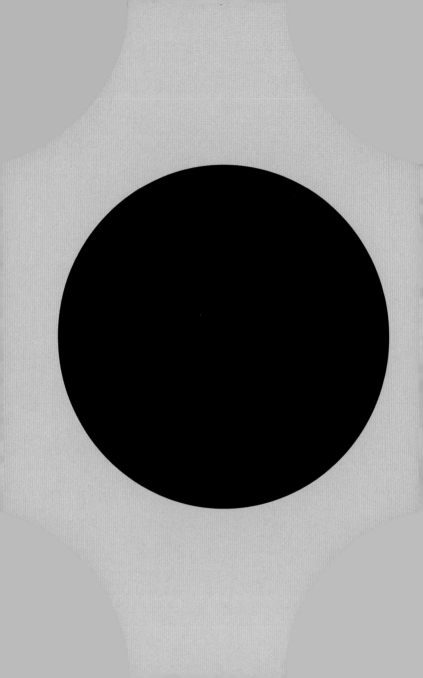

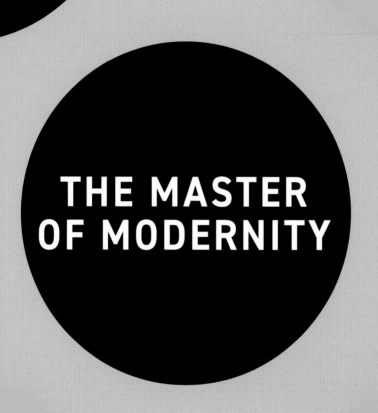

THE MASTER
OF MODERNITY

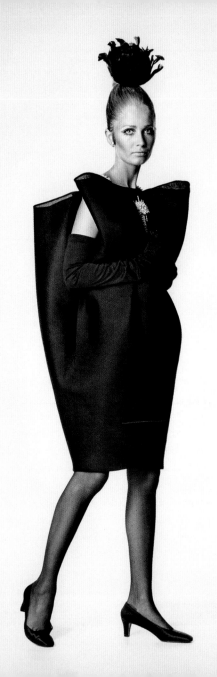

THE ARCHITECT OF HAUTE COUTURE

"Austerity and sobriety, balance and proportion, coherence and perfection, innovation and timelessness."
— Eloy Martínez de la Pera (art and fashion curator)

In many ways, Balenciaga's creations of the 1960s are best understood as a refinement of the designs, techniques and shapes he pioneered in the 1950s, highlighting his modus operandi: working and reworking ideas over time to test their limits and perfect them. Many of the silhouettes produced by Balenciaga in his final years as haute couturier are those for which is best remembered and the ones that were instrumental in earning him the accolade given by Hubert de Givenchy – he was the "architect of haute couture".

While Balenciaga's experiments with volume, which characterized his oeuvre during the 1950s, retained a sense of airiness, his 1960s work took on a more austere character. He presented more rigid architectural and moulded shapes which were achieved through a combination of new materials and mathematically refined patterns. The geometric shapes favoured by Balenciaga were constructed from cylindrical and spherical patterns and the joining of half circles. Yet while the finished product, devoid of all surface decoration so as not to distract

OPPOSITE Balenciaga "Envelope" dress, *Vogue*, September 1967

from the pure line of the silhouette, might appear minimal or straightforward, it was anything but. In fact, the perfect balance of his creations barely do justice to the complexity of their inner workings – each aspect, every detail, every cut and stitch was carefully planned out, worked and reworked to realize the master's vision.

Balenciaga's work from this period is often referred to as minimalist, positioning it alongside art and architecture, to which it has indeed been compared ever since. It has been suggested that his increasingly abstract experiments with form were paralleled by an increasing engagement with the world of contemporary art through his friendships with art collectors, and that the work of artist Joan Miró was particularly influential.

Although this is one way of framing the creations that defined the final phase of Balenciaga's career, it is perhaps more useful to think of these designs as the culmination of his ideas and craftsmanship. Indeed, the former "explanation" would imply a departure from his earlier influences and design themes, while thinking of them as the designs of a "young man with all the knowledge" (as described by Pauline de Rothschild, a socialite and Balenciaga customer) not only acknowledges that his design inspirations in the 1960s were a continuation of those that went before, but also highlights the garments' innovative and visionary qualities and honours the highly developed pattern-making and sewing skills that went into making them. They were the work of someone with a young eye and spirit as well as the skills and experience of a seasoned master. As historian Eloy Martínez de la Pera puts it: "his constant search for perfection translates to the rigorous, almost obsessive process of creation that seeks the most special aspects of the fabrics, cut and body and in which finishes, and sometimes inappreciable details, are essential for devising the perfect attire for imperfect bodies, making them beautiful."

OPPOSITE Balenciaga dark blue silk dress and cape, early 1960s

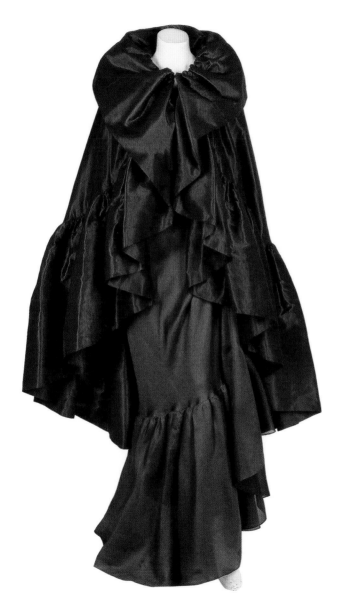

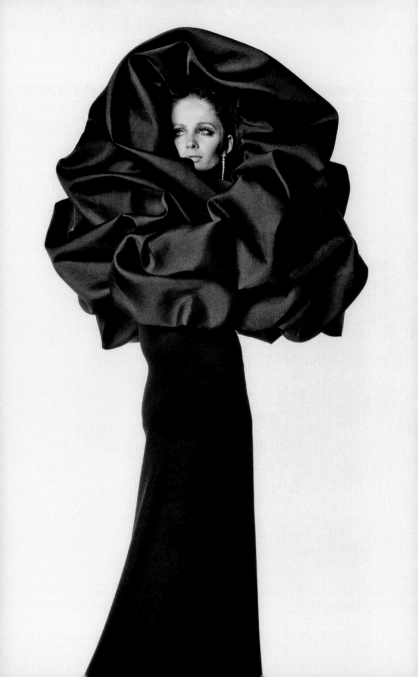

As we have seen, his tailoring work took on stylistically architectural tendencies, in both his arresting evening and occasion wear and his daywear suits. Balenciaga's dresses and coats at times moved closer to sculpture than clothing and yet remained – with a few exceptions – comfortable to wear. In this period, he returned to his earlier explorations of the garment as a capsule, involving the creation of sculptural space between the body and the clothing, an idea rooted in traditional Japanese pattern-cutting. From 1962 in particular, this translated as a move into increasingly abstract shapes that go beyond the body and resulted in truly novel, yet refined and timeless, silhouettes that enveloped the body but did not constrain it. Nor were the garments or silhouettes constrained by the body.

It should be emphasized that these creative leaps were both driven and underpinned by Balenciaga's deep knowledge of fabric and his use of materials. For his coveted tailored daywear suits he favoured mohair and wool mixes and substitutes (whose creation he was often closely involved with), while for his sculpted evening and formal wear he worked in silk faille and, more importantly, gazar, a fabric that he commissioned in 1958. Gazar was developed by the Swiss textile firm Abraham and was thicker and more pliable than other silks on the market due to its high-twist, double silk thread, which also gave the material a crisp, smooth texture. The fabric was perfect for both Balenciaga's love of highly ornate embroidery work (which decreased but far from disappeared in his custom-made work of the 1960s) and his need for a material that was capable of supporting his new architectural shapes. Gazar allowed Balenciaga to create volume through its inherent qualities rather than having to rely on supporting under-structures. His 1967 envelope dress and his chou wrap from the same year perfectly illustrate the structural possibilities of gazar, the dress being aptly described by curator and historian Alexandra

OPPOSITE Balenciaga chou wrap of crumpled black gazar that wraps around the head like a huge rose, *Vogue*, September 1967

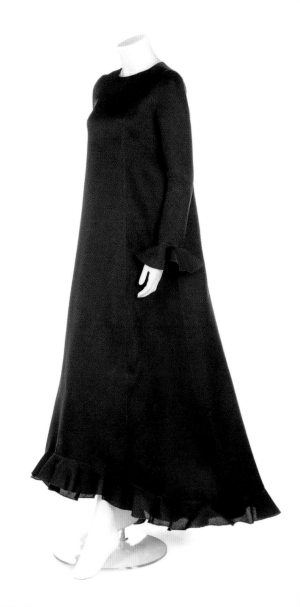

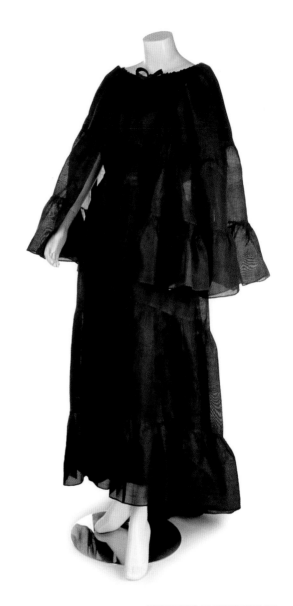

OPPOSITE Balenciaga
black gazar evening
gown with flounces
to cuffs and trained
hem, 1967

RIGHT Balenciaga
black couture gazar
evening gown and
cape, 1962

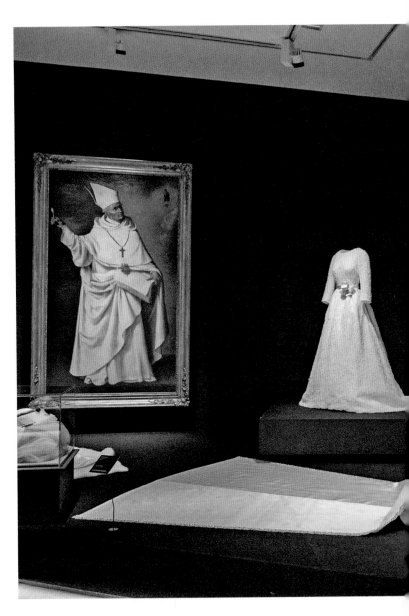

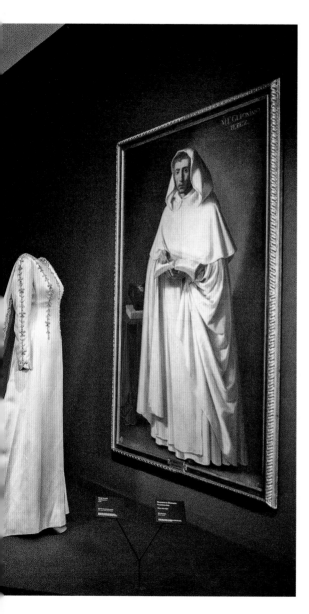

LEFT Cristóbal
Balenciaga's final
creation: María del
Carmen Martinez-
Bordiú's wedding
dress, 1972

Palmer as a "study in cloth; a science experiment in gravity and structure".

Although a continued use of the descriptive labels "architectural" and "modern" for Balenciaga's creations during this time are aesthetically correct, they also obscure his design references. As noted earlier, they suggest a rupture with his design past when, in fact, there is a clear continuation of inspiration and references in his work throughout his career right up until his final collection. Arguably, Balenciaga's work in the 1960s is his most modern-looking, especially to contemporary eyes, but it should be stressed that he also continually returned to historic painting and costume as sources of inspiration. He presented his own conceptual and modern interpretations of the voluminously draped costumes portrayed in seventeenth-century Spanish painting, and many of his creations owed a clear debt to historic liturgical vestments in their austere simplicity and silhouette – for example, a dress and ruffle-shoulder cape from 1965 in deep blue gazar evokes El Greco's late-sixteenth-century painting "The Virgin Mary" and Bartolomé Esteban Murillo's seventeenth-century painting of the Virgin Mary, "The Immaculate Conception of El Escorial". Moreover, Balenciaga's wedding dresses recall the robes of friars, as depicted by artist Francisco de Zurbarán; a 1960 red satin ensemble is indebted to artist Francisco Goya's painting of Cardinal Luis Maria de Borbón y Vallabriga; his 1967 black gazar evening gown and cape resembled a monk's habit; and his single-seam wedding dress of the same year featured a headdress that bore a close resemblance to a nun's veil. However, while his references may have been rooted in history, their translation into fashion was never outdated.

It has been argued that Balenciaga did not understand the social upheavals which had started changing the fashion landscape by the late 1950s and would come to dominate the 1960s. In terms of the fashion business, haute couture was fast falling out of favour, with the young increasingly turning their backs on Parisian exclusivity in preference for an expanding ready-to-wear market. This may well be true, but it would be wrong to extend that to Balenciaga's creative output or to think that, design-wise, he was outdated, old-fashioned or irrelevant. In fact, Balenciaga, more than many of his haute couture contemporaries, continued to experiment with new shapes, fabrics and techniques, and the results were truly innovative right until he closed his fashion house in 1968. His penultimate collection featured short suits, one- and no-seam dresses, and extraordinary trapezoidal evening dresses.

Balenciaga's position as an innovator in an outdated system is best illustrated by his 1968 work for Air France. He was asked to redesign the flight attendant uniform, a prestigious commission that evidenced his position as one of the fashion greats and a name known the world over. He created stylish summer and winter uniforms that looked as if they could have come straight out of his haute couture collections. There is no doubt they were elegant and expertly cut. However, this was 1968 and soon a wave of protests, strikes and political and social revolution would sweep across Paris and the rest of the world. Elitist elegance was no longer the order of the day and was now associated with the outdated world that the young were trying to discard. Staff and press alike condemned his creations as irrelevant and not fit for purpose. Fashion designer Ted Lapidus lamented Air France's choice and stated that Balenciaga's creations were "ravishing for getting out of a Rolls Royce or attending a soirée, but not for walking down the aisle of a Boeing". A harsh verdict that perhaps says more about the zeitgeist in which the uniforms were launched than the designs themselves, but nevertheless a low and undeserving note on which to end such an illustrious and important career.

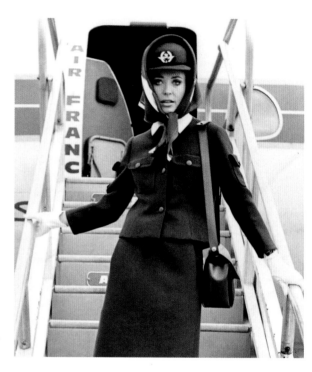

RIGHT AND OPPOSITE Air France flight attendants wearing the company's new uniform created by Balenciaga, December 1968

Seeing clearly what was on the horizon and sensing there was no room for haute couture in the modern world, while also suffering from ill health, Balenciaga retired and closed his salon in May 1968, days after violence erupted on the streets of Paris. He came out of retirement briefly in 1972 to create the wedding dress for General Franco's granddaughter María del Carmen Martinez-Bordiú y Franco. The dress was made in Madrid under his strict, hands-on supervision. Two weeks later, Balenciaga passed away at the age of 77.

Women's Wear Daily titled their story on his passing simply as "The King is Dead". He was laid to rest in the cemetery of his beloved native Getaria.

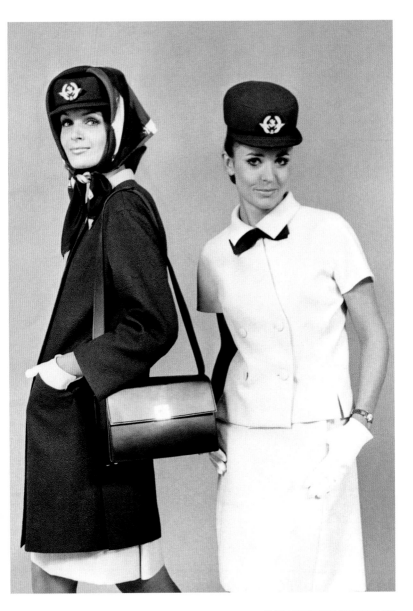

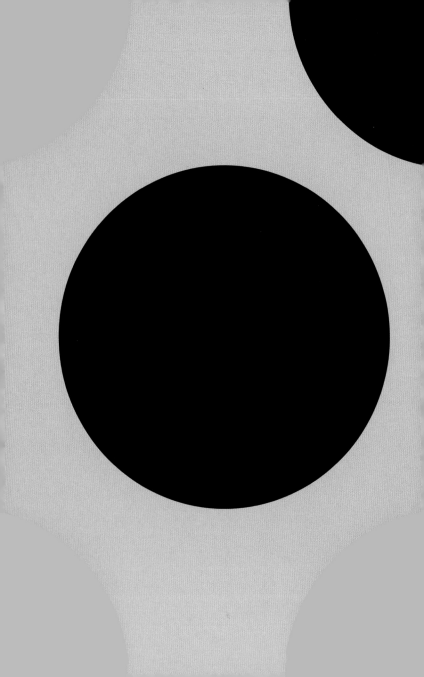

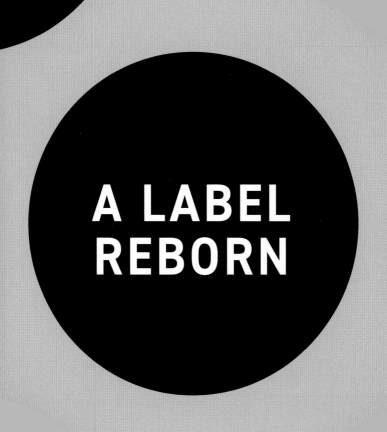

A LABEL
REBORN

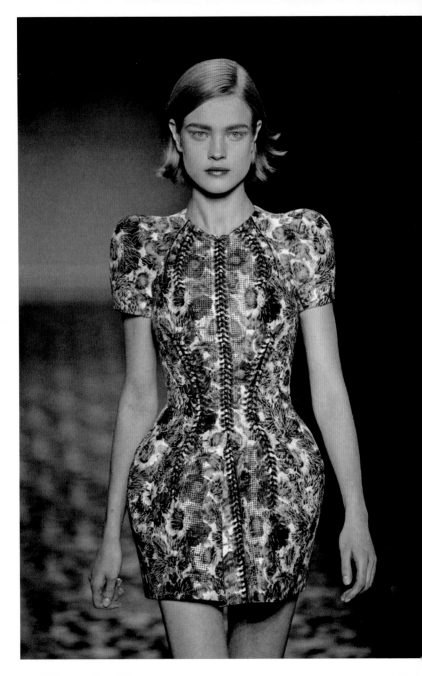

BALENCIAGA
AFTER
BALENCIAGA

When Balenciaga closed his salon in May 1968, regrettably his staff had to find out through the press. This was not because he had failed to inform his workers but because the termination letters that he sent them did not arrive for weeks and weeks due to the strikes that were crippling France at the time. Both the press and his devoted customers were full of praise for his achievements and lamented his retirement; it is said that socialite and long-time Balenciaga customer Mona von Bismarck took to her bedroom for three days to mourn.

Unlike today, designers who had founded their business in the early decades of the twentieth century did not expect their houses to survive them, and, indeed, many famous names disappeared completely post-closure. While couture production ceased when Balenciaga closed his atelier doors, his perfumes continued to be retailed after the closure and the house name remained in the ownership of his heirs until 1978, when they sold it to the German pharmaceutical company Hoechst AG.

Seven years later, Balenciaga was sold again, this time becoming part of the Jacques Bogart perfume group. It was

OPPOSITE Balenciaga bell-shaped dress, ready-to-wear, Spring 2008 during their ownership that serious efforts were made to re-establish the name as synonymous with high-end tailoring combined with classic elegance, by the appointment of Michel Goma as head designer. Goma had trained at couture houses such as Patou and Jeanne LaFaurie in the 1950s and '60s and was known for the immaculate cut of his designs. But Balenciaga the brand would not be associated with haute couture again until 2021 as its fashion revival had meant a shift to high-class, ready-to-wear clothes. In a way, this helped the brand make the transition and compromise required in the modern fashion landscape which had been refused by the master himself.

Goma deliberately mined the brand's archive for inspiration and reworked the originals into elegant modern classics for professional women, so following in its founder's footsteps. He became known for silhouettes that were well-sculpted, simple and minimalist, yet elegant and refined.

In an effort to raise the brand's profile the Bogart group closely controlled which retail outlets were allowed to stock Balenciaga. The strategy paid off and by the early 1990s the brand had a loyal fanbase once again.

In 1992 Goma was replaced by Josephus Melchior Thimister, who had trained at Lagerfeld and Patou. Like Goma, he consciously chose to reference the original Balenciaga oeuvre and specifically the semi-tailored look. Thimister quickly became known for his exquisite cutting skills and minimalist style – just like his predecessor, he favoured references from Balenciaga's later years. He contributed further to the elevation of the brand's profile, and when he left in 1997 to start his own label Balenciaga was again a relevant brand worn by celebrities and high-profile women around the world.

Thimister's successor, Nicholas Ghesquière, had joined the brand two years earlier to work on its Asian licences. Like Goma

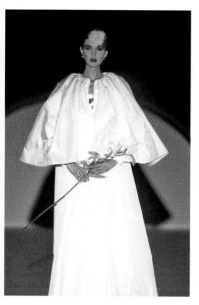

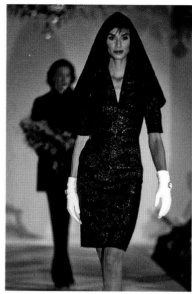

ABOVE LEFT
Balenciaga dress with
matching cape, ready-
to-wear, Fall/Winter
1989–1990

ABOVE RIGHT
Balenciaga hooded
dress, ready-to-
wear, Fall/Winter
1996–1997

and Thimister, he had earned his couture stripes – in his case, at Jean Paul Gaultier. In 1997, aged 25, he was promoted to head the house and his highly lucrative collections saw Balenciaga not only becoming a household name but also a favourite among the young and fashionable. This was in part down to his canny strategy for selling accessories. Ghesquière realized that aside from perfumes a brand's bread-and-butter business came from the sale of accessories and, specifically, the growing popularity of It bags. In 2000, he introduced the First bag, which was followed by the City bag not long after. Both were huge commercial successes, not least because they were seen on the arms of a host of celebrities, including Nicole Richie, the Olson twins, Sarah Jessica Parker and Sienna Miller. All these celebrities had serious fashion clout. As darlings of the paparazzi, they were featured daily carrying their bags while going about

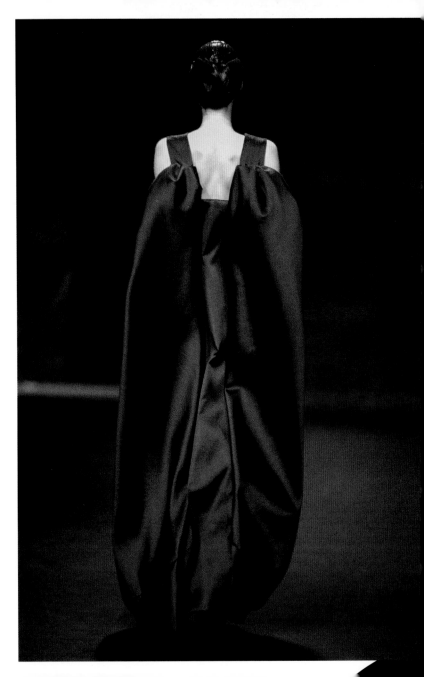

their business, fast making Balenciaga bags the most desirable accessories around and vastly improving the brand's finances.

Ghesquière never personally knew Balenciaga nor was he around during the master's heyday, having been born only a year before his death, but he familiarized himself with his oeuvre and often paid homage to it in his designs. While these design nods were possibly not as explicit as his predecessor's ability to make history relevant to contemporary audiences through his own personal vision and interest in new materials, they nevertheless drew a clear link between the two.

In 2001, the brand became part of Gucci, which itself became part of the Kering Group in 2004. In the same year, Ghesquière launched the Edition collection of "original designs reworked and reissued to suit the mood of fashion".

In 2012, Ghesquière moved to Louis Vuitton and was replaced by Alexander Wang, who was the first creative director at Balenciaga to come from a ready-to-wear background instead of a couture one. His three-year stint saw the brand cementing its move into designer branded goods, with a proliferation of high-profit items such as T-shirts and trainers making up a significant part of the brand's offerings.

Although to many the choice of Wang – who brought a decidedly street- and youth-wear aesthetic and experience with him – seemed weird and mismatched with the Balenciaga heritage, he nevertheless managed to create interesting and commercially viable collections which featured historic references that were updated with a sporty American twist. Kering's aim in hiring Wang was to "imbue a sense of modernity and youthful energy to the house", and while original brand devotees may have objected, there is no doubt he managed to achieve exactly that: he significantly widened the Balenciaga customer base and made the brand relevant to a young new audience.

OPPOSITE Balenciaga evening dress, ready-to-wear, Fall/Winter 1997–1998

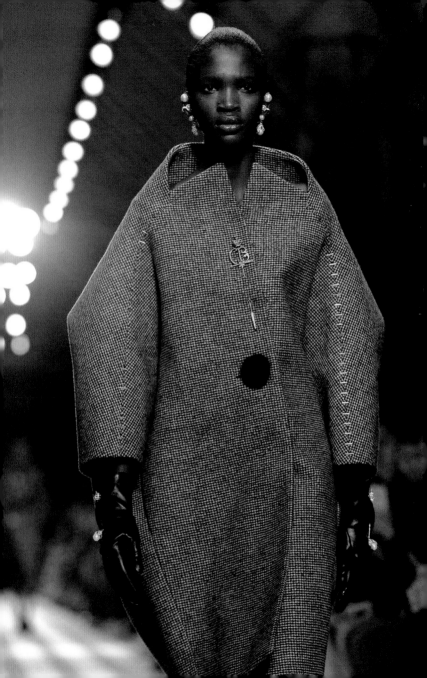

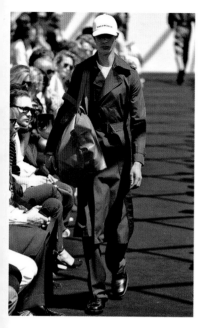
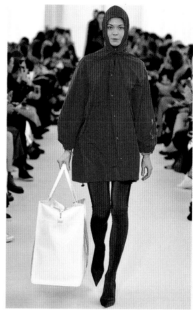

OPPOSITE Balenciaga rounded tweed coat with stand-up collar, ready-to-wear, Fall/Winter 2015–2016

ABOVE LEFT Balenciaga trench coat and the divisive blue "IKEA" bag, menswear, Spring/Summer 2017

ABOVE RIGHT Balenciaga raincoat dress with purple "pantashoes", ready-to-wear, Spring 2017

After Wang's departure another potentially left-field appointment got the fashion world all excited. In 2015, Demna Gvasalia, who had founded his cult streetwear brand Vetements with his brother Guram only a year earlier, took over as creative director. In his first year at the helm of Vetements he had become the darling of the fashion world. Some considered Gvasalia an odd choice for Balenciaga and accused the house of being driven more by a desire for cult status and profits than a respect for the brand's heritage. Closer examination, however, shows that although there may have been a sea of difference between the two aesthetically, when it came to business practices, Balenciaga and Gvasalia were aligned in many ways.

Vetements had already adopted several of Balenciaga's own tactics and incorporated them into their own business strategy:

they showed outside the traditional fashion calendar, just as Balenciaga had done, and the distribution of the brand was tightly controlled and limited, to retain control and exclusivity. But, most importantly, this was an anti-fashion stance that was specifically focused on critiquing a consumer culture obsessed with novelty – exactly what the master had eschewed himself.

The show notes to Gvasalia's first collection explained that this was a "reimagining of the work of Cristóbal Balenciaga—a wardrobe of absolute contemporaneity and realism imbued with the attitude of haute couture. A translation, not a reiteration. A new chapter." Classics were reinvented through streetwear and high-end tailoring was combined with hooded sweatshirts.

Gvasalia's reign at the house has seen him reinterpret the archives, and often deconstruct original silhouettes to reveal their complexity and heritage. In 2017, to celebrate the house's

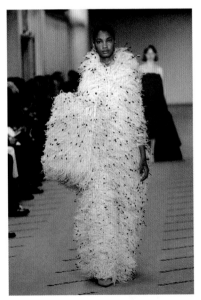

BELOW LEFT
Balenciaga ostrich feather dress, ready-to-wear, Fall/Winter 2017–2018

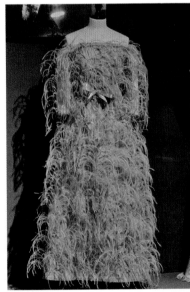

BELOW RIGHT
Balenciaga ostrich feather dress, 1965

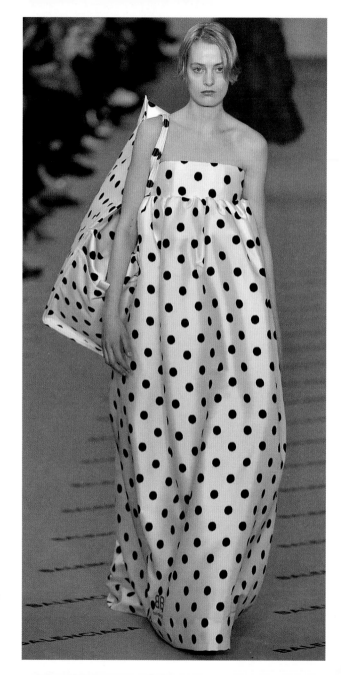

RIGHT Balenciaga
polka dot dress,
ready-to-wear, Fall/
Winter 2017–2018

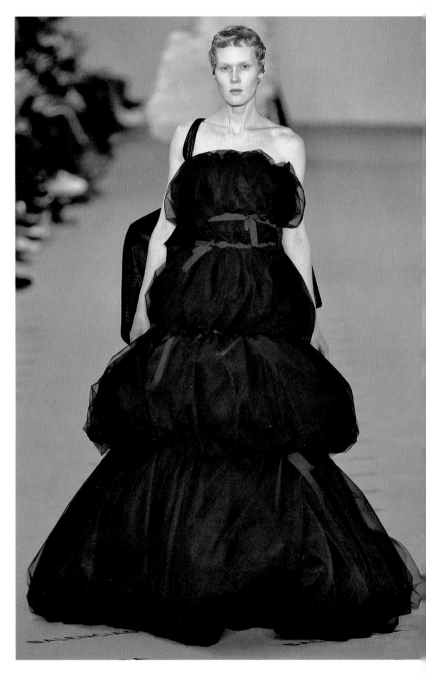

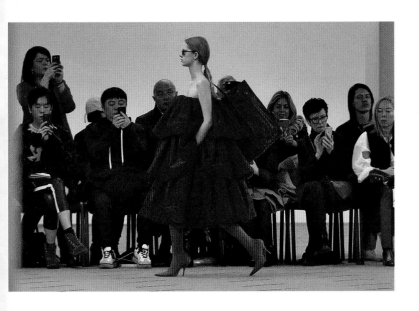

centenary, Gvasalia created nine spectacular Balenciaga couture dresses that were based on his study of the brand's archive and lookbooks, evidencing not only a deep understanding of the brand's heritage, but also an acknowledgement of the need to modernize and stay relevant.

The summer of 2021 saw the Balenciaga name make a return to the haute couture calendar after a 53-year hiatus, with a collection that was both modern and a clear homage to the master, with references to his original oeuvre through cut, colour palette, embellishments, fabric choices and experiments with draping and volume. While stylistically and commercially things have progressed, developed and changed significantly since 1968, the DNA of Balenciaga's founder nevertheless continues to run through the creations of the new generation of designers, whose work, like Balenciaga himself, still attracts a cult following.

OPPOSITE Balenciaga balloon dress, ready-to-wear, Fall/Winter 2017–2018

ABOVE Balenciaga baby-doll dress, ready-to-wear, Fall/Winter 2017–2018

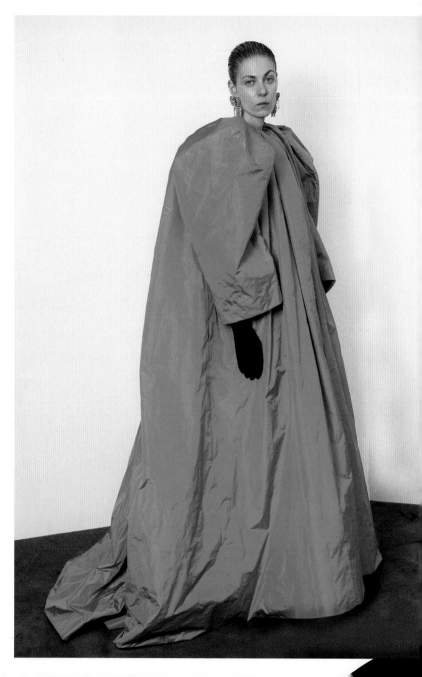

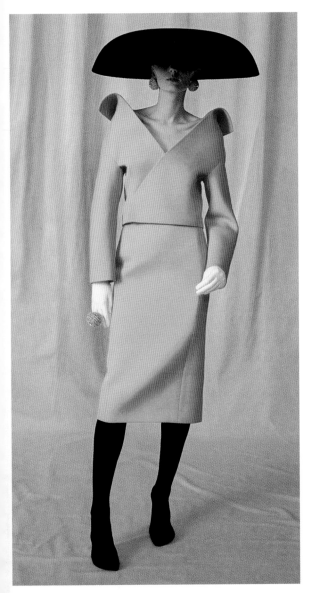

OPPOSITE Balenciaga
voluminous emerald
green coat, haute
couture, Fall 2021

LEFT Balenciaga
sculpted orange dress,
haute couture, Fall
2021

A LABEL REBORN 155

INDEX

(Numbers in *italic* refer to
pages on which captions
appear)

A Pygmalion *56*
Abraham 131
afternoon dress *44*, *47*,
    62, 95
afternoon suit 75, *75*
Air France uniform 137, *138*
Allurez, Miren 95
alpaca dress *109*
Amaya, Carmen 96
Andalusian Dancer dress *24*
Avenue George V 14, 19

B.E. Costura 14
baby-doll dress 80, *83*, 85,
    113, *153*
bags 37, *40*, 145, 147, *149*
Balenciaga and Spain 95
Balenciaga, C. 11
Balenciaga y Compañía 12
balloon dress 75, *86*, *153*
Balmain, Pierre 72
Basque Country 9, 11
bata de cola dress 96
bell-shaped dress *143*
Bergdorf Goodman 20
Biarritz 11, 56
Bismarck, Mona von 143
Bizcarrondo, Nicolás 19
Bogart, Jacques perfume
    group 143–4

bolero 43, 48, 92, 95, *95*, *132*
Boulanger, Louise 59
Bowles, Hamish 95, 101
Breitner, George Hendrik *64*
Brenot, Raymond 95
Britannia and Eve *31*
broadcloth coat *27*
bullfighter snoods 95
butterfly print white silk
    crepe evening dress *39*

Cáceres 101
Callot Soeurs 11, 12, 59,
    60, *62*
cape-coat *79*
capes 38, *60*, 95, 101, *107*,
    113, *128*, *133*, 136, *145*
Casa Gómez 10
Casa Torres, Marquesa de 9
Celada, Eloy Martínez de la
    Pera 107
Chanel, Coco 11, 59
Charlotte Observer, The 80
Chéruit 12
chiffon *24*, *62*
chou wrap *131*
City bag 145
cocoon coat 72, 75
cotton summer dress *50*
Courier-Journal, The 76
Courrèges, André 107
crepe
    afternoon dress *44*
    de chine underdress 85

dress *43*
evening dress *40*
summer suit *39*

D'Attainville, Wladzio
    Jaworowski 19
Dancing evening coat *59*
day dress *60*
daywear suits 131
dinner dress, black faille *31*
dinner dress, wool and
    satin *21*
Dior, Christian 72, 75, 107
Doré, Gustave 96
double-breasted tweed suit *85*
Doucet 12
dress and cape *145*

EISA 29, 50, *50*
    B.E. Costura 14
    Costura 13, 14
    matador bolero *95*
    veil *116*
    velvet evening gown *119*
Eizaguirre, Martina (mother)
    9, 10, 13
embroidered white lawn
    dress *33*
envelope dress *127*, 131
evening dress 14, *98*
evening gown *111*, *133*, 136
evening gown with bustle *23*
evening jacket *123*
evening wear 131

evening wrap coat *115*
Fath, Jacques 72
First bag 145
flamenco dresses 96, *96*
flight attendant uniforms
   137, *138*
Flores, Lola 96
Fortuny, Mariano 59, *66*
Franco, María del Carmen,
   Martinez-Bordiú y 138
Frankfurter Illustrierte 86
"French Newcomers" 20

Gaultier, Jean Paul 145
gazar 96, 116, 131, *131*,
   133, 136
Gazette du Bon Ton, La 59
Getaria 9, *13*, 138
Ghesquière, Nicholas 144,
   145, 147
Girl in a White Kimono 64
Givenchy, Hubert de 127
Goma, Michel 144
Goya, Francisco 23, 24, *103*,
   118, 136
Grands Magasins du Louvre,
   Les 10, 11, 56
Greco, El 118, 136
Gucci 147
Gvasalia, Demna 149, 150,
   153
Gvasalia, Guram 149

handkerchief linen dress *27*
Harper's Bazaar 20, 38,
   92, 95
haute couture 11, 19, 56,
   71, 91, 127, 137, 138,

144, 150, 153, *155*
Hoechst AG 143
hooded dress *145*
house-coats *56*

IKEA bag *149*
"Immaculation Conception
   of El Escorial, The" 136
Indianapolis Times 76
Infanta dress 20, *91*, *92*
Isabel Alfonsa, Infanta 12

jackets *19*, 29, *29*, *33*, 38,
   43, 44, *47*, 48, 50, 75, 85,
   92, 95, 105, *109*, 118, *123*
jacquard afternoon dress *62*
Jewish Chronicle, The 71

Kering Group 147
Kimono-style *55*, *56*, 59, 64

lace dress *111*
lace-over-taffeta sheath *98*
lace, white 23
LaFaurie, Jeanne 144
Lagerfeld, Karl 144
Lanvin kimono-style
   ensemble *55*
Lanvin, Jeanne 59
Lapidus, Ted 137
Lepape, Georges *59*
Lizaso, Benita and Daniela 12
Los Angeles Times 71
Madrid 14, 92
Mainbocher dresses *60*
Maison Worth 11
mantilla 113
mantle coat 75

María Cristina de Borbón,
   Queen 12
Marshal Fields & Company
   20
Martina Robes et Manteaux
   12–3
Martinez-Bordiú, Mariá del
   Carmen *135*
matador jacket 48, 92
Middy line tunic 76, *76*
Miró, Joan 128
moire evening coat *107*
montera 95
Morning Call, The 80
Murillo, Bartolomé Esteban
   136

Navarre 101
New Look 72
New York 50
New Yorker, The 76

Olson twins, the 145
organza apron dress *113*
ostrich feather dress *150*

Palmer, Alexandra 131–6
pannier dresses *103*
pantashoes *149*
Paquin 11, 12
Paris 11, 14, 19, 20, 43, 44,
   50, 56, *91*, 92, 138
   riots 138
   wartime 11, 38
Parker, Sarah Jessica 145
Patou 144
Pera, Eloy Martínez de la
   127, 128

Philadelphia Inquirer, The
   80, 85
plaid surah skirt and jacket 29
pleated and draped coat *121*
pleated silk Delphos dresses
   66
Poiret, Paul 59, *59*, 62
polka-dot dress *151*
printed dress *49*
printed moire Polonaise
   dress *31*
Province, The 50, 95

Quemada (tailor) 10

raincoat dress *149*
ready-to-wear 137, *143*, *145*,
   147, *149*, *150*, *151*, *153*
Redfern 12
Ricci, Nina *31*
Richie, Nicole 145
Romeo (tailor) 10
Rothschild, Pauline de 128

sack/chemise dress 80, *83*
Salamanca 101
Salt Lake Tribune, The 85
San Francisco Examiner 80
San Sebastián 10, *10*, 11, 13,
   50, 56, 92, 95
sculpted dress *155*
Second Republic 14, 19
sheer wool suit *37*
silk *19*, 24, *39*, *40*, 62, 66,
   80, 96, *107*, 113, *115*,
   116, *121*, *123*, *128*, 131
      crepe summer suit *39*
      dress *128*

faille coat *121*
   gazar bridal gown *116*
   tunic *80*
Sketch, The 24
Snow, Carmel 76
Soieries Illustrées, Les 56
Sorbet evening dress *62*
Spain 9, 29, 101
Spanish art exhibition,
   Geneva 23–4
Spanish Civil War 14, 19
*Spanish Costume:
   Extremadura* 101
Spanish lace skirt *24*
Sphere, The 33
strapless slipper satin dress *33*
striped cape-coat *79*
suit in grey with double flat
   pockets *39*
suit in light grey *47*

taffeta wrap dress *115*
tailored afternoon suit *75*
tailored outfits 12, 29, 38,
   47, 50 *75*, 85 131, 144
Tampa Bay Times 44
Tatler, The 109
Thimister, Josephus Melchior
   144, 145
Thurman, Judith 113
traje de luces see matador
   jacket
trench coat *149*
"Tres Nouvelles" dress design
   48
tulle 96, 113
Tunic line 80, *86*
tunic silhouette *79*

tunics 59, 76, *79*, 90, *86*, 101
tweed coat *149*

unfitted coat *71*

Vallabriga, Cardinal Luis
   María de Borbón y 118,
   136
Velázquez hat *103*
Velázquez, Diego 20, 23,
   24, *91*
velvet *19*, 38, 96, 113, *115*,
   119, *132*
Vértice 23
Vetements 149
Vigée Lebrun 29
Villar (tailor) 10
Vionnet, Madeleine 59
Vogue 19–20, 24, *27*, *29*, *31*,
   33, *37*, 38, *39*, *43*, 44,
   50, *60*, *75*, 76, *80*, *85*,
   103, 111, *127*, *131*
voluminous coat *155*
Vreeland, Diana 91
Vuitton, Louis 147

Wang, Alexander 147
wedding dresses 113, 118,
   135, 136, 138
Women's Journal 20
Women's Wear Daily 138
wool coat *72*
wool suit *100*
woollen skirt *47*
World War I 11
World War II 37

Zurbarán, Francisco de 136

BIBLIOGRAPHY

Arana, Ana Balda. "Cristóbal Balenciaga. Explorations in Traditional Spanish Aesthetics." *Costume* 53, no. 2 (2019): 161-185.

Arzalluz, Miren. *Cristobal Balenciaga*. V&A Publ., 2011.

Miren Arzalluz & Debo Kaat, eds. *Fashion Game Changers: Reinventing the 20th Century Silhouette*. Bloomsbury Publishing, 2016.

Balenciaga, C., Jouve, M.A. and Demornex, J., 1988. *Cristóbal Balenciaga*. Editions du Regard.

Bolton, Andrew, Barbara Drake Bohem, Marzia Cataldi Gallo, C. Griffith Mann, David Morgan, Gianfranco Cardinal Ravasi, and David Tracy. *Heavenly Bodies: Fashion and the Catholic Imagination*. Vol. 1. Metropolitan Museum of Art, 2018.

Bowles, Hamish. *Balenciaga and Spain*. Skira, 2011.

Geczy, A., 2013. *Fashion and Orientalism: Dress, Textiles and Culture from the 17th to the 21st Century*. A&C Black.

Join-Dieterle, C. ed., 1996. *Japonisme et mode*. Paris-Musées, Paris.

Martinez de la Pera, Eloy. *Balenciaga and Spanish Painting*. Fundacion Coleccion Thyssen-Bornemisza, 2019.

Miller, Lesley Ellis. *Cristóbal Balenciaga*. Batsford, 1993.

Nicklas, Charlotte. "Tradition and innovation: Recent Balenciaga exhibitions." *Fashion Theory* 17, no. 4 (2013): 431–444.

Piancatelli, Chiara, Piergiacomo Mion Dalle Carbonare, and Manuel Cuadrado-García. "Balenciaga: The Master of Haute Couture." In *The Artification of Luxury Fashion Brands*, pp. 141–162. Palgrave Pivot, Cham, 2020.

Reponen, Johannes. "BALENCIAGA: SHAPING FASHION." *Film, Fashion & Consumption* 6, no. 2 (2017): 165–168.

Rosés Castellsaguer, Sílvia. "Spanish Couture: In the Shadow of Cristóbal Balenciaga." *Fashion Theory* (2020): 1–22.

Zeitune, Leonardo Jacques Gammal. "Popularizing Haute Couture: A Balenciaga Brand Case Study." *Art and Design Review* 9, no. 1 (2021): 46–57.

CREDITS

The publishers would like to thank the following sources for their kind permission to reproduce the pictures in this book.

akg-images: 54; Album/Oronoz 93, 99, 150 (right); Les Arts Décoratifs, Paris/Jean Tholance 115

Alamy: incamerastock 58; Anton Oparin 149 (right)

Courtesy the author: 10, 13, 40, 45, 46, 47, 49, 86

© Cristóbal Balenciaga Museum: Getaria_ Spain 82, 94

Bridgeman Images: © Brooklyn Museum of Art 60; Chicago History Museum 121

Getty Images: AFP 78, 79, 87, 138-139; Walter Carone 73, 100, 112; Chicago History Museum 62, 63, 66-67, 106, 122-123; Alexis Duclos 145 (right); Estrop 150 (left); Keystone-France 70; Lipnitzki 8; Quim Llenas 134-135; Paul Popper/ Popperfoto 57; Pascal Le Segretain 148; Daniel Simon 146; Universal History Archive 65; Victor Virgile 145 (left), 149 (left), 151, 152, 153

Kerry Taylor Auctions: 15, 21, 39, 51, 83, 97, 110, 116, 117, 119, 120, 129, 132, 133

Mary Evans: 22, © Illustrated London News Ltd 25, 31, 33, 109

Shutterstock: Rene Bouet-Willaumez/ Condé Nast 27, 36, 42; Henry Clarke/ Condé Nast 74, 98, 111, 114; Carl Oscar August Erickson/Condé Nast 18, 90, 102, 103; Horst P Horst/Condé Nast 26, 30, 41, 81; George Hoyningen-Huene/Condé Nast 61; Frances McLaughlin-Gill/Condé Nast 84; Arik Nepo/Condé Nast 32; Cavan Pawson 142; Irving Penn/Condé Nast 126, 130; Robert Randall/Condé Nast 77; John Rawlings/Condé Nast 28; Xinhua 154, 155

Every effort has been made to acknowledge correctly and contact the source and/ or copyright holder of each picture and Welbeck apologizes for any unintentional errors or omissions, which will be corrected in future editions of this book.

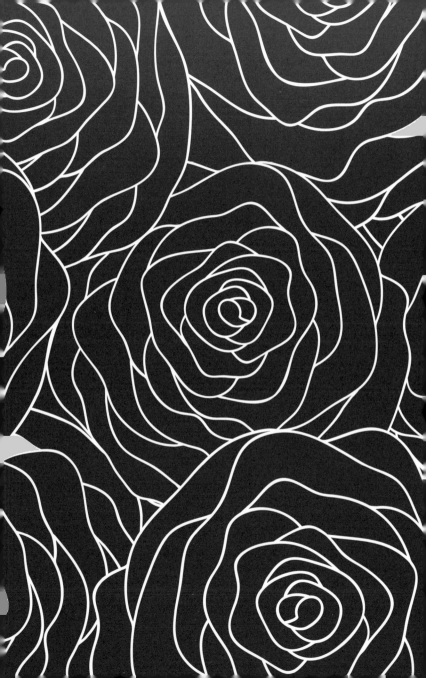

LITTLE BOOK OF

VALENTINO

Karen Homer is a fashion journalist and bestselling author. She has worked as a columnist for *The Times* and contributed to the *Telegraph*, *Harpers & Queen*, *Elle*, *World of Interiors* and *Vogue*. Homer is the author of *Little Book of Dior*, *Little Book of Gucci* and *Things a Woman Should Know About Style*. She lives in London.

Published by in 2022 by Welbeck
An imprint of Welbeck Non-Fiction Limited
part of Welbeck Publishing Group
Offices in: London – 20 Mortimer Street, London W1T 3JW &
Sydney – 205 Commonwealth Street, Surry Hills 2010
www.welbeckpublishing.com

Text © Karen Homer 2022
Design and layout © Welbeck Non-Fiction Limited 2022

A CIP catalogue record for this book is available from the British Library.

ISBN 978-1-80279-014-6

Printed in China

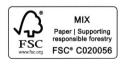

MIX
Paper | Supporting
responsible forestry
FSC® C020056

LITTLE BOOK OF

VALENTINO

The story of the iconic fashion house

KAREN HOMER

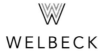

WELBECK

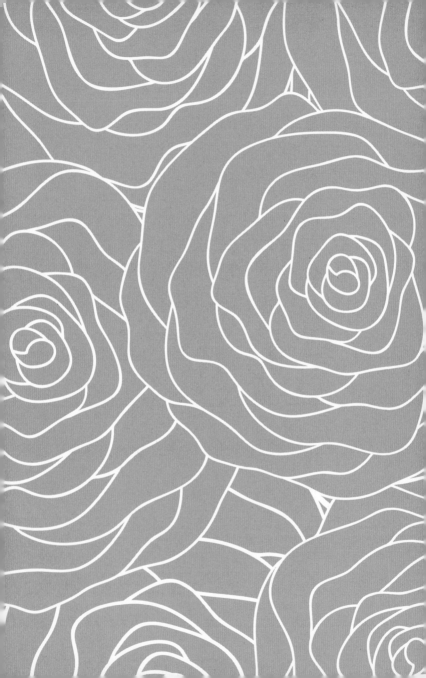

CONTENTS

INTRODUCTION....................................6

EARLY YEARS.......................................10

ATELIER VALENTINO..........................20

CELEBRITIES AND SOCIALITES 40

NEW YORK AND BEYOND..................58

HOMES AND INTERIORS.................106

SELLING UP BUT NOT OUT.............118

A NEW CHAPTER...............................134

INDEX...156

CREDITS...160

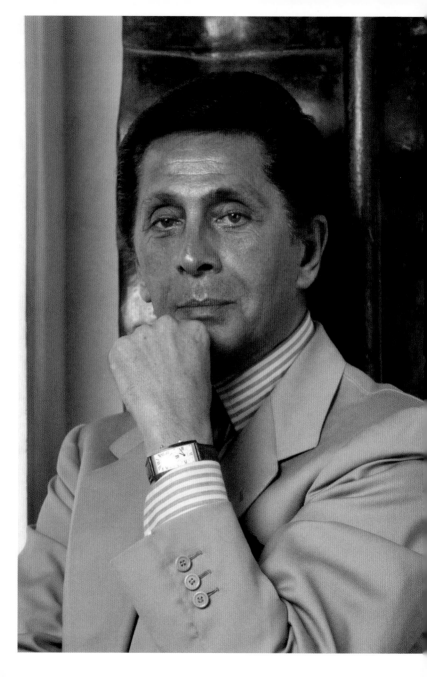

INTRODUCTION

"I know what women want. They want to be beautiful."

VALENTINO GARAVANI

There are few designers more synonymous with glamour than Valentino Garavani. Known simply by his first name, the Italian designer is the celebrity's favourite when it comes to Oscar gowns in "Valentino Red" or society wedding dresses in exquisite concoctions of lace and organza. He has enjoyed great success in the world of fashion, both critically and commercially, over a period of almost 50 years.

Named after the screen idol Rudolph Valentino, he was a child obsessed by the sirens of the golden age of cinema, so it is fitting that once Valentino opened his own atelier in Rome in 1959, his first big client was Elizabeth Taylor. His clientele soon grew to include other famous actresses and socialites, most notably the style icon Jackie Kennedy.

Valentino not only created wonderful clothes for these famous and beautiful women, but he also developed lifelong close friendships with many of them. Along with his partner

OPPOSITE Valentino Clemente Ludovico Garavani.

Giancarlo Giammetti, he quickly became a celebrity in his own right and cemented his status as one of the world's leading haute couture designers by delivering the elegant, tailored daywear and stunning, embellished evening gowns so beloved by his high-society clients.

During the 1970s, Valentino was taken under the wing of the legendary *Vogue* editor Diana Vreeland, and spent a considerable amount of time in New York, becoming part of the fashionable Studio 54 crowd alongside iconic names such as Andy Warhol, who later produced a series of screen prints of the designer. The following two decades saw a return to Rome, where Valentino produced biannual haute couture and ready-to-wear collections, managing to successfully navigate the fine line between his classic silhouette and the trends of the day, even when he confessed to hating the 1980s silhouette.

Despite some financial wobbles around the turn of the millennium, when the Valentino label was sold twice within a period of five years, Valentino himself continued to remain actively involved in the company until his retirement in 2008. In tribute, several retrospectives of his work were held along with the screening of a behind-the-scenes film, *Valentino: The Last Emperor*. All served to underline Valentino's huge achievements and importance within the world of fashion design.

After his retirement, the creative direction of Valentino was taken in hand by the designers Maria Grazia Chiuri and Pierpaolo Piccioli. Under their stewardship, the label has flourished in a modern era, appealing to a new raft of young celebrity clients while still retaining the heritage of Valentino and his old-school glamour. It may not look quite the same, but today's red-carpet gown is as likely to bear the label Valentino as ever.

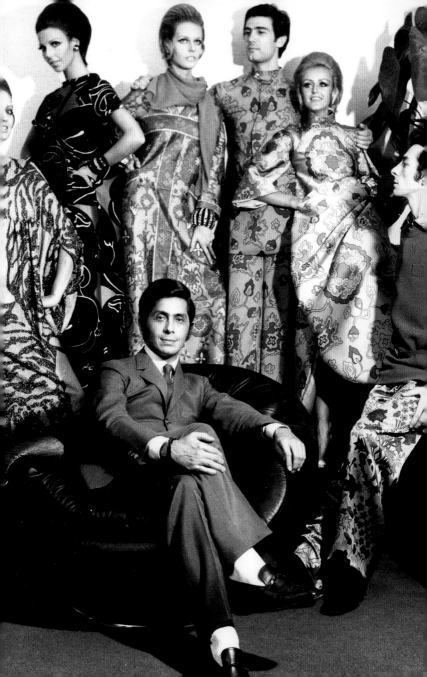

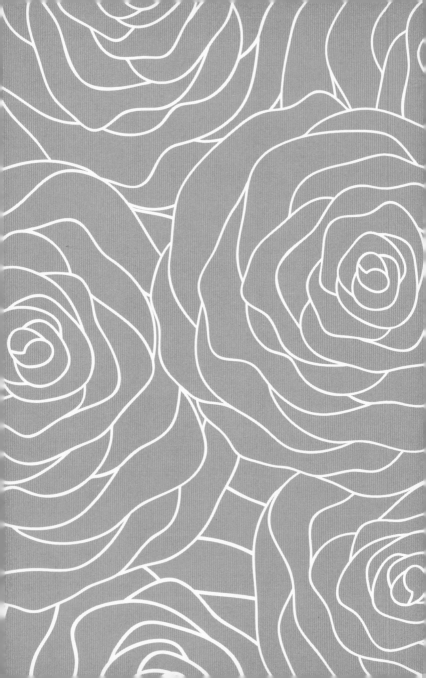

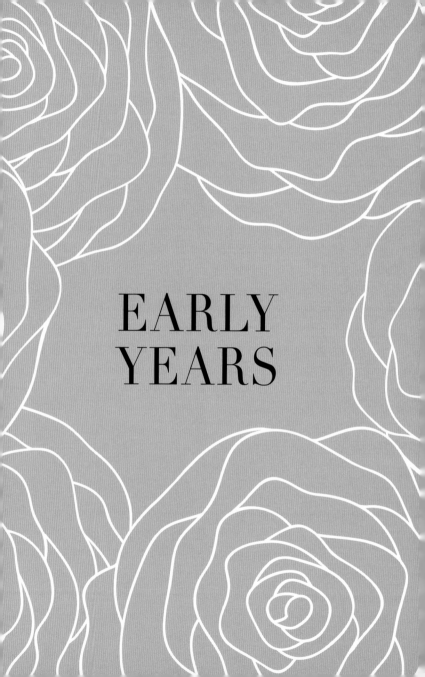

EARLY
YEARS

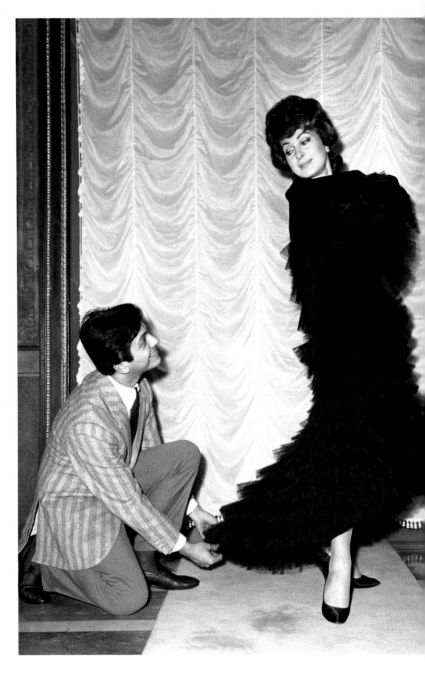

GLAMOROUS BEGINNINGS

Valentino Clemente Ludovico Garavani was born on 11 May 1932, in the small town of Voghera in the Lombardy region of Italy. As a child, he was transfixed by actresses such as Lana Turner, Hedy Lamarr and Judy Garland. In an interview for *System* magazine by Hans Ulrich Obrist in 2015, Valentino remembered visiting the cinema, aged just seven, with his older sister, to be captivated by "beautiful films with beautiful stars wearing beautiful dresses; for me at that time, they were like a dream"

This early passion for the cinema would remain central to Valentino throughout his career, not only as a source of design inspiration but also as a world where he found many of his muses. The love affair with performance continued even after his retirement in 2008: he went on to create costumes for the Paris Opera Ballet and the New York City Ballet. In 2016, along with his successors at Valentino, Maria Grazia Chiuri and Pierpaolo Piccioli, he created the costumes for Sofia Coppola's production of *La Traviata*.

OPPOSITE Valentino was devoted to Rome's glamorous Italian actresses from the very beginning of his career. Here he adjusts the hem of one of his dresses, worn by Silvana Pampanini in 1956.

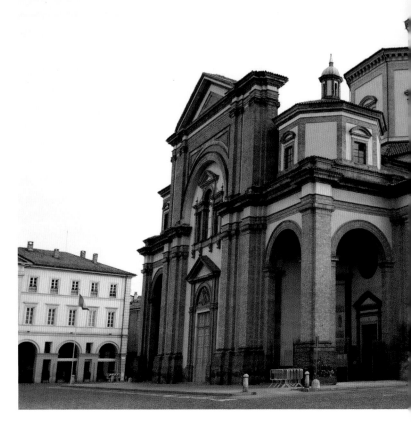

ABOVE Valentino
Clemente Ludovico
Garavani was born
on 11 May, 1932 in
Voghera, a small
town in the Lombardy
region of Italy,
pictured here in 2020.

As a child and young adult, Valentino was particularly captivated by the glamour of evening dresses, which he spent many hours sketching, an interest which anticipated his future success. He explained to Obrist: "My cousins used to dress very, very well, and every time they wore an evening gown, I was there staring at them."

Inspired to be a fashion designer for as long as he could remember, Valentino was as passionate about art as he was

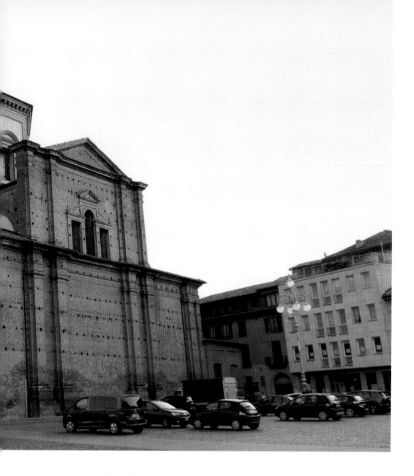

about dresses, and he moved to Milan in 1949 to study fashion illustration at the Santa Maria Institute. Aware that to become a serious designer he would need to study in Paris, he also took a course to learn French before moving there, where he studied at the École des Beaux-Arts and the École de Chambre Syndicale de la Couture Parisienne. Valentino was immediately captivated by the French haute couture houses that represented the pinnacle of the fashion industry. The culture of fashion

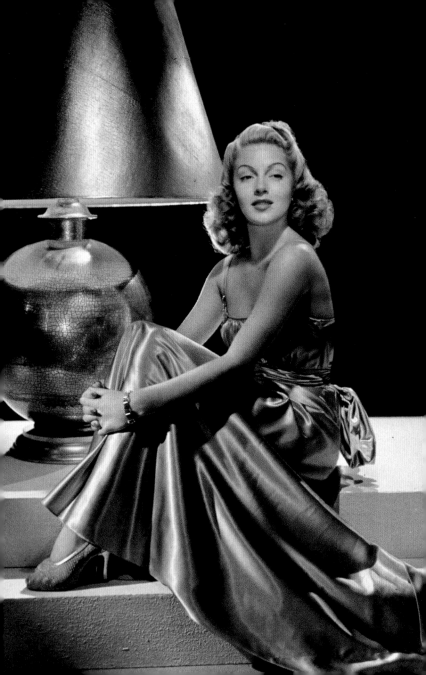

OPPOSITE A still from the 1940 musical *Two Girls on Broadway*, starring Lana Turner. The wonderful dresses worn by silver-screen stars were an inspiration to Valentino, who began visiting the cinema with his older sister when he was just seven years old.

RIGHT Judy Garland also captivated the young Valentino, who later recalled these screen images as being "like a dream".

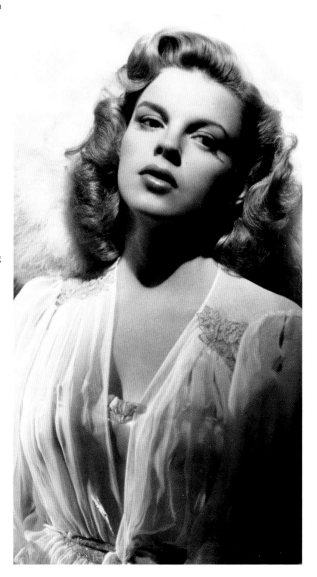

design at the time was extremely elitist, and most foreign designers, and in particular Italians, were looked down on as inferior. Nevertheless, Valentino was determined to succeed, soon proving his talent by winning the 1950 annual fashion prize sponsored by the International Wool Secretariat. His name is one of the first recorded by the textile institution, which subsequently awarded prizes to many of the most famous designers of the twentieth century, including Yves Saint Laurent, Karl Lagerfeld, Giorgio Armani and Ralph Lauren.

As a result of the prestigious prize, Valentino took up several apprenticeships with esteemed designers, including Jacques Fath and Balenciaga, as well as the society couturier Jean Dessès. At Dessès he spent five years learning the art of elaborate evening wear. He worked alongside an illustrator by the name of Guy Laroche, and in 1957, Laroche set up his own label, taking Valentino with him. For the next two years, Valentino learned how to manage the day-to-day running of a burgeoning fashion house. He told the curator, fashion historian and author Pamela Golbin: "I dealt with everything and learnt more and more. I handled all sorts of things – drawings, dressing the models for the runway, and getting into taxis to go and pick up dresses."

The experience was extremely valuable and gave Valentino the confidence to fulfil his dream: returning to Rome and opening his own atelier on the famous Via Condotti.

OPPOSITE Couturier Jean Dessès, with whom Valentino apprenticed and who first introduced him to the world of designing for celebrity clients.

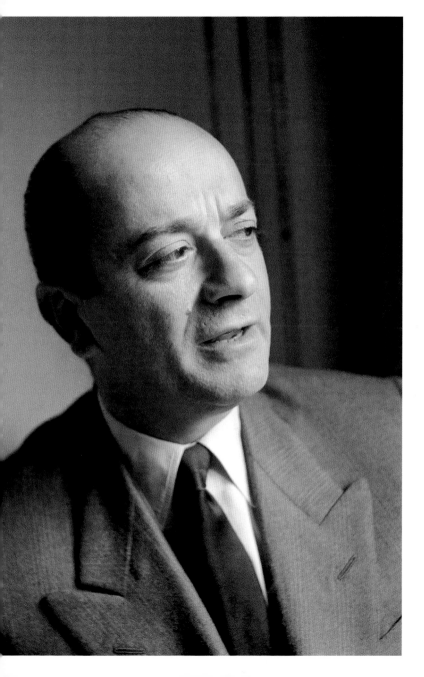

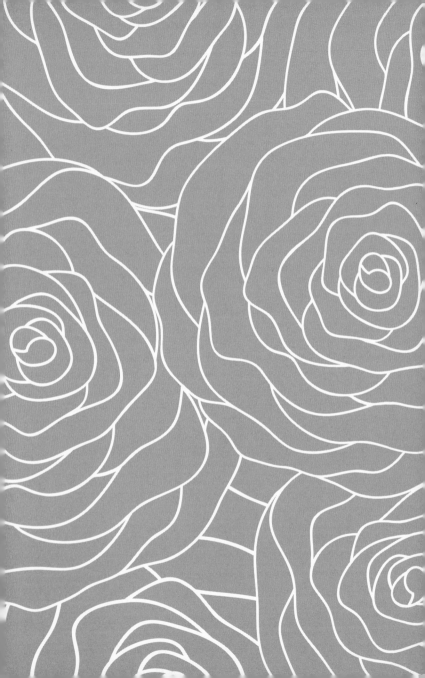

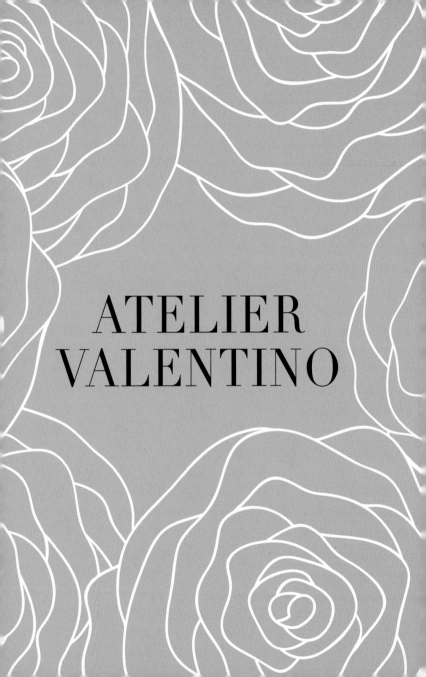

ATELIER
VALENTINO

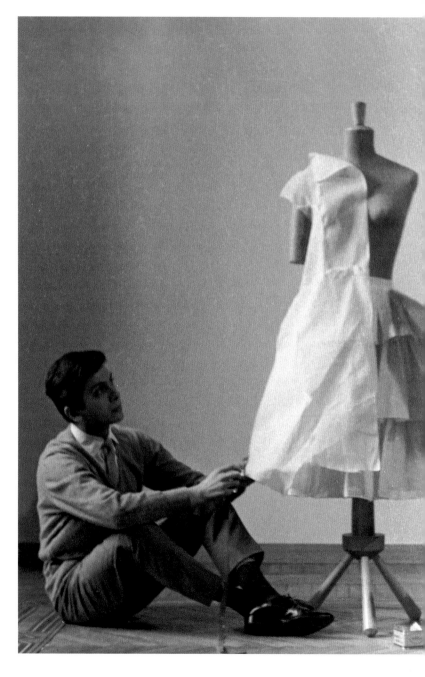

A DREAM
REALIZED

"I believe only in high fashion. I think a couturier must
establish his style and stick to it. The mistake of many
couturiers is that they try to change their line every
collection. I change a little each time, but never too much,
so as not to lose my identity."

VALENTINO GARAVANI, **Women's Wear Daily,** *1968*

In 1959, Valentino left Paris with the promise of financial
backing from his father and his father's business partner to
start his own label in his beloved Italy. Enthralled by the world
of haute couture, he opened his fashion house in Rome at 11
Via Condotti, modelling it on the ateliers and salons he had
so admired in Paris. Valentino had honed his design style too,
absorbing both the technical expertise and structural formality
that reigned at Dessès, and the more modern, colour-saturated
designs favoured by Guy Laroche.

OPPOSITE Valentino attends to a mannequin at his Rome atelier in 1959,
having finally realized his dream of opening his own fashion house.

His first collection was entitled "Ibis", and while the press gave it a good review, noting the influence of his Parisian internships, Valentino later admitted to Eugenia Sheppard that it was "full of ideas, but had no personality". However, looking back on the collection – which included "Fiesta", an elegant strapless cocktail dress of draped tulle, and the first to appear in the bold and now famous colour that became known as Valentino Red – it is easy to see his charismatic personality shining through. The 1959 dress has become a vintage icon and was worn again by Jennifer Aniston to the premiere of the film *Along Came Polly* in 2004.

Despite his misgivings about his debut collection, Valentino was determined to find his fashion voice and continued to pursue his dream of becoming a famous couturier. The following

BELOW Fashion buyers and press gave Valentino's debut collection positive reviews, although the designer himself later complained that it had "no personality".

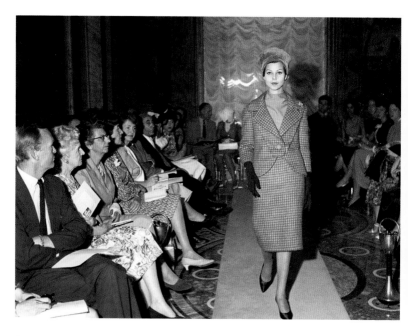

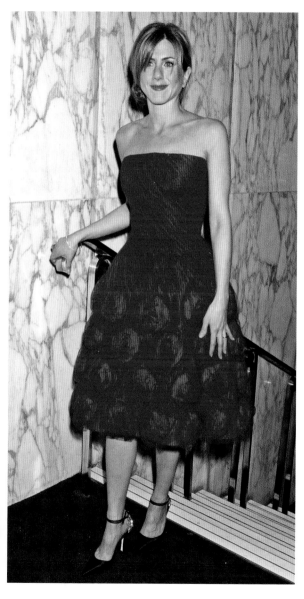

LEFT The first of Valentino's iconic red dresses was the "Fiesta" strapless cocktail dress with roses, from his debut collection in 1959. In 2004, over four decades later, it was worn by Jennifer Aniston to the premiere of *Along Came Polly*.

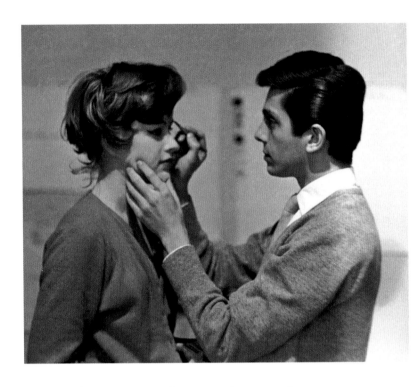

year, a serendipitous meeting with a young architecture student named Giancarlo Giammetti changed everything. Giammetti would become Valentino's partner for life, in both a personal and business capacity. For 12 years, they were romantically involved and later, the pair formed an inseparable bond. In a 2013 interview with *Vanity Fair*, which described the two as "blood brothers", Giammetti explained: "I was just 30 when the physical part of our relationship ended, and it was difficult in the beginning. We had to solve problems with jealousy."

Nevertheless, the love and respect the pair have for each other endures to this day. In 2011, Giammetti told the *Independent* that theirs is "a fraternal love…a relationship with nothing sexual

ABOVE A perfectionist, Valentino was as skilled with make-up as he was with fashion design, and in the early days could be found perfecting models' looks before a show.

in it. Yet a great love remains, ancient, surviving." Valentino also admitted that he and Giammetti were too different to survive as a romantic pairing: "Giancarlo and I understand each other, but his character is the opposite of mine."

Despite their somewhat unorthodox relationship, Giammetti has been intrinsic to the success of Valentino S.p.A. since the very beginning when the fledgling business faced ruin after Valentino's father's business partner withdrew his financial support. Giammetti abandoned his architecture training to work alongside Valentino and the two men moved the salon and atelier from Via Condotti to Via Gregoriana. Their new premises, where they occupied a spacious apartment on the first floor, soon started attracting the glamorous clients for which the house of Valentino would become known.

Italy in the early 1960s was the perfect setting for a designer whose early inspiration came from the glamour of the silver screen. Rome was the home of Cinecittà, roughly translated as

BELOW Rome's Cinecittà studios were the largest in Italy and from 1950 to the early 1970s hosted many famous films. Valentino gleaned great inspiration from the buzz around the studios and its glamorous actresses, especially Italian stars like Sophia Loren and Gina Lollobrigida, pictured here greeting the designer in 1970.

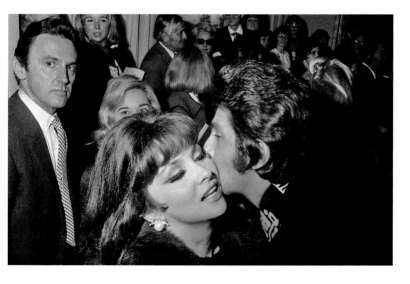

"Cinema City", with its stars including Gina Lollobrigida and Sophia Loren. Directors such as Visconti and Antonioni were taking full advantage of the city's romantic aspect in their films, especially after the success of Federico Fellini's *La Dolce Vita,* released in 1960. That same year, Elizabeth Taylor attended the premiere in Rome of Kubrick's *Spartacus* and was one of the first celebrities to visit Valentino's salon, buying a gown for the occasion and immediately sealing his reputation. It was the start of a long patronage and also a deep friendship.

In 1962, Valentino joined what was known as the Sala Bianca group of couturiers, an initiative set up by Count Giovanni Giorgini in 1951 to give credibility to young Italian fashion designers. From 1952, Giorgini arranged for this early group of just 15 designers to show their collections at the Sala Bianca in the Pitti Palace in Florence a week before the Paris collections to tempt buyers, a tactic that worked remarkably well. As a newcomer, Valentino was given one of the less coveted slots on the final day of the show – but his show was a hit, particularly among the American buyers, and it announced Valentino as a serious player in the world of fashion design. The fashion press took notice too, with a design from the collection featured on the cover of French *Vogue* – an unheard-of accolade for any foreign designer, let alone an Italian one.

The popularity of Valentino's designs among the American fashion buyers marked the beginning of financial profitability for the design house. The cost of producing clothes in Italy was low in comparison to France or America, allowing Valentino to supply department stores and boutiques at extremely reasonable prices. His cachet among American socialites also grew, with relationships forged with the likes of Gloria Guinness, Jackie Kennedy and her younger sister Lee Radziwill, and Nan Kempner. In 2006–07, when the Metropolitan Museum of Art staged a celebration of Kempner's

RIGHT Elizabeth Taylor with Kirk Douglas at the party in Rome for the film *Spartacus*. The actress is wearing a long, pleated, sleeveless Valentino gown with a decadent feathered detail at the bottom.

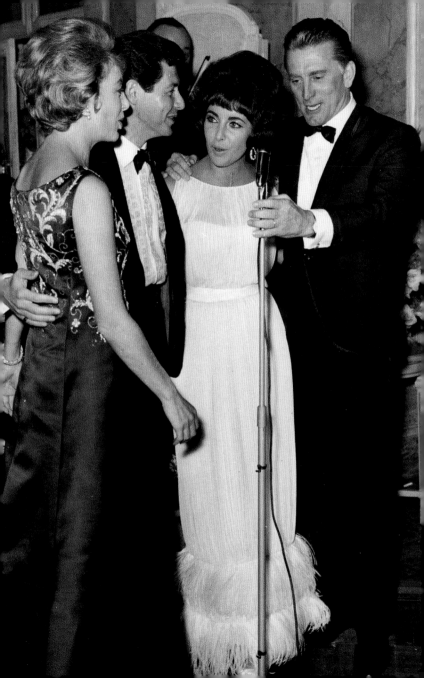

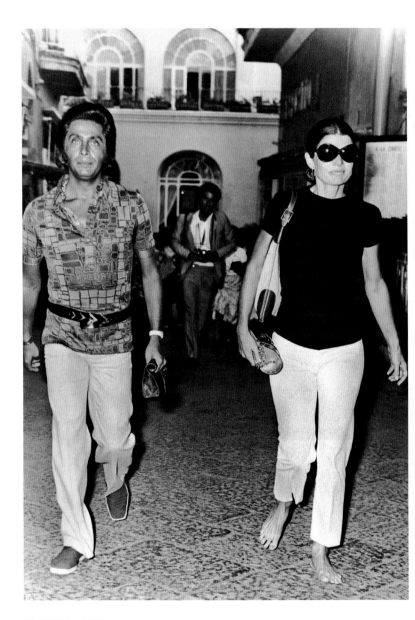

OPPOSITE Jackie
Kennedy Onassis
contributed hugely
to Valentino's early
success. The pair
are pictured here
in Capri in 1970,
the style icon
wearing her beloved
combination of black
and white, which so
inspired Valentino's
monochrome
palette.

OVERLEAF
Marisa Berenson
photographed at Cy
Twombly's Roman
palazzo for *Vogue* in
March 1968 wearing
an outfit from
Valentino's famous
White Collection.

style, Valentino explained: "Nan always looks so wonderful in my clothes, because she had a body like a hanger."

The relationship with Jackie Kennedy was extremely rewarding for Valentino, who started dressing the widowed first lady in 1964. She was one of the most photographed and stylish women of her generation, so her endorsement guaranteed success. In 2007, he told *Vogue*: "I owe so much to Jacqueline Kennedy. Meeting her meant so much to me. She became a very close friend. I designed her entire wardrobe, and she made me famous."

With his new fame came many more orders and increased financial security that allowed Valentino to expand. He opened a salon in Milan, which gave him the confidence to leave the Sala Bianca group and present new collections in his own Roman salon on Via Gregoriana. Seemingly unstoppable, Valentino received the Neiman Marcus Award, a prestigious American fashion prize, in 1967, and shortly afterwards he moved his salon further down the same street to a magnificent eighteenth-century palazzo.

Valentino's designs impressed throughout the mid 1960s as he experimented with a monochrome palette inspired by the black and white wardrobe commissioned by Jackie Kennedy. In 1967, Valentino was again inspired by Jackie Kennedy to make a collection of 12 white dresses, which provided the springboard for his legendary Collezione Bianca, or White Collection, which he presented for Spring/Summer 1968. The collection was extremely accomplished, exhibiting skilful flourishes in both structure and embellishment, and the fashion press went wild. *Vogue* enthused over "his crisp whites, his lacy whites, his soft and creamy whites, all shown together white on white".

The collection went down in history: Pierpaolo Piccioli, the current Valentino creative director, presented an homage in the

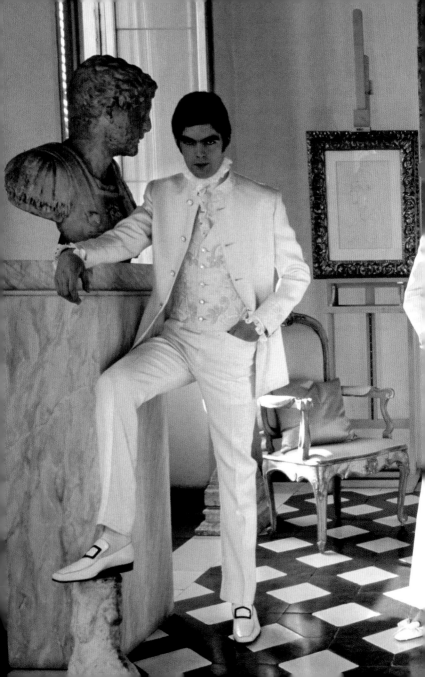

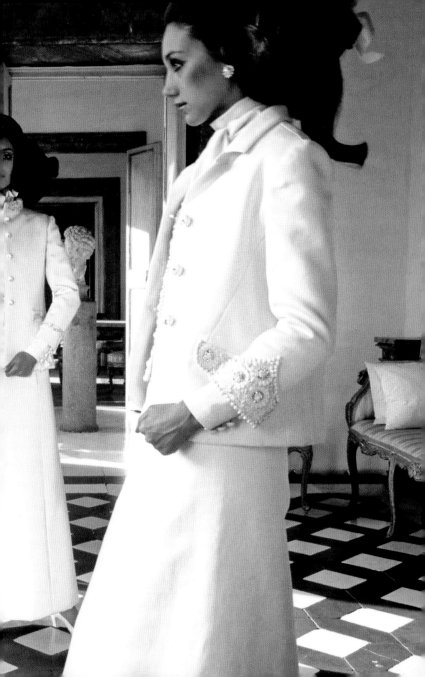

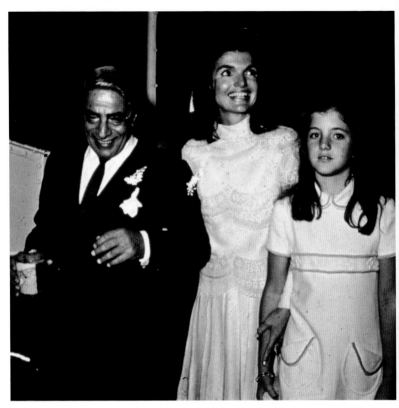

form of 12 white dresses for his Spring/Summer 2020 show. Perhaps the icing on the cake for Valentino himself was Jackie Kennedy choosing one of the dresses from the collection to wear for her second wedding, to Greek shipping magnate Aristotle Onassis, on 20 October 1968.

With his place among the top couturiers in the world confirmed, Valentino returned to open a boutique in Paris in May 1968, a decade after he had left. Finally, he was back in the rarefied world of French haute couture as a designer worthy of their respect.

ABOVE Jackie Kennedy Onassis pictured wearing a Valentino gown for her 1968 wedding to shipping magnate Aristotle Onassis. The couple are accompanied by 10-year-old Caroline Kennedy.

BELOW Valentino's Paris boutique proved immensely popular. Here, the designer helps Countess Maria Elena di Rovasenda with her many purchases.

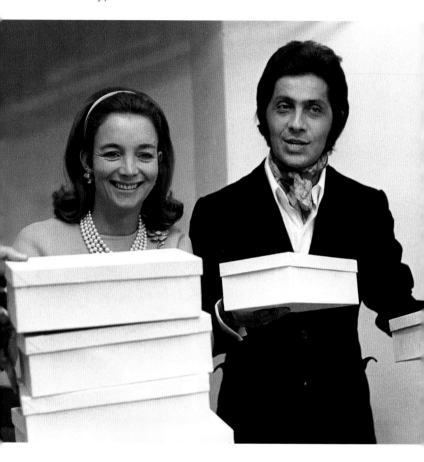

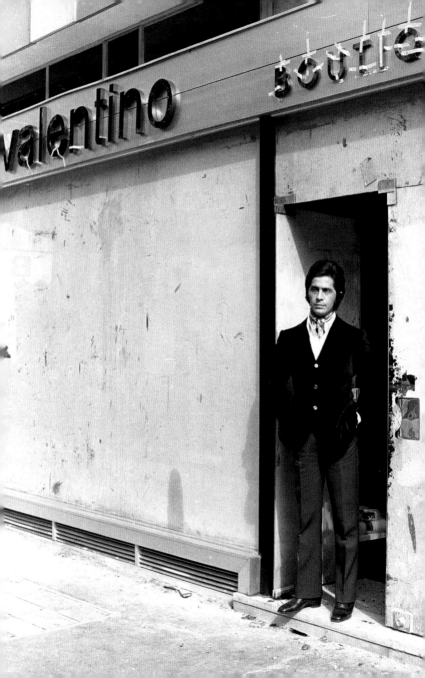

RIGHT By the end of
the 1960s, Valentino's
trademark glamorous
style was firmly
established. In 1967,
Marisa Berenson
modeled a vibrant
fuchsia pink Valentino
gown for *Vogue*.

OPPOSITE Valentino
standing in the
doorway of his first
Paris boutique, which
opened in 1968.

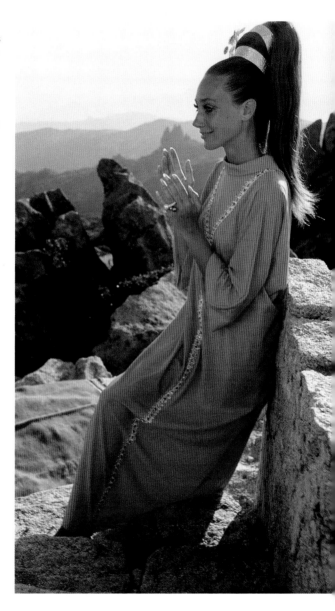

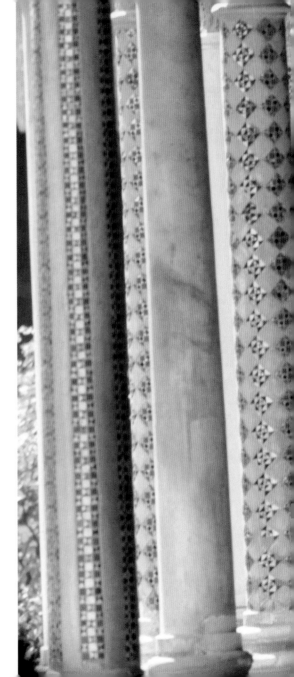

OPPOSITE In a 1967 shoot for *Vogue*, model Benedetta Barzini epitomizes Valentino's ostentatious Italian style in a red wool and lurex brocade evening dress against a backdrop of the Benedictine cloister in Monreale, Sicily.

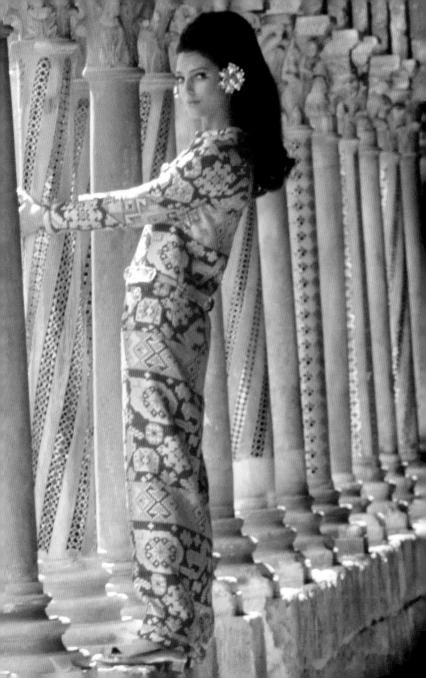

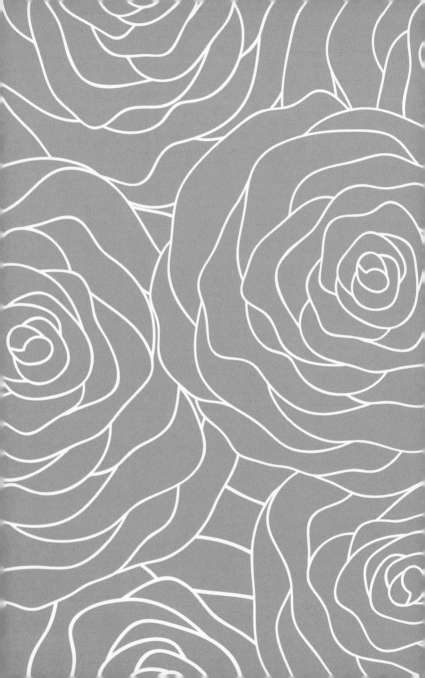

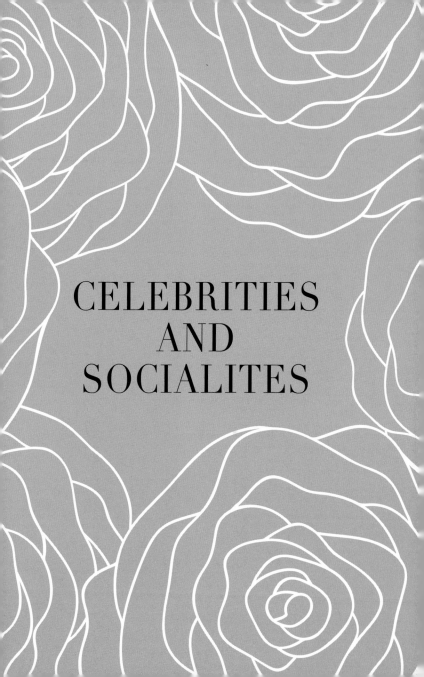

CELEBRITIES
AND
SOCIALITES

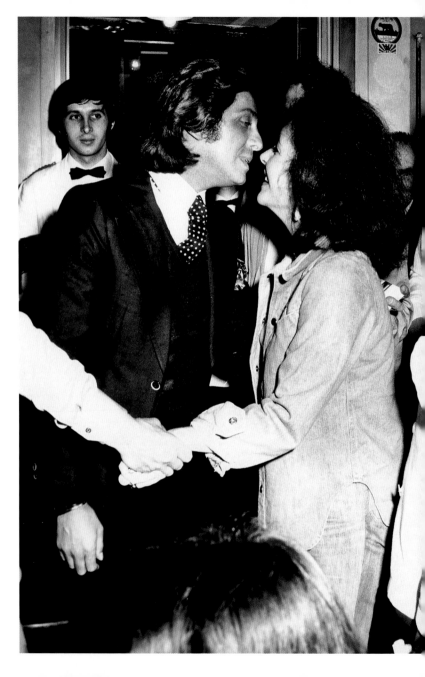

MUSES AND FRIENDS

Valentino has spent his career dressing the most glamorous women in the world, becoming many a celebrity's first choice of designer. He has also formed close friendships with several of his famous clients, regularly socializing with them and finding inspiration in designing for certain women who fulfilled the role of fashion muses.

Valentino was first introduced to the seductive glamour of celebrity clients early in his career, when he worked with the renowned couturier Jean Dessès. Born in Egypt to Greek parents, Dessès regularly created outfits for members of the Greek and Egyptian royal houses as well as the Greek shipping magnate Aristotle Onassis, who later married the widowed Jackie Kennedy. She chose a Valentino gown for the occasion.

The actress who had the earliest influence on Valentino's career was Elizabeth Taylor. The star, who was in Rome filming *Cleopatra*, had heard about an exciting new designer and asked to see his collection, with a view to wearing one of his gowns to the

OPPOSITE Elizabeth Taylor was one of Valentino's earliest muses and the pair remained friends until her death. Here, Taylor greets Valentino with a kiss at a restaurant in Rome in the 1970s.

premiere of the film *Spartacus*, starring her friend Kirk Douglas. As Valentino later recalled of their first meeting: "My mouth was open in front of this beauty. She was unbelievable."

Taylor did wear Valentino to the premiere, a white column gown from his Autumn/Winter 1961 collection. Thirty years later, in 1991, the actress paid tribute to her very first Valentino gown when she appeared at an anniversary celebration of the fashion house in Rome wearing a stunning white, off-the-shoulder dress.

Elizabeth Taylor became a lifelong client and friend of Valentino, although, true to her reputation as somewhat of a diva, was not shy about demanding complimentary dresses. The day after the *Spartacus* premiere gown received so much publicity, "she came to the fashion house," Valentino told the *Daily Telegraph* in 2014, "and wanted seven outfits. She said, 'Oh, you have so much publicity with me today – I deserve this, this, this, this.'"

Taylor was an excellent ambassador for Valentino's clothes, as was Sophia Loren, another close friend since the early days of the Rome atelier and a woman whose seductive style and glamorous Italian beauty he constantly cited as inspiration. But perhaps the most iconic of all his muses was Jackie Kennedy. In 2016, he told icon-icon.com how much she meant to him as both a friend and loyal patron: "She inspired me, supported me during difficult times. With her style, she was able to get people talking about me by getting them to talk about her."

Their relationship began when Kennedy went to Valentino to help her create a suitable mourning wardrobe after the assassination of her husband, John F. Kennedy, in November 1963. Valentino designed six dresses, all in black and white, which he acknowledges sparked a lifelong love of a monochrome palette and one which he returned to time and time again in his later collections.

OPPOSITE Sophia Loren was one of Valentino's favourite actresses from his early years in Rome and they stayed close, often attending events together such as this party in New York in 1992.

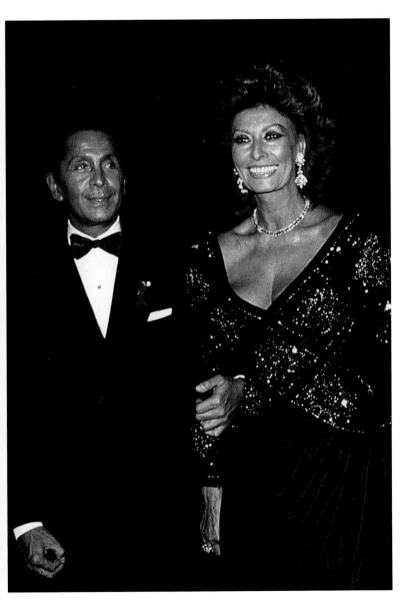

After Jackie's death in 1994, Valentino approached her children to see if he could buy back some of the many gowns he had made for her over the years. According to Isabel Jones, writing for *InStyle* in 2019, he considered them to be "among the most beautiful I've ever created".

Remarkably, he was told that many of her dresses, including a number of iconic Valentino creations, had been donated to a convent. Apparently, her son John told the dumbfounded designer: "We couldn't bear the thought of walking down the street and seeing people in her clothes, so we gave them away."

Jackie Kennedy helped Valentino become popular among a set of New York socialites who had great influence over what became fashionable, but it was Diana Vreeland, the legendary editor of *Vogue*, who sealed his reputation as a celebrity designer. Valentino credits her as being an important muse to him, especially with their mutual love of the colour red.

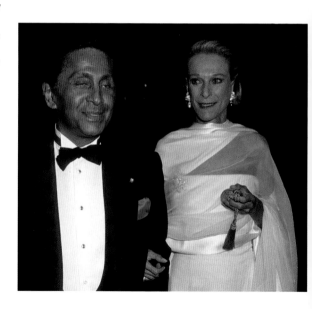

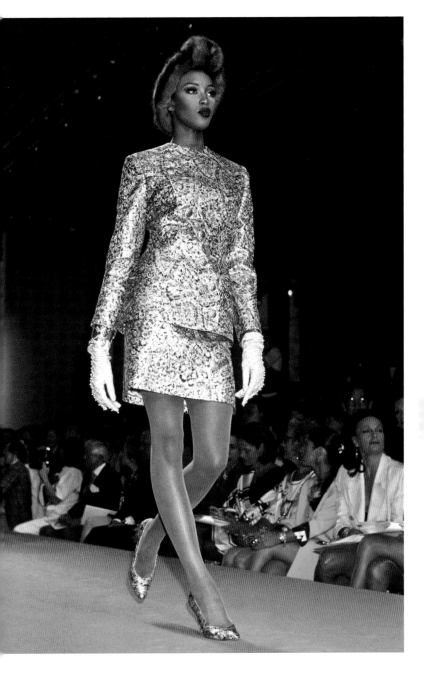

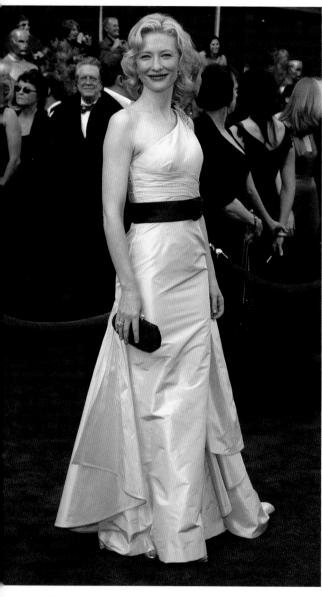

LEFT Cate Blanchett wearing belted yellow Valentino to the 2005 Academy Awards, when she was nominated for Best Actress for her performance in *The Aviator*.

OPPOSITE Victoria Beckham and Valentino at the 2018 Fashion Awards in partnership with Swarovski in London in 2018.

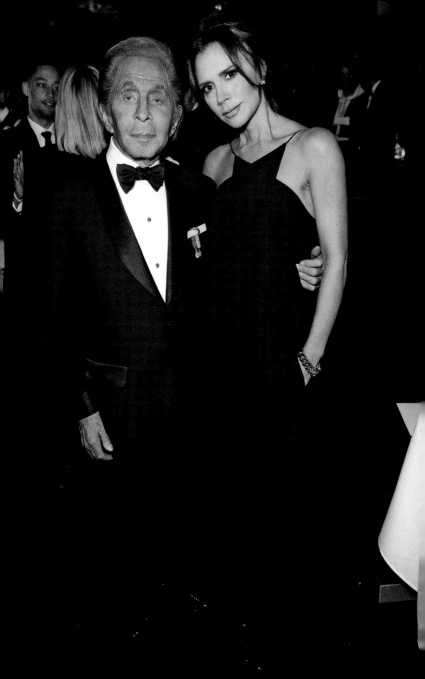

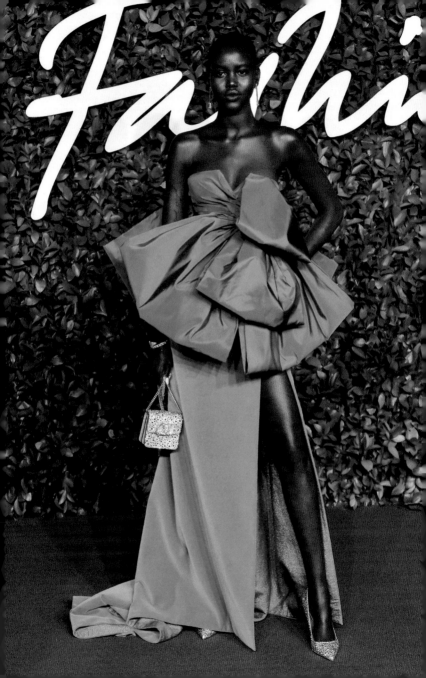

OPPOSITE More
recently, Pierpaolo
Piccioli has adopted
model Adut Akech as
his muse, shown here
arriving at the 2019
Fashion Awards in a
forest-green velvet
and taffeta dress by
the designer.

In 2017, he told HuffPost: "Diana Vreeland, we called her the
Chinese Empress because she loved China and the color red.
She was the most important lady in the world at the time, and
taught me a way to see and appreciate pictures. I learned a lot
from her."

Over the years, a number of models have inspired Valentino,
his two favourites being Gisele Bündchen and Naomi Campbell.
Indeed, Campbell closed the show for his final appearance before
he retired in 2008. She also returned to the Valentino catwalk
for Pierpaolo Piccioli's Spring/Summer 2019 haute couture
collection and stunned in the final outfit: a revealing black gown
with a semi-transparent chiffon bodice and voluptuous, black,
ruched taffeta skirt. Bündchen is close to Valentino to this day,
having appeared in many of his shows and campaigns from 1998
until her retirement in 2015.

Since Maria Grazia Chiuri and Pierpaolo Piccioli took the
helm at Valentino, many diverse modern icons have become
muses for the fashion house. Singer Florence Welch has
inspired many of the more bohemian, floral styles the pair have
created, while actress Olivia Palermo and her red-carpet outfits
represent the timelessly elegant aesthetic that is still so intrinsic
to Valentino. In 2019, Piccioli appointed model Adut Akech as
the face of Valentino, and that same year Janet Mock, award-
winning writer, director and producer of the television series
Pose and campaigner for transgender rights, became the face of
Valentino's VSLING bag.

VALENTINO RED

Since his first collection in 1959 and the strapless, rose-adorned bright red cocktail dress named "Fiesta", Valentino has included a stunning Valentino Red dress every season, and in 2000, a tribute to Valentino's four decades as a fashion designer presented 40 dresses in the couturier's signature bold hue at Rome's Piazza di Spagna.

RIGHT Claudia Schiffer wearing a Valentino Red gown with cutaway bodice to the Valentino 45th Anniversary Celebration Gala at the Villa Borghese in Rome in 2007.

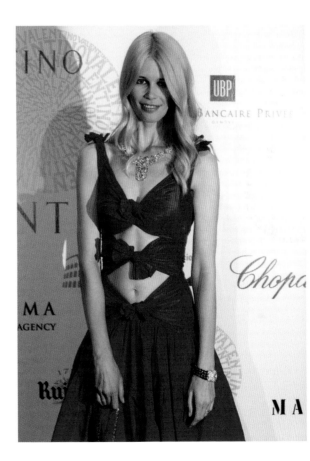

The shade, which Valentino told Hans Ulrich Obrist was "the first colour to have a big impact on me", is unique, and in 2012, the designer described his inspiration for creating it to *Marie Claire*: "When I was young, I went to see the opera *Carmen* in Barcelona and the whole set was red – the flowers, the costumes – and l said to myself, 'I want to keep this colour in my life.' So I mixed a shade with the people who make fabrics – it contains a certain amount of orange – and Valentino Red became an official Pantone colour."

Many celebrities have chosen a Valentino gown in the house's signature colour to appear on the red carpet. Some of the most memorable include Jennifer Aniston, who wore a classic, strapless, flowing version to the Oscars in 2013; Claudia Schiffer, who chose a gown with a cutaway bodice for the Valentino 45th Anniversary Celebration Gala in 2007; and Penelope Cruz, whose red column gown with rose detail wowed viewers at the David di Donatello Awards in 2004.

Other devotees who have worn Valentino Red include Emma Watson and Claire Danes as well as the actress Anne Hathaway, who is, says Valentino, "like a daughter" to him. She chose a vintage Valentino to wear to the Oscars in 2011, inspiring *Vogue* to comment: "The Oscars provided an interesting case study in Valentino then and now. Representing the 'then'

BELOW For the 2011 Academy Award ceremony Anne Hathaway wore a Valentino couture strapless red silk taffeta gown from 2002 with a puffed fishtail skirt featuring the designer's favourite rose motif.

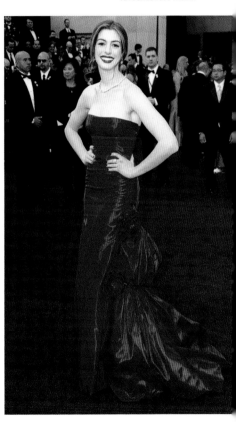

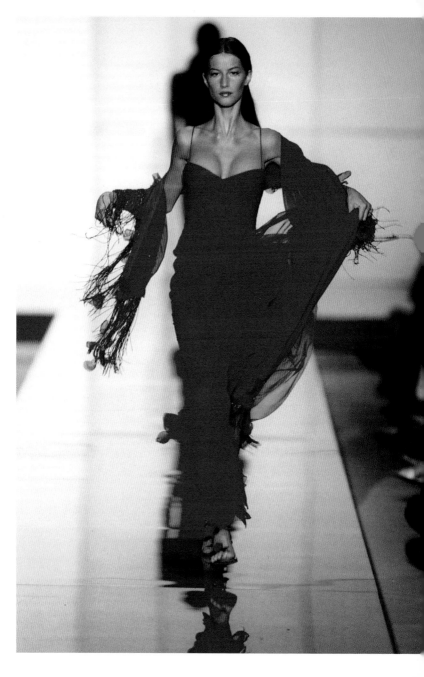

camp was Anne Hathaway in an archival red glamour gown dating to the mid-aughts. And in the 'now' corner: Florence and the Machine's Florence Welch in a high-necked, semi-sheer lace dress from the Spring haute couture collection by Maria Grazia Chiuri and Pierpaolo Piccioli."

Of course, it is not just Valentino's red gowns that appeal to celebrities, and plenty of memorable Oscar frocks can be attributed to the Italian designer: Julia Roberts wore vintage black and white Valentino to collect the award for Best Actress in 2001; Jennifer Lopez wore a Jackie Kennedy Onassis-inspired mint-green kaftan in 2003; and Cate Blanchett chose belted yellow Valentino in 2005. Looking further back, Sophia Loren wore a heavily embroidered Valentino to collect her Lifetime Achievement Award in 1991, and Elizabeth Taylor and Susan Sarandon have both donned the designer to attend the famous awards ceremony over the years.

OPPOSITE Gisele Bündchen wearing a Valentino Red gown for the Autumn/ Winter 1999 haute couture show in Paris.

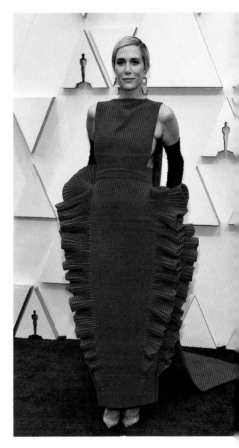

RIGHT A stunning example of a Valentino Red gown is this silk dress with extravagant ruching, given a modern twist by Kristen Wiig for the 2020 Academy Awards by the addition of long black gloves.

OPPOSITE Queen Máxima and King Willem-Alexander of the Netherlands were wed in 2002, the bride wearing a deceptively simple ivory Valentino gown in duchesse satin, with a high stand collar and three-quarter length sleeves.

WEDDING DRESSES

Given the showstopping quality of Valentino gowns, it is unsurprising that many women have chosen to wear them for their weddings. The first he designed was the high-necked, knee-length, off-white couture gown, embellished with intricate lace, in which Jackie Kennedy married Aristotle Onassis, but through the decades Valentino has created stunning gowns for Anne Hathaway, Courteney Cox, Jennifer Lopez and Elizabeth Taylor, who wore a pale-yellow lace gown for her eighth marriage to Larry Fortensky.

Ladylike and traditional, his designs have appealed to many European royals, including Queen Máxima of the Netherlands and Marie-Chantal, Crown Princess of Greece, who chose similar styles for their respective weddings. The designer even came out of retirement to oversee the creation of wedding gowns for his close friends Princess Madeleine of Sweden and Tatiana Santo Domingo, who married Andrea Casiraghi (grandson of Princess Grace of Monaco) in Gstaad in February 2014 wearing a dramatic, ruffled Valentino gown with matching long fur cape to combat the cold.

LEFT Jennifer Lopez married Chris Judd in 2001 wearing a Chantilly lace Valentino dress.

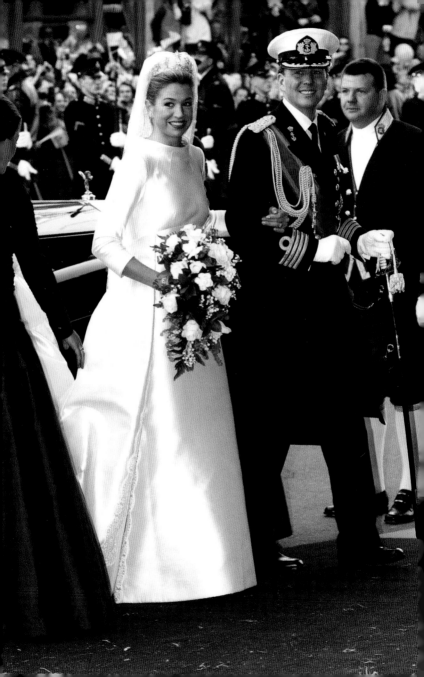

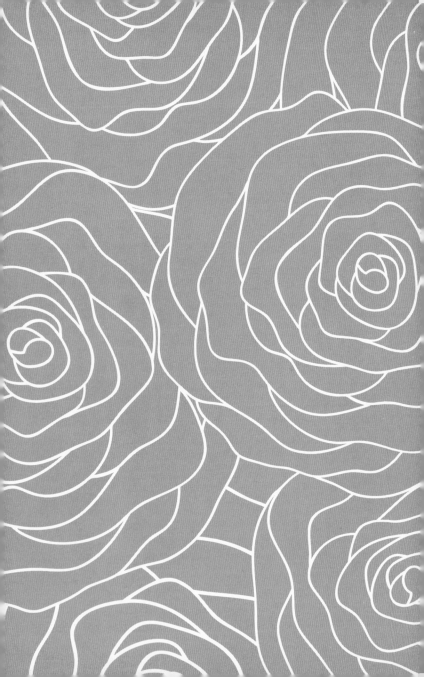

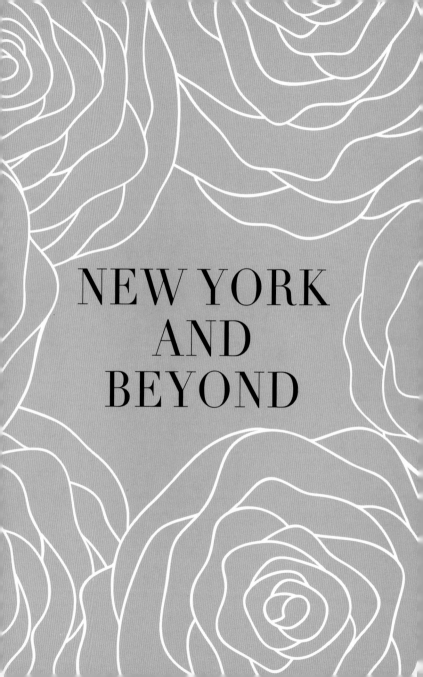

NEW YORK
AND
BEYOND

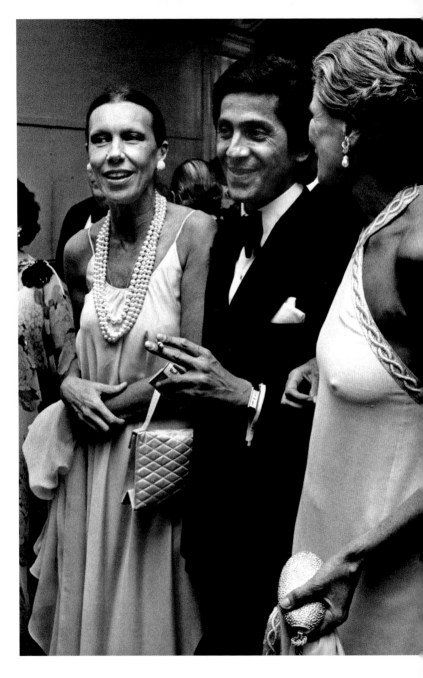

IN WITH THE IN-CROWD

At the beginning of the 1970s, Rome's deteriorating political situation made the city less attractive to the Hollywood elite who had flocked there during the 1960s.

Valentino's salon still saw biannual pilgrimages by American fashion buyers and press as well as clients happy to absorb themselves in the glamour of his new collections, but for the fashion house to move forward, a more international presence was essential.

With a keen eye for business, Giancarlo Giammetti decided to focus on expanding ready-to-wear by outsourcing production to the French garment manufacturer Mendès, which would streamline their operation and increase capacity. A highly reputable firm that worked with top fashion designers, including Yves Saint Laurent and Valentino's mentor Jean Dessès, Mendès was happy to take on Valentino – thanks to the designer's positive presence in the American market.

OPPOSITE Valentino, accompanied here by New York socialite Nan Kempner and Françoise de la Renta, arrives at a benefit show organized by the designer for the Special Olympics in 1976.

Another change made by the fashion house was to move the presentation of Valentino's ready-to-wear collections to Paris, although he continued showing his haute couture shows at his Rome salon. It was a bold decision. Most Italian designers stuck to their home turf in Milan because the French fashion world was notoriously hostile to outsiders, yet Valentino's Paris shows were successful, even if the audience were mostly Italians and Americans.

RIGHT AND OPPOSITE A 1976 charity show attracted many of Valentino's celebrity clients, including Jackie Kennedy Onassis, pictured here in the front row and afterwards chatting animatedly to Bobby Shriver.

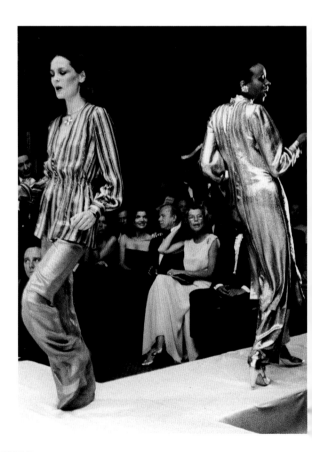

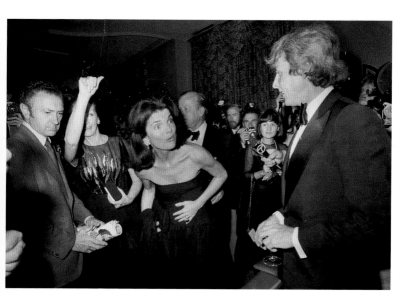

Valentino owed a lot to America. First, to the buyers who had flocked to place orders in the early days of his atelier, giving the designer the financial security he needed for his business to thrive, and second, to the country's socialites. As the decade turned, Valentino and Giammetti started to spend more time in New York, and in 1970, they opened a much-anticipated flagship store. Finding the right spot was essential. After first setting up on Fifth Avenue, Valentino moved his boutique uptown to 801 Madison Avenue, handily situated to cater to the Upper East Side ladies whose loyal patronage was essential to the image of his brand.

In a testament to Valentino's own celebrity and love of attention, the press excitedly reported the opening, which the *New York Times* likened to a Hollywood premiere, observing: "The main attractions were the architecture and the people last night at the opening for Valentino's porcelain and glass boutique

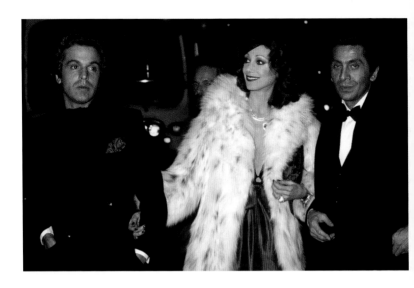

. . . and both could be admired from the outside. Because of the heat and the crowds, a lot of people brought their champagne out on the sidewalk . . . and if the crowds let up for a moment, they could always watch Naomi Sims and Marina Schiano, models who were posing in the big glass cylinder that is the shop's show window."

With his popularity showing no sign of flagging and a reliable manufacturer in place to fulfil big orders, Valentino expanded to open stores across the United States, in cities including San Francisco, Boston, Dallas and Palm Springs, where the launch of the Rodeo Drive store heralded another celebrity-filled party.

Already a designer with an excellent reputation, Valentino secured his place in the upper echelons of the fashion world thanks to the endorsement of Diana Vreeland, the legendary *Vogue* editor, and the pair remained lifelong close friends. The formidable fashion doyenne first met Valentino in 1964 and immediately gave him her seal of approval, telling him: "Even at birth, genius always stands out. I see genius in you. Good luck."

He told *The Cut* in 2015 that when he arrived in New York, Vreeland went out of her way to include him: "She did everything, just her calls in the morning, inviting us to the theater or a dinner with Andy [Warhol], to a performance of the Liquid Theater or just a dinner at Pearl's with Jackie [Kennedy], and I felt New York was at my feet."

Valentino's relationship with Andy Warhol was also an influential one. The men moved in the same social circles and were both regulars at the notorious nightclub Studio 54. In 1978, Valentino even held his birthday party at the Factory, Warhol's New York studio. Warhol also created four silk-screen prints of Valentino during the 1970s. Despite admitting to Hans Ulrich Obrist that he was "not crazy about them", the designer did eventually buy two.

The 1970s social scene was captured in Polaroids taken by

BELOW In 1977, Valentino held a circus-themed birthday party at Studio 54. Carlos Souza and Lorenzo Villarini were among the immaculately costumed guests.

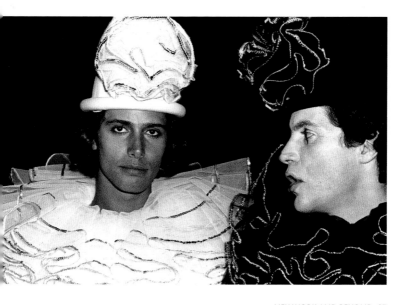

Valentino's partner Giancarlo Giammetti, who shared some of the shots from his personal collection in 2021 to honour the designer Halston. Alongside Halston and Andy Warhol, there are images of Liza Minnelli, Diane von Furstenberg, Bianca Jagger and Elsa Peretti, as well as many of Valentino himself.

Despite his profile as an avid socialite, Valentino was first and foremost a fashion designer. Throughout his career, he was remarkably consistent in his choice of prints, colours and silhouettes, only gently adapting his designs to nod to the trends of the era. Take, for example, the 1970s trend for peasant dresses popularized by the hippies and freethinkers of the time. The loose style was elevated to a new level of elegance by Valentino, who in 1971 created a whimsical off-white dress in flowing organza printed with poppies and wheat, matched with a wide-brimmed straw hat and adorned with silk poppies in his trademark red.

Flowers were a constant inspiration in his fashion designs. As in his homes and studio, where floral arrangements were always on display, his gowns featured a wide variety of printed and embellished flowers and were adorned by blousy organza facsimiles. A romantic at heart, the designer explained his obsession to Marie-Paule Pellé in 1991: "I have paid homage to all the flowers that I love so much through my creations of fabrics and dresses: that was my way of thanking all these marvels that have given me so much pleasure."

This slow evolution of Valentino's designs to accommodate changing fashions is exemplified by his journey through the 1970s. It began with a continuation of the elegant shift dresses and coats of his beloved 1960s, albeit with a slightly longer hemline. But soon, long jackets, wide harem-style trousers and kaftans started to appear, made in the brocades, paisleys and other elaborately printed fabrics Valentino so loved. He found inspiration in Gustav Klimt and the Ballets Russes and drew all

OPPOSITE In 1972 actress Raquel Welch was photographed for *Vogue* wearing a blue Valentino halterneck dress with a long trailing scarf. The gown's carefully pleated skirt shows Valentino's technical skills, while the design reflects the flowing style of the period.

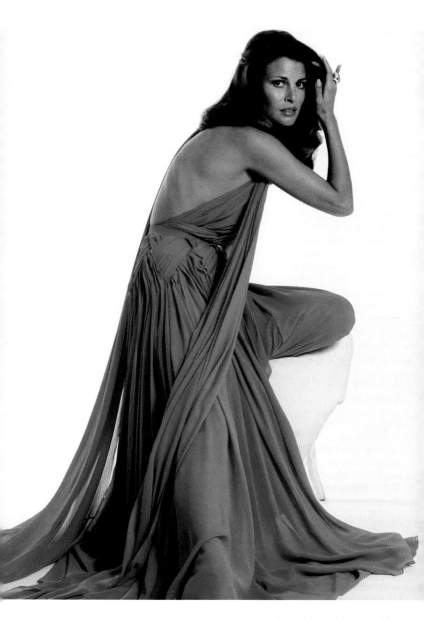

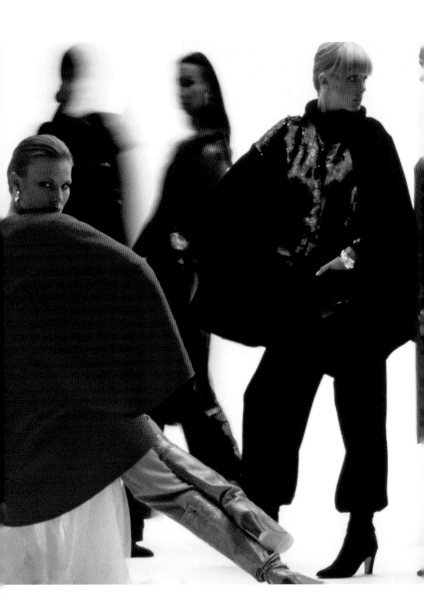

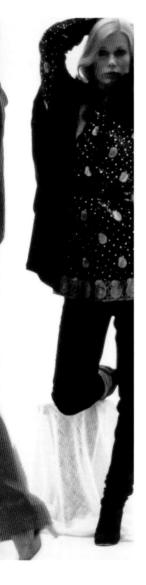

the threads together to create a 1970s silhouette, the essence of which remained true to Valentino's obsession with perfect tailoring and a detailed finish.

Another 1970s favourite of Valentino's was the asymmetrical flowing gown, subtly exposing shoulder, made from a draped silk crepe and edged with hand-sewn, glittering crystals. He did not, like some designers, fall prey to disco fever, always maintaining in his clothes a subtle elegance and femininity that would become his calling card for decades to come.

Other recurrent themes included animal prints, which lent themselves to the long, flowing kaftans and coats of the 1970s, and the black and white graphic patterns to which he so often returned in his designs. As the decade came to a close, the shape of the 1980s began to emerge: long, fitted skirts paired with blouson jackets flaring peplum-style at the waist and the shoulders gradually edging outwards. He also began to appreciate tweeds, a trend that continued throughout the following decade.

After a decade of glamour and regular parties in New York, and opening stores in Paris, London

LEFT Valentino's designs remained remarkably consistent throughout his career. However, he always tweaked his silhouette to reflect current trends. This 1976 *Vogue* editorial shoot features flowing red and black ponchos and wide trousers in Valentino's colour palette, but the shapes are very much of the decade.

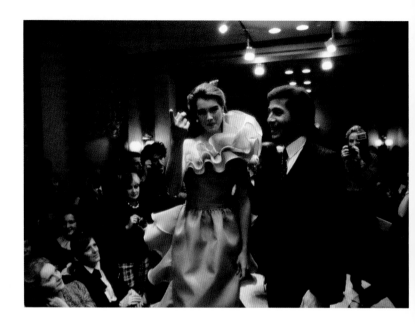

ABOVE Despite being just 15 years old at the time, actress and model Brooke Shields became Valentino's muse, and the star of the haute couture Spring/Summer 1981 catwalk show and campaign.

and Tokyo, Valentino returned in the 1980s to spend more time back in Rome. From a design point of view, he struggled, admitting he couldn't bear the 1980s silhouette. Speaking in 2014 as part of the *Fashion Icons with Fern Mallis* conversation series, he admitted: "I hated those dresses in the 80s, they were out of proportion with shoulders that didn't belong to the fit, they were all terrible, terrible!"

Nevertheless, his signature style seemed to capture something about the new decade and in February 1981, *Time* magazine ran photographs of the actress and model Brooke Shields, with the caption "The '80s Look". Within the issue was a shot of her wearing a red Valentino dress. Very much the face of the moment, Shields was fresh from filming *Blue Lagoon* when she starred in the Valentino haute couture Spring/Summer 1981 catwalk show and the subsequent campaign shot by celebrated

American fashion photographer Richard Ballarian. At the time, Shields was just 15 years old, yet she nevertheless projected a sophisticated glamour combined with a fresh-faced innocence that epitomized Valentino's ideal woman.

In 1982, encouraged by his friend and mentor Diana Vreeland, Valentino returned stateside to show his Autumn/Winter haute couture collection in New York rather than at his salon in Rome. The extravagant show, held before 800 select guests at the Metropolitan Museum of Art, was followed by an exclusive dinner for 300. In its review, the *New York Times* praised the designer: "Not everyone can give a party in the awesome, vaulting halls and galleries of the Metropolitan Museum of Art… Valentino is justly renowned as one of the great creators and purveyors of alluring, instinctively feminine evening clothes. As one admiring customer says, 'His clothes are

BELOW In 1982, Valentino showed his haute couture collection in New York for the first time, before an audience of 800 exclusive guests at the Metropolitan Museum of Art. Here, Andy Warhol, Lauren Hutton, Mikhail Baryshnikov and Brooke Shields applaud the designer.

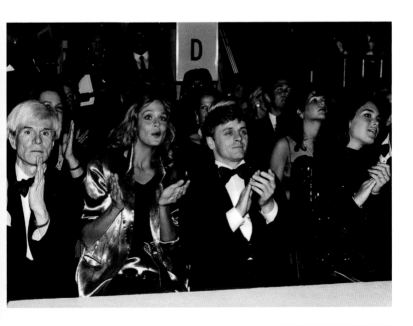

the essence of couture, made of the most luxurious fabrics and colors. One can wear them forever.'"

Valentino's success continued: as well as womenswear and menswear, he launched a range for young adults and children, named Oliver after his favourite dog. His ready-to-wear collections went from strength to strength, appealing to the independent 1980s woman who still wanted to remain feminine, preferring subtle shapes to other designers' severe power suits with the excessively oversized shoulders Valentino so despised. Even when he did present a suit, and bowed to the fashion moment by enlarging and squaring off the shoulders, it was more likely to be a dandyish pinstriped trouser suit, harking back to an older period in style, perhaps with a provocative slashed front and styled with a single red rose. His 1980s colour palette, centred around white, black, grey and red, was broken up by romantic gowns in dusky pinks.

As always, Valentino remained devoted to his love of tailoring and, most importantly, never lost his ability to showcase the elegance of the female form. In the early part of the decade, his two-piece outfits had long jackets, nodding to but just resisting the full inverted triangle demanded by the 1980s silhouette, atop full, flared skirts, while red tights offered a foil to black and grey. Gowns from the period include a gloriously full black and white dress modelled by supermodel Iman, the skirt falling in copious layers, the contrasting white high neck pleated into a wide ruff, its midsection pulled in tight to accentuate her long torso and tiny waist. Ruffles were always a longtime favourite of Valentino and sat perfectly within the decade's fashion aesthetic.

As the years progressed, Valentino embraced plenty of classic 1980s trends – including tweed suits, argyle prints, puffball skirts and shimmering sequins – and in 1983, a *Vogue* editorial much admired his glossy, red, sequinned sheath

OPPOSITE Despite famously declaring his hatred of 1980s fashion, Valentino nevertheless managed to combine his usual refined style with the decade's silhouette – epitomized here by a pale-yellow day suit from 1985, the shoulders only subtly squared off.

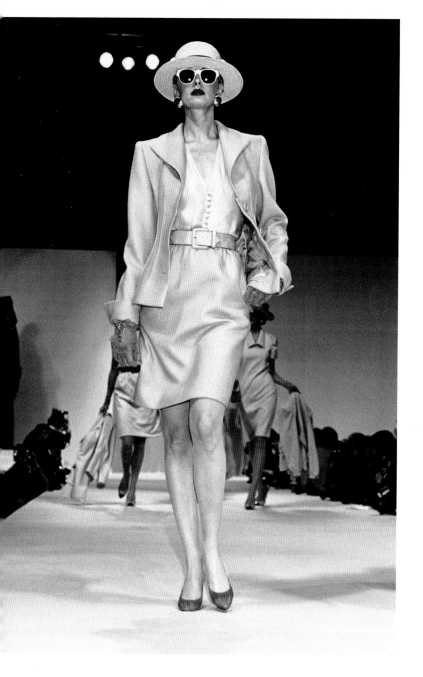

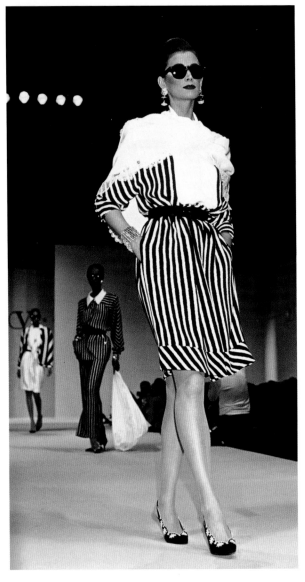

LEFT The monochrome palette was one that Valentino returned to time and time again. For Spring/Summer 1985, he presented several variations on the theme, including a striped, belted dress and a pair of wide-shouldered, double-breasted suits in reverse colourways.

dress that appeared almost liquid as it slid over the model's body. Black and white remained stalwarts for dresses, which in the 1980s most often came in the shape of cocktail dresses – including a stunning design from 1982 consisted of a black strapless bodice with a large bow at the back, billowing out into a balloon skirt in chequered black and white taffeta.

By the end of the decade, Valentino's outfits very much had the feel of what we now associate with 1980s fashions. A black suit from his Autumn/Winter 1989 collection, for example, featured a double-breasted jacket with square shoulders and large buttons, and a straight knee-length skirt. And the following year, as the decade turned, a collection of puffball cocktail dresses appeared for Valentino's Autumn/Winter 1990 show, epitomized by one of his favourite models Naomi Campbell strutting down the catwalk in a neat black dress, its bodice in ruched silk chiffon, the flared skirt adorned with black ostrich feathers and silver bow detail.

The 1980s saw key changes as well as increased recognition on the global stage for Valentino. In 1983, he relocated his Autumn/Winter haute couture show from his intimate salon to the nearby Piazza Mignanelli, an outdoor space large enough to easily accommodate a thousand guests. And in 1984, Valentino designed

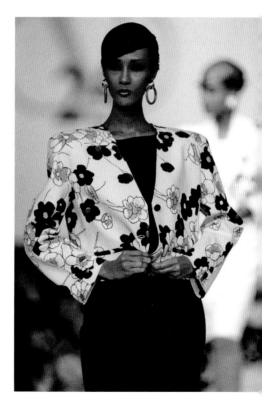

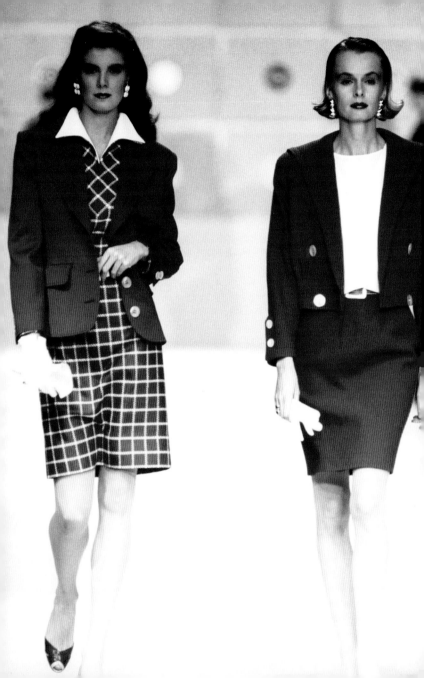

OPPOSITE
Valentino's challenge
during the 1980s
was to juxtapose the
severe fashions of
the decade with the
elegance for which
he was renowned.
These two red and
white outfits show
the designer's skill in
balancing trend with
his trademark style.

RIGHT A perfectly
tailored red, ochre
and brown plaid
suit with oversized
black buttons from
Autumn/Winter 1985,
made all the more
elegant by the model's
accent red leather
gloves and hat.

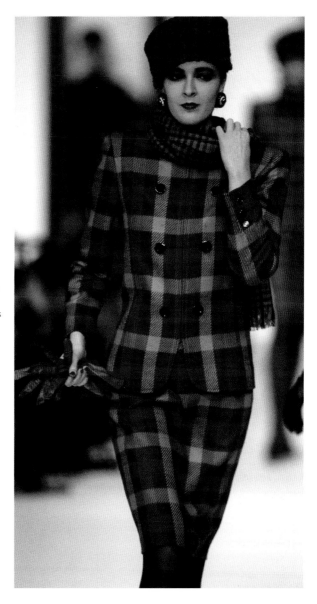

RIGHT Every
Valentino collection
included a striking
evening gown in his
trademark Valentino
Red. In 1985, a
figure-skimming
gown, slashed to the
waist, is teamed with
an oversized cape
and large statement
earrings.

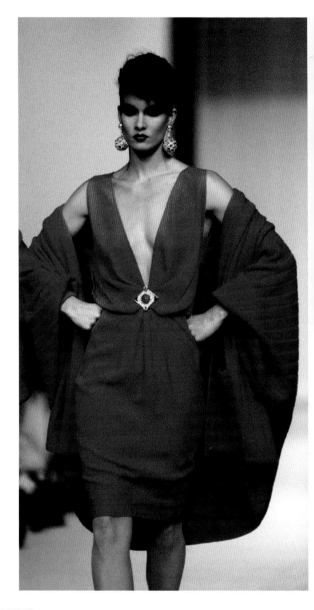

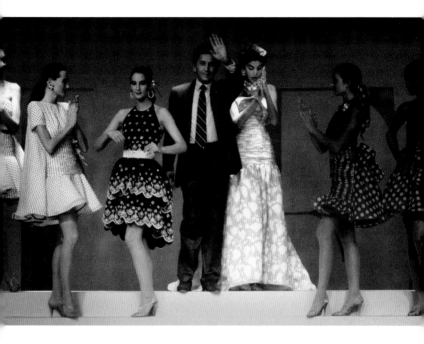

the outfits for the Italian Olympic teams and received an award from Italy's minister of industry.

The move to presenting his couture collections in the open-air setting of the Piazza Mignanelli was a great success, and Valentino continued showing against the backdrop of its impressive palazzo until 1989, when he moved his haute couture shows to Paris to join his ready-to-wear collections. In doing so, he finally realized his dream from the 1950s: to be welcomed into the elite group of top designers who truly belonged in the fashion capital of the world. At the end of the 1980s, the Palazzo Mignanelli became the home of Valentino's business operation, housing its management, atelier and showrooms, where they remain to this day.

ABOVE By 1988, on-trend frills and flounces and polka dots were becoming a mainstay of Valentino's designs, yet, as always, his offerings retained a dignity that other designers did not always master.

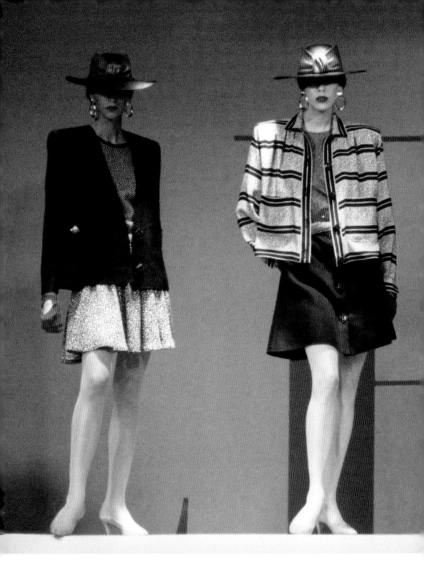

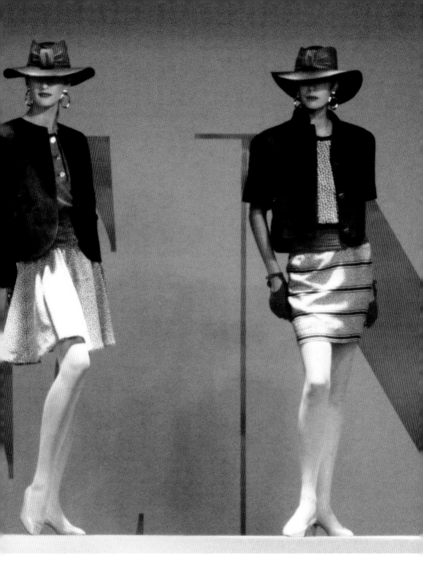

ABOVE This still from Spring/Summer 1988 shows Valentino's love of a bold
yet simple colour palette within a collection. Here, bold 1980s-style outfits in
navy and silver are offset with bows and buttons in his favourite pillar-box red.

The beginning of the 1990s marked three decades of Valentino, and in appreciation of all that the designer had achieved, a series of lunches, dinners, parties and two exhibitions were scheduled in Rome for June 1991. Praise was lavished upon the designer, with accolades arriving from Valentino's contemporaries including Hubert de Givenchy, Carla Fendi and Gianfranco Ferré. The retrospectives were widely admired, the *New York Times* confirming that they "establish him as a major player in shaping fashion in the last half of the 20th century".

Seeing Valentino's work from the previous 30 years in one retrospective bore out the fact that his style vision had remained extremely clear since his very early years as an apprentice to Jean Dessès. For the exhibition, drawings done by the then 19-year-old Valentino were recreated into a series of dresses for the exhibition, revealing a similar aesthetic to his later designs. As the *New York Times* put it: "As the work of 30 years was gathered

BELOW In 1991, an exhibition of 2,000 of Valentino's outfits, along with many of his original drawings, was held in Rome. Here, the designer is seen leafing through his sketchbook of illustrations, surrounded by mannequins wearing his designs from the previous three decades.

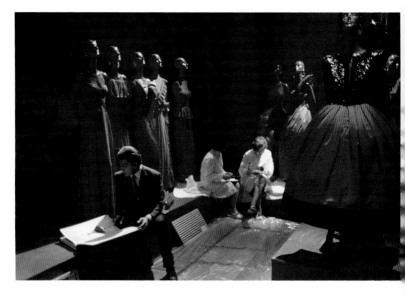

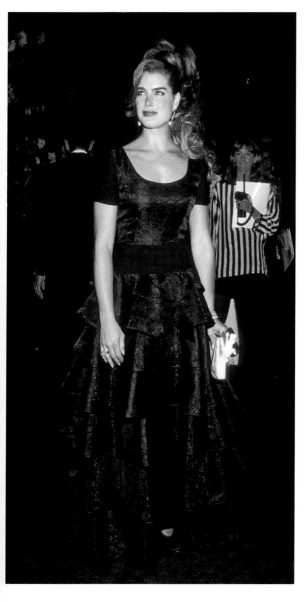

LEFT A series of exhibitions and galas were held in the early 1990s to celebrate 30 years of Valentino's success. Here, in 1992, Brooke Shields attends the gala Valentino: Thirty Years of Magic.

OPPOSITE Christy
Turlington walking
the runway for
Autumn/Winter 1990
in a high-necked
purple minidress
with exquisite lace
detailing.

together, grouped not chronologically but by themes, it was clear that Valentino had his basic ideas clearly in his head at the beginning of his career; he simply refined them as he went along, bringing more assurance and finesse to his work".

The conclusion on seeing the selection of outfits – including 2,000 from the Valentino archives and 700 contributed by clients – was that the "effect was cohesive as well as dazzling." It left "an impression of delicacy and sensitivity, of glamour as well as grandeur".

The early 1990s, trend-wise, had not moved on much from the short dresses of the late 1980s, which were still very much in vogue. As ever, Valentino refined his version of the look for his Spring/Summer 1992 ready-to-wear collection by adding scalloped edges to his bodices and choosing an array of girlish floral prints and pastel colours. More grown-up were the geometric-printed two-pieces, with belted unstructured jackets teamed with contrasting print trousers. Above all, everything was feminine, glamorous and exquisitely crafted.

Haute couture collections from this period saw Valentino indulge his love of unadulterated glamour: a young Christy Turlington walked the runway for Autumn/Winter 1990 in a purple minidress with exquisite lace detailing completed by a high Victorian-style neckline. And in his Spring/Summer 1993 couture collection, the traditional finale of a wedding dress came in the form of a corseted bodice flaring to clouds of white organza, all topped by an Edwardian-style hat and veil. Perhaps the most stunning from the 1990s was his Autumn/Winter 1994 all-black, high-neck blouse and skirt accessorized by a hat shaped like a pagoda, which was later included in the 2015 Metropolitan Museum of Art's Costume exhibition, China: Through the Looking Glass.

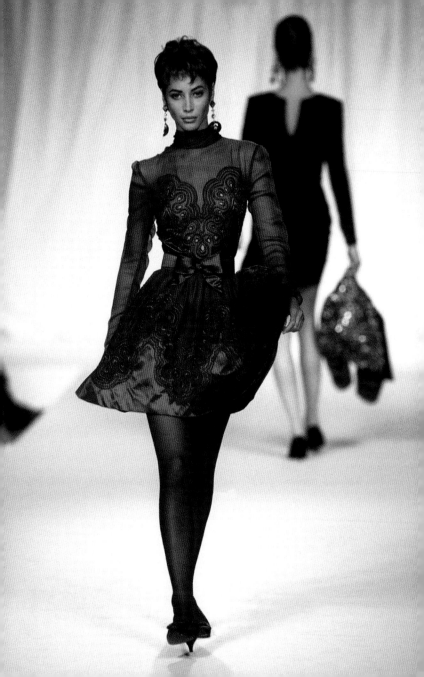

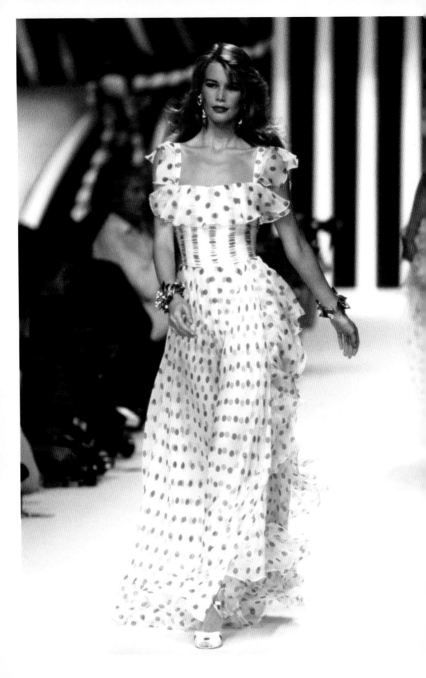

OPPOSITE Valentino's penchant for polka-dot patterns and ultra-feminine dresses with plenty of ruching are exemplified in this white and red chiffon gown worn by Claudia Schiffer for Spring/Summer 1992.

RIGHT Plaid became a favourite of Valentino's Autumn/Winter collections from the late 1980s. Here, Naomi Campbell wears a glamorous, fitted, black and white check day dress in 1992. The large bow is classic Valentino and the addition of gloves emphasizes the designer's love of old-fashioned, ladylike dressing.

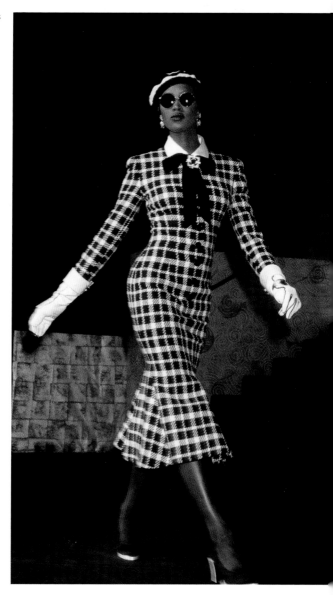

BELOW For Autumn/
Winter 1992, Christy
Turlingon wore a
minidress covered in
gold and black bugle
beads with accent
swirls of gold sequins.
A silk-lined brocade
coat and matching
hat complete the
decadent look that
sums up the house's
renowned glamour.

By the mid 1990s, the fashion for short, flared cocktail dresses was fading and a more sophisticated aesthetic taking its place. For Spring/Summer 1995, neutral trouset suits, the jacket slipped off to reveal Valentino's trademark deep V neckline, joined petal-front or peplum short skirts with contrasting black jackets. Later in the show, the hemlines dropped and corset-style camisole tops appeared beneath the tailored jackets of pinstripe and checked suits. The cropped bolero was a recurring theme, as were form-fitting dresses, all in a simple palette of black, white and beige.

The late 1990s saw many designers embrace the body-con dress, often using technical fabrics, but Valentino, as always, found a way to take a new trend and make it his own. In this case, he transformed a tight, overly sexualized aesthetic into a sculptural, form-fitting dress, elegant and simple, made from white silk and embellished with sequins or a rose-printed floral. Even when the designer did embrace the shine, as he did in his Spring/Summer 1998 couture show – which featured a gold lamé dress with a deeply plunging neckline, tightly belted and trimmed with crystals – the effect wasn't tacky but simply glamorous.

OPPOSITE For Autumn/Winter 1994
Valentino presented this outfit accessorized
by a hat shaped like a pagoda which was
later included in the 2015 Metropolitan
Museum of Art's Costume exhibition
entitled China: Through The Looking Glass.

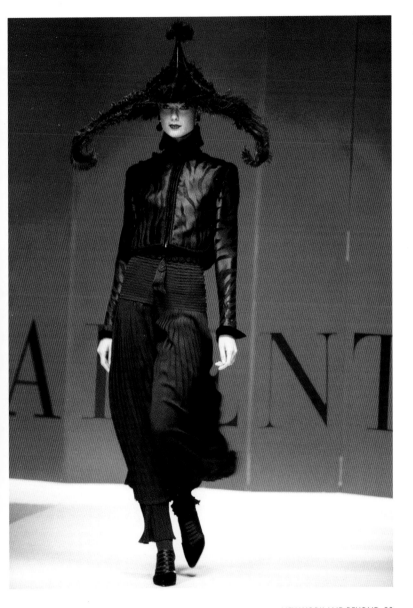

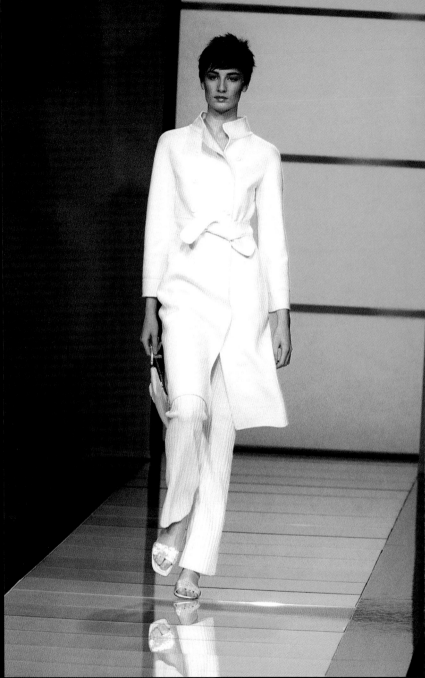

As the millennium approached, Valentino continued
doing what he did best – making clothes that made women
feel like film stars. His Spring/Summer 2000 collection
opened with a stunning all-white outfit, including a belted
cashmere coat reminiscent of the beautiful pieces he made for
Jackie Kennedy Onassis. Otherwise, the collection dazzled
with plenty of florals, from bold poppies emblazoned on
flowing trousers to a delicately embroidered lily-of-the-valley
appliqué. Colours ranged from orange polka dots to subtler
apricot and peach, and textures including lace and crystal
embellishments harked back to vintage Valentino. Entering
his fifth decade as one of the world's leading fashion designers,
Valentino was clearly still in his prime.

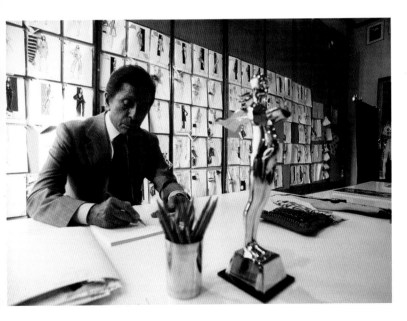

ACCESSORIES

Throughout the latter part of the twentieth century, Valentino's accessories lines were very much in keeping with his fashion aesthetic. Take, for example, the crocodile skin or beaded black evening bags from the 1980s with their jet chain strap, or the statement necklaces featuring the Valentino logo V. But unlike with other designers, there was less hype surrounding his accessories, especially compared to the attention his evening gowns garnered.

In part, this was due to the franchising arrangements that had been put in place during the 1970s. At the time, it was extremely popular for high-end fashion designers to offer licences to global partners in order to boost their profits and expand into new markets. It was a lucrative venture, with the Valentino name appearing on a wide range of accessories, including handbags, ties, belts and shoes. At one point, according to Giancarlo Giammetti, there were 40 franchises in Japan alone. However, as was the

BELOW The Rockstud motif has been hugely popular on handbags too, as exemplified in this white quilted version from 2019.

OPPOSITE An example of the cult Rockstud high-heeled pumps which have become a red carpet staple.

OVERLEAF The 2016 collection of brightly coloured leather cross-body bags with bohemian woven straps nevertheless maintains an edge of rock-star glamour with their metallic stud detailing.

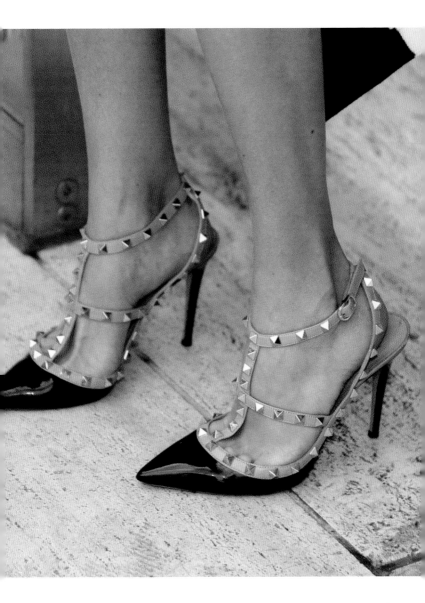

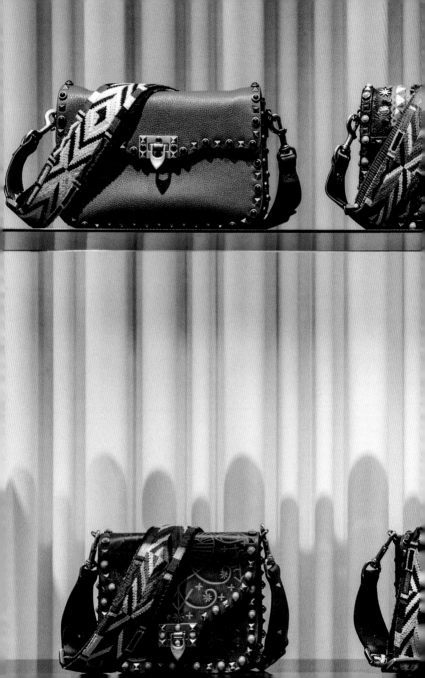

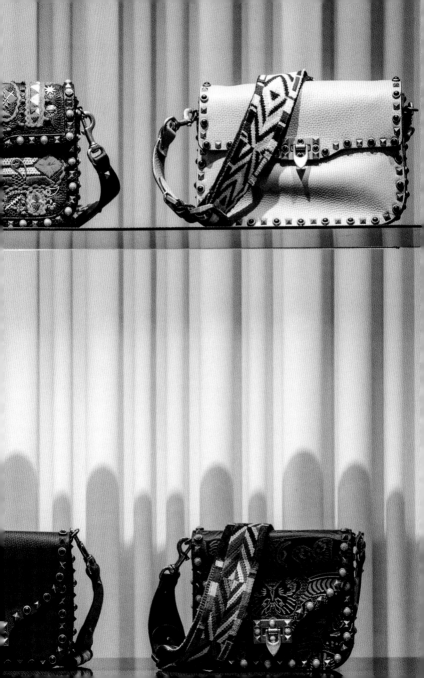

case with many other luxury fashion houses, Valentino and Giammetti felt that too many of these arrangements diluted the brand's image and, in subsequent years, the company brought much of its accessories design back under direct control.

The turning point came in 1999, when Valentino brought on board two designers who had previously created accessories at the luxury Italian fashion house Fendi. The duo, Maria Grazia Chiuri and Pierpaolo Piccioli, transformed the accessories at Valentino, bringing their quality into line with the expert design and glamour of the label's clothes. Soon, their bags were joining the list of the fashion world's most coveted "It" bags, and other items such as belts, jewellery and shoes became similarly sought-after. Since 2008, when Chiuri and Piccioli took over creative control of ready-to-wear and haute couture, a number of iconic styles have emerged.

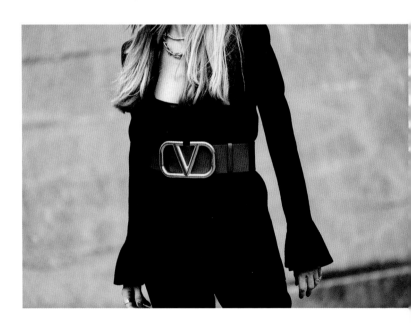

Unsurprisingly, accessories that bear the trademark V logo are some of the most popular. Belts are made from luxury leathers such as buffered cowhide and glossy calfskin, the gold emblem proudly displayed, while hats and gloves more discreetly show the wearer's discerning taste. Jewellery is popular too, with the label offering everything from miniature belts in the form of leather bracelets to charms and cufflinks.

The other extremely popular range, particularly among a new generation of younger customers, and one that epitomizes the uniquely Italian brand of glamour for which Valentino is renowned, is the Rockstud range. Shoes such as the killer-heeled Rockstud pump, a favourite of celebrities walking the red carpet, and bags in styles as varied as cross-body, clutch and tote cater for all occasions, the metallic studs adding just enough edginess to make a classic leather bag relevant again.

BELOW When Pierpaolo Piccioli took over creative design at Valentino in 2016, athleisure became part of the fashion house's repertoire, including previously unimagined designs such as this pair of trainers intricately woven from laces.

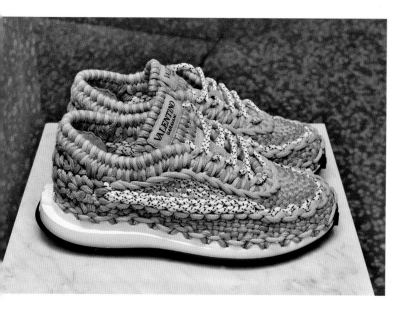

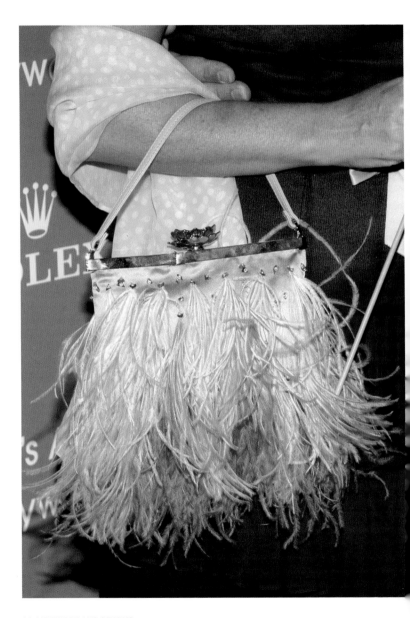

THE TWO VALENTINOS

Since the launch of his own label, Valentino has faced a unique problem when it came to his accessories lines, which is that he shared his name with another designer, Mario Valentino, a shoe and bag designer who had founded his own eponymous leather goods business in 1952. In 1979, to resolve the inevitable issue of customer confusion, the pair drew up a coexistence agreement which stated that Mario Valentino was permitted to "use and register the full name Mario Valentino or M. Valentino or Valentino or the letters MV or V exclusively on the outside, together with Mario Valentino on the inside".

During the ensuing decades, the mutual agreement more or less worked, but as Valentino Garavani grew to become one

OPPOSITE A turquoise Valentino evening bag with feather fringing shows a more delicate side to the brand's accessories.

BELOW A metallic black leather version of the Rockstud stiletto mixes classic Valentino elegance with a modern edge.

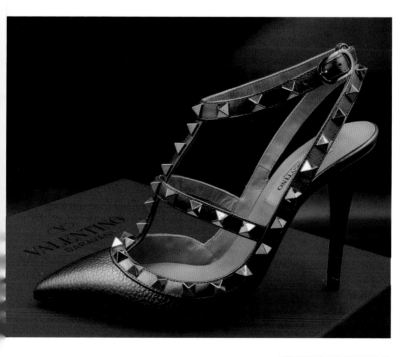

of the world's most famous designers, Mario Valentino was inevitably eclipsed. Mario Valentino passed away in 1991, but the business in his name continued, his products increasingly confused with those of Valentino Garavani, thus allowing the less well-known brand to benefit from the glamour and reputation of his internationally renowned competitor.

Ironically, early Mario Valentino bags were extremely well-crafted in quality leather and clearly marked with the correct designer's name. In fact, the house even employed some top designers, including Karl Lagerfeld and Giorgio Armani at the very beginning of their careers. But by 2013, a deluge of cut-price "Valentino" bags flooded the market, especially in the United States, all marked with the recognizable "V" logo of Valentino Garavani while the Mario Valentino name was hidden away and almost impossible to spot.

As a result, in 2019 Valentino S.p.A. took Mario Valentino and its American licensee Yarch Capital to court, accusing them of deliberately fostering misconceptions in their advertising campaigns by labelling products to take advantage of "Valentino's goodwill in the United States handbag market" and even going so far as to claim in marketing materials that Mario Valentino is "a top designer name that people worldwide are familiar with" – as reported by *The Fashion Law* on 23 July 2019.

The issue continues as Valentino Garavani bags become more and more popular. Sadly, it is necessary today to ensure that the Valentino bag you are buying comes from a reputable seller.

PERFUME

In 1978, Valentino joined many of his contemporary designers by releasing his first fragrance. Simply titled "Valentino", his debut

OPPOSITE A stunning feather-covered evening bag in rich orange and red hues from Autumn/Winter 2001 matches the model's silk fishtail gown perfectly.

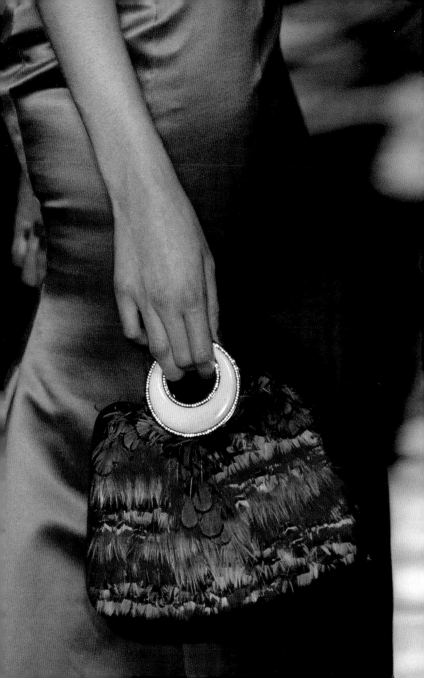

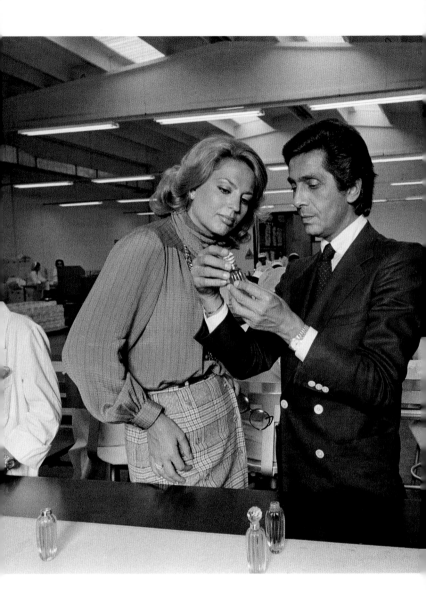

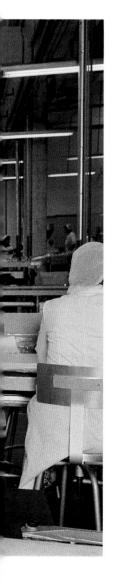

scent was created by Givaudan, a perfumer founded in 1895, which in 1946 started its now famous school to "train noses". Alumni include some of the greats of the twentieth century, such as Jean-Claude Ellena of Hermès and Jacques Polge, Chanel's former head perfumer.

The green and floral fragrance was designed to complement not just the glamour but also the romantic nature of the Valentino woman, and came in an elegant bottle created by Pierre Dinand, the man behind many of the world's most iconic perfume bottles.

Since then, the house of Valentino has released 39 fragrances for both men and women, all in keeping with the luxury aesthetic of the brand, many making an olfactory statement as grand as one of Valentino's beautiful gowns. Some of the most popular are Donna, V Ete and Valentina, created in 2011 by master perfumers Olivier Cresp and Alberto Morillas and presented in a perfectly round bottle adorned by a single, elegant flower. Scents for men include Valentino Uomo, Uomo Intense and Uomo Noir Absolu.

LEFT In 1978, Valentino released his first perfume. He is pictured here with the then president of Valentino perfumes, Ira von Fürstenberg.

OVERLEAF LEFT The flower-embellished bottle of Valentino Valentina.

OVERLEAF RIGHT In 2014, Valentino relaunched its classic men's fragrance Valentino Uomo.

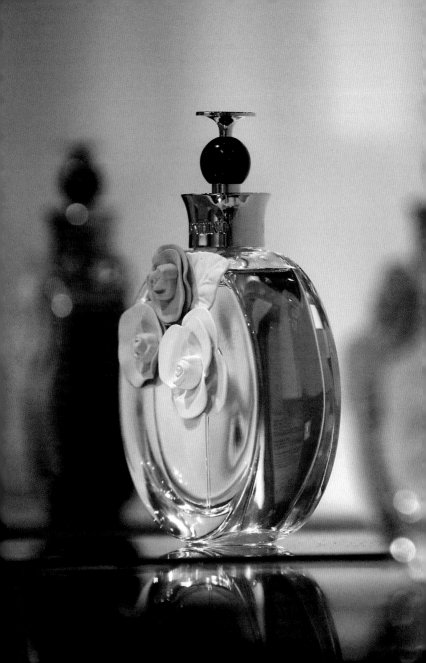

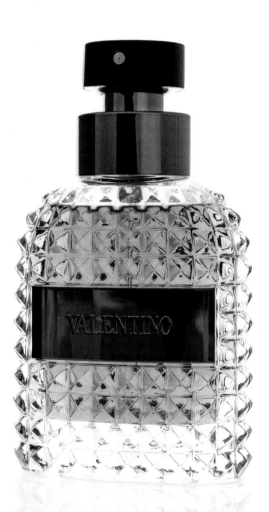

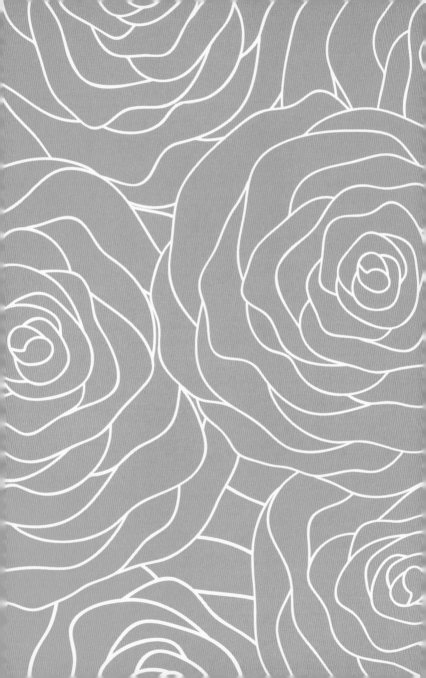

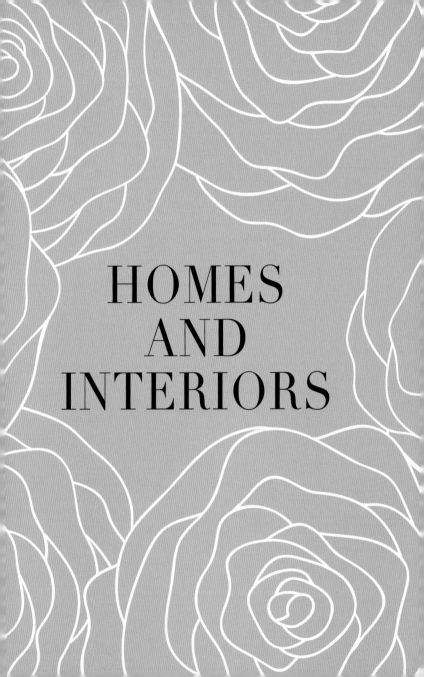

HOMES
AND
INTERIORS

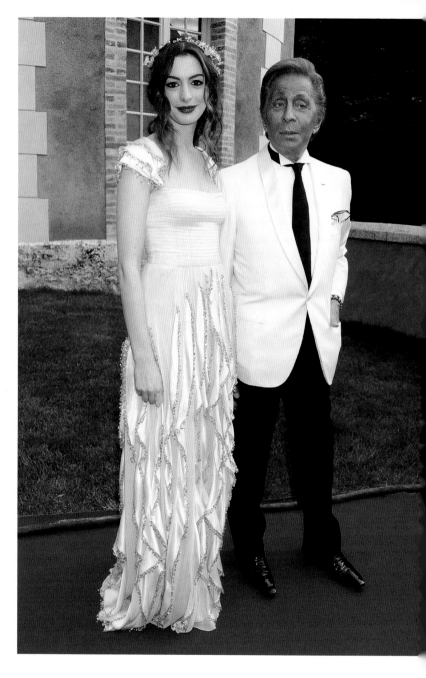

PARIS, ROME, LONDON, NEW YORK, GSTAAD

"It's certain that if I hadn't become a couturier,
I'd have been an interior designer."

VALENTINO GARAVANI,
Architectural Digest, *July 2016*

Valentino Garavani has often been dubbed the Emperor of Fashion – and rightly so, given his long career creating some of the most fabulous dresses in the world. But his taste for opulence is not limited to the catwalk, and Valentino is as well known for his extravagant interior style and lavish entertaining in his many homes around the globe.

Between them, Valentino and his long-time partner Giancarlo Giammetti boast prime residences in Rome, Paris, New York, London and Gstaad, which they share freely, although the pair are no longer linked romantically and have never officially lived

OPPOSITE Valentino and Anne Hathaway, wearing a beaded white Valentino gown, at his home outside Paris, Château de Wideville, where the designer hosted the 2011 Love Ball to raise funds for supermodel Natalia Vodianova's Naked Heart Foundation.

together. In the 2014 book *Valentino: At the Emperor's Table,* André Leon Talley, the designer's friend and former editor-at-large of *Vogue,* described how Valentino "designs his luncheons and dinners, in all of his homes, the way he has created crescendos and allegros vivace throughout his forty-plus-year career as one of the greatest haute couture designers and high-fashion leaders in the world".

CHÂTEAU DE WIDEVILLE

The grandest, and perhaps the favourite, of all Valentino's homes is the Château de Wideville, just outside Paris. The seventeenth-century, eight-bedroom house, with an estate comprising of 280 acres of exquisitely designed and manicured gardens, was originally built by Louis XIII's finance minister, and Louis XIV later installed one of his mistresses there. Valentino purchased it in 1995 and immediately worked with the legendary interior decorator Henri Samuel, then in his nineties, to decorate it. The style is classic Valentino, regal in a way befitting a château of such grandeur, yet still inviting, and showcasing his clear love of Chinese artefacts, including porcelain, figurines and a series of early nineteenth-century Chinese ancestor portraits looking down over the château's magnificent central curved staircase.

Always looking to create new and intimate spaces, Valentino restored the estate's pigeonnier into a workspace and hideaway described by *Architectural Digest* in 2012 as having "a decor redolent of 1920s Shanghai".

Valentino and Giammetti spend several months each year at Château de Wideville, hosting parties during Paris Fashion Week as well as other grand events, including the 2011 Love Ball to raise funds for supermodel Natalia Vodianova's Naked Heart Foundation.

OPPOSITE Had he not been a fashion designer, Valentino has always claimed that he would have been an interior designer – and his style is as flamboyant in both areas. This four-poster bed in his atelier was designed by Valentino in 1972.

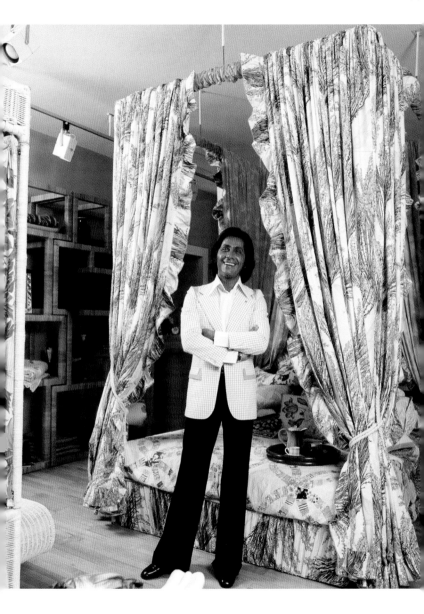

ROME: APPIAN WAY

With his business still based in Rome, the designer keeps a home there. Valentino's villa on the Via Appia Antica is far more than a "simple country house", as the designer has been known to describe it. Bought in 1972 and renovated in collaboration with the esteemed architect and set designer Renzo Mongiardino, the villa is an assault on the senses. Again, Valentino's love of chinoiserie is obvious in the form of wallpaper and ceramics, but his obsession with floral motifs is perhaps the most striking. The decor is a riot of colour, print and texture, with needlepoint carpets, rich embroidered velvet and lush oversized printed floral upholstery. On the wall hangs a red-accented Miró watercolour, a fitting tribute to Valentino's signature colour.

The interior design verges on the overwhelming but manages to work as a whole, just as Valentino expertly pulls together his extravagant catwalk collections. His delight, as well as his confidence, in his interior design skills is infectious. Speaking to *Architectural Digest* in 2016, he proclaimed: "If you have taste, you can mix it all together."

LONDON: HOLLAND PARK

In 2001, Valentino bought a townhouse in London's Holland Park, a discreet and extremely expensive enclave beloved of international celebrities. Describing the location to *ES Magazine* in 2014, the designer said: "It's perfect for me because I'm from a small town in northern Italy called Voghera, so I like places where you step out of the door and there is greenery and no traffic."

The house was decorated by Jacques Grange, the French interior designer well known for his ability to mix styles, and manages to combine rococo opulence with stark minimalism in a way few could achieve. The effect is pure Valentino, who also likes to juxtapose periods and styles to create a cohesive interior.

At first, it seems pure art deco, with 1930s furniture against a muted palette with black and white accent colours – but look more closely, and there is traditional nineteenth-century English furniture that nods to the heritage of the house. As with all of Valentino's houses, the walls are hung with stunning works of art – with a Francis Bacon, a Damien Hirst and a striking Andy Warhol offering well-considered notes of contrast.

NEW YORK: FIFTH AVENUE

The apartment that Valentino and his partner Giancarlo Giammetti currently share in Manhattan is situated in the prime real estate of Fifth Avenue, overlooking both the Frick Collection and Central Park, and it, too, was renovated by Jacques Grange. Giammetti bought it for $18.5 million in 2010, after the couple sold their previous, smaller residence in the city because Valentino realized that he would want to spend more time in New York after his retirement.

The light and airy space is filled with many precious artefacts and artworks – the entrance hall alone boasts a Mark Rothko and a pair of Tang dynasty horses. Again, the interior has an art deco feel, with bold black outlines to the walls and plenty of mid-century furniture by designers such as Karl Springer. Warmth is introduced by rosewood and walnut flooring, which extends to fill a lined hallway, and welcoming furniture has been specially designed by Grange and upholstered in a myriad of rich textures and prints, including a Pierre Frey tiger stripe.

Valentino and Giammetti's passion for art is most obvious in this space, their taste ranging from a pastel by Richard Prince (part of his Nurse series) to a Basquiat triptych, a Roy Lichtenstein and a David Hockney. The pair are serious collectors: a camouflage Andy Warhol hangs in the dining room and a Picasso takes pride of place in the sitting room.

It is clear from this latest project that Valentino's dedication to his homes is equal to that of his fashion design. Speaking in 2010, he admitted to *Vanity Fair*: "I am only good for two things in this world, designing dresses and the decoration of houses."

GSTAAD

The chalet that Valentino owns in the Swiss ski resort of Gstaad is one of his oldest homes and a favourite in which to spend Christmas and New Year with friends, skiing and socializing. Far more traditional in feel, it has a cosiness that belies the designer's reputation for liking only high glamour. The rooms are panelled in local wood, Irving Penn photographs line the walls and backlit shelves highlight his collection of European faiences, tureens and barbotines. A favourite table centrepiece when hosting his famous feasts is one of his nineteenth-century Meissen swans.

In *Valentino: At the Emperor's Table*, the designer explains how he loves to entertain, and the attention to detail that he gives his exquisite table settings, themed to fit the home in which they are served, is equal to that of any catwalk show.

ART

It is impossible to speak of Valentino's interior style without recognizing his extensive art collection. From his first major purchase of a "Picasso with beautiful colours" to the abstract expressionist Willem de Kooning, the figurative British painter Peter Doig, and the German visual artist Gerhard Richter, Valentino possesses a wide-ranging aesthetic taste.

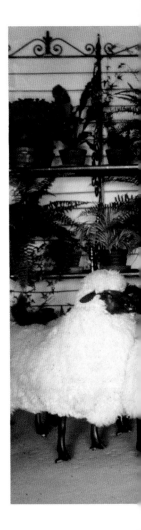

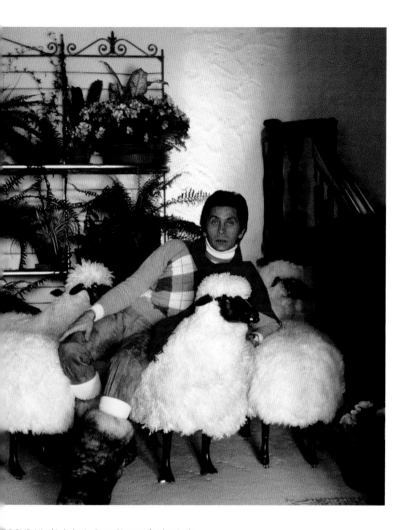

ABOVE His ski chalet in Gstaad is one of Valentino's oldest homes. Photographed in 1977, the designer reclines against the sheep sofa designed by French husband-and-wife artist duo Claude and François-Xavier Lalanne.

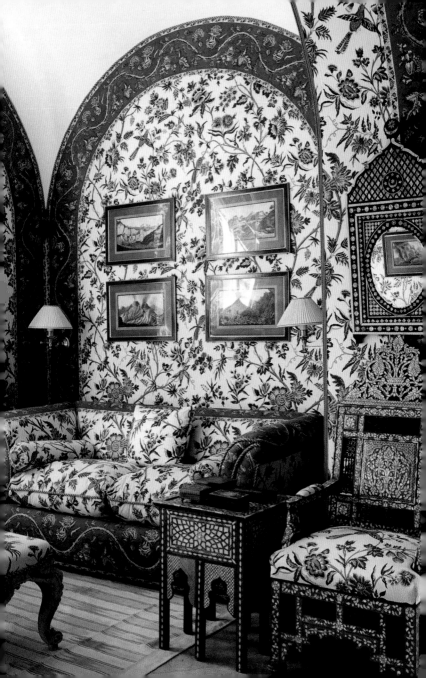

In a 2015 interview for *System*, Valentino spoke to Hans Ulrich Obrist, the Swiss art historian, curator and critic, about his love of beautiful paintings and bold colours. He also discussed his relationships with artists including Basquiat, who fell asleep after attending one of his catwalk shows, as well as Andy Warhol, who did a portrait of him in 1970 and with whom he socialized.

"When you see a beautiful painting, a Picasso or a Basquiat, you try and put it into your collection – especially Basquiat because I did a collection a not very long time ago in the 1990s where I showed several Basquiat details in the dresses . . . His use of colour is the strongest out of all those figures. He has always fascinated me."

As well as paintings, Valentino collects more sculptural pieces, one of the most unusual of which might be the life-size sheep by French husband-and-wife artist duo Claude and François-Xavier Lalanne. Over half a century of work, the artist duo have long been inspired by the animal kingdom while paying homage to the traditions of surrealism and art nouveau. The skin-covered bronze cast sheep were part of Sheep Station, the inaugural exhibition at Manhattan's Getty Station, the former filling station. The Lalannes' work was already a favourite of fashion designers including Karl Lagerfeld, John Galliano and Tom Ford, and flocks of the sheep have also found their way into the homes of Yves Saint Laurent and Marc Jacobs.

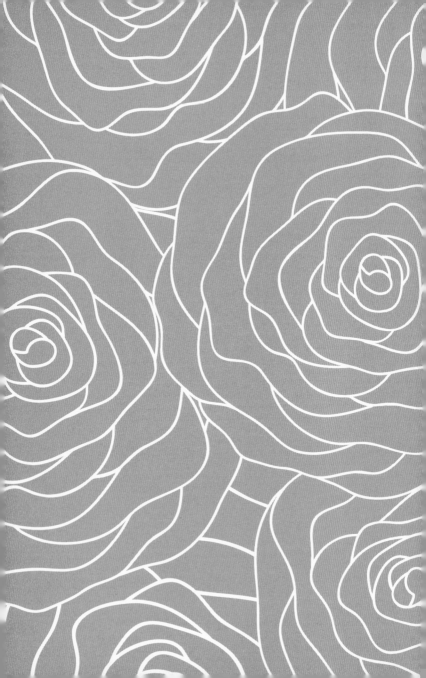

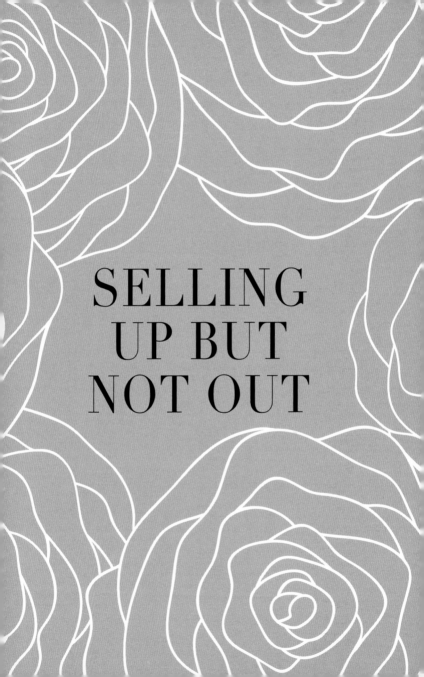

SELLING
UP BUT
NOT OUT

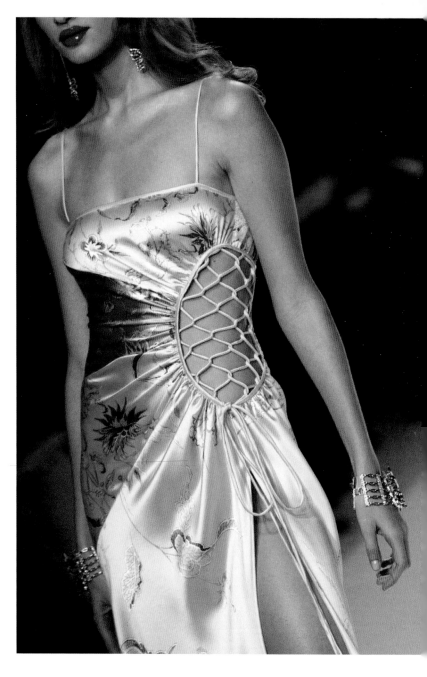

ONWARDS AND UPWARDS

In 1998, Valentino and Giammetti sold their company to Italian fashion and media conglomerate HdP S.p.A. for $300 million. Unfortunately, despite Valentino staying actively involved as designer and receiving plaudits for his seasonal collections, poor business decisions led to the brand failing to make a profit for several years, even registering a loss of €29 million in 2001.

As a result, Valentino S.p.A. was sold once again the following year, this time to the Italian textiles house Marzotto Apparel. Rumours at the time implied that the extravagant lifestyle enjoyed by Valentino and Giancarlo Giammetti, with their private jets and large entourage of staff, was partly to blame for the company's financial loss.

It is certainly true that the pair, renowned for their expensive tastes even within the notoriously big-spending fashion industry, have enjoyed a high-maintenance lifestyle. An insight into their exacting standards was given in *Vanity Fair* by Matt Tyrnauer, who also directed the documentary *Valentino: The Last Emperor.*

OPPOSITE Chinoiserie has always been a passion for Valentino in his homes and occasionally found its way into his fashion designs, such as on this yellow printed silk gown with cutaway detail from Spring/Summer 2004.

Watching the pair prepare to travel, Tyrnauer observed the three buses needed to get from the airport terminal to their private jet, "one to move Valentino, Giammetti, and staff, another for luggage, and a third to transport five of Valentino's six pugs".

He went on to note: "A staff of nearly 50 is employed to maintain Valentino's 152-foot yacht and his five homes." As John Fairchild, then editor-at-large at *Women's Wear Daily* and *W*, noted: "Valentino and Giancarlo are the kings of high living."

But this snippet of their rarefied existence was nothing new. Valentino had always enjoyed the high life, and his reputation for appreciating luxury himself imbued his clothes with extra glamour. Even when his business was going through a rocky patch, Valentino himself was being showered in praise and respect for his achievements, now stretching over four decades.

In 2000, to celebrate his long and successful career, a show featuring 40 Valentino Red dresses was presented at Rome's Piazza di Spagna. In 2003, playing on the reputation of Valentino Red, the fashion house launched the urban-focused REDValentino line. Standing for "Romantic Eccentric Dress", the line was designed to be edgy and streetwise and appeal to a younger shopper.

The new millennium saw no sign of Valentino's design brilliance fading as he presented his trademark combination of luxe evening dresses and beautifully tailored daywear, including suits for "ladies who lunch", which would not have looked out of place on any one of Valentino's socialite clients over the decades. As *Vogue* noted about the Autumn/Winter 2000 collection: "His real-life ladies lead a pampered limo life, apparently unchanged since the Duchess of Windsor's day."

In his collections during the early 2000s, Valentino continued the ethos of elegant clothes without overly indulging in the trends of the moment. A 1980s revival among his peers was flatly ignored by the Italian designer, his spring palette ranging from neutral white and beige, through greys to black, with the ever-present pop of red. He presented geometric stripes, checks and polka dots in black and white as well as simple monotone outfits that harked back to his breakthrough 1960s collections, and as always, there were exquisite gowns, embellished with crystals and embroidery or generously full, crafted from metres of organza.

Several of Valentino's collections, especially his haute couture, stood out. A notable example is Autumn/Winter 2002, when the designer presented a collection full of chinoiserie, something he has always had a passion for when it came to decorating his homes. Snakes, a symbol of elegance in Chinese mythology, were a central theme, worn as pieces of jewellery or even as a kind of dramatic headpiece. Coats and capes were elaborately embroidered with Eastern-inspired motifs and plenty of satin

BELOW Always hands-on, Valentino gives a model a last-minute adjustment backstage during his Spring/Summer 2005 show.

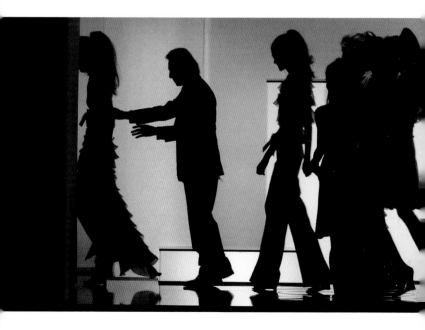

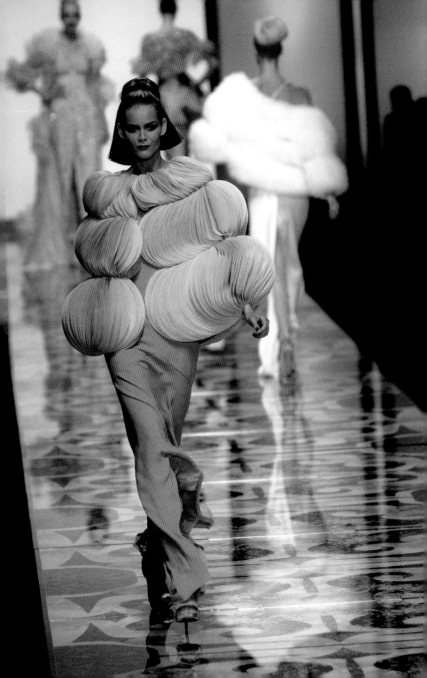

OPPOSITE In July
2007, Valentino
presented an haute
couture collection
that gave full rein to
his love of volume.
This memorable
haute couture pink
silk column gown
with oversized ruched
collar and cuffs has
become one of the
designer's most
famous contemporary
classics.

lent the show even more glamour than usual.

Here was a collection in which Valentino appeared to be nodding towards the "dark side", as *Vogue*'s show report noted, but "ultimately nothing diverted Valentino from his primary goal of making women look gorgeously pretty".

The same was true for his couture show for Spring/Summer 2005, a tongue-in-cheek homage to the global relevance of fashion. His outfits, given names like "Sevilla, No Bull" and "Courting Versailles" were not really about diversity of style, although the backdrop took the audience on a whistle-stop tour of some of the world's most iconic landmarks. It was, in fact, just Valentino putting on a show for his wealthy clientele, who were increasingly as likely to come from India or Russia as from Europe or America. The outfits were pure elegance, from ladylike suits for those who still lunch to fabulous gowns for evening soirées. The finale, entitled "Milano, Callas Forever", saw Naomi Campbell in an opera-worthy voluminous gown with a fitted bodice, overlaid with beaded appliqué lace and an organza tiered skirt edged with lace. One velvet shoulder strap finished things off perfectly. As *Vogue* put it, Valentino still designs for an "old-school wonderland where women are treated as creatures made of spun glass".

Valentino's final years before retiring in 2008 continued to display his brilliance at creating exquisite clothes to make women feel beautiful. Ready-to-wear collections focused on elegantly tailored daywear, with colour palettes ranging from beige, caramel and black tones in 2003 to Valentino's favourite monochrome in both 2004 and 2006. In between, Autumn/ Winter 2005 was a vision in Valentino Red, stunning when offset against jet black, with a re-emergence of the argyle print that he had returned to over the years. And, of course, every season included a series of seductive frocks, embellished, embroidered and inevitably destined for the red carpet.

Spring/Summer collections conjured up a more playful feel.

OPPOSITE
Valentino's frequent
references to the
silver-screen glamour
of the early years of
cinema has never
been more exquisitely
expressed than in his
penultimate collection
for Autumn/Winter
2007. A perfect
example is this
1930s-style moss-
green ruched silk gown
with beaded chiffon
sleeve detail.

In 2004, confections of lace and chiffon were presented complete with satin bows and butterfly motifs. But there was a more sophisticated nautical theme too, with outfits such as tailored white sailor trousers paired with a simple navy silk top – very much the kind of thing Jackie Onassis might have worn on her husband's yacht – and perfect for a new generation of socialites holidaying on Cape Cod.

A year later, Valentino presented a dramatic change in tone, offering a wardrobe designed for a globe-trotting traveller. The collection was a riot of sunshine-filled floral prints with a colour spectrum ranging from lime green and citrine to oranges and yellows, barely toned down by a muted terracotta reminiscent of the clay buildings of Morocco and Spain. All of this came in the form of chiffon dresses, swinging, pleated skirts and neat, beaded jackets.

For Spring/Summer 2006, as rumours about his impending retirement were circulating, Valentino returned to his pared-down black and white, broken up by a selection of Asian-inspired floral silk dresses, skirts and trouser suits. In Spring/Summer 2007, when old-school ladylike style was back in fashion, Valentino was in his element, with *Vogue* proclaiming that "the lifelong themes of his work – delicate dresses, lace, bows, and, of course, the color red – seem quite beautifully relevant at a time when so many edgier upstarts are stabbing around the territory".

And therein lies Valentino's brilliance. His ability to retain a consistent design ethos over a period of 45 years is both an extraordinary feat and the reason that Valentino has been so successful for so long.

Valentino's final show season was for Spring/Summer 2008. While the temptation might have been to offer a retrospective display of decades-old classics, Valentino showed a collection of eminently wearable, pretty, light and airy dresses that might almost have been called youthful. Nothing in his selection of colourful minidresses could be said to be old-fashioned or staid.

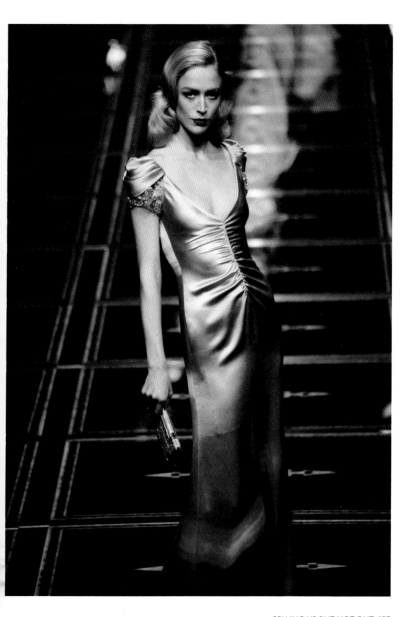

RIGHT Valentino finally retired after half a century in the business after his haute couture Spring/Summer 2008 show. Here he acknowledges the admiration from the audience for his extraordinary contribution to the world of fashion. He is surrounded by models wearing dresses in his iconic red.

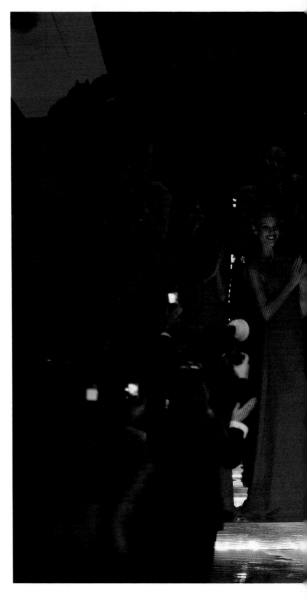

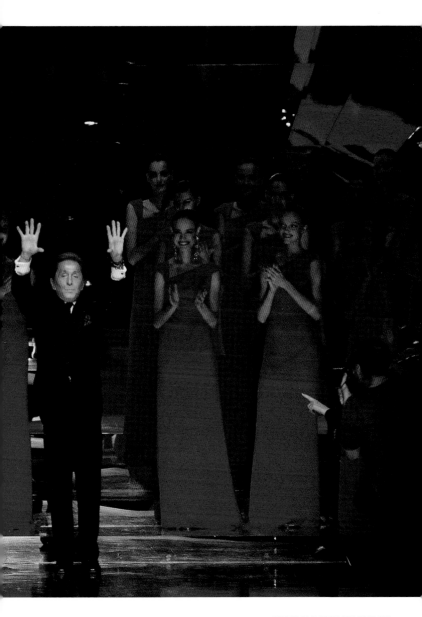

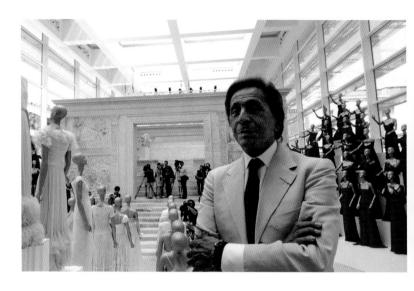

Instead, pale pinks gave way to yellows, purples and greens, and even a pink so bright it was almost neon. A multicoloured block stripe with a semi-transparent layer and a shiny, liquid, asymmetrical, off-the-shoulder, body-skimming dress were Valentino's way of saying he could still be modern. As the show progressed, he moved on to a series of cocktail frocks with the flamboyant twists he can never resist in the form of ruffles and ruches, bows and beaded fringes. Inevitably, some classics did emerge in the form of a series of black and white-polka dot outfits and, of course, the statement evening gowns.

Valentino's very last appearance, in a room filled with projections of models wearing gowns in his iconic red hue, was the haute couture Spring/Summer 2008 show. It was full of what his fans had come to expect. Aside from the flattering, tailored day suits, it was the exquisitely crafted gowns that most reminded the audience of why Valentino had been at the top of his game for so long. Made from the finest silk, taffeta and lace, semi-transparent veil-like layers of the most delicate floral embroidery lifted the more formal gowns to another level. Among the glossy gold, white and monochrome dresses, there were eye-catching pops of bright colour and bold oversized floral prints. The silhouettes ranged from an elegant 1950s knee-length black pencil skirt and contrasting flare-sleeved tailored short jacket, complete with elbow-length gloves, to a floor-length yellow floral-printed silk chiffon dress reminiscent of the Belle Époque, complete with oversized floral-trimmed hat. A culmination of decades of honing his favourite styles to perfection came together, and here was a show in which Valentino should rightly have taken pride.

In 2008, the exhibition Valentino: Themes and Variations, was held at the Museé des Arts Decoratifs in Paris. Curated by Pamela Golbin, it drew together his favourite recurring themes from throughout his long career. Showcasing his technical expertise, his love of ornamentation, and the ways in which he played with different lines and silhouettes over the years, experimenting with volume, pattern and texture, this was a remarkable collection of his most memorable dresses, and a fitting tribute.

VALENTINO: THE LAST EMPEROR

A celebrity in his own right, Valentino not only appeared in a cameo role in the 2006 film *The Devil Wears Prada*, but in 2008 was the subject of a documentary entitled *Valentino: The Last Emperor*.

Directed by Matt Tyrnauer, the short film offered a rare glimpse into the lives of Valentino and his business partner, one-time lover, and lifelong friend, Giancarlo Giammetti, in the two years preceding their retirement. The film's intention was to examine the ongoing struggle between the high art form of Valentino's haute couture and the challenges of navigating the world of business, represented by Giammetti, but it also revealed a story of the remarkable relationship between the two men as well as the genius and legacy of Valentino as a fashion designer.

Speaking to IndieWire in 2009, director Matt Tyrnauer said: "They have a relationship unlike any I have ever seen before. It's unique. People frequently say, Valentino and Giancarlo, it's like a marriage. Well, I'd say it's more than a marriage. It's a supernatural bond that has lasted for 50 years. They are part of the same person, really. So close, and so interdependent."

Valentino's status as one of the truly great designers of the twentieth century is summed up by an extraordinary capture by Tyrnauer of Karl Lagerfeld embracing a tearful Valentino backstage after his final show. The legendary German designer leans in to Valentino and says: "Compared to us, the rest just make rags."

As Tyrnauer put it, speaking to *Paper* magazine in 2020, "we were able to capture an immortal moment in the history of fashion. These were the last emperors – and they knew it".

Valentino retired in January 2008 but, along with Giammetti, has been far from idle. One of the pair's first projects was the founding of the Valentino Garavani virtual museum, a digital archive of his work that can be downloaded and viewed like a virtual museum tour. The pair now spend more time in New York than ever, thanks to Valentino's passion for ballet, and he creates costumes for the New York City Ballet. He also takes on commissions for very special clients, such as actress and friend Anne Hathaway, for whom he designed a wedding dress for her marriage to Adam Shulman in 2012.

"Definitely, we're not retired people," insisted Giammetti about himself and Valentino in an interview for *WWD* in 2012. "Any project that he and I have now is at a different pace. It's not under the stress of 'collection after collection after collection,'… Every project we have now is a bit more relaxed, I would say."

One project that the pair collaborated on in 2012 was the Valentino: Master of Couture exhibition at London's Somerset House. Curated by Patrick Kinmonth and Antonio Monfreda, the retrospective featured over 130 couture outfits from almost half a century of Valentino's designs. It included not only outfits but also personal photographs and clips of films that gave an extraordinary insight into Valentino's atelier and the complex techniques required to create couture clothes.

Since Valentino's retirement, the company has continued to struggle somewhat, requiring it to restructure its debts in 2009. Then, in 2012, Valentino S.p.A. was sold once again, this time to the Qatari royal family for €700 million. The move was supported by Valentino and Giammetti, who told *WWD*: "Sheikha Mozah is our client for a long time. Valentino personally did two weddings for the family."

By 2012, with investment secured from Qatar and a steady design hand under the artistic direction of Maria Grazia Chiuri and Pierpaolo Piccioli, Valentino felt confident that the continuation of his label would honoured as he wished, summing up his legacy as: "Precision, personality, courage."

BELOW Valentino and Giancarlo Giammetti continue to socialize globally after their retirement and are pictured here attending the Polo Cup in Greenwich, Connecticut in 2011.

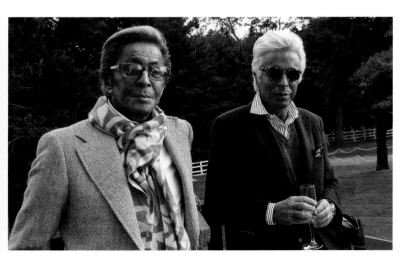

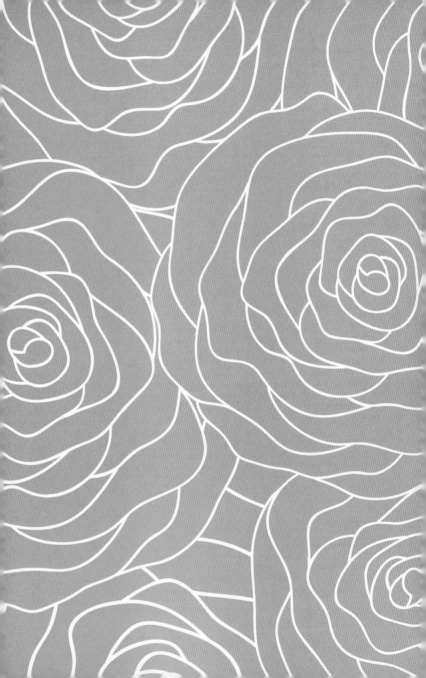

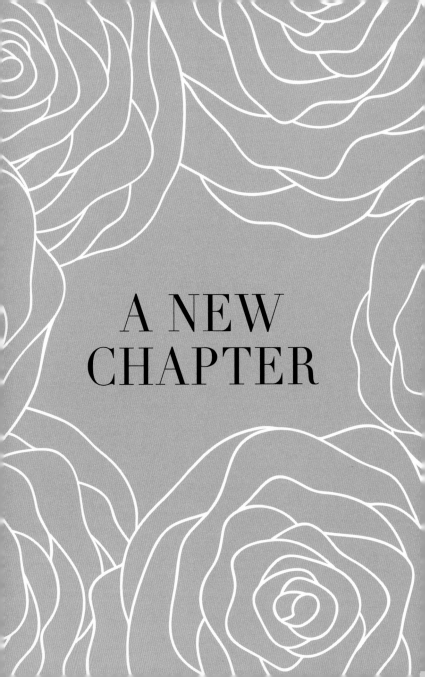

A NEW
CHAPTER

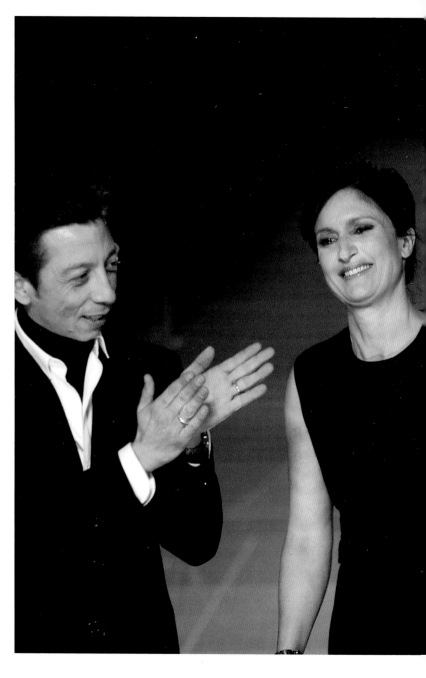

VALENTINO
AFTER
VALENTINO

In 2008, when Valentino retired, a surprise appointment was announced as his replacement: Italian designer Alessandra Facchinetti, a modern woman less than half Valentino's age. Sceptics immediately predicted a downturn in the quality of design, but Facchinetti's first show impressed the fashion press.

The *Guardian* reported: "Facchinetti silenced critics today with a collection that captured the air of refined seduction that is the essence of Valentino, while bringing the look bang up to date."

Vogue agreed: "Alessandra Facchinetti has big shoes to fill at Valentino. Today she slipped into them with the tact and sensitivity of a young Italian who appreciates the storied heritage of the house, but is quietly resolved to say something to a new generation."

OPPOSITE Maria Grazia Chiuri and Pierpaolo Piccioli acknowledging the applause from the audience after their debut show for Valentino, the Spring/Summer 2009 haute couture collection.

The collection pointed to a way in which a new, younger woman could wear Valentino with as much grace and elegance as the house's traditional older clients. It was full of wearable suits and dresses in a simple colour palette that must surely have won the approval of Valentino himself. Perhaps the only slight disappointments were Facchinetti's interpretations of the trademark Valentino Red chiffon dress. The versions she presented were perfectly accomplished but lacked the red-carpet panache that Valentino himself had always delivered.

But within months, despite the positive start, rumours began to surface that Facchinetti was not up to the job of taking such a powerful old fashion house and modernizing it. Then abruptly, the day after her second collection was shown, Facchinetti was fired. Perhaps the worst part was that Facchinetti did not realize she had been let go until reading it in the press. She issued a statement several hours after the news leaked, expressing her "deep regret" to learn of her dismissal from the press "since the company's top management has not yet seen fit to inform me."

In fact, this hiring and firing of fresh, young designers by old-school fashion houses has become commonplace. At Givenchy, John Galliano lasted just a year before defecting to Dior, his role at Givenchy filled by Alexander McQueen, and at Emanuel Ungaro, a single decade saw three designers – Giambattista Valli, Peter Dundas and Esteban Cortazar – start and quickly leave. Gallingly for Facchinetti, she had experienced the same at Gucci several years earlier, having succeeded Tom Ford in 2004 and then having been quickly fired, again after just two seasons.

Both Giancarlo Giammetti and Valentino expressed their agreement with the decision to fire her. Despite initial enthusiasm from Giammetti for the designer's first collection, he quickly changed his mind at her attempt "to pretend to transform and revolutionise the Valentino style".

For Valentino, it was Facchinetti's failure to respect his

OPPOSITE Chiuri and Piccioli's debut collection played it safe, very much keeping to the traditional style of the house of Valentino by presenting outfits such as this cream pleated silk gown.

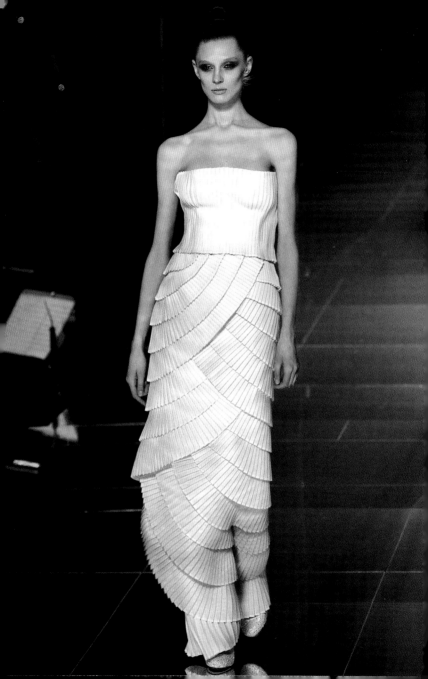

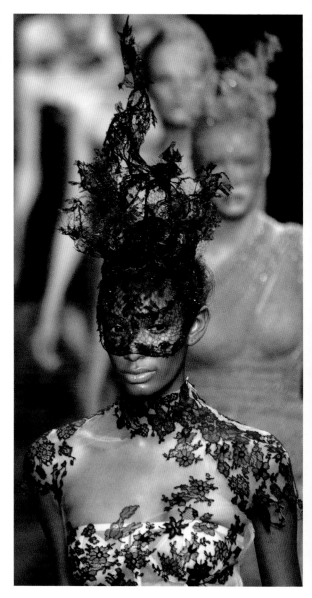

RIGHT For Autumn/
Winter 2009 couture,
a beautifully crafted,
black veiled headdress
complements a silk
chiffon gown with
delicate lace appliqué
over a fitted bustier.

legacy that was unforgivable, especially, he explained, when "there is an existing archive with thousands of dresses . . . [to] take inspiration from to create a Valentino product that is relevant today."

Stefano Sassi, chief executive since 2006 and the man widely credited for turning the brand's fortunes around, now announced the promotion of Maria Grazia Chiuri and Pierpaolo Piccioli, Valentino's heads of accessories. The appointment was clearly endorsed by Valentino himself; he had personally recruited the pair in 1999 from Fendi to revolutionize his fashion house's floundering accessories lines. The relationship, both between the two designers and the brand's business leaders, had been a success and the decision to appoint artistic directors from within was a cautious way to protect the house's legacy, especially after the drama of Facchinetti's abrupt departure.

The debut show for Chiuri and Piccioli was the Spring/ Summer 2009 haute couture collection. There was a great deal riding on their performance, with *Vogue* noting: "the house of Valentino needs to regain its sense of equilibrium". But with Valentino and his entourage applauding loudly from their front row seats, there was no doubt that the two new designers were determined to get it right this time.

If anything, the first designs presented by Chiuri and Piccioli erred on the safe side. The catwalk was filled with ladylike Valentino classics such as cream suits, silk and chiffon dresses and crystal-embellished coats with accents of red in the form of elegantly ruched and draped dresses. Even Valentino's signature oversized bows and flowers seemed mindfully included, illustrating how respectful the new pair of designers were determined to be of the grand master. Nevertheless, couture was never going to be the place where dramatic modernization took place and Chiuri and Piccioli's first ready-to-wear collection, where change was more likely, was awaited with eagerness.

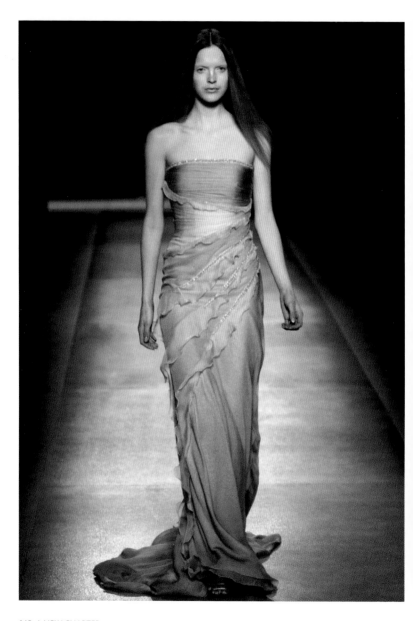

In fact, Autumn/Winter 2009, while still adhering strictly to the Valentino dress codes of old, didn't quite spark a revolution. The design duo's outfits, maintaining the 1960s theme of their couture collection, continued in a sedate, ladylike fashion, the only excitement coming in the form vibrant pops of jewel colours, such as emerald and turquoise. Loyal customers, often ladies of a certain age, must have been happy, but fashion watchers, eager to see how Valentino might be made more relevant to a modern audience under its new leadership, were left disappointed.

Six months later, however, things were looking very different. The Spring/Summer 2010 ready-to-wear collection suddenly had a much younger feel, full of tiny party dresses in draped and ruched organza, chiffon and silk as well as plenty of semi-sheer outfits that would most certainly frighten off the Valentino old guard. Shockingly, there wasn't even a red dress. As Pierpaolo Piccioli explained to *Vogue*: "We wanted to tell a new fairy tale. We're proud of the house heritage, but we wanted to give a personal point of view."

The pair had made the right call. Valentino needed to move forward to stay relevant in the fast-changing world of fashion where other traditional couture houses were shaking things up, and it seemed that Chiuri and Piccioli were the designers to do it. Even their Spring/Summer 2010 couture show, usually a place where tradition held greater sway, led with a futuristic collection of graphic prints and cyber-punk colours that definitely courted a younger clientele. Giancarlo Giammetti was less impressed, condemning it on his Facebook page at the time as a "ridiculous circus".

The contemporary feel continued over their next few collections as the new designers gained confidence. Unsurprisingly, accessories benefited first, being Chiuri and Piccioli's original brief at the fashion house, and the metal-stud motif, especially

OPPOSITE Within a couple of seasons, the Valentino collections started to have a younger, fresher feel. For example, this classic pink silk strapless gown with chiffon ruching and bugle beads is offset by futuristic blue make-up.

the Rockstud spike heel, has gone on to become a cult classic for Valentino. Dresses continued to use generous amounts of fabric drawn into copious drapes and ruffles, but more often than not, these were little party frocks rather than long gowns, offset by harder-edged cropped jackets in glossy leather. The endorsement of Chloë Sevigny, who wore a strapless ruffled lilac Valentino gown to the Golden Globes in 2010, certainly helped the house reach a new crowd.

Much debate ensued as to whether the new popularity of Valentino among bright young things would come at the cost of the brand's loyal, older clientele as well as its traditional reputation. Reviewing the Autumn/Winter 2010 couture show, *Vogue* admired the expert craftsmanship of the truncated, youth-oriented versions of classic Valentino but noted the lack of appeal to the house's former customer: "it was plain to see that Chiuri and Piccioli had done their research on classic couture shapes, however abbreviated they might be here. But that will be scant consolation to mournful clients of the ancien régime."

Young celebrities and socialites were regularly appearing on the front row, however, and a boost in sales reflected the appeal of Maria Grazia Chiuri and Pierpaolo Piccioli's modern expression of house classics. Valentino and Giammetti both expressed their support, applauding enthusiastically at shows and visiting the designers backstage. Giammetti even told *WWD* in 2012: "We think they are great designers. They have been able to bring the Valentino style up to today, in a very modern way but respectful of the past of the house."

With the younger customers reeled in, the most impressive skill exhibited by Chiuri and Piccioli was to incorporate the more traditional elements, using fabrics such as tweed and referencing themes that reached as far back as medieval dress, while still looking contemporary.

"Chiuri and Piccioli's signal achievement has been to turn

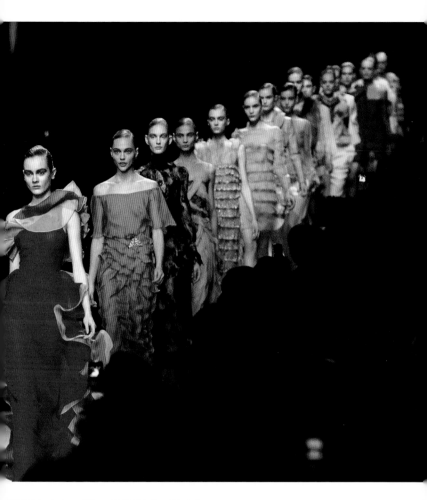

ABOVE By Autumn/Winter 2010, Chiuri and Piccioli
had begun to put their own contemporary mark
on Valentino, while still incorporating the house
trademarks – ruffles, pleats and adornments such as
sequins and bugle beads.

the old-fashioned into something new and irresistible," read the assessment by *Vogue* in 2011.

As their collections continued, the once stiff, ladylike formality of Valentino clothes continued to soften into a new girlishness. Pretty dresses were crafted from lace and full of the house's favourite florals themes as well as delicate embroidery, but the level of skill and attention to structure meant these were still dresses to fantasize over. Or as Piccioli told *Vogue* in 2011: "Fashion is a dream, and in this moment we need dreams."

While couture and evening wear continued to retain a level of glamour that only comes with a degree of formality, daywear

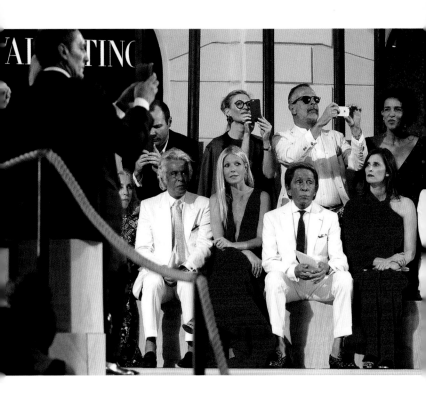

was a place where Chiuri and Piccioli could experiment with far less rigid silhouettes. The first inkling came in Autumn/Winter 2011, with the appearance of semi-sheer straight dresses and two-piece outfits composed of ribbed knit sweaters and tiered knee-length skirts, albeit cleverly crafted from lace or even, in one case, a lattice of lace superimposed onto leather.

The metal stud, the new house signature, appeared scattered in a way that crystals might have been in Valentino's day. Chiuri and Piccioli's fascination with leather, of the softest and most flattering kind, of course, continued the following year. For Autumn/Winter 2012, they presented a series of long and short dresses, skirts, a trouser suit and even a flowing cape made out of glossy hide.

Maria Grazia Chiuri and Pierpaolo Piccioli continued tactfully to challenge the traditional aesthetic of Valentino, most noticeably in their haute couture shows. For example, in Autumn/Winter 2012, the collection had a very different feel, concentrated on deep sensual blues and dusky purples, dark cousins to the statement red for which the house is so known. But floral motifs never waned and much use was still made of embroidery and brocade to ensure that the rarefied nature of couture clothes from one of the world's most elite fashion brands was not lost. In fact, the stunning gowns for which the house was so famed became only more impressive under the new guard, with elaborately beautiful embellishments and patterns.

Even when the pair went somewhat avant-garde, they were acknowledged for their spirit and creativity. For Autumn/Winter 2014 ready-to-wear, they took inspiration from Italian pop art, sending a brightly colourful and graphic collection down the catwalk. *Vogue* noted: "When Chiuri and Piccioli came out for their bow, Valentino Garavani and Giancarlo Giammetti stood to applaud and offer kisses of congratulations. The outpouring of affection felt like an appropriate recognition of the duo's talents. They are this house's beating heart."

OPPOSITE Maria
Grazia Chiuri and
Pierpaolo Piccioli
spent 17 years
together at Valentino,
eight as co-designers-
in-chief. Their final
joint collection,
greeted by rapturous
applause, was the
couture collection for
Autumn/Winter 2016.

Inevitably, things eventually change, and in 2016 it was announced that Chiuri would be leaving the brand to take over from Raf Simons at Dior and that Piccioli would continue as sole design director. Valentino CEO Stefano Sassi paid tribute to the duo's achievements at Valentino in a statement: "Everything achieved in these years would have been impossible without Maria Grazia Chiuri and Pierpaolo Piccioli's talent, determination and vision that together have contributed into making Valentino one of the most successful fashion companies."

Maria Grazia Chiuri and Pierpaolo Piccioli had spent 17 years at Valentino, the last 8 of which saw them assume the role of artistic directors. Adding the time they spent together at Fendi, their working relationship had lasted a quarter of a century; under their leadership, Valentino had been modernized without losing its heritage or identity, as well as reaching a new level of profitability.

Their final joint collection, the couture collection for Autumn/Winter 2016, was a stunning swansong. In acknowledgement of the four centuries since Shakespeare's death, it was an Elizabethan-themed extravaganza, full of ruffled collars, doublets and puffed-sleeve gowns, which paid tribute to the playwright's obsession with Renaissance Italy and the pair's own experience of living and working in Rome.

In a joint statement, Chiuri and Piccioli acknowledged their close working relationship and friendship, and also the importance of allowing one another to grow creatively: "After 25 years of creative partnership and of professional satisfactions we gave ourselves the opportunity of continuing our artistic paths in an individual way with the reciprocal desire of further great achievements."

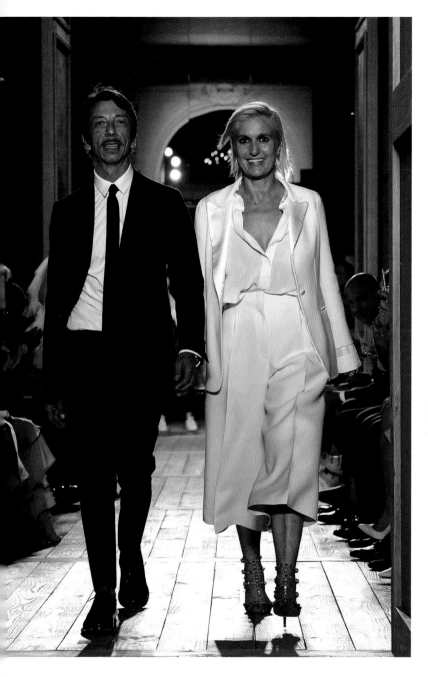

PIERPAOLO PICCIOLI

The huge success that Maria Grazia Chiuri and Pierpaolo
Piccioli had achieved at Valentino left many nervous about
whether Piccioli could continue to reach the same standards
alone. They needn't have worried. His first collection after his
long-time collaborator's departure, for Spring/Summer 2017,
was a triumph. Inspired by the Hieronymus Bosch triptych *The
Garden of Earthly Delights*, it also paid homage to British
designer Zandra Rhodes, with whom Piccioli had spent time
looking through her archives as he researched his collection.
The result was a wonderfully romantic series of bright fuchsia-
pink and red outfits, adorned with delicately embroidered
birds, flora and fauna. His daywear was also praised for taking
pastoral nostalgia and mixing it up with crisp white shirts for a
thoroughly modern feel, causing *Vogue* to enthuse: "In short, he
aced it, not only meeting expectations but surpassing them too."

Since his debut, Piccioli has gone from strength to strength
at Valentino. Stepping into the limelight as sole designer
has clearly released new depths of creativity within him. His
first couture collection took Greek myths and architecture
as its theme, offering long white pleated column dresses and
classical draped gowns worth of any goddess. Since then, he has
continued to offer collections of clothes researched and curated
to a level worthy of an art historian, referencing widely from the
Renaissance to Victoriana.

With biannual seasonal presentations spanning the range
from the more casual resort collections to the pinnacle of
elaborate design represented by haute couture, Piccioli has
been unafraid to mix luxe with athleisure, as illustrated in the
juxtaposition of tracksuits and mink coats for his resort wear.
Haute couture necessarily tips the scale towards elegance and
refinement, but even here, bright colours and graphic prints
make all his clothes thoroughly modern.

OPPOSITE For
Autumn/Winter 2019,
and in homage to
Valentino's love of the
voluminous ruffled
gown, Pierpaolo
Piccioli dressed model
and muse Adut Akech
in an extravagant
purple creation.

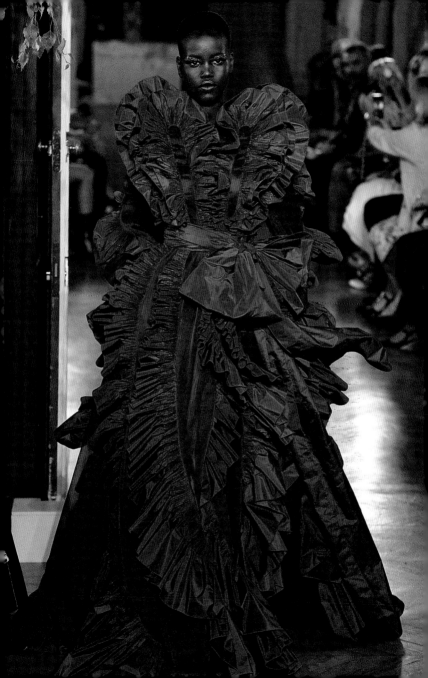

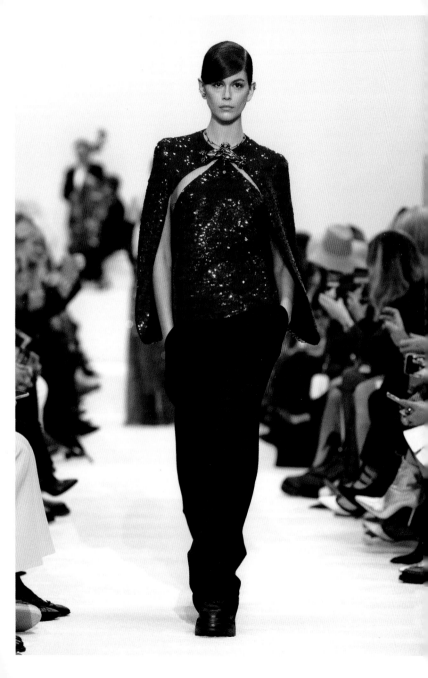

Like Valentino did before him, Piccioli clearly enjoys playing with volume and elaborate adornment within his silhouettes. For Spring/Summer 2018 couture, a voluminous faille coat in ochre yellow was presented complete with a turquoise ostrich feather hat. More feather headgear concoctions followed, some trailing excess strands like a kind of a sea creature. The colours were bright and clashing, full of purple, pink and yellow. It was a more flamboyant glamour than the house of Valentino is known for, but it worked, offering something new and exciting in a fashion world that has too often seen it all before.

Like for many designers, the COVID-19 pandemic and the restrictions imposed on traditional catwalk shows by lockdown conditions have necessitated a new way of conceptualizing fashion. For his Autumn/Winter 2020 couture show, Pierpaolo Piccioli offered a collaboration with photographer and film-maker Nick Knight, entitled Of Grace and Light.

The capsule collection of just 16 looks, all in white, drew obvious comparisons to Valentino's legendary all-white collection of 1968. It was part digital and part physical, staged in Studio 10 of Rome's legendary Cinecittà, yet again reaching far back into Valentino's own early dreams of silver-screen glamour. Knight's film featured trapeze-borne models in gowns that were more sculpture than dress, reaching far beyond the limitations of the female form, giving them surreal, Alice-in-Wonderland proportions. Next, curtains were opened to show the real-life models, balancing on high ladders so that the dresses with their metres of fabric could cascade to the floor. With just a small audience in attendance, it was all live-streamed via Zoom, a magical fantasy and perfect escapism from the dire global situation.

As his journey at Valentino continues, Piccioli has challenged the traditional haute couture system more and more. In an increasingly gender-neutral world, sending male models

OPPOSITE Piccioli has continued the legacy of Valentino's elegant womenswear while still making it feel current – illustrated perfectly by this combination of black tailored trousers and an electric-blue, batwing-sleeved sequinned top, modelled by Kaia Gerber.

Taking
Valentino throughly
up to date, Piccioli has
juxtaposed athleisure
with classic Valentino
tailoring over the
last few seasons. This
brightly printed blue
shirt combination
for Spring/Summer
2020 menswear has a
streetwear feel to it,
as does the matching
bag.

down a couture catwalk broke one barrier, as did his blending of what might be considered casual athleisure wear with the highly structural and embellished clothes we associate with high fashion. Playing with new shapes and silhouettes takes Valentino into a more modern era, but continues to honour the tradition of the house.

Interviewed by *Vogue* before his Spring/Summer 2021 couture show, Piccioli explained: "My idea is to witness the moment... To me, the essence of couture is the ritual, the process, the care, the humanity. That's what makes couture timeless, special."

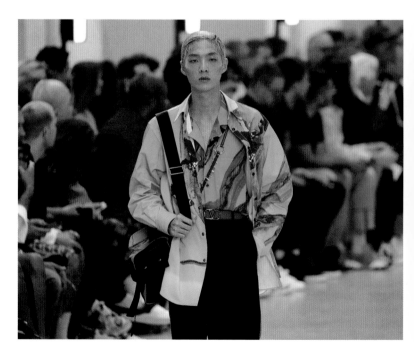

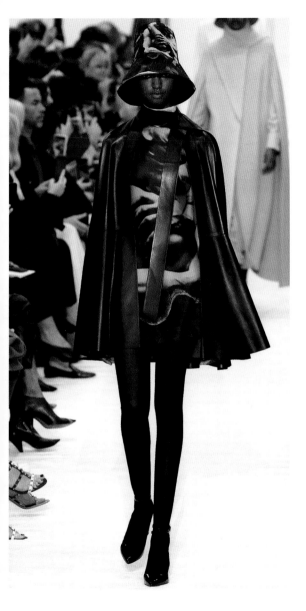

LEFT Leather, a mainstay of the luxury Valentino label since its inception, has been crafted in a very different way by Piccioli, as shown by this black cape over a graphic printed silk tunic with matching hat for Autumn/Winter 2019.

INDEX

(Page numbers in *italic* refer to photographs and captions; **bold** to main subjects)

Academy Awards *48*, 53, *53*, 55, *55*
accessories **92–7**, *99*, 143–4
Akech, Adut 51, *51*, *150*
Along Came Polly 24, *25*
American fashion 28
Aniston, Jennifer 24, *25*, 53
Appian Way *112*
Architectural Digest 110, 112
Armani, Giorgio 100
Art 114, *117*
ateliers 7
    Fifth Avenue 63
    Madison Avenue 63
    New York 63
    Rome 7, 23, 44, 62, 70
    Palazzo Mignanelli 75
    Paris 34, *35*, *37*, 62
    Rodeo Drive 64
    Via Condotti 18, 23, 27
    Via Gregoriana *8*, 27, 31
athleisure *97*, *154*
Aviator, The 48

bags 51, 92, *92*, 96, 97, *99*, 100, *100*, *154*
Balenciaga 18
Ballarian, Richard 71
Ballets Russes 69

Baryshnikov, Mikhail *71*
Barzini, Benedetta *38*
Beckham, Victoria *48*
Berenson, Marisa *37*, *64*
Blanchett, Cate *48*, 55
Blue Lagoon 70
Bosch, Hieronymous 150
brocade evening dress *38*
Bündchen, Gisele 51, *52*, 55

Campbell, Naomi *45*, 51, 75, *87*, 123
cape *155*
Capri *117*
Carmen 53
Château de Wideville *109*, **110**
chiffon cape *45*
China: Through the Look- ing Glass 84, *88*
chinoiserie *121*, 123
Chiuri, Maria Grazia 8, 13, 51, 55, 96, 133, *137*, *138*, 141, 143, 144, *145*, 147, 148, *148*, 150
Cinecittà studios 27–8, *27*, 153
Cleopatra 43
Collections
    40th anniversary 52
    Autumn/Winter 1961 44
    Autumn/Winter 1962 *45*
    Autumn/Winter 1982

71, *71*
    Autumn/Winter 1983 75
    Autumn/Winter 1985 *77*
    Autumn/Winter 1989 75
    Autumn/Winter 1990 75, 84, *84*
    Autumn/Winter 1994 84, *88*
    Autumn/Winter 1999 *55*
    Autumn/Winter 2000 *122*
    Autumn/Winter 2001 *100*
    Autumn/Winter 2002 123
    Autumn/Winter 2007 *126*
    Autumn/Winter 2009 *140*, 143
    Autumn/Winter 2010 144, *145*
    Autumn/Winter 2011 147
    Autumn/Winter 2012 147
    Autumn/Winter 2014 147
    Autumn/Winter 2015 *146*
    Autumn/Winter 2016 148, *148*
    Autumn/Winter 2019 *155*
    Autumn/Winter 2020 153
    celebration 2000 122, *130*
    Ibis (1959) 24, *24*, *25*
    Spring/Summer 1981 70, *70*
    Spring/Summer 1985 *74*
    Spring/Summer 1988 *74*
    Spring/Summer 1992 84, *87*
    Spring/Summer 1993 84
    Spring/Summer 2000 91, *91*

Spring/Summer 2004
    121, 126
Spring/Summer 2005
    123, *123*
Spring/Summer 2006
    123, 126
Spring/Summer 2007 126
Spring/Summer 2008
    126, *128*, 130
Spring/Summer 2009
    137, 141
Spring/Summer 2010 141
Spring/Summer 2018 153
Spring/Summer 2019 51
Spring/Summer 2020 *154*
Spring/Summer 2021 154
Coppola, Sofia 13
Cresp, Olivier 103
Cut, The 65

Daily Telegraph 44
Danes, Clare 53
David di Donatello Awards 53
day suit *72*
de la Renta, Françoise *61*
Dessès, Jean 18, *18*, 23, 43,
    61, 82
Devil Wears Prada, The 131
Dinand, Pierre 103
Dolce Vita, La 28
Douglas, Kirk *28*, 44

École de Chambre
    Syndicale de la Couture
    Parisienne 14
École des Beaux-Arts 15
Ellena, Jean-Claude 103
ES Magazine 112
Exhibition 82, *82*

Faccinetti, Alessandra 137, 138

Fairchild, John 122
Fashion Awards *48*, *51*
*Fashion Icons with Fern
    Mallis* 70
Fashion Law 100
Fath, Jacques 18
feathers 28, 75, 153
Fellini, Federico 28
Fendi, Carla 82, 96, 141, 148
Ferré, Gianfranco 82
Fifth Avenue **113–4**
Florence 28
flowers 66
frills and flounces *79*
Fürstenberg, Ira von 103

Garavani, Valentino 7, *7*,
    8, *91*, 99, 100, 109,
    109, *123*
    30 Years of Magic 82, *83*, 84
    45th Anniversary Gala *52*
    2005 Academy Awards *48*
    2018 Fashion Awards *48*
    accessories **92–7**
    American fashion 28
    Andy Warhol 65, 66
    Appian Way **112**
    Art 115
    ateliers 7, 8, 18, *23*
    bags 92, *92*, 96, 100
    Brooke Shields 70–71,
        70, *71*
    Capri *117*
    Château de Wideville
        109, **110**
    colours *80*
    Diana Vreeland 64–5, 71
    early years 13–15, *13*, *14*,
        17, 18, *18*
    Elizabeth Taylor 43, *43*, 44
    expanding ranges 72

Faccinetti 138
Fifth Avenue **113–4**
flowers *75*
franchising 92
Giancarlo Giammetti 8,
    26–7, 61, 63, 66, 96,
    109, 110, 113, 121–2,
    131–3, *133*, 138,
    143–4, *146*, 147
Gstaad chalet **114**, *115*
HdP spA 121
Holland Park **112–3**
homes 109–114, *109*
interior designer *110*
Jackie Kennedy Onassis
    44, 91, *91*
Mario Valentino 99, 100
Mendès 61
muses 43, 44, *70*
Nan Kempner *61*
new millennium 91, *91*
Oliver range 72
outsourcing production 61
perfume 103, *103*
residences 109–114, *109*,
    115
retirement 125
Rockstud 92, 98
Sala Bianca group 28, 31
selling up 121–33
Sophia Loren 44, *44*
V logo 92, *96*, 97, 100
Valentino Red 52–5, *52*,
    122, *128*
Valentino SpA 27, 100
wedding dresses 56, *56*
*Valentino: The Last
    Emperor* (documentary)
    131–33
*Garden of Earthly Delights,
    The* 150

Garland, Judy 13, *17*
Gerber, Kaia *153*
Giammetti, Giancarlo 8, 26–7, 61, 63, *64*, 66, 96, 109, 110, 113, 121–2, 131–3, *133*, 138, 143–4, *146*, 147
Giorgini, Count Giovanni 28
Girls on Broadway 17
Givaudan 103
Givenchy 138
Givenchy, Hubert de 82
Golbin, Pamela 18, 131
Golden Globes 144
Gowns 7, *8*, *28*, *34*, *37*, 44, 46, 51, *52*, 53, *53*, 55, *55*, 66, *66*, 69, 72, *78*, *87*, *100*, *109*, *121*, 123, *125*, *126*, 130, *130*, 131, *138*, *140*, *143*, 144, 147, 148, 150, *150*, 153
Grange, Jacques 112
Gstaad chalet **114**, *115*
Guardian, The 137
Gucci 138
Guinness, Gloria 28

Halston *64*, 66
halterneck dress *66*
Hathaway, Anne 53, *53*, 55, 56, *109*, 132
HdP spA 121
headdress *140*
heels 97, 144
Holland Park **112–3**
HuffPost 51
Hutton, Lauren *71*

icon-icon.com 44
Independent, the 26

IndieWire 132
InStyle 45
International Wool Secretariat 18

Jagger, Bianca 66
jewellery 97
Jones, Isabel 45
Judd, Chris *56*

Kempner, Nan 28, 31, *45*
Kennedy, Jackie *see* Onassis
Kennedy, John F. 44
Kinmonth, Patrick 133
Klimt, Gustav 69
Knight, Nick 153
Kubrick, Stanley 28

Lagerfeld, Karl 100, 132
Lalanne, Claude and François-Xavier *115*, 117
Lamarr, Hedy 13
Laroche, Guy 18, 23
leather *155*
leather belt *96*, 97
Lollobrigida, Gina 27, *27*
London 112–3, 132
Lopez, Jennifer 55, *56*
Loren, Sophia *27*, 28, 44, *44*
Love Ball *109*, 110

Marie Claire 53
Marzotto Apparel 121
Máxima, Crown Princess *56*
Mendès 61
Metropolitan Museum of Art 28, 70, 71, *71*, 84, *88*
Milan 14, 31
minidress *87*

Minnelli, Liza 66
Miró, Jean 112
Mock, Janet 51
Monfreda, Antonio 133
Mongiardino, Renzo 112
monochrome palette 44, *74*, 75
Monreale *38*
Morillas, Alberto 103
Musée des Art Decoratifs 131

Naked Heart Foundation *109*, 110
Neiman Marcus Award 31
New York 63, 65, 113–4
New York City Ballet 13
New York Times 63–4, 82, 84

O'Connor, Erin *91*
Obrist, Hans Ulrich 13, 14, 53, 65, 66, 117
Of Grace and Light 153
Onassis, Aristotle 34, *34*, 43
Onassis, Jackie 7, 28, 31, *31*, 34, *34*, 43, 44, 45, *62*
Oscar gowns 7
Oscars *see* Academy Awards

Palazzo Mignanelli 75
Palermo, Olivia 51
Paltrow, Gwyneth *146*
Pampanini, Silvana *13*
Paper magazine 132
Paris 15, 23, 34, 110, 131
Paris Opera Ballet 13
peasant dresses 66
Pellé, Marie-Paule 66
Peretti, Elsa 66

perfume **103**, *103*
Piazza di Spagna 52
Piazza Mignanelli 75
Piccioli, Pierpaolo 8, 13, 31, *51*, 55, 96, 133, *137*, *138*, 141, 143, 144, *145*, 146, *146*, 147, 148, *148*, **150**, *150*, **153–4**, *153*, *154*, *155*
Pitti Palace 28
plaid *87*
plaid suit *77*
Polge, Jacques 103
polka dots *87*
ponchos *69*
Pose 51
pumps *92*, 97

Radziwill, Lee 28
red dress 138
REDValentino 122
Rhodes, Zandra 150
Roberts, Julia 55
Rockstud 92, *92*, 97, *99*, 144
Rome 7, 31, 70, 82, *82*, 112, 153
Rovasenda, Countess Maria Elena di *35*
Rubell, Steve *64*

Saint Laurent, Yves 61
Sala Bianca group 28, 31
Samuel, Henri 110
Santa Maria Institute 15
Sarandon, Susan 55
Sassi, Stefano 141, 148
Schiffer, Claudia 53, *87*
Sevigny, Chloë 144
sheath dress 75
Sheep sofa *115*

Sheppard, Eugenia 24
Shields, Brooke 70–71, *70*, *71*, *83*
shoes 92, 96, 97, 99
Shriver, Bobby *62*
Somerset House 132
Souza, Carlos *65*
Spartacus 28, *28*, 44
Stiletto *99*
Studio 54 – *64*, 65, *65*
studios *see* ateliers
Swan Lake 45
System 13, 117

Talley, André Leon 110
Taylor, Elizabeth 7, 28, *28*, 43–4, *43*, 55
Time 70
Traviata, La 13
trousers, wide *69*
Turlington, Christy 84, *84*, *88*
Turner, Lana 13, *17*
Tyrnauer, Matt 122, 131, 132

Ungaro, Emanuel 138

V logo 92, *96*, 97, 100
Valentino Red 24, *25*, 52–5, 52–5, *52*, *53*, 55, *78*
Valentino spA 121, 133
Valentino Uomo 103
Valentino, Mario 99, 100
Valentino: At the Emperor's Table 110, 114
Valentino: Master of Couture exhibition 132–3
Valentino: The Last Emperor 8, 122, **131–3**
Valentino: Themes and

Variations exhibition 131
Vanity Fair 26, 114, 122
velvet and taffeta dress *51*
Villa Borghese *52*, 53
Villarini, Lorenzo *65*
Vodianova, Natalia *109*, 110
Voghera 13, *14*
Vogue 8, 28, 31, *38*, 45, 53, 64, 72, 75, 110, 137, 141, 143, 146, 147, 154
Von Furstenberg, Diane 66
Vreeland, Diana 8, 45, 51, 64–5, 66, 71
VSLIN bag 51

W 122
Warhol, Andy 8, 65, 66, *71*, 117
Watson, Emma 53
wedding dress 43, **56**, *56*
Welch, Florence 51, 55
Welch, Raquel *66*
Wiig, Kristen 55
Willem-Alexander, Crown Prince *56*
Women's Wear Daily 23, 122
WWD 132, 133, 144

CREDITS

The publishers would like to thank the following sources for their kind permission to reproduce the pictures in this book.

Alamy: dpa picture alliance 93; /Alberto Grosescu 94-95; /Reuters/Regis Duvignau 155; /Reuters/Charles Platiau 154

Getty Images: Slim Aarons 115; /Carlo Allegri 48; /Arnal/Picot/Gamma-Rapho 85, 86; /Bassignac/Buu/Gamma-Rapho 120; / Benainous/Rossi/Gamma-Rapho 123; /Dave Benett 25, 108; /Bettmann 19, 34, 63; /Joe Buissink/WireImage 56; /Stephane Cardinale/ Corbis 50; /Pascal Chevallier/Gamma-Rapho 116; /Alain Dejean/Sygma 102; /Antonio de Moraes Barros Filho/WireImage 127; /Darren Gerrish/BFC 49; /Gianni Girani/Reporters Associati & Archivi/Mondadori Portfolio 35; /Ron Galella Collection 46, 60, 62, 64, 83; / Gianni Giansanti/Gamma-Rapho 82, 91; / Francois Guillot/AFP 128-129, 136, 139, 144-145; /Frazer Harrison 53; /Rose Hartman 45, 65; /Anthony Harvey 57; /Keystone/ Hulton Archive 29; /Patrick Kovarik/AFP 140; /Licio d'Aloisio/Reporters Associati & Archivi/Mondadori Portfolio 24; /Stephen Lovekin/FilmMagic 98; /Thierry Orban 101;

/Franco Origlia 52; /Robin Platzer/Images 71; /Marisa Rastellini/Mondador 9, 70, 111; /Reporters Associati & Archivi/Mondadori Portfolio 26; /Bertrand Rindoff 47, 73, 74; / Rafael Roa/Corbis 6; /Pascal Le Segretain 152; /Daniel Simon/Gamma-Rapho 54, 75, 77, 78, 79, 80-81, 89; /Simon Stevens/ Gamma-Rapho 90; /Amy Sussman 55; /Eric Vandeville/Gamma-Rapho 124, 130; /Pierre Vauthey/Sygma/Sygma 87; /Elisabetta Villa 146; /Victor Virgile/Gamma-Rapho 76, 88, 151; /Franco Vitale/Reporters Associati & Archivi/Mondadori Portfolio 12, 22

Shutterstock: Alinari 42; /AP 30; /ArdoPics: 14-15; /Henry Clarke/Condé Nast 32-33, 37, 38-39, 67; /Creative Lab 96; /Jonathon Hadfield 99; /Keith Homan 105; /G Jacopozzi/AP 27; /Duane Michals/Condé Nast 68-69; /NeydtStock 92; /Report 97; / Snap 16-17

Every effort has been made to acknowledge correctly and contact the source and/ or copyright holder of each picture and Welbeck Publishing Group apologizes for any unintentional errors or omissions, which will be corrected in future editions of this book.

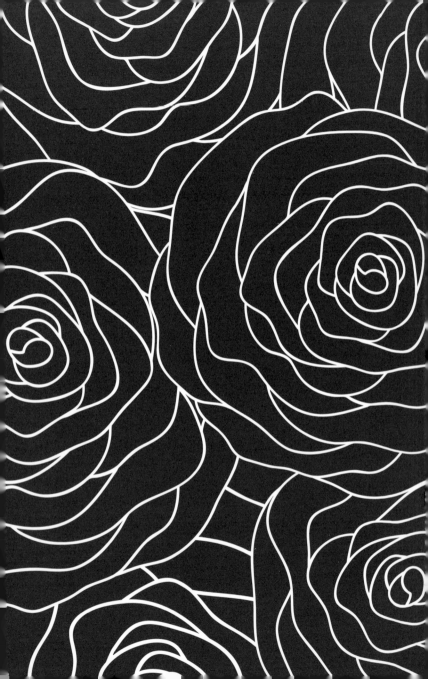